D0848323

The Fifth Monarchy Men

Released from
Samford University Library

THE FIFTH
MONARCHY MEN

*A Study in Seventeenth-century English
Millenarianism*

✠

B. S. CAPP

FABER AND FABER
3 Queen Square
London

Samford University Library

First published in 1972
by Faber and Faber Limited
3 Queen Square London WC1
Printed in Great Britain by
Butler & Tanner Ltd Frome
All rights reserved

ISBN 0 571 09791 X

© *B. S. Capp, 1972*

Annex
914.203

DA
425
.C25

for
Elizabeth

73-05069

73-05063

Contents

Preface

This book is a modified version of my Oxford D.Phil. thesis, submitted in 1969. I have resisted the temptation to undertake a complete rewriting, to avoid the not unusual consequence of an increase in length and a decrease in readability. But as a result, the book will no doubt reflect some of the limitations of the thesis form.

I would like to thank Professor Hugh Trevor-Roper and Professor Austin Woolrych, the examiners of the original thesis, for their helpful criticisms and suggestions, and Professor Woolrych especially for his encouragement for its subsequent publication. A number of corrections and modifications I owe to the prolific and helpful correspondence of Dr. Peter Toon of Ormskirk. But for the assistance of Dr. Van Den Berg of the Free University, Amsterdam, and Professor H. J. Schoeps of Erlangen, even my brief foray into the vast unexplored field of continental millenarianism would have been impossible. My greatest debt, which I cannot hope fully to acknowledge here, is to my former supervisor at Oxford, Mr. Keith Thomas of St. John's College. From him I have received, for five years, a ceaseless stream of valuable references, suggestions, keen criticism and constant encouragement.

The Biographical Appendix will, I hope, be of some value to researchers in other radical movements during the Interregnum. The relationships between the radical groups cannot be established satisfactorily until the interchange of personnel as well as ideas can be studied. For this, a laborious but vital first step must be the compilation of checklists of early Levellers, sectarians and so on.

The original spelling, capitalization, punctuation and use of italics have been retained except in the rare instances when change was necessary to make clear the sense. Dates are according to the Old Style, but the year has been taken to begin on 1 January. All books cited were published in London unless otherwise stated. I have generally cited the State Paper *Calendars*, except where the originals contain additional material of importance.

I owe a special debt of gratitude to my wife for her constant encouragement, and for her patience at my prolonged preoccupation with such a 'hare-brain'd and irreligious Crew'.

Two important new books, relevant to this theme, have appeared since this work was sent to press: C. Hill, *Antichrist in seventeenth-century England*, and K. V. Thomas, *Religion and the Decline of Magic* (both 1971).

University of Warwick   *December 1971*

CHAPTER ONE

Introduction

The English Revolution of 1640 was the result of a multitude of interlocking causes, both secular and religious. There had been widespread dissatisfaction, for example, at both the extravagance and the popery of the Stuart Court. Royal policies, too, had aroused great resentment, especially the crown's attempts to raise revenue through extra-Parliamentary methods, such as Ship Money, and its conspicuous lack of concern for the Protestant cause in the Thirty Years' War, one of the dominating issues in the 1620s and 30s. The Laudian exaltation of the powers of monarchy and divine-right episcopacy had provoked deep antagonism, and Laud's policy of enforcing strict conformity with the provisions of the Elizabethan Settlement destroyed the unity of the loose but comprehensive Church which had been able to contain hitherto most Puritan clergy: Puritans were driven out, some into exile, all into total hostility against the Laudian Church in which they saw idolatry and Popery thinly disguised.

Thus from the outset of the Revolution, there was a twofold preoccupation: a desire for liberty in place of tyranny, and for godliness in place of idolatry. Accordingly there emerged two currents of radicalism, one secular and the other religious. In the early stages, when the slogans of liberty and godliness signified a largely negative programme of destroying Stuart innovations, unity could be maintained. Some persons, such as Oliver Cromwell, were indeed able to belong to both movements—perhaps the key to Cromwell's greatness and success. But under the stress of war, the two concepts developed and were endowed with a far more radical content, from which in time most of Parliament's original supporters recoiled in alarm, and which revealed the fundamental disparity in the nature of the Revolution.

The demand for liberty reached its apogee at the end of the 1640s with the emergence of the Leveller movement, advocating a wide extension of the franchise, and of the smaller, but still more radical, communist movement, the Diggers. The ultimate development of the search for godliness came in the early 1650s with the evolution of the Fifth Monarchist movement. The Fifth Monarchists were a political and religious sect expecting the imminent Kingdom of Christ on earth, a theocratic regime in which the saints would establish a godly discipline over the unregenerate masses and prepare for the Second Coming. They were, it will be argued later, only part of a wide current of belief in some form of imminent Kingdom of Christ. But the Fifth Monarchists were unique, amongst the major groups, in that millenarianism formed the basic core of their doctrines, and was indeed the *raison d'être* of the movement. It was unique, too, in claiming the right and indeed the duty of taking arms to overthrow existing regimes and establish the millennium, and also in its detailed formulation of the political, social and economic structure of the promised kingdom.

To their contemporaries in the mid-seventeenth century, the Fifth Monarchists appeared as violent revolutionaries, hiding behind a façade of saintliness. Cromwell is said to have remarked that '*they had tongues like Angels, but had cloven feet.*'[1] English millenarian movements since the eighteenth century have been generally insignificant, arousing ridicule rather than alarm. But the Fifth Monarchists were closely linked to the mainstream of political affairs in the years after the execution of Charles I in 1649. Oliver Cromwell was himself a fellow-traveller until 1653, and his sometime deputy, Major-General Harrison, was an enthusiastic supporter. During the nominated 'Parliament of Saints' in 1653 it was indeed possible to regard the Fifth Monarchists as being on the threshhold of supreme political power, and it is impossible to doubt the fear they aroused during the 1650s. Only after the Restoration in 1660 did ridicule begin to overshadow anxiety. Abraham Cowley's comedy *Cutter of Coleman Street* (1663), a savage satire of the movement, is said to have played to packed audiences at double prices—an eloquent testimony to public preoccupation.[2]

The Fifth Monarchists did not outlast the seventeenth century, and denominations such as the Baptists and Congregationalists have tended, naturally, to minimize their early associations with the

[1] Anon., *The Protector (So called,) In Part Unvailed* (1655), p. 17.
[2] H. Newcome, *Diary*, ed. T. Heywood (Chetham Soc., xviii, 1849), p. 8n.

movement. Consequently, the 'never to be forgotten Sect' of 1661[1] had already passed into oblivion by the beginning of the eighteenth century. Millenarianism had little to offer to future political and intellectual trends (except that it supported the novel concept of progress), and in the age of Bacon and Hobbes it can easily be seen as anachronistic, a mediaeval relic. Perhaps this explains why, whereas millenarian movements in primitive societies are subjected to a scholarly analysis, the Fifth Monarchist movement is still brushed aside as an interlude of insanity, the product of 'ill made brains and disturbed fancies, strongly tinctured with an hypocondriack melancholy'.[2] Sir George Clark dismissed Thomas Venner, one of the most militant of the self-styled saints, as a 'crack-brained enthusiast'. G. P. Gooch thought that 'one pamphlet alone had pretensions to sanity' (ironically choosing Venner's manifesto). H. N. Brailsford and Herschel Baker found the Fifth Monarchists respectively 'picturesque' and 'ludicrous'. Professor Trevor-Roper, who describes three prominent European millenarians as 'crackpots', has labelled as hypocrites the group surrounding the Welsh Fifth Monarchist, Vavasor Powell, a mere 'knot of Tammy demagogues'. In a recent study of the English Revolution, Professor Roots apparently found the Fifth Monarchists unworthy of mention.[3] Modern writings have proliferated on those radical seventeenth-century movements, notably the Levellers and Diggers, which in some respects anticipated modern ideas. The Fifth Monarchists, however, have attracted only two historians. In 1911 Miss Louise Brown published a solid and reliable account of the movement during the Interregnum. Her book was concerned, though, less with the nature of Fifth Monarchism than with its role in the political history of those years. Recently, in 1966, P. G. Rogers attempted a wider view, but the brevity of his book and a very incomplete use of available sources made the analysis somewhat unsatisfactory.[4]

The ridicule of the Fifth Monarchists by many modern historians

---

[1] Anon., *Londons Glory, or, the Riot and Ruine of the Fifth Monarchy Men* (1661), p. 6.
[2] J. Hall, *Confusion Confounded* (1654), p. 3.
[3] Sir G. N. Clark, *The Later Stuarts* (2nd edn., Oxford, 1955), p. 22; G. P. Gooch and H. J. Laski, *English Democratic Ideas in the Seventeenth Century* (New York, Evanston and London, 1959), p. 225; H. N. Brailsford, *The Levellers and the English Revolution* (1961), p. 120; H. Baker, *The Wars of Truth* (London and New York, 1952), p. 85; H. R. Trevor-Roper, *Religion, the Reformation and Social Change* (1967), pp. 286 and n., 365; I. Roots, *The Great Rebellion 1642–1660* (1966).
[4] L. F. Brown, *The Political Activities of the Baptists and Fifth Monarchy Men* (1911, reissued New York, 1965); P. G. Rogers, *The Fifth Monarchy Men* (1966).

stems from an assumption that they were an irrational movement, beyond the pale of analysis. The millenarian concept as such, of course, cannot be brushed aside as abnormal or unimportant. Such ideas have been a recurring theme in many parts of the world throughout history. They sustained the Jews during the Maccabean revolt of 165 B.C. They swept through China in the Taiping rebellion of 1850–65 and have recurred frequently in Brazil, for example, and in the Cargo cults of Melanesia, where the islanders awaited the return of the dead, bearing riches, to set up paradise.[1] Wherever religion or folk-lore presented a Messiah or lost hero, a millenarian movement was possible. Any form of crisis, whether through conquest, plague, social disruption or religious innovation, was likely to produce such a movement. Mediaeval Christian Europe combined all these elements, and experienced a long series of millenarian movements from about 1100 onwards. The most radical support came from the poorest elements in town and country, with the destruction of the 'godless' landowners and clergy seen as the first step towards New Jerusalem. Christ and the 'Emperor of the Last Days', sometimes named as St. Louis of France or the Emperor Frederick II, played the same role of providing inspiration and justification.[2]

Western Europe in the sixteenth and seventeenth centuries represented, of course, a very different social and intellectual milieu, and to some extent this might justify dismissing the Fifth Monarchists as 'irrational'. But rationality is a very subjective concept. The modern belief that it is synonymous with explanations based upon scientific materialism is valid only for the present age. By such a definition, indeed, the sixteenth and seventeenth centuries as a whole must stand condemned. Though science was making great advances, the influence of the supernatural on human affairs was accepted almost universally, by educated and ignorant alike. No one doubted that the hand of God was to be seen in the outcome of wars, in the visitations of plague and in the fortunes of each individual. The Devil was equally active. Both on the continent and to a lesser extent in England, the period saw a massive preoccupation with witchcraft, magnified on the continent into a gigantic league with Satan. Thousands were tortured and executed. Such beliefs were

---

[1] See, for example, S. Thrupp, *Millenial Dreams in Action* (The Hague, 1962); P. Worsley, *The Trumpet Shall Sound* (1957).
[2] N. Cohn, *The Pursuit of the Millennium* (1962 edn.), *passim*.

not confined to the ignorant or obscure. Calvinists and Jesuits, princes and academics, amongst them James I and Bodin, believed in witchcraft and advocated its extermination by force.[1]

The same period saw a widespread interest in astrology. From the early days of printing, a flood of almanacs appeared annually, predicting from the conjunction of the stars not merely the weather to be expected but the approach of plague, the death of kings, and the results of wars. In 1649 William Lilly's almanac *Merlinus Anglicus* sold 18,500 copies. During the civil war, rival astrologers predicted the fortunes and victory of their respective sides.[2] The Anglican Church accepted that men were influenced by the stars under which they were born, and though it criticized some of the prophetic claims of the astrologers, this probably had little effect. A critic complained in 1561 that the people were so dependent on astrologers 'that scarce would they ride or go any journey, unless they consulted with these blind prophets, or at least with their prophecies'.[3]

Prophecies of all kinds were widespread. On the continent, the *Prognosticatio* of 1488, a collection of ancient prophecies and astrological predictions published by Johannes Lichtenberger, astrologer to the Emperor Frederick III, attracted widespread interest in the early sixteenth century. Ancient prophecies, including the prophecy of a Third and Golden Age by the twelfth century Calabrian abbot, Joachim of Fiore, were applied to many of the French and Imperial rulers of the period, especially the French kings Charles VIII and Henry IV and the Emperors Frederick III, Maximilian and Charles V.[4] Prophecies could thus serve as royal propaganda. But in England, for example, where there were popular prophecies both of the Galfridian type (using animals symbolically) and of the Sibylline (which played on words and letters), prophecies were also used to justify rebellion. The prophecy of the 'mouldwarp', or mole, which can be traced back to the early fourteenth century, and told of a

1 See, for example, Trevor-Roper, *Religion, the Reformation and Social Change*, pp. 90–192. By far the best discussion of witchcraft, astrology, prophecies and providence in England in this period is now to be found in K. V. Thomas, *Religion and the Decline of Magic* (1971).
2 H. R. Plomer, 'A Printer's Bill in the 17th Century', *The Library*, N.S., vii (1906), p. 42; H. Rusche, 'Astrology and Propaganda from 1644 to 1651', *Eng. Hist. Rev.*, lxxx (1965), pp. 322–33.
3 P. H. Kocher, *Science and Religion in Elizabethan England* (San Marino, California, 1953), chaps. 4, 10; S. R. Maitland, *Notes on the Contributions of the Rev. George Townsend* (1841–2), ii, 106.
4 W. E. Peuckert, *Dit Grosse Wende* (Darmstadt, 1966), pp. 103–19; M. Reeves, *The Influence of Prophecy in the late Middle Ages: A Study in Joachism* (Oxford, 1969).

proud and cowardly king who would be driven from the land, was utilized by Percy, Glendower and Mortimer in opposing Henry IV, and revived in the reign of Henry VIII to justify the Pilgrimage of Grace.[1] In societies where there was no concept of progress and the existing order was presented as that imposed by God, prophecies were naturally popular as a means of justifying change. The fact that an upheaval had been predicted suggested that it was preordained, and that it was part of God's overall plan. Accordingly, men were 'prone to believe any thing they would have, and any words that seem that way, they lay hold on; never regarding though the ground be foolish, and the coherence with the rest repugnant to their construction'.[2] William Lilly used the prophecy of the White King, purporting to have been written in the seventh century and describing the end of monarchy, to justify Parliament in the civil war. Charles I, he wrote, '*hath already acted such thing as the* White King *must*'. The *Prophecy of the White King* sold 1800 copies in three days.[3]

Even prophecies relating to events already past, or foretelling only disasters, seem to have been popular. Mother Shipton's prophecy of the fall of Wolsey, said to have been written before the event, probably dated from 1641. Yet it won widespread interest and acceptance, and the Great Fire of London of 1666 was seen by Prince Rupert as the fulfilment of one of her prophecies. The prophecy of Otwell Binns, describing tub-preachers, the Irish rebellion, and the king's breach with Parliament, purported to date from 1600, but was probably written after the events it described.[4] In an age of political and social change and insecurity, perhaps any prophecy served a need in suggesting that events could be foretold and thus reduced to some order. If foreknowledge was interpreted as proof of preordination, then even disasters could be accepted as part of a divine, cosmic plan. There may be a similar explanation for the popularity of the numerous pamphlets relating news of monstrous births, clouds which rained blood, babies who prophesied, and battles in the sky between flocks of birds. These too were seen as auguries of some impending disaster, and satisfied a

[1] M. H. Dodds, 'Political Prophecies in the Reign of Henry VIII', *Modern Language Review*, xi (1916), pp. 276–84.
[2] J. Mede, *Works* (1672), pp. 878–9.
[3] W. Lilly, *A Prophecy of the White King* (1644), p. 19; Lilly, *A Collection of Ancient and Moderne Prophecies* (1645), p. 26; H. Rusche, 'Prophecies and Propaganda, 1641 to 1651', *Eng. Hist. Rev.*, lxxxiv (1969), p. 760.
[4] *D.N.B.*, Mother Shipton; anon., *Sixe strange Prophesies* (1643), sig. A2–3v., A4–v.

need for sensationalism at the same time as suggesting a supernatural control of human affairs.[1]

Throughout the mediaeval period, the belief in the miraculous
powers of saints and holy relics had been a fundamental of the popular religious mind. Such beliefs survived in the Counter-Reforma-
tion, and were even institutionalized, with official records of local
wonders being kept in 'Books of Miracles'.[2] The leading Protestant
Churches swept away the cult of saints, but failed to destroy the
faith in miracles. In England, belief in the supernatural healing
powers of the 'King's Touch' appears to have reached its height in
the seventeenth century. Moreover, the practice of healing miracles
was revived by the sects of the civil war period, and the most successful sect, the Quakers, was the one which laid most emphasis on
miraculous healing.[3]

This widespread belief in the role of supernatural forces in human
affairs was quite consistent with contemporary rationality. Mechanical explanations of phenomena were as yet inadequate to challenge
the primary role of supernatural causation and, in any case, they
were not widely known. Moreover, the relationship between
scientific and supernatural explanation was not one of simple
confrontation. The greatest progress in contemporary science was
made by the Neo-Platonists, with their belief in a universe of spirits
and magical forces, and their interest in the compilations of Hermetic magic. Paracelsus and his disciples combined a grasp of experi-
mental method with an active interest in alchemy and magic. His
English disciples included John Thornborough, bishop of Worcester,
a practising alchemist, and Walter Charleton, a Fellow of the Royal
Society, who argued that 'we must quit the dark Lanthorne of
Reason' and seek knowledge by illumination.[4]

The recent appearance of a number of new books suggests that
the barrier formed by the view of millenarianism as an irrational
and therefore insignificant force is at last being swept aside. They
share a common theme in stressing the normalcy and the wide
extent of millenarianism in England in the seventeenth century,

[1] Rusche, 'Prophecies and Propaganda', pp. 755–6, 764 and n., gives examples
of such wonders, used to serve Puritan and royalist ends respectively.
[2] H. G. Koenigsberger and G. L. Mosse, *Europe in the Sixteenth Century* (1968), pp.
169, 172.
[3] Cf. H. J. Cadbury, *George Fox's 'Book of Miracles'* (Cambridge, 1948), esp. the
Introduction.
[4] A. G. Debus, *The English Paracelsians* (1965), pp 103–5 and *passim*; P. M.
Rattansi, 'Paracelsus and the Puritan Revolution', *Ambix*, xi (1963), pp. 24–31.

and they see the Fifth Monarchists, rightly, as only one aspect of a much wider current. The collection of essays edited by Dr. Peter Toon, *Puritans, the Millennium and the Future of Israel* (1970), traces the academic rediscovery and the dissemination of millenarianism amongst several movements. Professor J. F. Wilson, in *Pulpit in Parliament* (1969), emphasizes the importance of millenarianism in the sermons preached before the Long Parliament in the 1640s, and argues that the founding of gathered, Independent Churches represented a 'specific anticipation of a broader reign of Christ'.[1] Dr. William Lamont has made a far greater (though more suspect) claim in his *Godly Rule* (1969): that 'millenarianism meant not alienation from the spirit of the age but a total involvement with it', and he includes both King James I and Archbishop Laud within his millenarian band.[2] It becomes clear that the furore produced by the Fifth Monarchists in the seventeenth century sprang not from the fact that they held millenarian ideas, but that they developed a potent and dangerous synthesis in which these ideas became the justification for violent political action and sweeping social changes.

The claim that millenarianism was a broad and important movement in England in the mid-seventeenth century does not, of course, explain why it developed, nor why the Fifth Monarchists detached themselves from the main stream of such believers to form a separate group; an attempt to do this will be made in the next two chapters. But these developments seem less surprising when we recognize the widespread preoccupations with the Biblical prophecies of Daniel and Revelation. Daniel's vision of the rise and fall of four successive, degenerating world-empires, after which would follow a kingdom that would endure for ever (Dan. vii), exerted for centuries a fascination over Christian Europe. By the late Middle Ages the four were normally interpreted as Babylon, Assyria, Greece and Rome. Since Rome was construed to include the Holy Roman Empire, the theory provided valuable propaganda for the Imperialist cause, which it guaranteed would flourish until the end of the world—the everlasting kingdom beginning, it was held, after the Last Judgement. Early critics of the interpretation came, predictably, from countries hostile to the Empire. The theory of four world-empires had also a much wider appeal: it provided

[1] Pp. 195, 229 and *passim*.
[2] P. 13 and *passim*. I have discussed these works in '*Godly Rule* and English Millenarianism', *Past and Present*, 52 (1971).

a means by which the whole, anarchic course of history could be reduced to a simple and satisfying pattern, and by which a divine, if inscrutable, purpose was given to all events.[1] The concept too blended with the widespread theory of a Roman Golden Age from which all later history represented a continuous decline lasting till the world's end. The division of Europe by the Reformation and the ensuing wars seemed to presage the impending dissolution of all things. A typical English writer early in the seventeenth century saw decay in the four elements of fire, water, air and earth; all plants were feebler, and men were 'not so long lived, nor of that goodly tall and strong constitution of body, as in former ages'.[2]

Others besides the Holy Roman Emperor had aspirations towards universal monarchy, and the sixteenth and seventeenth centuries saw attempts to reinterpret Daniel's prophecy, to prove that the eternal, Fifth Monarchy was already in being. Thus the Dominican monk, Sylvester Prierias (1460–1523), master of the papal palace at Rome, claimed that the papacy was the Fifth Monarchy, in being now and for ever. In a sermon preached in 1639, Thomas Goodwin, a prominent English Independent minister, claimed that the Jesuits believed firmly in a 'fifth Monarchy; onely they do apply it and appropriate it to themselves, and call that kingdom ... *Regnum Jesuiticum*'. In 1679, during the furore over the alleged Popish Plot to kill Charles II, William Bedloe attributed the whole design to the Jesuits, who had 'long been Big with the Project of a Fifth-Monarchy, intending to make all the World slavishly to truckle to their Tripple Crown'd Idol at Rome'.[3] But Tommaso Campanella (1568–1639) hailed the king of Spain as the universal monarch, a theory which Milton in 1641 thought it necessary to refute. Spain was widely held to have aspirations of this kind. Vermuyden's Paper, the basis of a projected Anglo-Dutch alliance in 1653, contained the reminder that 'the Spaniard hath been busy this hundred years ... to settle him into a fifth monarch'. The anonymous *Brief Description of the future History of Europe* (1650) claimed that Spain had been seeking

[1] G. Huppert, 'The Renaissance Background of Historicism', *History and Theory*, vi (1966), pp. 55–7. For a typical mid-sixteenth century exposition of Daniel's vision, see J. Sleidan, *De Quatuor Summis Imperiis*, frequently published in English in the ensuing century and a half.
[2] V. Harris, *All Coherence Gone* (Chicago, 1949), *passim*; H. Baker, *The Wars of Truth*, pp. 65–78; anon., *The Generall Signes and Fore-runners of Christs comming* (?c. 1620), *sig.* A4v.
[3] L. E. Froom, *The Prophetic Faith of our Fathers* (Washington, D.C., 1946–54), ii. 267, 484; T. Goodwin, *A Sermon of the Fifth Monarchy* (1654), pp. 25–6; W. Bedloe, *A Narrative and Impartial Discovery of the Horrid Popish Plot* (1679), *sig.* Av.

for a hundred and seventy years, and Sweden more recently, to establish themselves as the Fifth Monarchy. Later in the century, Eva Fröhlichinn, the wife of a Swedish noble, was prophesying a Fifth Monarchy to be established largely by Charles XI of Sweden. Campanella revised his interpretation in his later years, claiming now that Spain was the Fourth Monarchy about to be destroyed by France and the Pope, who together would establish the Fifth.[1]

The concept of a Fifth Monarchy was thus widely known. In Ben Jonson's *Alchemist* (1613), the worldly knight, Sir Epicure Mammon, expecting to become master of the secrets of alchemy,

talk'd

> *Of a fifth monarchy I would erect,*
> *With the Philosopher's Stone . . .*[2]

An Anglican minister could write casually in 1682 that Christ had been crucified because the Jews had 'pretended . . . to the *Romans*, that He intended to set up a Fifth Monarchy'.[3] The phrase was used, for example, in the millenarian prophecies of the Baptist, Henry Jessey, in 1647, and of the Presbyterian, Nathaniel Stephens, in 1656. It was used, too, in 1664 by the Cambridge Platonist, Henry More, who taught that '*The Reformed parts of Christendom are . . . the real* Fifth Monarchy'.[4]

Millenarianism, then, was only one aspect of an almost universal belief in the constant intervention of supernatural forces in the affairs of individuals and of nations. And the Fifth Monarchy Men represented only one attempt amongst many in the period, in many nations, to utilize the Biblical prophecies to justify the erection of one supreme world power. But they seem to have been unique in expecting this kingdom to arise from amongst the saints, ordinary citizens and soldiers. Whereas prophets such as Campanella provided valuable propaganda support for the government concerned, the Fifth Monarchy Men seemed to stand for revolution and anarchy.

---

[1] T. Campanella, *A Discourse Touching the Spanish Monarchy* (1654), pp. 10–12; M. Reeves, *The Influence of Prophecy in the late Middle Ages: A Study in Joachism* (Oxford, 1969), pp. 387–8; F. A. Yates, *Giordano Bruno and the Hermetic Tradition* (1964), pp. 360–97; J. Milton, *Complete Prose Works*, i, ed. D. M. Wolfe (New Haven and London, 1953), p. 582; T. Birch, ed., *A Collection of the State Papers of John Thurloe* (1742), ii. 126; anon., *Brief Description*, p. 33; H. Corrodi, *Kritische Geschichte des Chiliasmus* (Frankfurt and Leipzig, 1781–3) iv. 24.

[2] Jonson, *The Alchemist*, IV. iii.

[3] M. Barne, *A Discourse Concerning . . . Christ's Kingdom* (1682), p. 32.

[4] H. Jessey, *The exceeding Riches of Grace* (1647), sig. A4; N. Stephens, *A Plaine and Easy Calculation of the Name . . . of the Beast* (1656), sig. a1v; H. More, *A Modest Inquiry into the Mystery of Iniquity* (1664), p. 204.

CHAPTER TWO

The Origins and Rise
of Millenarianism to 1649

The origins of seventeenth-century millenarianism are to be found in the tensions created by the Reformation, and in the new exegesis of the prophetic texts which these tensions produced. The vision of a New Jerusalem, contained especially in the books of Daniel and Revelation, gave a millenarian outlook to the early Church. At the popular level, Cerinthus and his sect at the end of the first century A.D. looked forward to a thousand years' reign of luxury and ease. Many of the Early Fathers, such as Irenaeus, Tertullian, Lactantius and Cyprian, indulged in a similar if more spiritual vision. This teaching was undermined by St. Augustine, who imposed a metaphorical interpretation. The thousand years' reign became merely the work of the church on earth, and the first resurrection from the dead (Rev. xx. 6) denoted only the change from sin to purity.[1] The Augustinian interpretation was accepted generally until the Reformation period.

The Reformation itself produced important changes in the approach to Daniel and Revelation. The vision of Daniel consisted of four beasts, representing world empires (generally accepted in this period as Babylon, the Medes and Persians[2], Greece, and Rome). The last beast had ten horns, or kings, and a little horn which destroyed several of the ten. After the destruction of the last beast, the kingdom was given to the saints for ever—the 'Fifth Monarchy'. No dates were given, but there were cryptic references to a time of woe lasting 1290 days, and a fullness of joy beginning after 1335 days.[3] The prophecies of Revelation were still more involved. They described the reign of the Beast as lasting for 1260 days or 42 months.

[1] E. L. Tuveson, *Millenium and Utopia* (Berkeley and Los Angeles, 1949), pp. 1–17.
[2] Or Assyria.   [3] Dan. vii and xii, *passim*.

Two beasts persecute the saints, one from the earth with two horns, the other from the sea, with seven heads and ten horns. Two witnesses who testify against them are killed, lie dead for $3\frac{1}{2}$ days and then rise again. During this persecution, God encourages the saints by punishing His enemies—the opening of the seven seals, the blowing of the seven trumpets and the pouring out of the seven vials of wrath. After this, Satan is bound for a thousand years; Christ and the saints reign for a thousand years, and then, at the end of the world, follows the battle of Armageddon, in which Satan is slain, and then Last Judgement begins.[1]

In 1522 Luther accepted the Augustinian interpretation. But by 1545 he had come to accept that Daniel and Revelation were genuine, if obscure, historical prophecies, and that the Fourth Monarchy and the Beast both represented the papacy. The thousand years were a literal period of time, but were already over, having begun at the time of Christ. Though the Protestants might be comforted by the vials of divine wrath, Luther held that persecution would continue until the end of the world, which was imminent. Calvin was very cautious, accepting only that the Beast was the papacy, but many of the leading figures of the Reformation, such as Bullinger, Oseander and Melancthon, accepted a position close to that of Luther.[2]

There were several reasons for the popularity of this new exegesis. The Protestant emphasis on the letter of Scripture instead of tradition and authority, and the new interest in the ideas of the early, 'pure' church, led naturally to a re-examination of Augustinian orthodoxy. Luther himself was influenced by Lollard and Hussite tradition, for they had in many respects preceded him in his new position.[3] Renaissance writers were attracted by a cyclical theory of history, and found support for their beliefs in Daniel's concept of history as the rise and fall of a series of basically similar world empires.[4] To prove that the Pope was Antichrist was naturally good propaganda for the Reformers, but the new exegesis had a far deeper attraction. Every Protestant was confronted with the funda-

---

[1] Rev. vi–viii, xi–xiii, xvi, xx–xxii.

[2] Tuveson, *op. cit.*, pp. 17, 24–9; T. F. Torrance, 'The Eschatology of the Reformation', *Scottish Journal of Theology*, Occasional Paper no. 2, pp. 36–62; L. E. Froom, *The Prophetic Faith of our Fathers* (Washington, D.C., 1946–54), ii. 255–79. Froom's work is coloured by his own adventist beliefs, but on historical eschatology he is a sound guide.

[3] Torrance, 'Eschatology', p. 43.

[4] F. E. Manuel, *Shapes of Philosophical History* (1965), pp. 46–69.

mental problem of why God had allowed the Roman church to persecute the truth for a thousand years. By accepting the biblical prophecies, a complete answer was found: the whole of history was the working-out of an inscrutable but divine plan, leading to an inevitably just conclusion.[1] Illyricus re-wrote history to present this thesis, which was adopted by John Foxe in his *Acts and Monuments* (1563), itself a major source-book.

The prophecies also explained the chaos following the Reformation, which seemed without parallel in the history of the church. The Bible predicted that the last days would be a time of woe, with wars, corruption and decay.[2] Interpreters were quick to point out that this prophecy appeared to be in progress. The wars and disputes, and the threat of destruction by the Emperor, Spain and France seemed to betoken the end of the world, and there was an almost universal Protestant belief in the imminent dissolution of all things.

The new interpretation of the prophecies spread to England quite rapidly. Protestants who fled abroad under Henry VIII and Mary accepted the new ideas and translated the commentaries which contained them. In the 1540s George Joye translated the expositions by Oseander, Melancthon and Oecolampadius. Many other translations followed under Elizabeth, including in 1574 a compendium of the work of sixteen continental Protestants, arguing that the vials were in progress and that Christ's coming was imminent.[3] English Protestants, including Latimer, Sandys, Jewel, Bale, Hooper and Cranmer, adopted this position.[4]

One of the returning Marian exiles was John Foxe, whose *Acts and Monuments* gave English apocalyptic ideas their greatest impetus. It narrated the history of the church, showing how in all ages true Christians had recognized the Pope as Antichrist. Foxe used not only the biblical prophecies themselves and the works of the Early Fathers, but the testimony of the great mediaeval heresies, the Albigenses, Waldenses, Hussites and Lollards, and of individual seers such as Joachim of Fiore, to look forward to the fall of the Pope, and the Turks, and a period of bliss when this world ended.

---

[1] S. A. Burrell, 'The Apocalyptic Vision of the Early Covenanters', *Scottish Historical Review*, xliii (1964), pp. 4–5.

[2] For example, II Tim. iii. 1–13.

[3] G. Joye, *The exposicion of Daniel* (Geneva, 1545); A. Oseander, *The coniectures of the ende of the worlde*, trans. Joye (1548); A. Marlorat, *A Catholike exposition upon the Revelation*, trans. A. Golding (1574).

[4] Tuveson, *op. cit.*, pp. 49–50; Froom, *Prophetic Faith*, ii. 355–419.

Where possible he used English sources, including a sermon of 1388 by Ralph Wimbledon proclaiming that the world was about to end. Any prophecy which was conceivably relevant was included, such as the sayings of Merlin, the Sibylline oracles (which were said to have foretold the careers of Huss and Jerome of Prague) and Turkish prophecies. Foxe was not a millenarian, but later writers who were, including Fifth Monarchists, drew heavily upon his work.[1]

Luther and the early writers had confessed that whilst accepting the Biblical prophecies as genuine, they found them obscure and sometimes incomprehensible.[2] But naturally men wished to know exactly how far the prophecies had progressed. Many Calvinists, seeing themselves as especially favoured by God, claimed to have been favoured with prophetic powers. John Knox asserted that 'God hath revealed unto me secretes unknowen to the worlde, and . . . hath made my tong a trumpet to forewarne realmes and nations . . . of mutations and chaunges'.[3] The Fifth Monarchist, Mary Cary, declared that 'all Saints have in a measure a spirit of Prophesie'.[4] Thus commentators began to claim that each political event could be identified with complete confidence in Daniel and Revelation. Marlorat identified the first vial of wrath (Rev. xvi. 2) as the venereal disease which struck the French army during the Italian wars at the end of the fifteenth century, and several others adopted this position.[5] John Mayer, minister of Little Wratting, Suffolk, thought the first vial referred to the Albigenses and Waldenses; the Puritan, Henry Burton, thought it signified Luther.[6] The exiled Italian Protestant, Jacobus Brocard, argued that the seventh and last vial was already in progress.[7] As early as 1597 one writer had fixed on 1666 as the date when Antichristian Rome would fall, a prophecy which later found widespread support, and there was general agreement that Christ's coming was imminent.[8] The most important of these writers was John Napier of Merchistoun, the

---

[1] J. Foxe, *Acts and Monuments*, ed. J. Pratt (1877), iii. 301ff, 721, iv. 116–17. For Fifth Monarchist use of Foxe, see Note 1 (p. 45).

[2] Froom, *Prophetic Faith*, ii. 277.

[3] Maitland, *Notes on the Contributions*, part ii, p. 116.

[4] M. Cary, *The Little Horns Doom & Downfall* (1651), p. 106.

[5] Marlorat, *op. cit.*, f. 225–*v.*; J. Mayer, *Ecclesiastica Interpretatio* (1627), p. 465; G. Gifford, *Sermons upon . . . Revelation* (1599), pp. 307–8; J. Trapp, *A Commentary or Exposition upon . . . Revelation* (1647), p. 556.

[6] Mayer, *op. cit.*, p. 474; H. Burton, *The Seven Vials* (1628), p. 14.

[7] J. Brocard, *The Revelation of S. Ihon reveled*, trans. J. Sanford (1582), f. 140.

[8] T.L. (i.e. T. Lupton), *Babylon is Fallen* (1597), p. 26. Cf. anon., *A Prophesie that hath Lyen hid, Above these 2000 yeares* (1610), p. 45. See below, pp. 213–14.

Scottish laird who invented logarithms, who reconciled for the first time all the prophetic numbers and identified all the seals, trumpets, woes and vials. Napier concluded that Rome and her allies would fall by 1639, and that the world would end about 1688.[1]

Despite the pleasure with which it anticipated the punishment of God's enemies, the apocalyptic school was definitely pessimistic in outlook. There was no hope of real improvements before the end of the world. The thousand years' reign was either a figurative expression or had ended in 1000 or 1300. But this view of the thousand years was the only matter in which the apocalyptic school differed from the millenarian, which expected a reign of the saints on earth before the end of all things—and the chronology of Revelation was by no means self-evident.

The first millenarian development after the Reformation was in Germany and at a popular level. As early as 1520 a vagrant priest, Thomas Müntzer, established himself at Zwickau near the Bohemian border, and declared that the elect must rise up and annihilate the godless to prepare for Christ's coming and the millennium. He won a considerable following among the local weavers, mine-workers and peasants. The most important movement was in 1534–5 when the Anabaptists won control of the city of Münster and proclaimed it as the New Jerusalem. Its programme included polygamy, a ferocious legal code based on the statutes laid down in the Old Testament, and the abolition of the private ownership of money and many other goods; the social order was inverted completely. In June 1535 the New Jerusalem was captured by an army of mercenaries raised by the bishop of Münster, and the saints were put to the sword.[2]

Münster involved only the lower orders of society; its leader, John of Leyden, was a former tailor, and its only effect on orthodox eschatology was to discredit millenarianism. But in time, reputable theologians did move towards a millenarian position without drawing any radical social or political conclusions. The study of the early history of the Church brought to light the fact that many of the Early Fathers, such as Tertullian and Irenaeus, had been millenarians, and this weakened the charge that such a belief was a new and seditious heresy. In the mid-seventeenth century Nathaniel Homes

---

[1] J. Napier, *A Plaine Discovery of the whole Revelation* (Edinburgh, 1593), *passim.*
[2] Cohn, *Pursuit of the Millennium*, pp. 251–306; G. H. Williams, *The Radical Reformation* (1962), chap. xiii.

justified his millenarian ideas by printing several hundred pages of excerpts from Early Christian and Jewish writers. Baxter shrank from describing so many saints as heretics.[1] Moreover, the continued survival of the world, the victory of Henry of Navarre over the Guises, the defeat of the Spanish Armada, and the successful rebellion of the Dutch gave grounds for a more optimistic outlook. Napier, who described these events, foresaw a period between the fall of Rome and the end of the world which could not be other than happy.[2] Professor Collinson describes the general belief of Elizabethan Puritans in 'some kind of apocalyptic victory which would bring in the discipline'.[3]

The first to reinterpret the prophecies in this light was Thomas Brightman (1562–1607), a minister educated at Cambridge, with strong Presbyterian views.[4] In his commentary, published abroad in 1609, Brightman argued that although there were still many afflictions to come, there would be a thousand years' reign on earth, which had already begun. The millennium was the purified Presbyterian church, beginning about 1300 with Marsilio of Padua and then Wyclif, and destined to reach a glorious climax with the conversion of the Jews and the ruin of bishops, papists and Turks.[5] Brightman had some lay supporters, including among the gentry the Osborne family who gave him hospitality, but his work was published abroad and made its greatest impact only after 1640.[6]

A very different position was taken by Johannes Alsted (1588–1638), professor of Philosophy at Herborn. He argued that the establishment of the millennium would involve a sudden and total transformation of the world. According to his system, the first three vials were poured out between 1517 and 1625; the last four would be between 1625 and 1694, when the last judgement would begin. The saints would be raised from the dead, and the elect would reign on earth for a thousand years. Alsted's adoption of this revolutionary

---

[1] N. Homes, *The Resurrection Revealed* (1654), *passim*; R. Baxter, *Which is the True Church* (1679), p. 163.

[2] Napier, *op. cit.*, pp. 179–86.

[3] P. Collinson, *The Elizabethan Puritan Movement* (1967), pp. 389–90.

[4] *D.N.B.*; B. G. Cooper, 'The Academic Re-discovery of Apocalyptic Ideas in the 17th Century', *Baptist Quarterly*, xviii (1959–60), pp. 352–6; P. Toon, *Puritans, the Millennium and the Future of Israel* (1970), pp. 26–32.

[5] Brightman, *Apocalypsis Apocalypseos* (Frankfort, 1609); English trans., *The Revelation of St. John Illustrated* (4th edn., 1644), esp. pp. 824–5; Brightman, *An Exposition of the 11th Chapter of Daniel* (1644), *passim*.

[6] F. Osborne, *Traditional Memoirs* (1658), p. 34, cited by H. R. Trevor-Roper, *Religion, the Reformation and Social Change* (1967), p. 248n.

eschatology seems to have been caused by the early disasters of the Thirty Years' War, which drove him into exile, and threatened the very existence of Protestantism. In these circumstances, Brightman's millennium, to be achieved by gradual reforms, seemed neither relevant nor possible.[1]

The first important English millenarian of this kind was Joseph Mede (1586–1668), a celebrated Cambridge theologian who stayed inside the Anglican Church, and was a friend of Archbishop Ussher. Almost certainly influenced by Alsted, Mede systematized all the prophecies and concluded that there was to be a thousand years' reign on earth, and that it was entirely in the future; it would be *'in and during the day of judgement; which day of judgement should continue a thousand years, beginning with the ruin of Antichrist'*.[2] In later years, the Fifth Monarchy Men drew heavily on all three of these writers.[3]

Despite press censorship, millenarian ideas did circulate in pre-revolutionary England. In 1586 Ralph Durden, a minister educated at Cambridge, was imprisoned for predicting the downfall of the Tudor monarchy, which he identified as the Beast of Rev. xvii. He prophesied that he would lead the Jews and all the saints to rebuild Jerusalem, and would defeat all the kings of the earth, who 'shall be obedient to us, and pay us tribute' for a thousand years. A mark on his thigh was final proof that he was the messianic king of Rev. xix. 16 who had 'on his thigh the name written, KING OF KINGS, AND LORD OF LORDS'. Durden apparently submitted, for he remained for many years a minister in Essex.[4] A work by John Wilkinson, a Brownist minister imprisoned for many years, was published posthumously in 1619 and concluded with the promise of Rev. xx. 4, that the saints would reign with Christ a thousand years.[5] John Stoughton, a London minister who died in 1639 and had been in the circle of the Puritan earl of Warwick, claimed in a tract published

[1] J. Alsted, *The Beloved City*, trans. W. Burton (1643), pp. 13–19; R. G. Clouse, 'The Influence of John Henry Alsted on English Millenarian Thought in the Seventeenth Century' (U. of Iowa Ph.D. thesis, 1963; microfilm in Dr. Williams's Library), pp. 108–205; Cooper, 'Academic Re-discovery', pp. 358–62.

[2] *D.N.B.*, Mede; Cooper, 'Academic Re-discovery', *Bapt. Quart.*, xix (1961–2), pp. 29–34; Mede, *The Key of the Revelation*, trans. R. More (1643), p. 121, 2nd pagin., p. 129; Mede, *The Apostacy of the latter Times* (1641), sig. A2–v.; Clouse, 'Influence of Alsted', pp. 207–13.

[3] See Note (pp. 45–6).

[4] J. Strype, *Annals of the Reformation* (Oxford, 1824), II. i., pp. 693–4, II. ii., pp. 479–87; J. Venn and J. A. Venn, *Alumni Cantabrigienses . . . to 1751* (Cambridge, 1922–7), ii. 77.

[5] J. Wilkinson, *An Exposition of the 13. Chapter of the Revelation* (1619), sig. A1v., p. 37.

after his death that despite appearances, the princes were about to rise up, destroy the Pope and the Habsburgs and establish the last millennial age.[1] In a sermon preached in the early 1640s, the Independent minister Thomas Goodwin declared he had been a millenarian for twenty years.[2] Goodwin had been convinced by one Wood, whom he called the first English millenarian. This was probably Tempest Wood, born about 1575, educated at Christ's College, Cambridge, and vicar of Lavington (alias Lenton), Lincs., from 1601. In the 1620s Wood sent his 'elaborate Meditations' on Revelation to Mede, with whom he had a long correspondence.[3] Wood may well have been the Lincolnshire vicar who was reported in 1629 to believe that Christ and the saints would eat and drink during a future reign on earth.[4] The exiled Independent church at Arnhem, to which William Bridge and Sidrach Simpson belonged, was later said to have consisted of 'crassi *Chiliastae*'.[5] John Mayer noted in 1627 that many men believed in the reign of the saints on earth.[6]

When authority began to crumble in 1640, these men emerged into view. In *A Glimpse of Sions Glory* (1641), Thomas Goodwin wrote of the dawning new world, and William Kiffin, later one of the leading Baptists, added an epistle. Goodwin declared that at present 'the saints have but little in the World; now they are the poorest and meanest of all', but soon 'the World shall be theirs'.[7] Jeremiah Burroughes, another Independent, predicted a future reign on earth, and argued that the prophetic texts were otherwise incomprehensible.[8] Also in 1641, John Archer prophesied a kingdom of heaven on earth, established by Christ in person and governed by the saints. Whereas at present 'all the world groanes under tyranny and oppression of Kings', all earthly monarchies would be destroyed. It would be a time of universal peace and riches, heralded by the fall of Rome, which would occur in 1666. Archer had been a London

---

[1] J. Stoughton, *Felicitas Ultimi Saeculi* (1640), *passim*; Trevor–Roper, *op. cit.*, pp. 258–9.

[2] T. Goodwin, *The World to Come* (1655), p. 30.

[3] Ibid., p. 19; J. Mede, *Works* (1672 edn.), pp. 581–605; Venn and Venn, *Al. Cantab.*, iv. 454.

[4] Mede, *Works*, pp. 773–4.

[5] G. Hornius, *Historia Ecclesiastica et Politica* (Leyden and Rotterdam, 1665), p. 268, cited by G. F. Nuttall, *Visible Saints* (Oxford, 1957), p. 148n.

[6] Mayer, *Ecclesiastica Interpretatio*, pp. 503–4.

[7] Goodwin, *Glimpse*, p. 28; for Goodwin's authorship, see J. F. Wilson, 'A Glimpse of Syons Glory', *Church History*, xxxi (1962), pp. 66–73; Toon, *op. cit.*, pp. 131–6.

[8] J. Burroughes, *Moses his Choice* (1641), pp. 485–7.

lecturer in 1629, but was silenced by Laud. In 1631 he was presented by the Feoffees for Impropriations to All Saints', Hertford, but in 1638 it was reported that he had already been absent for over a year, and was not likely to return. Probably he had already fled abroad, and he became pastor of the church at Arnhem. He died abroad, in or shortly before 1642.[1] Robert Maton, another minister, published in 1642 his belief that Christ would shortly return, restore the Kingdom of Israel, and reign on earth. Like Goodwin, and probably others, Maton 'was always in his heart a Millinary, which he never discovered in publick till the Rebellion broke out'.[2] William Bridge asserted in 1641 that *'I shall not prophecie if I say, The sword is now drawne, whose anger shall not be pacified till* Babylon *be downe, and* Sion *rais'd'*.[3] Henry Burton, whilst a prisoner on Guernsey (from 1637 to 1640), announced his expectation that 'Christ alone may reigne' and that God would 'subject the Kingdome to Christs Government'.[4] In the 1630s, millenarian beliefs were adopted by James Toppe, a Baptist minister and schoolmaster of Tiverton, who expected Christ to appear and reign in person.[5]

Though few of the laity ventured into print on the interpretation of the prophecies, apocalyptic and millenarian ideas certainly spread among them. At the highest level, the future James I had declared in 1588 that the Pope was Antichrist, and that the last age was at hand.[6] Many of the commentaries mentioned above were dedicated to laymen of high standing, such as the earls of Leicester and Essex, and Sir Walter Mildmay, Chancellor of the Exchequer.[7] One of the few lay interpreters was Lady Eleanor Douglas who, though thought insane and put in Bedlam, shared many of the characteristics of radical Puritanism. In 1633 she predicted the execution of Charles I, and in 1625 she had declared that the last judgement was only $19\frac{1}{2}$ years hence. She identified James I as the little horn (Dan. vii. 8). To symbolize her scorn for episcopacy, she poured tar over the alter at Lichfield Cathedral.[8] The fact that

---

[1] J. Archer, *The Personall Reigne of Christ upon Earth* (1642, 1st edn. 1641), p. 53 and *passim*. For his career, see Biographical Appendix.

[2] R. Maton, *Israels Redemption* (1642); A. Wood, *Athenae Oxonienses* (1691), ii. 123.

[3] W. Bridge, *Babylons Downfall* (1641), sig. A3.

[4] H. Burton, *The Sounding of the Two Last Trumpets* (1641), pp. 43, 88.

[5] W. H. Burgess, 'James Toppe and the Tiverton Anabaptists', *Trans. Bapt. Hist. Soc.*, iii (1912–13), pp. 193–211.

[6] James I, *A Fruitefull Meditation* (1603 edn.), sig. A4v., B3v.

[7] The works of Brocard, Gifford and Marlorat respectively.

[8] E. Audley (later Douglas), *A Warning to the Dragon* (1625), esp. p. 100; Douglas, *The Excommunication out of Paradise* (1647), p. 16; *Bethlehem Signifying the House of*

the apocalyptic sermon preached by Ralph Wimbledon in 1388 went through at least sixteen editions between 1550 and 1635 testified to a much more widespread lay concern over the world's end.[1] The sermons at Paul's Cross were used by the government from 1534 as propaganda to persuade the population that the Pope was Antichrist, and about to fall.[2] The interests of the preachers were no doubt reflected in their sermons and conversation. The Puritan, Richard Rothwell (1563–1627), was so concerned with Daniel and Revelation that, despite a warning from Whitgift, 'he seldom preached abroad out of any other Scriptures'.[3] Ben Jonson, in *The Alchemist* (1613), alluded to a Puritan preoccupation with Daniel's Four Monarchies.[4] William Gouge described a common 'superstitious practise', by which people 'sit up all night at certaine times of the yeere, keeping themselves awake with talking one with another, playing on instruments, . . . upon a conceit that Christ will come in iudgement on some of those nights . . . and they would not then be found asleepe'.[5] It was thought necessary in 1552 to include in the liturgy three articles condemning millenarian ideas and the associated beliefs that hell was only temporary, and that the damned would be pardoned after the thousand years. The related idea of the soul's sleep or death was an ancient heresy, held also by such eminent figures as Luther and Milton. But amongst the Anabaptists of the 1530s and the English sects of the 1640s and '50s, it became an element in lower-class radicalism. To attack the doctrine of hell was to weaken a vital sanction by which the structure of society was maintained, and the belief was made a criminal offence by the Blasphemy and Heresy Ordinance of 1648.[6]

The appearance of pseudo-prophets is further evidence, though of an indirect and general kind, of lay millennial excitement. Though

---

Bread (1652), p. 5; S. G. Wright, 'Dougle Fooleries', *Bodleian Quart. Rec.*, vii (1932), pp. 95–8; cf. C. J. Hindle, *A Bibliography of . . . Lady Eleanor Douglas* (Edinburgh, 1936), pp. 1–10.
 [1] A. W. Pollard and G. R. Redgrave, *Short Title Catalogue . . . 1475–1640* (1950), p. 601.
 [2] M. Maclure, *The Paul's Cross Sermons* (Toronto, 1958), *passim*.
 [3] S. Clarke, *A Generall Martyrologie . . . Whereunto are added two and twenty Lives* (1660), 2nd pagination, p. 87.
 [4] Jonson, *The Alchemist*, IV. iii.
 [5] W. Gouge, *Workes* (1627), part ii, p. 234.
 [6] *The Two Liturgies . . . of King Edward VI*, ed. J. Ketley (Parker Soc., xiv, Cambridge, 1844), p. 537; Gouge, *Workes*, pt. ii, p. 295; R. Overton, *Mans Mortalitie*, ed. H. Fisch (Liverpool, 1968), esp. the Introduction; C. H. Firth and R. S. Rait, eds., *Acts and Ordinances of the Interregnum* (1911), p. 1135. Cf. D. P. Walker, *The Decline of Hell* (1964).

the sanity of many of these prophets may be doubted, the very forms their delusions took testify to the character of popular ideas and preoccupations. In 1555 two women were punished for claiming that a new-born child had proclaimed that 'the kyngdom of God is at hand'. On 10 April 1561 William Geffrey was whipped through the streets of London for claiming that one John Moore was Christ. Two days later a man was put in the stocks for claiming to be 'kynge of all kynges'. In 1562 one Elizeus Hall of Manchester went to London, claiming to be a messenger sent by God to the Queen. He was imprisoned, and died in 1565. In 1586 John White, a shoemaker of Rayleigh, Essex, claimed to be John the Baptist.[1] The most notorious of these prophets was William Hacket, a malt-maker, who in 1591 declared that Christ had returned in him, and was about to fulfil all prophecies. Two gentlemen who supported him, Coppinger and Arthington, proclaimed the news and invited people to call on Christ at one Walker's house in Broken Wharf. Hacket, they said, was to be king of Europe. A 'mightie concourse of the common multitude' followed them through the city, chanting their slogans, led by 'a great multitude of lads and young persons of the meaner sort'. Hacket was taken and executed.[2] In 1628 Edward Francklin, Esquire, was put in Bedlam after proclaiming in church that his brother was God, his son Christ, and one Lady Dyer was the Holy Ghost. A Warwickshire woman thought she was the 'Mother of God and of all things living.'[3] Two London weavers, Farnham and Bull, claimed in 1636 to be the two witnesses of Rev. xi. 3, asserting that the millennium was imminent and that even if executed, they would rise again on the third day and reign as king and high priest in Jerusalem. They both died of the plague in prison.[4] Had the authorities been less firmly in control, such instances would surely have multiplied, as they did after 1640.

Another element in the origins of Fifth Monarchism was the idea of the elect nation. Apocalyptic and millenarian ideas blended

[1] *The Diary of Henry Machyn*, ed. J. G. Nichols (Camden Soc., xlii, 1848), pp. 88, 255; J. Stow, *A Summarie of the Chronicles of England* (1598), p. 299; R. Holinshed, *The Laste volume of the Chronicles of England* (1577), p. 1815; Strype, *Annals of the Reformation*, I. i, pp. 400, 433–5, I. ii, p. 196, III. i, pp. 37–8.
[2] R. Cosin, *Conspiracie, for Pretended Reformation* (1592), pp. 55–8 and *passim*; *Cal. S.P. Dom., 1591–4*, pp. 75–6.
[3] R. Hunter and I. Macalpine, *Three Hundred Years of Psychiatry, 1535–1860*, (1963), pp. 103–5, 144.
[4] T. Heywood, *A True Discourse of the Two infamous upstart Prophets* (1638), *passim*; anon., *False Prophets Discovered* (1642), *passim*; *Cal. S.P. Dom., 1637–8*, pp. 66, 188, 606.

with the intense nationalism of the period and with the Calvinist concept that only the predestined few, the elect, would be saved. England was the only major Protestant state, and this produced the belief that it was an elect nation destined by God to play a great part in destroying Rome to hasten the world's end, or in setting up the millennium. This doctrine was popular from the time of John Foxe, who showed how the earliest British kings had maintained the true religion, and how God had chosen the Englishman Wyclif as harbinger of the Reformation.[1] John Aylmer, a Marian exile and later bishop of London, argued that England produced Wyclif, who 'begate Husse, who begat Luther, who begat the truth. What greater honor could you or I have, then that it pleased Christ as it were in a second birth to be born again of men among you?' 'God is . . . English' and Elizabeth was 'gods chosen instrument.'[2] Even the continental reformer Martin Bucer of Strassburg accepted the claim. His description of a Christian utopia, *De Regno Christi*, was an account of what England might become under Edward VI.[3] English events predominated in most interpretations of the prophecies. Brightman explained the first vial of wrath as Elizabeth's expulsion of papists and the third vial as Cecil's legislation against the Jesuits.[4] Mede saw this legislation and the defeat of the Armada as the third vial.[5] Robert Parker (*c.* 1564–1614), a radical Puritan minister who died in exile, explained the sixth vial as England, soon to make a way for the sacking of Rome and the conversion of the Jews.[6] Another minister, Richard Bernard, claimed that God had honoured England 'above all other places in the Christian world': the first Christian emperor was Constantine, born in England; the first Christian king was (the mythical) Lucius, king of England; and Wyclif was the first exponent of the truth. The defeat of the Armada, and the success of the Dutch and Huguenots were proof that the cause of God and England was one.[7]

The cautious foreign policy of the Stuarts, especially their refusal to enter the Thirty Years' War, was a severe blow to the theory of the elect nation. Commentators such as Mede turned to

---

[1] W. Haller, *Foxe's Book of Martyrs and the Elect Nation* (1963), esp. chap. 7.
[2] J. Aylmer, *An Harborowe for Faith-full . . . Subiectes* (Strassburg, 1559), pp. 99, 122.
[3] C. Hopf, *Martin Bucer and the English Reformation* (Oxford, 1946), pp. 100–3.
[4] Brightman, *Revelation*, pp. 524, 532–3.
[5] Mede, *Key of the Revelation*, 2nd pagin., p. 116.
[6] R. Parker, *The Mystery of the Vialls Opened* (1651), p. 14.
[7] R. Bernard, *A Key of Knowledge* (1619), pp. 127–9, 279.

Gustavus Adolphus as God's champion and the angel who poured out the fourth vial.[1] But the speed with which the theory reappeared after 1640 shows that it was only dormant.

The evolution of millenarian ideas was perhaps helped by a half-remembered precedent of the Lollards. Their leaders had identified the Papacy as the Beast and Antichrist, and their apocalyptic ideas were set down by Foxe.[2] A millenarian vision of a Lollard victory emerged at a more popular level, and chiliastic hopes have been recorded in East Anglia and Gloucestershire (early fifteenth century), at Newbury in the 1490s and in London and Wiltshire in the early sixteenth century.[3]

The tension produced by the Reformation thus combined with nationalism, Protestant literalism, Calvinist elitism and perhaps Lollard tradition to produce widespread apocalyptic and millenarian beliefs. The civil war, breaking out in 1642, soon came to be seen as the decisive apocalyptic or millenarian struggle, intensifying earlier excitement. The war did not break out over primarily religious conflicts, but there was a long tradition among Puritans of interpreting all political events in an apocalyptic or millenarian sense. There was also a natural tendency for all forces discontented with the Stuart regime to coalesce in opposition to it, whatever the origins of that opposition. Although religion was not at first involved, there were several considerations leading Puritans to support the Parliamentary cause. Queen Henrietta Maria and many courtiers were Catholics, and to many the Laudian church seemed distinctly Catholic in spirit. Instead of trying to neutralize Puritan discontent, Charles identified his cause with that of the Church of England. Radical Puritans had begun long since to denounce the Anglican as well as the Catholic Church as part of Antichrist. Even Brightman had seen the episcopal church as merely luke-warm Laodicea (Rev. iii. 14–16).[4] John Wilkinson argued that every Anglican minister accepted the Mark of the Beast (Rev. xiii. 17) by receiving letters of orders from a bishop.[5] Lady Eleanor Douglas saw Archbishop Laud as the beast from the bottomless pit (Rev. xvii. 8).[6]

[1] Mede, *Key of the Revelation*, 2nd pagin., p. 117; anon., *The Swedish Discipline* (1632), sig. A4v. and *passim*.
[2] Foxe, *op. cit.*, iii. 132, 291.
[3] J. A. F. Thomson, *The Later Lollards* (Oxford, 1965), p. 241.
[4] Brightman, *Revelation*, p. 124.
[5] Wilkinson, *Exposition of the 13. Chapter*, pp. 24–5.
[6] E. Douglas, *The Dragons Blasphemous Charge against Her* (1651), p. 3.

John Cotton, a leading New England Puritan, described Anglicanism in 1642 as the kingdom of the Beast, and expected its collapse under the fifth vial.[1] Henry Burton described the bishops as the 'Limbes' of Antichrist, and John de la March, a Presbyterian gaoled with Burton on Guernsey, claimed they were God's two persecuted witnesses (Rev. xi. 3) and that all episcopal officials were parts of Babylon.[2] Thus the effect of the king's proclamation was to transfer to himself part of the millenarian odium already felt towards the church. This was evident in a pamphlet of 1642 which argued that as bishops sprang from the Antichristian Papacy, the king in defending them became the agent of Antichrist.[3]

. The effect of the traditional use of military imagery by Puritan preachers was probably a further help in transforming the war into a crusade. Though they spoke of spiritual warfare, the concept of Puritan duty as a military struggle must have encouraged this view of literal warfare in 1642. 'The world is the great field of God,' declared Thomas Taylor in 1618, 'in which Michael and his Angels fight against the dragon and his angels.' Simeon Ashe argued in 1642 that 'when we were baptized we took press money, and vowed to serve under the colors of Christ'.[4] John Spencer, groom to Lord Saye and Sele, asserted in 1642: 'Here you must look for fight if ever you would come to heaven . . . The Lord hath told you, *in the last dayes there should be terrible times*, . . . do you not already perceive the very drops of blood begin to fall? . . . Christ seems now to set up his glorious standard.'[5]

These considerations combined to lead many Puritans to find a millenarian meaning in the war. Some, like Spencer, later a Fifth Monarchist, seem to have been convinced immediately, whilst others explained the war as both a defensive struggle against the king's evil counsellors and a war of the Lamb against the Beast, with adherence to the king tantamount to saying 'that the Devil is to be obeyed, and God is to be punished'.[6]

The extensive freedom of the press in the 1640s allowed for the first time the publication of the major millenarian works in England

[1] J. Cotton, *The Powring out of the Seven Vials* (1642), vial 5, p. 5.
[2] Burton, *Sounding of the Two Last Trumpets*, p. 33; J. de la March, *A Complaint of the False Prophets Mariners* (1641), sig. a1–v., p. 6.
[3] Anon., *The Camp of Christ, and the Camp of Antichrist* (1642), *passim.*
[4] M. Walzer, *The Revolution of the Saints* (1966), pp. 277–80.
[5] J. Spencer, *The Spirituall Warfare* (1642), pp. 3, 12, 13. For Spencer see the Biographical Appendix.
[6] Anon., *Englands Alarm to War against the Beast* (1643), tit. pag., sig. B1, p. 16.

and in English. Brightman's work appeared in 1644, preceded by several short, popular versions, sometimes in verse.[1] Alsted's *Diatribe* was translated for the first time, and a summary was also published.[2] Mede's *Clavis Apocalyptica* was translated in 1643, and several of his other millenarian writings were published.[3] Napier's commentary reached its fifth edition in 1645, and it also circulated in two popular versions.[4] The almanacs of Lilly and others such as John Vaux helped to spread apocalyptic ideas, and the newspapers proclaimed that 'Antichrist is falling.'[5] Moreover the works of Paracelsus and Boehme, both of whom held millenarian beliefs, were translated in the years after 1640.[6]

The conviction that God's saints were engaged in a millenarian struggle in England brought the prompt reappearance of the theory of the elect nation. Milton in 1641 remarked on the '*Precedencie* which GOD gave this *Iland*, to be the first *Restorer* of *buried Truth*'.[7] The very turmoils of the war were seen as refining England's character. 'If this *British Northern* nation bee the people chosen of *God* to accomplish the last wonders of the world,' Christopher Syms asked, 'was it not necessary the nation it self be first purged?'[8] Even the cautious Presbyterian, Herbert Palmer, could see the new Reformation as 'the great expectation of the world' and the Independent Hugh Peter visualized the army of the elect nation conquering the world to establish the millennium.[9] William Bridge and Peter Sterry were enthusiastic believers in the theory, but the most exalted view was that of the visionary William Sedgwick, who described England as the 'bosome of the earth where the divine glory chooseth to treasure up his richest *Jewels*: . . . Nothing heer but is spoken by God, made by the *Word* of God; and doth again

---

[1] Brightman, *Revelation of St. John*; anon., *Brightmans Predictions and Prophecies* (1641); *A Revelation of Mr. Brightmans Revelation* (1641); *Sixe strange Prophecies* (1643), sig. A4; *Reverend Mr. Brightmans Iudgement* (1643).
[2] Alsted, *Beloved City* (1643); anon., *The Worlds Proceeding Woes* (1642).
[3] Mede, *Key of the Revelation* (1643 and '50); *A Paraphrase of . . . St. Peter* (1642 and '49); *The Apostacy of the Latter Times* (1641); *Daniel's Weekes* (1643).
[4] Anon., *Napiers Narration* (1642); J. Booker (? = H. Burton), *The Bloudy Almanack* (1647).
[5] J. Vaux, *Vaux. 1643. A Prognostication* (1643), sig. B2–v.; *Certaine Informations*, 27 (17–24 July 1643), p. 209.
[6] D. Hirst, *Hidden Riches* (1964), pp. 76–109; P. M. Rattansi, 'Paracelsus and the Puritan Revolution', *Ambix*, xi (1963), p. 24.
[7] Milton, *Complete Prose Works*, i. 526.
[8] C. Syms, *The Swords Apology* (1644), p. 10.
[9] H. Palmer, *The Duty and Honour of Church-Members* (1646), sig. A3; R. P. Stearns, *The Strenuous Puritan* (Urbana, 1954), p. 330.

speak God: . . . to make *England* a happy Canaan, Father, Son and Spirit agree to dwell in it.'[1]

The crucial development was the adoption and dissemination of millenarian views by Puritan preachers. The speed of this change is only explicable on the assumption that these beliefs were already widespread and were released and intensified, rather than created, by the war. The Scottish Resident in London, Baillie, complained that not only the sectaries but even the gravest of the Presbyterians 'such as Twisse, Marshall, Palmer, and many more, are express Chiliasts'.[2] In a recent detailed study of the fast sermons of the 1640s, Professor J. F. Wilson remarks that millenarianism was 'the most striking and fundamental characteristic of the formal preaching before the Long Parliament'—the majority of the preachers, of course, being Presbyterians.[3] The millenarian wave caught up large numbers of ministers, of Presbyterian, Independent and Baptist views alike. The diary of a cautious Essex Presbyterian, Ralph Josselin, vicar of Earls Colne, suggests that his whole family was preoccupied with millenarian expectations by the early 1650s. In 1650, for example, his thoughts were 'much that god was beginning to ruine the kingdom of the earth, and bringing christs kingdom in'. The following year, his five-year-old daughter dreamed that Christ had appeared in the parish church and later came to her bed and said 'he should come and rayne upon the earth 10000 years'.[4] A complete statistical examination of the extent of the millenarian wave is not possible, but a rough guide can be obtained using the collections of the London bookseller George Thomason, by examining the new works of ministers living in England and supporting Parliament in the civil war in the period 1640–53, the greatest years of the movement.[5] In this period some 112 ministers published three new works, a number which ensures that the most important clergy are included and their ideas fairly represented. Of these no less than 78, or just under 70%, can be identified as millenarians: they believed in an imminent kingdom of glory on earth, either a literal thousand years' reign, or (often in the case of Presbyterians) a period of 'latter-day glory', and often explained the civil war as its precursor.

[1] W. Bridge, *Christs Coming* (1648), sig. A4; P. Sterry, *Englands Deliverance* (1652), p. 34; W. Sedgwick, *The Leaves of the Tree of Life* (1648), pp. 2–3.
[2] R. Baillie, *Letters and Journals* (Edinburgh, 1775), ii. 156.
[3] J. F. Wilson, *Pulpit in Parliament* (London and Princeton, N.J., 1969), p. 195.
[4] A. Macfarlane, *The Family Life of Ralph Josselin* (Cambridge, 1970), pp. 185–6, 190.
[5] G. K. Fortescue, *Catalogue of the Pamphlets . . . Collected by George Thomason* (1908).

Moreover, since not all the works of all the authors have been examined, this is probably less than the true total. Well over a third were not sectaries but Presbyterians. Only four writers denounced millenarian ideas altogether, though several rejected the physical return of Christ and resurrection of the martyrs whilst accepting a millennial kingdom to come.[1]

Moreover, the millenarianism of many of these preachers, including the Presbyterians, was very unlike the calm and academic speculations of Mede, who had even hoped to see the fall of Rome without bloodshed.[2] Many had suffered persecution at the hands of the bishops and some had been forced into exile. Consequently their joy in the happy age to come was equalled or surpassed by their pleasure at the dreadful fate about to overtake their enemies. William Bridge urged upon the House of Commons a policy of simple revenge: 'enquire after this Babylonish company, and . . . repay them according to their demerits. *An eye for an eye, a tooth for a tooth, burning for burning, . . . and blood for blood.*'[3] Henry Jessey, the Baptist, looked forward to when God 'shortly will bring down every high thing'.[4] Many of the ordinary laymen who were attracted to millenarianism may have been drawn primarily by the wish to humiliate their superiors and oppressors.[5]

To achieve the ruin of their enemies and the establishment of New Jerusalem, the preachers called for the zealous prosecution of the war: the millennium, the war, and the cause of God were presented as the same struggle. The Presbyterians were as bellicose as any. 'In vain are the high Praises of God in your Mouths', asserted Charles Herle, 'without a *Two-edged Sword* in your hands.'[6] Edmund Calamy declared that 'The Cause you manage is the Cause of God; . . . He that dies fighting the Lords Battle, dyes a Martyr.'[7] Stephen Marshall assured Parliament that 'All Christendom except the Malignants in England, do now see that the Question in *England* is, whether *Christ*, or *Antichrist*, shall be *Lord* and King.'[8] Even the cautious Richard Baxter could urge on the soldiers against the bishops as 'the Military Instruments of the Devil'.[9] Some of the

---

[1] For details and names, see Note on pp. 46–9.
[2] Mede, *Key of the Revelation*, 2nd pagin., pp. 28–9.
[3] W. Bridge, *Babylons Downfall*, p. 10.
[4] H. Jessey, *The Exceeding Riches of Grace Advanced* (1647), sig. A6v.
[5] See below, pp. 142–3.
[6] R. L'Estrange, *The Dissenter's Sayings* (1681), p. 42.   [7] *Ibid.*, p. 41.
[8] L'Estrange, *The Dissenter's Sayings: The Second Part* (1681), p. 73.
[9] *Ibid.*, p. 25.

Scottish Presbyterians felt the same millenarian hopes about the war. Rutherford and Gillespie, two of the leading ministers, were both enthusiasts. There too the concept of the elect nation played its part in heightening expectations—though naturally the elect nation was Scotland.[1]

Many of the preachers joined the army as chaplains and some preached before Parliament.[2] Many of the leading politicians and officers seem to have accepted their millenarian views. Cromwell and Sir Henry Vane certainly did, and Baillie thought them no better than the Münster Anabaptists.[3] Oliver St. John was the patron of the Anglo-German millenarian Hartlib, whose avowed aim was *'the advancement of the Kingdom of Jesus Christ'*.[4] Lord Brooke, one of the early Parliamentary leaders, who died in 1643, was said to have boasted that he 'should see the millenary fooles Paradise begin in his life time'.[5] The translation of Mede was by Richard More, a Member of Parliament, and Alsted's *Beloved City* was dedicated to Sir John Cordwell, Alderman of London. Sir John Wray, a Lincoln-shire Member, had long possessed an apocalyptic work of Robert Parker, later published in 1651.[6] Parker's son Thomas published a millenarian tract which was dedicated to Philip, earl of Pembroke.[7] Burroughes dedicated a millenarian work to the earl of Warwick who was to help God 'set up Ierusalem as the praise of the earth'.[8] William Prynne hailed the earl of Essex, the Parliamentary general, as the 'Generall of the Lord of Hosts', who was to set up Christ's kingdom.[9] A Parliamentary memorandum on the proposed Treaty of Uxbridge in 1644 reflected that all the prophecies spoke of great tribulations immediately before Christ's kingdom. 'So that the more our perswasions are, that we fight against the beast,' and that the beast was about to fall, 'the stronglier we may conclude that the contrary power shall overcome.' A compromise peace was therefore advised as the best way to stave off the ravages of the beast.[10]

---

[1] S. A. Burrell, 'The Apocalyptic Vision of the Early Covenanters', *Scott. Hist. Rev.*, xliii (1964), pp. 1–24.

[2] L. F. Solt, *Saints in Arms* (1959), *passim*; Trevor-Roper, *op. cit.*, pp. 294–344.

[3] Baillie, *Letters and Journals*, ii. 260.

[4] (A. von Frankenberg), *Clavis Apocalyptica* (1651), sig. *3.

[5] W. Chestlin, *Persecutio Undecima* (1648), p. 56. I owe this reference to Dr. Robin Clifton.

[6] R. Parker, *Mystery of the Vialls*, sig. A1v. I owe this point to Professor Trevor-Roper.

[7] T. Parker, *The Visions and Prophecies of Daniel* (1646).

[8] Burroughes, *Moses his Choice*, sig. A2v.

[9] W. Prynne, *The Popish Royall Favourite* (1643), sig. ¶2.

[10] *Thurloe* (1742), i. 54. I owe this reference to Mr. Blair Worden.

The celebrated continental scholar and millenarian, Comenius, and his associates John Dury and Samuel Hartlib, were in close contact with Cromwell and other Parliamentary leaders.[1] Among millenarians who became Fifth Monarchists, John Carew was a member of the Council of State, and the army officers Harrison, Overton, Rich and Danvers all held the rank of colonel or above.[2] John Cook, the prominent Independent lawyer, was far from hostile: the Independent, he wrote, 'knows no hurt in a million of millenary-like errours; who would not be glad to see Jesus Christ?'[3] A striking illustration of the widespread interest in millenarian ideas was provided later, in January 1654, by the numerous distinguished visitors to the Fifth Monarchist prophetess, Anna Trapnel. They included Col. Sydenham of the Council of State, Cols. West, Bennett and Bingham (all sometime Members of Parliament), Thomas Allen, later Lord Mayor of London, Lady Darcy and Lady Vermuyden.[4] Milton too seems to have been swayed for a time by millenarian hopes.[5]

Even royalists shared some of the apocalyptic and millenarian spirit. An Anglican author in 1642 quoted Alsted, Mede and John Archer to prove the imminence of the millennium. He dedicated the work to Henry, viscount Newark, a prominent royalist, and inserted a commendatory note from Seth Ward, later bishop of Exeter and Salisbury.[6] Joseph Hall thought there could be no millennium, on the grounds that the world was about to end. In 1651 a friend of Bishop Duppa had identified Antichrist (probably as Cromwell), and expected the world to end within two years. Duppa thought 'it might be so, for every body might see that the world was now drawn low, and in the dreggs'. Another royalist explained the two witnesses who would die and then rise again (Rev. xi. 3–12) as the execution of King Charles who would rise again in the person of his son.[7]

---

[1] M. Spinka, *John Amos Comenius* (Chicago, 1943); R. F. Young, *Comenius in England* (1932); Trevor-Roper, *op. cit.*, pp. 249–93.

[2] For all these see Biog. App.

[3] J. Cook, *What the Independent would have* (1647), p. 2, quoted in G. F. Nuttall, *The Holy Spirit in Puritan Faith and Experience* (2nd edn., Oxford, 1947), p. 114.

[4] A. Trapnel, *The Cry of a Stone* (1654), pp. 2–3, 7; G. F. Nuttall, *James Nayler: a Fresh Approach* (1954), pp. 10, 14 and *passim*. For Trapnel see Biog. App.; see also the distinguished visitors to the convert Sarah Wight: Jessey, *Exceeding Riches*, (1647) *passim*.

[5] A. E. Barker, *Milton and the Puritan Dilemma* (Toronto, 1942), pp. 194–6.

[6] T.B., *Nuncius Propheticus* (1642), *passim*.

[7] J. Hall, *The Revelation Unrevealed* (1650), pp. 224–7 and *passim*; Sir Gyles Isham, ed., *The Correspondence of Bishop Brian Duppa and Sir Justinian Isham, 1650–60* (1955), pp. 37–8; E. Hall, *Lingua Testium* (1651), *passim*.

In Scotland, prominent lay millenarians included General David Leslie, who envisaged a European crusade to establish the millennium, and Archibald Johnston of Warriston, Scottish commissioner to the Westminster Assembly. A minority group of the Remonstrant faction of the Presbyterians, led by Johnston and James Guthrie, remained millenarians in the 1650s. In 1655 they were described as 'Fifth-monarchy-presbiterians', but apart from a belief in the millennium and the rule of the godly, the only feature they had in common with the English movement was a violent hostility to the Cromwellian regime.[1]

Inevitably, the excitement and the millenarian ideas passed down to the common people and were reshaped in accordance with the people's own and different hopes. One development in the civil war period was the emergence of a large number of popular prophets in the tradition of Hacket. In 1644, for example, a labourer named Rowland Bateman claimed to be both the Son of God and Abraham, and said the king was his son Isaac. He announced that he must be hanged, and would rise again on the third day, and that the millennium would begin in nine years' time. Despite the confusion of his ideas, there were fears about the 'many severall sorts of People that hourly flocke unto him'.[2] Nicholas Nelson was sent to the Gatehouse in 1647, after saying 'he is the Lord's Anointed for this Kingdom, to lead them that are the Lord's as Moses led the Israelites out of Egypt; and that the King is a murderer.'[3] Rhys or 'Arise' Evans, a Welsh tailor who had been a self-appointed prophet since the 1630s, stood up in St. Botolph's, Bishopsgate, in 1647 and proclaimed that he was Christ. For a time he belonged to Chamberlen's Fifth Monarchist congregation, but later became a royalist propagandist.[4] Several women claimed to be with child by the Holy Ghost, and that their child would be the Messiah.[5] John Robins, a Ranter, claimed to be God the Father, and found a number of disciples.[6] A sect arose at Andover in 1649 led by a rope-maker

[1] C. Hill, *Puritanism and Revolution* (1962 edn.), p. 130; Burrell, *art. cit.*, pp. 20–1; *Thurloe*, iv. 557.

[2] Anon., *Beware of False Prophets* (1644), *passim*.

[3] Cal. Middx. Sessions (typescript in Middlesex Record Office), ii. (1644–52), p. 83; I owe this reference to Mr. K. V. Thomas.

[4] *D.N.B.*, Rhys Evans; anon., *Strange Newes from New-Gate* (1647), where Evan Price was perhaps an error for Rhys Evans; Minutes of the Lothbury Church, Bodl. MS. Rawlinson D 828, f. 18.

[5] Anon., *A List of Some of the Grand Blasphemers* (1654), brs.

[6] Anon., *A List of Some of the Grand Blasphemers* (1654), brs.; *All the Proceedings at the Sessions of the Peace holden at Westminster* (1651), *passim*.

named William Franklin, who had deserted his wife to live with Mary Gadbury, who sold pins and laces and was accused of keeping a brothel. They moved to Hampshire (the land of Ham, Psalm cv. 23), and Franklin announced that he was Christ and about to establish the millennium. His 'very plausible' tongue won many converts, including a local minister. His followers also claimed to have visions, and ascribed to themselves such roles as John the Baptist, the two witnesses and the angels who were to destroy God's enemies, among whom were listed several unpopular local figures. Franklin was arrested and recanted in 1650, when his sect already numbered five or six hundred.[1] George Foster, claiming to be the voice of God, declared that the chosen people of all lands would gather in Jerusalem to inaugurate the millennium.[2] Lodowick Muggleton, claiming that he and his friend John Reeve were the two witnesses, founded a sect which lasted for several centuries.[3] The London goldsmith, Thomas Tany, claimed descent from Henry VII and Aaron, High Priest of the Jews, demanded the crowns of England, France, Naples, Rome and Jerusalem, and proclaimed that he was to lead the Jews back to Israel. In 1655, inspired by a vision to kill all the Members of Parliament, he attacked the House single-handed, wearing an ancient costume and armed with a rusty sword. The doorkeeper was wounded, and Tany was sent to prison.[4]

Bizarre as these prophets seem, many were able to win popular support, and the sense of divine intervention in their daily lives was the same feeling which inspired many to millenarian enthusiasm. Many contemporaries testified that such enthusiasm was widespread amongst ordinary people. One author complained as early as 1642 that 'millenaries are most frequent with us; men that looke for a temporal Kingdome, that must begin presently and last a thousand yeares . . . to promote that Kingdom of Christ, they teach that all the ungodly must be killed, that the wicked have no propriety in their estates . . . This doctrine filleth the simple people with a furious and unnaturall zeale.'[5] The two heresiographers, Edwards

[1] H. Ellis, *Pseudochristus* (1650), *passim*; Cohn, *Pursuit of the Millennium*, pp. 336–9.
[2] G. Foster, *The Pouring Forth of the Seventh and Last Viall* (1656); Foster, *The Sound of the Last Trumpet* (1650), both *passim*.
[3] *D.N.B.*, Muggleton; J. Reeve and L. Muggleton, *A Transcendent Spiritual Treatise* (1652), pp. 4–5.
[4] T. Tany, *Hear, O Earth* (1654), brs.; *Thearauiohn High Priest* (1652), *passim*; *Thau Ram Tanjah* (1654), brs.; *The Nations Right* (1651), p. 1; *A Perfect Account*, 209 (3–10 Jan. 1655), p. 1666.
[5] Anon., *A Short History of the Anabaptists* (1642), pp. 54–5.

and Pagitt, both included the expectation of an earthly reign by the saints 'in outward glory and pomp' as a popular heresy.[1] Another wrote in 1645 of the increasing belief in a time of 'prosperity, peace, riches, plenty, wealth, and glory, with such supreme power and Majesty, as never any Monarch in this world had before'.[2]

As early as May 1643 the soldiers at Wallingford were repeating a rumour that 'Christ shall come into the world and destroy King Charles, and that the Earl of Essex is accounted for John the Baptist'.[3] One William Bowling of Cranbrook, Kent, expounded the text 'this day shalt thou be with me in Paradise' (Luke xxiii. 43) as 'when I come personally to reign upon earth a 1,000 years, at that day shalt thou be with me in my Kingdom'. Philip Tandy, from near York, was confident that 'within these very few yeers I shall see him whom our soul loveth'.[4] Often the preachers directed their millenarian teaching at the lower classes. John Brayne, a minister at Winchester, had a vision that Christ would begin to reign 'first in England, where the meanest people, that are now despised, shall have first the revelation of Truth'. Thomas Goodwin presented this vision to the army.[5] Goodwin himself taught that 'God intends to make use of the common People in the great Worke of proclaiming the Kingdome of his Sonne'.[6] In 1647 William Sedgwick declared that Christ would come to judgement within a fortnight, and was said to have claimed that Christ had appeared in his study at Ely.[7] Several years earlier, in 1643, a preacher told the Commons that 'the generall talk throughout the household'—probably in London— 'among the domesticks, is, that Christ their King is comming to take possession of his Throne'.[8] Hugh Peter spoke of the universal interest, 'Some looking to the prophesies that concern *Gog* and *Magog:* some casting their eye upon the drying up of *Euphrates,* . . . and most men disputing the slaying of the two witnesses; as much conducing to Gods designe in bringing about . . . the fifth Monarchy.'[9]

[1] T. Edwards, *Gangraena* (1646), i. 23; E. Pagitt, *Heresiography* (2nd edn., 1645), p. 44.
[2] J. Graunt, *Truths Victory* (1645), p. 44.
[3] *Journal of Sir Samuel Luke*, ed. I. G. Philip (1947), p. 76, quoted in C. Hill, *Puritanism and Revolution*, p. 326.
[4] Edwards, *Gangraena* (1646), iii. 36, 55.
[5] Anon., *A Vision, which One Mr. Brayne . . . had in September, 1647* (1649), brs.
[6] Goodwin, *Glimpse of Sions Glory*, p. 6.
[7] *The Clarke Papers*, ed. C. H. Firth (Camden Soc., new ser., xlix, liv, lxi, lxii, 1891–1901), i. 4.
[8] H. Wilkinson, *Babylons Ruine* (1643), p. 21.
[9] H. Peter, *Gods Doings and Mans Duty* (1646), p. 9; cf. Rev. xi. 7, xvi. 12, xx. 8.

The belief that Doomsday or the millennium would arrive 'such a day in such a week' was 'the common talk about London, and so consequently over England'.[1]

Thus by the mid-1640s the excitement arising out of the Reformation and intensified by the civil war had created millenarian hopes at all levels of society. The Fifth Monarchists, drawing upon the works of Brightman, Mede, Alsted and Archer, emerged from this wave of excitement, and stood within the line of millenarian development.[2] But by the time they emerged, millenarianism was already shrinking. The millenarian vision was by its nature flexible, appealing in different forms to different social groups. For the Presbyterians, following Brightman, it meant the universal establishment of that church: 'The kingdom of our Lord is come, when . . . Religion is countenanced, and Kings become nursing fathers to the Church; all the Saints do not become Magistrates, but God maketh Magistrates Saints or friends to them who are so.'[3] The events of the early 1640s were consistent with this vision, but it disappeared with the triumph of the largely sectarian New Model Army and the purge of the Parliamentary Presbyterians in 1648. Those millenarians who were socially conservative shrank from these developments. Worst of all, the execution of Charles in January 1649 seemed to herald not New Jerusalem but a New Münster.

NOTE 1

(see pp. 26, 29)

The use made by Fifth Monarchist writers of Foxe and the academic millenarians and John Archer

FOXE was cited by, among others:
C. Feake, *The Genealogie of Christianity* (1650), *sig*. D3.
J. Rogers, *Ohel* (1653), p. 23.
J. Pendarves, *Arrowes against Babylon* (1656), p. 1.
H. Danvers, *Theopolis* (1672), p. 211.

BRIGHTMAN
J. Rogers, *Ohel*, p. 24.

[1] Anon., *Doomes-day* (1647), pp. 5-6.
[2] See Note, p. 45-6.
[3] J. Durham, *A Commentarie upon the Book of the Revelation* (3rd edn., Amsterdam, 1660), p. 712.

H. Danvers, *Theopolis*, p. 2.
J. Canne, *Truth with Time* (1656), p. 19.
J. Tillinghast, *Generation-Work* (2nd part, 1654), p. 253.
B. Stoneham, *The Voice of a Cry* (1664); p. 30.

MEDE
C. Feake, *Genealogie*, sig. D3.
J. Tillinghast, *Knowledge of the Times* (1654), p. 57.
Anon., *A Door of Hope* (1661), p.1.
J. Canne, *Truth with Time*, p. 4.
V. Powell, *The Bird in the Cage* (1661), p. 35.

ALSTED
V. Powell, *Bird in the Cage*, p. 35.
J. Tillinghast, *Knowledge*, p. 57.
J. Canne, *The Snare is Broken* (1649), pp. 20-1.
Anon., *Vavasoris Examen* (1654), p. 18.

ARCHER
W. Aspinwall, *Legislative Power* (1656), p. 50.
J. Tillinghast, *Knowledge*, p. 57.
V. Powell, *Bird in the Cage*, p. 35.
M. Cary, *The Little Horns Doom* (1649), p. 17.

NOTE 2
(see pp. 38–9)
*The extent of millenarian ideas among ministers publishing
three or more works, 1640–53*

Denominations are indicated (sometimes tentatively) as P = Presbyterian, I = Independent, B = Baptist, FM = Fifth Monarchist. Sources are given for all but Fifth Monarchists. Quakers, whose millennium was often an internal spiritual kingdom, are not included.

(i) AUTHORS SHOWING MILLENARIAN IDEAS:
Simeon Ashe (P) . . . signed the millenarian tract by H. Whitfield, *Strength out of Weakness* (1652), sig. a2.
John Arrowsmith (P) . . . his *A great Wonder in Heaven* (1647), p. 44.
John Bastwick (P) . . . R. L'Estrange, *The Dissenter's Sayings* (1681), 2nd part, p. 54.
John Bond (P) . . . *ibid.*, p. 56.

John Brayne (? Seeker) . . . anon., *A Vision, which one Mr. Brayne . . . had*(1649.)

William Bridge (I) . . . *Christs Coming* (1648).

Thomas Brookes (I) . . . *The Glorious day of the Saints Appearance* (1648), pp. 3–6.

Cornelius Burgess (P) . . . *The Necessity and Benefit of washing the Heart* (1645), p. 35.

Jeremiah Burroughes (I) . . . *Moses his Choice* (1641), sig. A2–v., pp. 485, 487.

Henry Burton (P later I) . . . *The Sounding of the Two Last Trumpets* (1641), p. 88.

Richard Byfield (P) . . . *The Power of the Christ of God* (1641), sig. A1.

Edmund Calamy (P) . . . L'Estrange, *op. cit.*, pt. i, pp. 35, 41.

John Canne (I/FM)

John Cardell (I/FM) . . . J. Spittlehouse, *The Royall Advocate* (1655), p. 44.

John Caryl (I) . . . L'Estrange, *op. cit.*, pt. ii, p. 31.

Thomas Case (P) . . . *ibid.*, p. 56.

Peter Chamberlen (B/FM)

Francis Cheynell (P) . . . L'Estrange, *op. cit.*, pt. ii, p. 69.

Thomas Coleman (P) . . . *ibid.*, p. 34.

Thomas Collier (B) . . . *A Vindication of the Army-Remonstrance* (1649), sig. A3.

Richard Coppin ('Universalist') . . . *Saul Smitten* (1653), p. 31.

Francis Cornewell (B) . . . *The Vindication of the Royall Commission of King Jesus* (1644), p. 12.

Walter Cradock (B) . . . *The Saints Fulnesse of Joy* (1646), p. 31.

William Dell (?Seeker) . . . *The Way of True Peace* (1649), sig. A2, A3v.

Henry Denne (B) . . . *The Man of Sin Discovered* (1645).

John Durant (I) . . . *The Salvation of the Saints* (1653), pp. 184–7, 191–2.

John Dury (irenicist) . . . *Israels Call to March out of Babylon* (1646), sig. A2–3v.

William Erbery (Seeker) . . . *The Babe of Glory* (1653)

William Goode (P) . . . *Jacob Raised* (1647), pp. 8, 10.

John Goodwin (I) . . . *Dis-satisfaction Satisfied* (1654), p. 10.

Thomas Goodwin (I) . . . *A Sermon of the Fifth Monarchy* (1654).

William Gouge (P) . . . *The Progresse of Divine Providence* (1645), sig. A4, p. 29.

Thomas Grantham (B) . . . *Christianismus Primitivus* (1678), p. 5.

William Greenhill (I) . . . *An Exposition of the five first Chapters of . . . Ezekiel* (1645), p. 134.

Charles Herle (P) . . . L'Estrange, *op. cit.*, pt. ii, p. 59.

Gaspar Hickes (P) . . . *The Glory and Beauty of Gods Portion* (1644), p. 42

Thomas Hill (P) . . . *The Season for Englands Self-Reflection* (1644), sig. A2–v.

Paul Hobson (B) . . . signed millenarian *Confession of Faith, Of those Churches . . . called Anabaptists* (1644), sig. A2v, B2v.

Nathaniel Homes (B) . . . *A Sermon . . . before . . . Foote* (1650).

George Hughes (P) . . . *Vae-Euge-Tuba* (1647).

William Jenkyn (P) . . . L'Estrange, *op. cit.*, pt. ii, pp. 56–7.

William Kiffin (B) . . . signed Baptist *Confession of Faith* (1644), sig. A2v, B2v.

Thomas Killcop (B) . . . *ibid.*

Hanserd Knollys (B) . . . *An Exposition of the first Chapter of the Song of Solomon* (1656), pp. 43–5.

Christopher Love (P) . . . L'Estrange, *op. cit.*, pt. ii, p. 62.

Thomas Manton (P) . . . *Meate Out of the Eater* (1647), p. 3.

Samuel Marshall (P) . . . L'Estrange, *op. cit.*, pt. ii, pp. 27, 48, 53.

Thomas Mocket (?P) . . . *The Churches Troubles* (1642), p. 57.

Matthew Newcomen (P) . . . *Jerusalems Watch-men* (1643), pp. 6, 28.

Philip Nye (I) . . . L'Estrange, *op. cit.*, pt. ii, p. 34.

John Owen (I) . . . *A Sermon . . . concerning the Kingdome of Christ* (Oxford, 1652).

Herbert Palmer (P) . . . L'Estrange, *op. cit.*, pt. ii, p. 56.

Thomas Parker (I) . . . *The Visions and Prophecies of Daniel* (1646).

Hugh Peter (I) . . . R. P. Stearns, *The Strenuous Puritan*, p. 330.

Vavasor Powell (I/FM)

Robert Purnell (B) . . . *Good Tidings for Sinners* (1649), pp. 22–3.

Samuel Richardson (B) . . . signed *Confession of Faith* (1644), sig. A2v, B2v.

Francis Roberts (?P) . . . *Clavis Bibliorum* (4th edn., 1675), p. 581.

John Rogers (I/FM)

John Saltmarsh (Seeker) . . . L. F. Solt, *Saints in Arms* (1959), pp. 73–4.

Lazarus Seaman (P) . . . *Solomons Choice* (1644), sig. A2v, A3v.

William Sedgwick (Seeker) . . . *Zions Deliverance* (1642).

John Shaw (P) . . . *Brittains Remembrancer* (York, 1644), sig. B5.

Sidrach Simpson (I) . . . signed Whitfield, *Strength out of Weaknesse,*
sig. a2.

Peter Sterry (I) . . . *England's Deliverance* (1652), pp. 38–40.

John Strickland (P) . . . L'Estrange, *op. cit.,* pt. i, p. 42.

William Strong (I) . . . *XXXI Select Sermons* (1656), pp. 2–3.

John Tombes (B) . . . *Saints no Smiters* (1664), p. 26.

John Trapp (P) . . . *A Commentary or Exposition* (1647), p. 584.

Thomas Valentine (P) . . . *Christ's Counsell* (1647), pp. 19–20.

George Walker (P) . . . *A Sermon Preached . . . Jan. 29th 1644* (1645),
p. 18.

Thomas Watson (P) . . . L'Estrange, *op. cit.,* pt. ii, p. 31.

Jeremiah Whittaker (I) . . . signed Whitfield, *op. cit.,* sig. a2.

Jeremiah White (I) . . . L'Estrange, *op. cit.,* pt. ii, p. 55.

Henry Wilkinson (P) . . . *Babylon's Ruine* (1643).

Francis Woodcock (P) . . . *Christ's Warning-Piece* (1644).

Hezekiah Woodward (I) . . . *Inquiries into the Causes of our miseries*
(1644), sig. Av.

(ii) AUTHORS NOT SHOWING MILLENARIAN IDEAS:

Robert Bacon	Thomas Gataker
Thomas Bakewell	John Geree
Richard Baxter	John Graunt
John Biddle	Thomas Hall
Thomas Blake	Robert Harris
Christopher Blackwood	Richard Hollingworth
Samuel Bolton	William Hussey
John Brinsley	John Ley
Anthony Burgess	John Lightfoot
Daniel Cawdry	Nicholas Lockyer
Humphrey Chambers	Thomas Moore sr.
Samuel Clarke	Obadiah Sedgwick
John Collinges	William Spurstowe
Richard Culmer	Samuel Torshell
Calibute Downing	Richard Vines
Samuel Eaton	John Webster
Thomas Edwards	Thomas Whitfield

Of these, only four—Edwards, Graunt, Hall and Lightfoot—
actually condemned millenarianism, though several in list (i),
including Gouge, rejected a literal reign of a thousand years and the
physical return of Christ, whilst accepting an imminent Kingdom of
Christ on earth.

Samford University Library

The Beginnings of the Fifth Monarchy Movement and the Barebones Parliament, 1649–53

The execution of the king in January 1649 was viewed with dismay by the majority of the population. But to the most militant of the godly, the removal of King Charles symbolized the clearing of the way for King Jesus. William Dell was alleged to have said that Charles 'was no king to him, Christ was his king'.[1]

On the day after the execution, John Owen, later Vice-Chancellor of Oxford, preached before the Commons. He placed the events of the previous day in their context by explaining that '*As the days approach for the delivery of the decree, so the shaking of Heaven and Earth, and all the powers of the World, to make way for the establishment of that* kingdom which shall not be given to another people . . . *must certainly grow.*'[2] Three weeks later the regicide, Col. Tichborne, rejoiced that the Lord's 'great and glorious workings in these our dayes doth seem to point out that time to be neere at hand; when God himselfe doth shake the whole Earth and heavens' to set up a 'righteous and peaceable Kingdome of Christ'.[3] John Brayne's vision of the fall of all kings was published in 1649.[4] Lady Eleanor Douglas, who had proclaimed an imminent millennium, seeing '*the day of Judgement clothed in the Parliaments likenesse*', was released from confinement and her prophecy of the king's execution was reprinted. One of her prophetic tracts was read before the Commons.[5] Edward Haughton, lecturer

---

[1] A. G. Matthews, *Calamy Revised* (Oxford, 1934), p. 161.
[2] J. Owen, *A Sermon preached to the Honourable House of Commons* (1649), sig. A3.
[3] R. Tichborne, *The Rest of Faith* (1649), pp. 1, 45.
[4] Anon., *A Vision, which One Mr. Brayne . . . had* (1649).
[5] E. Douglas, *Sions Lamentations* (1649), p. 8; *From the Lady Eleanor, Her Blessing* (1644), pp. 22, 25–6; *Before the Lords second coming* (1650), tit. pag.; *Strange and Wonderfull Prophesies* (1649), reprinted in *Fugitive Tracts* (1875), 2nd ser., no. 20.

at Horsham in Sussex, explained 'upon what account the late *Charls* fell, these wars on foot being indeed part of the Battel you read of in the 16. and 19. Chapters of the *Revelations*: I say . . . that he with his armies fell, as the Popes second.'[1] John Eliot, a prominent New England Puritan, wrote that '*Much is spoken of the rightful Heir of the Crown of England, and the unjustice of casting out the right heir; but Christ is the only right Heir.*' Nathaniel Homes and Peter Sterry shared his view.[2]

Those saints who later became Fifth Monarchists saw the execution in the same light. The Welsh evangelist Vavasor Powell saw Charles as the King of the North who stumbled (Dan. xi. 15, 19). In doggerel verses probably written in or soon after 1649, Powell also justified the king's execution on the grounds of having broken all Ten Commandments: Charles was guilty of papal idolatry, swearing, Sabbath breaking and even filial disobedience—

> *He disobeyed his parent, all men this know,*
> *It was a sin, although but soe & soe.*

Powell concluded that

> *of all Kings I am for Christ alone,*
> *For he is King to us though Charles be gone.*

John Rogers, lecturer at Thomas Apostle's in London, saw Charles as one of the toes of the image in Dan. ii, destroyed by Christ.[3] John Spittlehouse, assistant to the Marshal-General (who controlled military security), argued that Charles was a part of Antichrist, destroyed 'as soon as the fatal blow was given'.[4] Mary Cary, the Fifth Monarchy prophetess, identified Charles as the little horn.[5] John Canne, chaplain to Col. Overton, argued in 1649 that the execution was 'Gods work, . . . don in Gods way'. A few years later he asserted that '*The high Court of justice . . .* before which the last of our kings had his tryal and sentence, was no other, then that *throne of God*, men-

---

[1] E. Haughton, *The Rise, Growth, and Fall of Antichrist* (1652), sig. A5v.
[2] J. Eliot, *The Christian Commonwealth* (1659), sig. B1v.; N. Homes, *A Sermon . . . Preached Before . . . Thomas Foote* (1650), p. 17; P. Sterry, *England's Deliverance* (1652), pp. 38–40.
[3] *Calendar of State Papers, Domestic, 1653–4*, p. 305; Nat. Lib. Wales MS HM2.14/ 7a, b: 'Of ye late K.Charles of Blessed Memory, by Vavasar Powell'; J. Rogers, *Ohel or Bethshemesh* (1653), p. 25. For Powell and Rogers, see Biog. App.
[4] J. Spittlehouse, *The first Addresses* (1653), p. 23; *Rome Ruin'd by Whitehall* (1650), sig. b1v. For Spittlehouse, see Biog. App.
[5] M. Cary, *The Little Horns Doom* (1651), p. 6. For Cary, see Biog. App.

tioned in *Dan.* 7.9, 10.' 'Here began the Lord God Almighty, to call Kings and Kingdomes to an account.'[1]

Christopher Feake, vicar of Christ Church, Newgate, from 1649 but formerly a minister at Hertford, taught at Hertford in 1646 that there was in monarchy 'an enmity against Christ, which he would destroy'.[2] But no one dared to publish such views until immediately before the king's execution. Joseph Salmon, a Ranter in the army, urged the army to be 'the Executioners of that beast (Monarchy) which they had formerly wounded, and whose wound the Parliament had . . . salved over'.[3] An anonymous Scottish pamphlet claiming the support of the Scottish gentry urged Parliament to remove Charles. 'The *quarrel* is whether Jesus shal be *King* or no,' the author argued. 'O that *England* may never seek the death of crowned King Jesus! may never co[m]ply with dying Antichrist . . .'[4]

Once the execution had taken place, the most radical millenarians in the sects and the army ventured to express their approval, and to rebuke the army officers for having so nearly apostatized. The 'wel-affected' saints of Blackburn recorded that their *'dying, sinking hopes'* had been raised by Pride's Purge (of the Parliamentary Presbyterians), the execution of the king and the abolition of the Lords.[5] The first Fifth Monarchist petition, the *Certain Quaeres*, subscribed by the saints throughout Norfolk, was published on 19 February 1649 and began with an attack on the officers for trying to reach a settlement with the king. The signatories hoped the army would never be *'instrumental for the setting up of a meer natural and worldly government, like that of Heathen Rome and Athens (as too many late overtures have caused us to fear)'*.[6] William Dell's congratulations to the army contained a rebuke. He spoke of the army as 'through a *blessed necessity*, being *now* doing *that* work of God, which *once* you had little minde to, *viz.* The *procuring* the *Peace* of the Kingdom, by subduing the *great* enemies of Peace.'[7] Christopher Feake also later condemned the army for attempting to preserve the monarchy.[8]

---

[1] J. Canne, *The Golden Rule* (1649), sig. A2v.; *A Voice From the Temple* (1653), pp. 14–15. For Canne, see Biog. App.
[2] T. Edwards, *Gangraena* (1646), iii. 148. For Feake, see Biog. App.
[3] J. Salmon, *A Rout, A Rout* (1649), p. 13. On Salmon, see Cohn, *Pursuit of the Millennium* (1962), pp. 346–9.
[4] Anon., *Plaine Scottish, or Newes from Scotland* (no date), p. 7.
[5] *Perfect Occurrences*, 118 (30 March–6 April 1649), p. 934.
[6] *Certain Quaeres* (1649), pp. 3–4.
[7] W. Dell, *The Way of True Peace and Unity* (1649), sig. A3v.
[8] C. Feake, *A Beam of Light* (1659), p. 19.

Nevertheless, the death of Charles was a great triumph for the saints, and they saw it as the beginning of a world-wide revolution, in which all kings would be destroyed. Spittlehouse thought God had used England 'as a Theater to act a president of what he intends to do to all the Nations'.[1] Hugh Peter told the Commons in 1648 that he knew 'by Revelation' that '*This Army must root up Monarchy, not only here but in France, and other kingdoms round about; . . . This Army is that Corner stone cut out of the Mountain, which must dash the powers of the earth to pieces.*'[2] John Canne expected that the Lord would 'eminently appear, . . . *overthrowing the Thrones of Kingdoms* every where in Europe'.[3] In a sermon graphically entitled *The Shaking and Translating of Heaven and Earth*, John Owen assured the Commons that God would 'sooner or later shake all the *Monarchies* of the Earth'.[4] John Durant, a preacher at Canterbury, thought that 'In a few years I beleeve a man may in sober speech ask, *Where is the King of England? where is the King of France? where is the King of Spaine? where is the Danish, Swedish, Hungarian, &c.* power?'[5] John Rogers agreed that kings would collapse 'over all the *World* ere long, till not one be left'.[6]

Many felt with Hugh Peter that England was not only the first of God's nations, but the instrument by which the godly revolution was to be carried to all lands.[7] Spittlehouse warned the rulers of Rome to 'beware of *Nol Crumwels* Army, lest Hugh Peter come to preach in *Peter's* Chaire'.[8] One Thomas Banaster wrote that by England 'the Sword of the Lord' was to be 'sheathed in the sides of all Kingdoms by a civill war; *England*, thou hast begun to drink blood, and thou shalt yet drink one draught more to all the world, and they shall pledge thee round in a bowl of blood again'. He asked the kings of the world and all worldly men, 'How many times have you said, Hallowed be thy Name, Thy Kingdom come? you little know what you said, . . . you prayed for the Lords Power, Justice, and Judgement to fall upon you; behold it is come according to your desire.'[9] Wars were to be millenarian crusades, and the Fifth Monarchists saw the Dutch War of 1652–4 in this light. Vavasor

1 Spittlehouse, *First Addresses*, p. 5.
2 R. P. Stearns, *The Strenuous Puritan* (Urbana, 1954), p. 330. Cf. Dan. ii. 34.
3 Canne, *Voice From the Temple*, p. 29.
4 J. Owen, *Shaking and Translating* (1649), p. 19.
5 J. Durant, *The Salvation of the Saints* (1653), p. 293.
6 Rogers, *Ohel*, introduction, p. 23.
7 See C. Hill, *Puritanism and Revolution* (1962 edn.), pp. 123–52.
8 Spittlehouse, *Rome Ruin'd*, p. 339.
9 T. Banaster, *An Alarm to the World* (1649), pp. 7–8, 14.

Powell was rebuked because he 'durst call the States of Holland Embessadors, drunkards, and wish them to go home with this Answer, That Sion is built'.[1]

With the execution of the king, millenarian zeal in the army reached a peak. Col. Hewson, Governor of Dublin and a member of Rogers's congregation, rejoiced that God had made the army 'his sharpe threshing instruments to thresh the Nations'.[2] The fervour was illustrated best by the Declaration of Musselburgh, published by the soldiers and junior officers in 1650 during the invasion of Scotland. Lamenting the apostasy of the Scots (who had accepted Charles II), they claimed they fought 'having these things simply in our eye, namely, the destruction of Antichrist, and the advancement of the Kingdom of Jesus Christ'. They justified the execution of Charles as one of the ten horns of the beast (Rev. xvii), and declared they had 'proclaimed Jesus Christ, the King of Saints, to be our King by profession'. When God destroyed 'those his enemies that will not suffer Jesus Christ to be King . . . let not Scotland, nor any other Nation say, What dost thou?' It was, as Feake said later, 'as if *they were Fifth-Kingdom-men at the highest rate*'. Moreover, Cromwell himself commended the paper as 'a plaine, simple spirituall one'.[3] There was close liaison between the soldiers and the gathered churches. The troops in Scotland in 1650 wrote to Feake, Simpson and other church leaders.[4] In the summer of 1650 a number of officers, including Barkstead and Goffe, called on the godly to hold a day of seeking God to lament the darkening of His cause. The Congregationalist church at Sandwich wrote back that it was convinced that God was using the army to establish the kingdom of the saints. Many other congregations and garrisons took part.[5] In Wales the links were especially strong. Major-General Thomas Harrison was the head of the Commission for the Propagation of the Gospel in Wales, and was a millenarian.[6] Vavasor Powell was the most prominent minister on this body. When Harrison in 1651 was given the task of containing the invading Scottish army, the Welsh saints

---

[1] A. Griffith, *Mercurius Cambro-Britannicus* (1652), p. 13. On Fifth Mon. foreign policy, see below, pp. 151–5.
[2] *Severall Proceedings in Parliament*, 90 (12–19 June 1651), p. 1379.
[3] Anon., *Declaration of the English Army in Scotland, To the People in Scotland* (1650), pp. 3–5; Feake, *Beam of Light*, p. 30; W. C. Abbott, *The Writings and Speeches of Oliver Cromwell* (Cambridge, Mass., 1937–47), ii. 302.
[4] Anon., *A Declaration of several of the Churches of Christ* (1654), p. 9.
[5] Worcester College, Oxford, Clarke MS. 18, fos. 8–10, 42–4v., and *passim*.
[6] For Harrison, see Biog. App. For the Commission, see below pp. 57–8.

rushed to his assistance. Led by Powell, Morgan Llwyd of Wrexham, Walter Cradock and Jenkin Jones, these 'eminent Pauls of our time' raised horse troops from their congregations and joined Harrison in Cumberland. Sixty of them under Llwyd, Capt. Hugh Pritchard and one Capt. Taylor arrived early in June, and one of Harrison's soldiers reflected that 'surely the presence of the Lord (which we desire more then the increase of our forces) usually attends such'.[1] The saints left behind supported them with letters and prayers. 'The Faith of the Saints here', wrote Llwyd's church at Wrexham, 'is much raised to a confident expectation of the greate works of God (by you worms) to thresh the mountains: we would not Idolize men, but rejoyce that we see our King hath girt on his sword, and goeth out Conquering and to Conquer.' The saints of Powell's churches in Radnor and Montgomery wrote that 'doubtless you are called to bring the King of Righteousness . . . to his Crown'.[2] When God's cause triumphed at the battle of Worcester, the Wrexham church wrote 'we conclude . . . Who can be against us if God of heaven be for us?'[3]

Despite any misgivings before the execution of the king, the saints were confident afterwards that the government, in the hands of the Rump would set up Christ's Kingdom in England. William Rowse wrote from his ship, the 'Love in the Hope', to Speaker Lenthall that 'me thinks I see the kingdome of Jesus Christ begin to flourish, while the wicked . . . do now perish and fade like a blowne-off-blossome'.[4] William Dell told the Commons that when 'all, *almost, that is* great, *and* honourable, *and* noble, *and* Royall, *and* wise, *and* learned' was hostile to God's plan, '*How* highly *are you* honored *of him, and how* happy *are you, that* You *yet are found for it.*'[5] Powell was a loyal admirer of the regime, and the soldiers at Musselburgh delivered a specific rebuke to the Scots for referring to the Rump as 'a pretended Parliament'.[6]

The saints' discontents, probably shared by all the radical millenarians, were set out in a second petition from Norfolk in 1649 seeking '*the advancement of Iesus Christ, the inlargement of his Kingdome*

---

[1] C. H. Firth, *Cromwell's Army* (1902), p. 328n.; *Mercurius Politicus*, 53 (5–12 June 1651), p. 862. For Llwyd, see Biog. App.

[2] *Merc. Pol.*, 58 (10–17 July 1651), pp. 924–5.

[3] *Perfect Passages*, 40 (7–14 Nov. 1651), pp. 320–1.

[4] *Severall Proceedings*, 111 (6–13 Nov. 1651), p. 1714 (pagination erratic).

[5] Dell, *Way of True Peace*, sig. A2.

[6] V. Powell, *Saving Faith Set Forth* (1651), sig. A3v.; anon., *Declaration of the English Army*, p. 6.

here on earth'. It is worth quoting at some length. The saints complained that

> Still we see the scandalous and ignorant Clergy in many places,
> and where the godly Pastors are placed, much discouraged by the
> troublesome gathering of their maintenance by way of tythes . . .
> still we see the Lords Day as much broken as ever, still we see
> swearing, lying, Cursing, and Drunkenesse, . . . still we see all
> Schools (almost) as well Universities as others, to abound with
> disaffected teachers, to the utter interruption of Godlynesse: still
> we see Lawyers to grow rich, by and of the ruines of poor men,
> by bringing to tryall things of no value: still we see Lords of
> Mannours to exact fines according to their own wills upon poor
> Tennants, urging that unparallel'd Oath of Fealty and Homage;
> and so of free born English, still made slaves by the marks of the
> Conquerour; . . . still we see the taxes to continue, and to lye as
> heavy upon us, as upon those who were the causers of them.[1]

This list includes most of the concerns of the later Fifth Monarchist
movement: to purge the clergy, abolish tithes, reform the law and
impose a puritanical morality, reduce taxes and remove the privileges of the rich. This petition did not mention some further major
proposals: to transfer government from the 'carnal men' to the saints;
to destroy the national church altogether; and to invert the social
order altogether, as well as reforming its minor abuses.

Filled with enthusiasm in 1649, the saints had expected Parliament
to implement this revolution. But it soon became apparent that the
Rump was not a gathering of saints but a cautious and worldly
body, and some accordingly began to transfer their hopes to Oliver
Cromwell. Dr. Peter Chamberlen, surgeon to Charles I and later to
Charles II, and pastor of a congregation in Lothbury Square,
greeted the Rump hopefully, and in April 1649 published some projected social reforms which he hoped it would undertake.[2] But in
1650 he lamented to Cromwell, then in Scotland, that 'Were there
the same integritie with us at home as with you abroad, surely the
Lord would bless us . . . Your counsels, at this distance, are soon
forgotten; every man seekes his own . . . What will the end of these
things bee?'[3] A few months later he told the Commons, in a tract,
that though God had honoured them at first, now there was only

---

[1] *A Perfect Diurnall of some Passages in Parliament*, 294 (12–19 March 1649), pagin.
hopelessly erratic.

[2] P. Chamberlen, *The Poore Mans Advocate* (1649). For Chamberlen, see Biog.
App.

[3] J. Nickolls, *Original Letters and Papers . . . of Mr. John Milton* (1743), p. 36.

chaos and dishonour. 'Would you now die like men, or live the Sons of God?' he asked them. 'Remember whereto you are exalted. Remember from whence you are fallen. Do the first works, and let the last be better then the first.'[1]

John Canne shared Chamberlen's disillusion. After the victory at Dunbar in 1650 he had declared that '*the Parliament of* Englands *Cause* . . . hath been proved sufficiently to be . . . the *Cause of GOD*'.[2] But he came to feel that the Parliament men were not true saints. In executing the king they had done God's work, but 'not that our Statesmen thought so, or so intended'. In 1653 he wrote of the Rump that 'taking no heed to walk in the law of the Lord God of Israel, but *flying upon the spoile* . . . God at last rejected them'.[3] Spittlehouse had been cynical about Parliament since 1650. 'There is an *Unum necessarium*', he wrote, addressing the Commons and the Council of State, 'which is farr from their [worldly men's] thoughts, and I feare not very neare yours (viz. the flourishing of the kingdome or Church of Christ) which ought to be your chiefe object to adorne'. Until this was done, 'you obstruct the descending of the new Jerusalem'.[4] Daniel Border, the millenarian Baptist editor of the *Faithful Scout*, wrote in 1652 of the Rump: 'Ye have promised Haulcion dayes; but I fear a monstrous Age.'[5]

In Wales the disillusioned tended to turn to Harrison, a fervent millenarian who was at the head of the Commission for the Propagation of the Gospel in Wales, in which Vavasor Powell had a prominent role. Powell and his colleagues launched a fierce attack on scandalous ministers, though it seems likely that ministers with episcopalian sympathies were deemed scandalous *ipso facto*. The commissioners were accused of driving out all the clergy and teachers and growing rich on forfeited revenues. In reply, Powell asserted that 'many hundreds (if not thousands) have been converted in Wales', and that those ejected were 'un-preaching Curates, or scandalous in their lives'.[6] When confidence in the Rump was shrinking, the Commission seemed vitally important to the saints as the sole remaining

1 P. Chamberlen, *Plus Ultra: To the Parliament of England* (1651), broadsheet.
2 J. Canne, *Emmanuel, or God With Us* (1650), p. 44.
3 Canne, *Voice From the Temple*, pp. 14–15.
4 Spittlehouse, *Rome Ruin'd*, sig. A4, A5v.
5 *Faithful Scout*, 95 (5–13 Nov. 1652), p. 743.
6 A. Griffith, *Mercurius Cambro-Britannicus*; *A Perfect Diurnall of some Passages* . . . *of the Armies*, 125 (3–10 May 1652), pp. 1847–9. On the Commission, see S. R. Gardiner, *History of the Commonwealth and Protectorate* (1903 edn.), ii. 249–51; R. T. Jones, 'The Life, Work, and Thought of Vavasor Powell (1617–1670)' (Oxford Univ. D.Phil. thesis 1947), pp. 62–107.

means of implementing at least part of the godly revolution. Any surviving faith in the Rump was shattered on 1 April 1653 when it rejected a bill to prolong the Commission, which accordingly expired.[1]

Harrison's ideas satisfied even the most radical Welsh saints, but some of the most perceptive saints in London soon realized that Cromwell was no more likely than the Rump to meet their demands. Hitherto the saints had felt that the godly revolution to prepare for Christ would be undertaken by Parliament or the army. They had felt no need to do more than bear witness to the coming kingdom and remind the government of its divine mission. They had not thought it necessary to form any specifically millenarian movement to prepare the way for this kingdom, and had even taught that ordinary citizens should not meddle in politics. In 1649 John Canne told the Presbyterians that 'I cannot finde, either in Scripture, or other History, that any Ministers of Jesus Christ . . . did ever before Your time . . . deny the lawfulnesse of the Government under which they lived.' In 1651 a group of Independent and Baptist ministers, including Feake and John Simpson (minister of St. Botolph's, Bishopsgate), affirmed that *all People in Every Nation as well Members of Churches, as others . . . are to submit to the Civill Commands, not onely of such Rulers as are faithfull, but even to Infidels*.[2] But now, in a mood of disillusion, it became apparent that unless the saints formed their own active organization to remove the apostate regime by propaganda or even violence, the millennium would never arrive. The Fifth Monarchist movement emerged as a reaction to fading, not rising expectations, and was in many respects 'an attempt to rally and organize what could be marshalled from the . . . millenarian impulses of the sixteen-forties'.[3]

The Fifth Monarchist movement first took shape shortly after the battle of Worcester in 1651, when 'divers *Officers and Members* of several Congregations' met Cromwell at Suffolk House, to urge him to 'press forward in promoting that *glorious Cause* . . . and particularly, to quicken the Parliament to do some *honest and honourable works*'. After two meetings they found that Cromwell preferred other advice, and went no more. Instead, in December 1651, they met together at

[1] Gardiner, *Comm. and Protect.*, ii. 251.
[2] J. Canne, *The Improvement of Mercy* (1649), p. 12; anon., *A Declaration of divers Elders and Brethren* (1651), p. 3.
[3] J. F. Wilson, 'Comment on "Two Roads to the Puritan Millennium"', *Church History*, xxxii (1963), p. 341.

Allhallows the Great in Thames Street, where Feake, Simpson and Henry Jessey were weekday lecturers, 'to pray for a new Representative, and to preach somewhat against the old'. Feake recorded that within half an hour the gathering had reached agreement on six objectives, or '*General Heads of Prayer*', the first being that 'whatsoever stood in the way' of Christ's kingdom 'might be utterly pulled down, or brought to nothing'. They sought also the removal of ungodly magistrates and ministers, the ending of divisions among the godly, the fulfilling of promises made by Parliament and the army, and that the negotiations with the Dutch might produce nothing contrary to 'the Cause of Christ and his Kingdom, now carrying on in these Nations'. The first Fifth Monarchists were met with hostility by the government, army leaders and leading Independent churchmen. They were attacked by Owen, Thomas Goodwin, Philip Nye and Sidrach Simpson when they gave an account of their ideas at a meeting at Fleetwood's lodgings in Somerset House. Their belief that the current government, and all regimes not in the hands of the saints, were 'pieces of the fourth monarchy' was condemned because it 'cut the sinews of all Magistracy whatsoever'.[1]

The Independent leaders stated that their intervention had failed, but very soon 'divers *Leading men* fell off, who at the first rejoyced and joyned in' the meeting. About the time of the outbreak of war with the Dutch (in June 1652), Feake and others had to begin again, summoning messengers from six London churches to London House and later to Blackfriars, probably at St. Anne's, where Feake held a lectureship. (Blackfriars claimed to be independent of the municipal authorities, on the basis of the mediaeval abbey's rights of sanctuary, and was accordingly a centre for dissident groups of all kinds.) There they heard the scriptures expounded, wrestled with the Lord 'for the fulfilling of his Word', and dealt with other matters 'of General advancement to the *Cause of God* in these Nations and beyond the Seas'—a reference to the Dutch war. Cromwell and the Grandees were 'wonderfully displeased'.[2]

William Erbery, a Welsh millenarian and mystic, twice intruded into the Fifth Monarchists' meetings at London House in November

---

[1] Feake, *Beam of Light*, pp. 39–43; W. Erbery, *The Bishop of London* (1653), p. 1; Bodleian MS. Carte 81, fos. 16–17: circular letter, 9 Jan. 1654; MS. Carte 81, fol. 214: anonymous letter, probably by Philip Nye, 1663/4; cf. L. F. Brown, *The Political Activities of the Baptists and Fifth Monarchy Men* (1911), pp. 19–21.

[2] MS. Carte 81, fol. 17; Feake, *Beam of Light*, pp. 43–6; J. Stoughton, *Ecclesiastical History of England* (1867), ii. 67.

1652, and described them as utterly chaotic. He said the saints had 'founded a Structure of two stories high: not a Pulpit and Reading-Pue, but a *stately frame of wood to preach and pray* in two distinct Forms', one for the Independents and one for the Baptists. Erbery felt called upon to make violent interruptions, and only escaped being ejected by a hasty departure.[1]

Prominent among the earliest leaders of the Fifth Monarchists were Feake and John Simpson. Erbery also mentioned George Cockayne, Independent minister of St. Pancras, Soper Lane, and a Mr. Knight, perhaps Isaac Knight, rector of Fulham. Among the army officers present were Major William Packer and Captain John Spencer, formerly notorious as a tub-preacher.[2] Vavasor Powell, who was in London early in 1653, may have joined them. John Rogers, lecturer at St. Thomas Apostle's, admired the Fifth Monarchist meetings as an '*unparalleled exercise*', but was not allowed to participate, which he attributed to the '*self-conceit*, and *self-seeking*' of the leaders, who also spurned his own meetings. Their real reason was probably that Rogers, like Canne, Spittlehouse and others, still retained a firm faith in Cromwell as the saints' champion.[3] Many of the officers later connected with the Fifth Monarchists were serving outside London. Adjutant-General Allen and Capt. John Vernon were in Ireland, where they had helped the rigid Baptists to break up Rogers' mixed Baptist and Independent church at Dublin in 1651–2.[4] Capt. Edmund Chillenden was serving with Whalley's regiment in Scotland, though in April 1651 he was enlisting recruits in Coleman Street, London, and was involved there in 1652 in some sort of machination against the Rump. He wrote to a friend that Parliament was 'resolved to sit to perpetuity, but I hope they will have a sooner period than is dreamt of. Be silent in this; you shall hear more.'[5] Col. Henry Danvers was at this time still governor of Stafford.[6]

The Fifth Monarchists and the many discontented elements in the army intensified the attack on the Rump in the first months of 1653.

---

[1] Erbery, *Bishop of London*, pp. 1–7.

[2] *Ibid.*, pp. 3, 7. For all these, see Biog. App., and for Knight and Cockayne see Matthews, *Cal. Rev.*, pp. 311, 124.

[3] Rogers, *Ohel*, introd., p. 69.

[4] Rogers, *Ohel*, p. 302. He cites Vernon by name, and 'A.G.A.' probably stands for Adj.-Gen. Allen. For Allen and Vernon, see Biog. App.

[5] *A Perfect Diurnall*, 70 (7–14 April 1651), p. 954; Hist. MSS. Comm., li, *Leyborne-Popham MSS.*, p. 104. For Chillenden, see Biog. App.

[6] *Cal. S.P. Dom.*, *1650*, p. 211; *ibid.*, *1651–2*, p. 566. For Danvers, see Biog. App.

Early in January soldiers and 'army preaching-men' at Allhallows called for a new Parliament, but were silenced by army and government authorities. At Blackfriars in March three officers attacked the Rump after a series of such preachings which had, according to a royalist newswriter, 'scandalized the whole parliament'. In the same month, the Rump postponed making any decision over the Dutch war 'that they might gaine a breathing time upon the preaching people, who are now very violent'. The speakers at Blackfriars were now preaching 'that they intended speedily to destroy that accursed parliament at westminster'. In April they demanded no peace with the Dutch 'or any Prince of the earth', and at Somerset House a young glazier predicted that his congregation 'should ere long see a greater destruction fall on the Parliament than ever befell the Cavaliers'. The 'preaching party' decided that Cromwell himself must go, for 'they must have both a new Parliament and General before the work be done; . . . these are not the people that are appointed for perfecting of that great work of God, which they have begun'.[1]

Major-General Harrison was not mentioned as attending these meetings, where his presence could hardly have escaped notice. But his position as the hero of the preachers and the most violent critic of the Rump was well-known. Indeed, he had sponsored several who became Fifth Monarchist leaders as preachers before the Commons: Powell in February 1650, John Simpson in 1651 and Christopher Feake in 1652. Only Powell's sermon, preached before he became disillusioned with the Rump, proved acceptable to the auditory; a motion to give the customary vote of thanks to Simpson was defeated.[2] Harrison was far more ready than Cromwell to take violent action against the Rump. A royalist agent went so far as to claim that the army and Parliament were divided into two factions following the two officers, and that Harrison's supporters were predominant in the army and 'doubted not but to bring their designe about before midsomer'. There was a rumour that Harrison had enlisted four thousand of the 'preaching people' in North Wales, which he denied when questioned by Cromwell. But it was perhaps a fear that Harrison might try to establish a power basis in Wales, as well as

---

[1] C. H. Firth, 'Cromwell and the Expulsion of the Long Parliament in 1653', *Eng. Hist. Rev.*, viii (1893), pp. 528–9; Bodl. MS. Clarendon 45, fos. 223, 204: newsletters, 1 April, 18 March.

[2] H. R. Trevor-Roper, *Religion, the Reformation and Social Change* (1967); *C.J.* vi. 357, 374, 544, 549, vii. 173.

stories of the corruption of the Welsh commissioners, that had led the Rump to reject 'Major Harrisons Act for propagating the Gospell in Wales'.[1]

The royalist agents appear to have exaggerated the differences between Cromwell and Harrison, which certainly existed, but were over methods rather than objectives. Cromwell complained that Harrison's followers were urging him to dissolve the Rump by force, 'the consideration of the issue whereof makes my hairs to stand on end'. But both officers felt a total distrust of the Rump, which they shared with the army as a whole. Throughout 1652 the army had expressed its dissatisfaction at the failure of the Rump to carry out reforms, and its refusal to allow fresh elections. The crescendo of Fifth Monarchist and army prayer meetings in 1653 made the issue pressing, and the Rump's alleged plan to replenish its numbers by a series of by-elections, thus postponing indefinitely a dissolution, led Cromwell to feel that action was essential. On 20 April 1653 he took his seat in the House, condemned the Rump's proceedings and, calling in a troop of soldiers, dissolved it by force.[2]

The dissolution of the Rump was welcomed almost universally, especially by the saints. It was reported that 'the pulpitt men of Blackfriers predicate alowd the Generall's wisdome for grubbing up the wicked Parliament, not leaving a rotten roote thereof'.[3] Vavasor Powell proclaimed that henceforth 'law should streame down like a river freely', and then went back to North Wales to justify the change. He found a favourable response in Montgomery, and the gathered churches in the county of Radnor, where his influence was strongest, sent their congratulations to the government.[4] John Spittlehouse rushed into print within four days of the dissolution with an enthusiastic defence of the army's action.[5] Addresses and petitions poured in from the godly. On 25 April an unknown gathered church expressed confidence that Cromwell, 'whome we look upon as our Moses', would 'advance the Scepter of our Lord Jesus'.[6] The commander-in-chief in Scotland, Robert Lilburne, and his

---

[1] Firth, 'Cromwell and the Expulsion', pp. 529–31; MS. Clar. 45, fos. 206–*v*; 204*v*; 269: newsletters, 25 March, 18 March, 8 April 1653.
[2] Gardiner, *Comm. and Protect.*, ii. 223–37, 245, 248–65.
[3] D. A. Johnson and D. G. Vaisey, *Staffordshire and the Great Rebellion* (Staffs. Records Committee, 1964), p. 73.
[4] Firth, 'Cromwell and the Expulsion', p. 533; *The Moderate Publisher*, 133 (13–20 May 1653), p. 1070; *The Perfect Diurnall*, 182 (30 May–6 June), pp. 2750–1.
[5] J. Spittlehouse, *The Army Vindicated* (24 April) 1653.
[6] *Severall Proceedings*, 187 (21–8 April), p. 2954.

officers expressed their belief that the work now was 'the setting up of Kingdom of Jesus Christ' which they expected Cromwell to begin.[1] Paul Hobson and the Baptist church at Durham, Colonel Overton, the governor of Hull, and John Portman, secretary to the Naval Commissioners, all wrote expressing their hopes that Christ's kingdom was dawning.[2]

There was naturally a great wave of public speculation as to what was to replace the Rump, and how any new representative should be chosen.[3] The saints themselves were not united. The Norfolk petition of 1649, the *Certain Quaeres*, and a tract of 1651 entitled *A Model of a new Representative*, had advocated that the gathered churches alone should elect a new Parliament.[4] But many of the saints had not yet accepted what was later to be the standard Fifth Monarchist belief, that none except themselves was loyal to Christ's kingdom. On 25 April John Rogers held a meeting of 'hundreds' at St. Thomas Apostle's. He hailed Cromwell as 'the great *Deliverer* of his people', and argued that God had chosen the general to select personally the new assembly. Rogers hoped it would be based on the Old Testament sanhedrin with seventy members, or alternatively one member from each county.[5] Spittlehouse was even more enthusiastic about the Lord General. His first thoughts were that the only 'real Members of this Commonwealth are included in the Congregational Churches, and the Army, and their well-wishers'. Asking 'Whether it be the proper work of the Congregational Churches . . . to *rule the Nations* . . . in a Magistratical employment', he concluded it was 'altogether improper'. God had ordained that the army alone should rule the kingdom. Representatives should be chosen by and from the army; moreover only officers should have a vote, as 'a means to keep the private Souldiery at quiet'. Fifth Monarchism was never an egalitarian movement. In a later pamphlet, dated 19 May by Thomason, Spittlehouse urged that there should be no elections of any sort and that Cromwell, a second Moses, should have total freedom of choice. He was the 'chief Ruler

[1] *Mercurius Politicus*, 153 (misprint for 155), (26 May–2 June), pp. 2477–8.
[2] *Severall Proceedings*, 188 (28 April–5 May), pp. 2959–60; R. Overton, *More Hearts and Hands* (1653); *Cal. S.P. Dom.*, *1652–3*, pp. 292, 392, 425. For Overton and Portman, see Biog. App.
[3] For the debate see A. H. Woolrych, 'The Calling of Barebone's Parliament', *Eng. Hist. Rev.*, lxxx (1965), pp. 492–513.
[4] Anon., *Certain Quaeres*, p. 6; *A Model*, p. 3.
[5] J. Rogers, *To His Excellency the Lord Generall Cromwell. A few Proposals relating to Civil Government* (1653), brs.

appointed by God over us', and to criticize him was to criticize God. Spittlehouse, a soldier against the Stuarts for eight years, was accepting Cromwell as an absolute ruler by divine right.[1] In June a petition signed by several hundreds in Norwich and Norfolk, on behalf of 'thousands of others', urged Cromwell alone to select godly men for the new assembly.[2] The saints of Newcastle described the decision that Cromwell and the officers were to choose the representatives as 'such a mercy as goes beyond what we would have believed that our eyes should ever have seen'.[3]

The new assembly, often known as the Barebones Parliament after a member named Praise-God Barbone, was in fact chosen by Cromwell and the officers.[4] But many of the saints had not wanted to give Cromwell, or the army as a whole, any such powers. Several Norfolk churches, including those of Christopher Pooley at Wymondham and Richard Breviter at North Walsham, both prominent Fifth Monarchists in the mid-1650s, ventured to nominate people they wished to be in the new assembly.[5] From Denbigh came a petition bearing 153 signatures, urging Cromwell to allow the gathered churches to nominate the members. It was signed by Morgan Llwyd, and by John Browne and John James, both of whom later sat in the Barebones Parliament.[6] In fact, however, the North Welsh members were nominated by Harrison and Powell, without a vote of any sort, although Harrison did invite comments on their choice.[7] William Aspinwall, formerly a prominent figure in the Massachusetts Bay Colony, was content that the army, as the 'Lambs Military Officers', should hold power and 'demolish the Kingdom of Antichrist', providing they were holy men, 'throughly purged'. But he wanted minor officials to be recommended by the congregations.[8] The gathered church meeting at the 'Chequer without Aldgate', to which Chillenden belonged, suggested that treble the required number of members should be chosen, apparently by the Presbyterian, Independent and

---

[1] Spittlehouse, *Army Vindicated*, pp. 3, 6, 1 (misprint for 9), 11; *A Warning-piece Discharged* (1653), pp. 10, 13, 24. For Fifth Mon. views on society and government in general, see chap. 6, below.

[2] *Severall Proceedings*, 194 (9–16 June), p. 3070.

[3] *A Perfect Diurnall*, 180 (16–23 May), pp. 2718–19.

[4] Woolrych, 'Calling of Barebone's Parliament', *passim*.

[5] J. Nickolls, *Original Letters and Papers of State* (1743), pp. 124–5. For Pooley and Breviter, see Biog. App.

[6] *Ibid.*, pp. 120–1. For Browne and James, see Biog. App.

[7] C. H. Simpkinson, *Thomas Harrison, Regicide and Major General* (1905), p. 297.

[8] W. Aspinwall, *A Brief Description of the Fifth Monarchy* (1653), pp. 4, 6, 7. For Aspinwall, see Biog. App.

Baptist churches, and then selected by lot.[1] The most determined opposition to Cromwell came predictably from Feake and the meetings at Blackfriars. Looking back from 1659, Feake saw the outcome of the Barebones experiment as the betrayal of the saints by hypocrites in the army. All they had done was to '*pretend to roll the Government of this Nation upon the Saints*, . . . as if they would *introduce the Kingdom of Christ*, or the fifth Kingdom'. But when the saints set about this task, and '*the work and Cause prospered in their hands*', the army drove them out.[2] Feake seems to have been almost as suspicious before the assembly met. On 5 May the French ambassador wrote that the Anabaptist preachers, probably meaning Feake and Simpson, were declaring that this was still nothing like the promised reign of the saints.[3] Feake was said to have preached at Christ Church on 8 May that 'although the General had fought their Battles with successe, yet he was not the Man, that the Lord had chosen, to sitt at the Helme'.[4] At the Monday meetings at Blackfriars on 16 and 23 May, the preachers urged 'by revelation' 'the necessity of Monarchy in this Nation but bestowed it . . . on a new Line', presumably King Jesus.[5] Powell was absent in Wales at this time, involved in a storm of his own making when he raised a troop of horse consisting of several hundreds of his saints, only to have it disbanded by the sheriff of Montgomery.[6] But his own and Simpson's views were probably close to those of Feake.

The position of Major-General Harrison is far from clear. One writer thought he was so close to Cromwell, and 'so much his Excellencys Creature of late, that he is now esteemed a property of his'. It was also reported that some accused 'his Saintship for double dealing with the Brethren, and that all along, as they trusted him, he discovered all to the General'.[7] But the royalist newswriters also spoke of great enmity between the two officers. On 6 May Harrison was reported to have written to a friend 'that the Lord had now at last made the General instrumentall to put the power into the hands of his people . . . contrary to his intentions; that it was the Lord's worke & no thanks to his Excellency'. This may have referred only

---

[1] Nickolls, *Original Letters*, p. 122.
[2] Feake, *Beam of Light*, pp. 48, 50.
[3] Public Record Office, Baschet Transcripts, P.R.O. 31/3/90, f. 662–*v*.: Bordeaux to Brienne, 5/15 May 1653.
[4] MS. Clar. 45, f. 380–*v*.: newsletter, 13 May 1653.
[5] MS. Clar. 45, fos. 400, 436*v*.: newsletters, 20 May, 27 May.
[6] *Ibid.*, f. 484*v*.: newsletter, 3 June.
[7] *Ibid.*, fos. 399*v*., 380*v*.: newsletters, 20 May, 13 May.

to friction over who was to nominate the Welsh members, as Professor Woolrych suggested, but it certainly points to some disagreement.[1] Harrison was thought to have the support of a third of the army, and a royalist claimed that in June some of Cromwell's associates had tried to cajole Harrison into resigning his commission, urging that 'such a pretious pillar was not to be hazarded in the continuall rage of warre'. However he stood firm, and even offered to serve without pay if necessary. This may well have been merely rumour, but Cromwell did ban 'Harrisons gathered Churches at Blackfryers' about this time and attempted in vain to silence Feake.[2] The royalist agent's most extreme report was in mid-May when he wrote that Harrison had preached to the gathered churches 'that there would speedily be a King again; but not one of the former Race, nor such carnall persons, as some eminent in present power; but a man after Gods owne heart, and a King anointed with the Spiritt'. The agent thought that Harrison was seeking the crown for himself, but in fact he was probably referring to King Jesus. Shortly after the fall of the Rump he had told the Council of Officers that he was 'assured the Lord General sought not himself, but that King Jesus might take the Scepter'.[3] Though the two officers may have had some premonition of the differences which later brought them into mutual antagonism, at this stage they were firmly united on essentials. Both looked forward with confidence to the meeting of the saints.

The assembly met for the first time on 4 July, and Cromwell addressed the members in emotional terms before handing over power. 'Truly you are called by God to rule with Him, and for Him,' he said. 'I confess I never looked to see such a day as this . . . when Jesus Christ should be so owned as He is, at this day.' For 'this may be the door to usher in the things that God has promised; which have been prophesied of . . . some of us have thought, That it is our duty to *endeavour* this way; not vainly to *look* at that prophecy in Daniel, . . .'[4] The House published a declaration with a strongly millenarian tone, comparing the age to that immediately before the

[1] Firth, 'Cromwell and the Expulsion', p. 529; Woolrych, 'Calling of Barebone's Parliament', p. 499.

[2] Johnson and Vaisey, *Staffordshire and the Great Rebellion*, p. 73; MS. Clar. 46, fos. 9, 32v.: newsletters, 24 June, 1 July.

[3] MS. Clar. 45, f. 380; J. Heath, *Flagellum* (2nd edn., 1663), p. 134.

[4] Abbott, *Writings and Speeches*, iii. 61, 63–4 (my italics). For the Barebones Parliament see Gardiner, *Comm. and Protect.*, ii. 286–328; H. A. Glass, *The Barbone Parliament* (1899).

birth of Christ. It expected Christ's 'glorious coming, who is King of kings, and Lord of lords, . . . who is still to ride on prosperously, conquering, and to conquer, till he hath subdued all his enemies'.[1] Some of the free-men of London presented a remonstrance during the first week, urging the members to 'accomplish the grand design of your professed Lord and Master Jesus Christ, in these Overturning, Overturning, Overturning dayes, . . . indeavour the erecting of the Kingdom of Jesus Christ to the uttermost parts of the earth'. Parliament was to launch a crusade against Rome, and was advised that 'the most facile way thereunto is, by invading France and Holland, and so erect your Standard before the Towers of *Babylon*'.[2] Part of this remonstrance was derived from a tract published by Spittlehouse on 5 July, in which he laid down a programme for the inauguration of Christ's kingdom.[3] On 4 August a number of justices from Kent presented a petition against tithes in which they noted that 'though the Kings of the Earth have bin unwilling that the anointed Jesus should reign, . . . yet . . . the day of the accomplishment of the Promises . . . is dawned'.[4] Similar expressions came from the churches at Exeter, Bideford and Luppit, in Devon, and from Gloucester.[5]

The feeling that the reign of the saints was beginning spread far beyond the churches. At the end of June a worried customs official in Hull wrote that a purge of the staff was in progress, and that the Fifth Monarchist John Canne 'has such influence with the Council of State that he can place or displace whom he likes'.[6] Even the Leveller, John Lilburne, imprisoned in Newgate, thought it worth appealing for help to Feake, whom he had never met.[7] Feake himself forgot his doubts for a moment, and introduced at Christ Church a jubilant hymn he had composed:

> *How pleasant are the dayes of ioye*
> *to Sions children all;*
> *With trembling wee rejoyce to see*
> *proud Babylon downe fall.*

1 *Severall Proceedings*, 199 (14–21 July), p. 3142.
2 *The Moderate Intelligencer*, 10 (4–11 July), pp. 109–10.
3 Spittlehouse, *First Addresses*, p. 4.
4 *Mercurius Politicus*, 165 (4–11 Aug.), p. 2636.
5 *Mercurius Politicus*, 168 (25 Aug.–1 Sept.), pp. 2696–7; *A Perfect Account*, 138 (24–31 Aug.), pp. 1100–1.
6 *Cal. S.P. Dom., 1652–3*, p. 426.
7 J. Lilburne, *The Afflicted Mans Out-Cry* (1653), title page.

The Beginnings of the Fifth Monarchy Movement

An enemy remarked with some pleasure that in the absence of Fifth Monarchist music, Feake had been obliged to use 'Prelatical Tunes'.[1]

The Barebones Parliament has been divided by Glass and by Gardiner into two clear parties, one radical, the other moderate. On the basis of a division list, published later in June 1654, showing those members for and against the national ministry and the universities, Gardiner ascribed the members to one or other of the parties, concluding that 'there were therefore 84 Moderates and 60 of the Advanced Party' (or 81 : 61, according to Glass).[2] But this classification is of little help, for it was recognized as early as 1 August that the 'radical party' was itself divided.[3] Only twelve Fifth Monarchists can be identified, Harrison and the regicide, John Carew, being the best-known. Francis Langden and John Bawden sat for Cornwall, Col. Danvers for Leicester, Jacob Caley for Ipswich, and Arthur Squibb, a member of the Committee for Sequestrations, for Middlesex. Col. John James, a former Governor of Worcester, John Browne, a regicide, Hugh Courtney, Richard Price and John Williams were all supporters of Powell and Llwyd and represented Wales.[4] Thomas Baker, Sheriff of Shropshire in 1649, was a benefactor of Powell, and may have belonged to the group, and there were possibly others on the fringe.[5] Of the group of twelve, five were sometime members of the Council of State, six were justices of the peace, two had been Sheriffs, and nine held army or militia commissions. Thus even the most radical elements hardly deserved the royalist criticism, surprisingly shared by Spittlehouse, that the members were 'such pitifull Creatures as were never heard of till these times made them infamous . . . no better then Attorneys, Tanners, Wheelwrights, and . . . the meanest sort of Mechaniques'.[6] The Fifth Monarchist members acted together as a group. They never appear on opposite sides in the lists of tellers in Parliamentary divisions, nor in the only extant complete division list.[7] They discussed tactics amongst themselves and with the Blackfriars preachers.

[1] 'Mr. Feake's Hymne: August ye 11: 1653 Christ Church', MS. amongst Thomason Tracts in Brit. Mus., E 710 (13); J.N., *Proh Tempora! Proh Mores!* (1654), p. 6.
[2] Glass, *Barbone Parliament*, p. 64; Gardiner, *Comm. and Protect.*, ii. 290, 307–10. The original list is printed in *A Collection of the State Papers of John Thurloe*, ed. T. Birch (1742), iii. 132 (henceforth *Thurloe*).
[3] *Thurloe*, i. 393. [4] See Biog. App. for all these.
[5] H. T. Weyman, 'Shropshire Members of Parliament', *Trans. Shrops. Arch. Soc.*, 4th series, xi (1928), pp. 177–8.
[6] MS. Clar. 45, fos. 381*v*.–2; Spittlehouse, *First Addresses*, p. 2.
[7] *Commons' Journals*, vii (1813), pp. 282–363; *Thurloe*, iii. 132.

68

Cromwell said later that 'the persons that led in the meeting were Mr. Feake and his meeting in Blackfriars, Major-General Harrison, and those that associated with him at one Mr. Squibb's house; and there were all the resolutions taken that were acted in that House day by day'. A member of Barebones agreed that it was Squibb's house 'where most of their imaginations were formed and shaped'.[1] The Fifth Monarchist and other members attended the Blackfriars meetings, and actually taught there.[2] The Blackfriars preachers commented on Parliamentary affairs, and moderate members were 'unsainted and condemned into the fourth Monarchy, and looked upon as obstructors of Reformation, . . . if not thorough paced to all the Principles of Reformation held forth by Mr. *Feake* and others . . . and stickled for by some in the House'.[3]

Even if the Fifth Monarchists acted together, they comprised a mere twelfth of the membership. But there were many other members of a radical outlook who shared some of their aspirations. Moreover, the moderates did not constitute a united party. Barebones was an assembly of individuals and very small groups, with no true parties. In no less than 32 of the 67 recorded divisions at least one pair of the tellers was a combination of one of the supposed radicals and a supposed moderate. A member might be a moderate on law reform but a radical over religious matters, or *vice versa*. The situation was so fluid that the prominent 'moderates' Sir Gilbert Pickering, Sir Charles Wolseley and Walter Strickland acted as 'radical' tellers with Carew, Courtney and Harrison respectively, two of the divisions being on law reform.[4] This fragmentation made it impossible to predict the outcome of any vote, especially as absenteeism was a serious problem. Though there were nominally 144 members, only once between the end of July and mid-November did the numbers recorded reach ninety.[5]

The assembly began quite favourably for the Fifth Monarchists. They obtained places on most committees, and on 14 July Williams and Courtney were added to the Council of State.[6] The saints con-

---

[1] Abbott, *Writings and Speeches*, iv. 489; L.D., 'An Exact Relation', *A Collection of Scarce and Valuable Tracts . . . of the late Lord Somers*, ed. Sir Walter Scott (1809–1815), vi. 283.

[2] L.D., 'Exact Relation', p. 273; anon., *A True State of the Case of the Commonwealth* (1654), p. 20.

[3] Anon., *An Answer to a Paper entitled A True Narrative* (1653), p. 3.

[4] *C.J.*, vii. 282, 304, 335.

[5] *C.J.*, vii. 344.

[6] Glass, *Barbone Parliament*, pp. 91–2; *C.J.*, vii. 284–5.

centrated on securing major law reforms and the destruction of the national church. The removal of the existing law and church was a pre-requisite for the establishment of the millennium: they were 'Out-works of *Babylon*', which 'must be taken down before there could be a coming at the main fort', and since there was widespread discontent with both, any attack was likely to attract considerable support.[1] On 15 July there was a radical motion for a vote on whether to abolish immediately the system of tithes, the financial basis of the state church. This was defeated, but the radicals forced a debate lasting four days, when the whole issue was referred to a committee. Harrison acted as a teller on the radical side, and was presumably prominent in the debate; he was placed on the committee, along with Squibb, Danvers and Courtney.[2] On 27 July Carew was a teller for the radical side in a motion that there should be total freedom of preaching in public places, another effort to undermine the national church. This too was defeated, by eleven votes.[3] The cause of religious reform was thus checked, but it was not yet despaired of. John Rogers attended the tithes committee's meetings, to give evidence against the system, despite being attacked by the 'rude rabble'. In September Spittlehouse submitted a tract to the committee, expressing confidence that tithes would soon be abolished.[4]

With religious affairs now removed to committee, attention was transferred to the law. There was widespread interest in law reform, and a committee had been established on 20 July, with a largely moderate membership. But attempts were now made in the main body of the House to secure immediate and far-reaching changes. On 5 August a resolution was passed without a division that the court of Chancery should be abolished, and a bill drawn up to this effect.[5] The radicals may have chosen a time when few of their opponents were present, but there was clearly strong feeling against Chancery. When the law debate was resumed on 19 August the moderates tried to secure an adjournment, but failed, and a motion was carried that there should be a completely new body of law. Courtney and Squibb were among the tellers for the majority, as well as the 'moderate' Wolseley. A new committee was established

---

[1] *A True State*, pp. 14–15. For Fifth Monarchist views on the law and the church see chaps. 7, 8, below.

[2] *C.J.*, vii. 285–6.

[3] *C.J.*, vii. 290.

[4] J. Rogers, *Sagrir* (1653), *sig.* b3–c2; J. Spittlehouse, *An Explanation of the Commission of Jesus Christ* (1653), *sig.* A2.

[5] *C.J.*, vii. 286, 296.

to prepare a bill, with Harrison, Squibb and Barbone among its members.[1] But by mid-October the new legal term had begun, and no bill had appeared. Harrison and other impatient members suggested that Chancery should be suspended at once for a month, and this motion was carried by three votes. But when a bill was introduced to this effect, its opponents rallied their forces and defeated it by the casting vote of the Speaker.[2]

Another of the Fifth Monarchists' objectives was, allegedly, to destroy the army which was seen as 'the great Impediment in the way of *their Monarchy*'. They attempted this first by opposing the bill to renew the assessment, the tax which financed the army. Defeated in this, they tried to force a change in the army leadership by attacking the officers as '*Janisaries*', and urging the Blackfriars preachers, whose 'Patrons' they were, 'to cast dirt upon all persons in Trust and Power, in the Army and elsewhere, by proclaiming them to be *Pensioners of Babylon*'.[3] This account was from a very hostile source, and it is unlikely that the saints wished to destroy the army in which many still held commissions and which had been seen for several years as the most hopeful instrument of Christ. But there probably were attacks on some officers. Another account of the assessment debate stated that the 'dissenters' accused the officers, like the Rump, of growing rich on forfeited estates, and demanded that they should serve without pay to lower taxes. Harrison, as noted already, was alleged earlier to have offered to serve without payment. The 'dissenters' also argued that assessment by counties was an unfair mode of taxation, and should be altered.[4]

The deep divisions and the confused situation inside the House produced discontent very rapidly. Some felt, unjustly, that Cromwell had called the assembly merely as an opportunity to assume supreme power, and some members refused to furnish the lodgings provided for them because they felt they would not be there long enought to justify the expense.[5] A royalist agent reiterated the message that 'Cromwel and the Parliament can not, nor will agree' on 5 August and 2 and 16 September, 'so that you may shortly expect a dissolution'.[6] The French ambassador repeated a rumour that the

---

[1] *C.J.*, vii. 304.   [2] *C.J.*, vii. 335.
[3] *A True State*, pp. 19–20.
[4] Gardiner, *Comm. and Protect.*, ii. 313 and note; see p. 66, above.
[5] MS. Clar. 45, f. 398; Sir John Birkenhead, *Bibliotheca Parliamenti Libri Theologici* (1653), p. 7; MS. Clar. 46, f. 112: newsletter, 22 July.
[6] MS. Clar. 46, fos. 158v., 230v., 274–v.: newsletters, 5 Aug., 2 and 16 Sept.

army leaders and Parliamentary moderates would ally to purge the Anabaptists.[1]

The Fifth Monarchist group was itself becoming discontented, since nothing had been achieved. Moreover, their opponents had rushed through a bill to establish a High Court of Justice. A motion to introduce this bill had been defeated on 28 September, with Squibb and Barbone as tellers for the Noes, who feared such a court might be used against radicals as well as royalists. But on 21 November, whilst the saints were absent at the Blackfriars prayer-meeting, the bill was introduced and pushed through all its stages in the course of a single morning.[2]

The Fifth Monarchists' discontents had begun long before this episode, and since August they had been highly suspicious of Cromwell's negotiations with the Dutch. The saints saw the Dutch war as a means of both hastening the millennium and securing economic advantages, and Feake warned that if Cromwell came to terms, 'God's vengeance would follow upon such a heathenish peace.' In November, Harrison and his supporters were said to 'rail and preach every day' against the negotiations.[3] The failure to secure law and church reform also produced bitterness, so that by September the '*murmuring people*' were abusing not only the Rump but the Barebones Assembly 'for treading in their *steps*'.[4] The leading saints drew back from the regime. Harrison attended ninety-nine Council meetings from May to July, but only seven from August to December, and Carew behaved similarly. Williams and Courtney were not re-elected to the new Council on 1 November.[5] Harrison was said to be 'under a cloud' in October, and intending to 'leave this place, and to come no more'. The Fifth Monarchists wrote to 'the Churches all the Nation over, to blast that part of the House that agreed not with them; and at a set meeting at a Members house', doubtless Squibb's, there were consultations on whether 'to leave the House and Remonstrate against them as hinderers of Reformation and not fit to Govern the Nation any longer'.[6]

[1] P.R.O. 31/3/92, f. 30: Bordeaux to de Brienne, 14/24 Nov. 1653.
[2] *C.J.*, vii. 325, 353–4; L.D., 'An Exact Relation', p. 273; Gardiner, *Comm. and Protect.*, ii. 317–18.
[3] *Thurloe*, i. 441–2, 534, 612. On Fifth Monarchist foreign policy, see below pp. 151–5.
[4] A. Evans, *The Bloudy Vision of John Farley* (1653), sig. A4–v.
[5] *C.J.*, vii. 343–4; *Cal. S.P. Dom., 1652–3*, pp. xxxiv–xl; *ibid., 1653–4*, pp. xxxvi–xxxvii.
[6] Hist. MSS. Comm., xliii, *Somerset MSS.*, p. 158; *Thurloe*, i. 612; *Answer To a Paper*, p. 3.

The saints outside the House were as disillusioned as those within. The preachers heaped 'scandalous and scurrilous aspersions' upon Parliament, the Council and the army, and 'peremptory predictions of their remove or downfall, and the bringing in of another interest and other persons to predominate'.[1] Spittlehouse was arrested for writing seditious petitions against Thurloe, and Peter Chamberlen was arrested on a charge of threatening to assassinate Cromwell. By good fortune, 'as from the Lord', the witnesses failed to agree, and Chamberlen was released.[2] At Blackfriars on 28 November Feake and his colleagues denounced Cromwell as 'the man of sin, the old dragon, and many other scripture ill names'. Exasperated at last, Cromwell summoned the preachers two days later and accused them of casting ill odour on the government. Feake retorted that it was the General's 'tampering with the king, and his assuming an exorbitant power, which made these disorders; and so held forth the fifth monarchy'. Cromwell then tried an alternative approach, setting Peter Sterry to preach 'obedience, as the most necessary way to bring in the kingdom of Christ'. This produced predictably little response.[3]

Cromwell and many moderate members may well have been hoping that the extremists would secede, but this did not happen. It became apparent that the cause of the Fifth Monarchists, hitherto defeated, was not wholly lost. On 3 November a bill for the abolition of Chancery, providing alternative arrangements for equity cases, was at last introduced, and was read twice and committed. On 17 November a major step was taken when a motion was carried to take away the right of lay patrons to present to benefices, and a bill was ordered.[4] The tithes committee reported at last on 2 December, but only increased the Fifth Monarchists' dissatisfaction by its recommendation that the system of tithes should be retained. Harrison apparently said that he would 'rather submit his judgement in the case than prove pertinacious where he finds better judgements patronise it'. But most of the saints were determined to oppose the report and forced a debate lasting four days, at the end of which they defeated the first clause by two votes, with Danvers acting as teller. The clause had provided for a body of commissioners (who were named) who were to eject unfit ministers and approve all new ones.

[1] *Thurloe*, i. 591.
[2] *Cal. S.P. Dom., 1653–4*, pp. 277, 294, 446; Church Book of Lothbury Square, Bodl. MS. Rawl. D 828, f. 16.
[3] *Thurloe*, i. 621; P.R.O. 31/3/92, f. 65: Bordeaux to de Brienne, 1/11 Dec.
[4] *C.J.*, vii. 346, 352.

Its opponents objected to it probably both as an instrument of a continuing state church, and because it consisted largely of Presbyterians and cautious Independents.[1]

The moderates were reminded forcibly that they were still unable to control the assembly, and despaired of ever doing so. The vote against tithes was a vote against property, and highly alarming. Accordingly, the moderates assembled in the House early the following Monday morning, 12 December, before most of their opponents had arrived, and despite fierce criticism from Harrison, who was present, resolved to surrender their power to Cromwell. Wolseley, who took a leading part in this, had earlier been in favour of radical law reforms but declared that the recent vote had endangered property and that law itself was likely to be destroyed. About thirty-five members remained in the House but were driven out by a party of soldiers under Col. Goffe. He derided them as 'but a degree above a Conventicle', and was alleged to have added that Parliament 'was not so fit for them as Mr. Squibb's house'.[2]

The apologists of the resignation claimed there had been in Barebones a radical party, comparable to the Münster Anabaptists, seeking 'the plucking up of all *Ecclesiastical* and *Civil* policy, laying all waste that they might enter and devour at pleasure'. One correspondent believed that 'if the house had sate a weeke longer, law and the ministry had been voted down'. A former member claimed the radicals had sought to establish the fifth monarchy, ruling 'by a Divine and extraordinary right' which would give them authority 'to possess all mens properties and Estates'. It would have produced 'blood and confusion'.[3]

These charges contained some truth. There had been an attack on the state church, and although property itself had not been questioned, tithes and the right to present to benefices, which were seen as forms of property, had been condemned. A former member who defended the Parliament's record denied they had sought the 'destroying of the law, or putting it down'; they had wished only for a 'reducing the wholesome, just, and good laws into a body, from them that are useless and out of date'.[4] This may have been true for most, but in November John Rogers had stated that 'It is not enough to

---

[1] *C.J.*, vii. 361; Hist. MSS. Comm., xliii, *Somerset MSS.*, p. 159.
[2] L.D., 'Exact Relation', p. 283 and note; J. Hall, *Confusion Confounded* (1654), p. 6; *A True State*, p. 22; Gardiner, *Comm. and Protect.*, ii. 326–8.
[3] Hall, *Confusion Confounded*, p. 7; *Thurloe*, i. 754; *Answer To a Paper*, p. 2.
[4] L.D., 'Exact Relation', p. 278.

change some of these *Lawes*, and so to *reforme* them (as is intended by most of you) . . . O no: that wil be to poore *purpose*, and it is not *your worke* now, which is . . . bringing in the *Lawes* of *God* given by *Moses* for *Re-publique Lawes*.'[1] By confusing the small Fifth Monarchist group with radical members as a whole, it was easy to hang the label of fanaticism around the necks of all.

With the fall of Barebones, the Fifth Monarchists went into permanent and unwavering opposition. They reviled Cromwell for accepting the resignation of the assembly and so disrupting the reign of the saints. But the Barebones Parliament had been only a very rough approximation to the saints' reign. The bitterness with which they saw its fall sprang probably from their realization that the new regime would be far less favourable to the Kingdom of Christ.

[1] Rogers, *Sagrir*, sig. A4–*v*.

CHAPTER FOUR

The Distribution and Composition of the Fifth Monarchy Men

The Fifth Monarchists were an essentially urban movement. The London area was dominant throughout: it contained at least twenty-nine groups in the second half of the century, though their frequent migrations, dissolutions and re-formations prevent exactness, and membership probably overlapped. Only about forty-three groups are recorded for the rest of the country, excluding Wales, although the records are less complete.[1] In the 1650s the Fifth Monarchists were confined largely to the southern half of England. There were eight groups in Norfolk and Suffolk, and Devon and Cornwall were important areas. In Wales, Fifth Monarchist ideas emanated from Vavasor Powell and Morgan Llwyd, who were based at Radnor and Wrexham respectively. Powell was a great evangelist who established a further twenty churches, but it is not possible to determine how many of these can be called Fifth Monarchist.[2] North of the Midlands there was only one real centre, embracing Liverpool, Manchester and Cheshire. In addition, there were isolated strongholds at Hull and Sheffield. Large parts of the country seem to have been untouched by Fifth Monarchist ideas, including most of the North, South Wales, many parts of the Midlands and the traditionally Puritan county of Essex.[3]

After 1660 this distribution altered. London remained predominant, but Fifth Monarchist activities ceased in North Wales and East Anglia. Itinerant preachers from London visited Devon and attempted also to win over the North. They won considerable support in Yorkshire, Durham and Westmorland, mainly among disaffected and militant Baptists and former soldiers, with whom they engineered the Yorkshire plot of 1663.[4]

[1] See Appendix II for a list of all known Fifth Monarchist groups.
[2] T. Crosby, *The History of the English Baptists* (1738–40), i. 377; see below, p. 109.
[3] See Appendix II.   [4] See below, pp. 207, 209–10.

Apart from these regional centres, Fifth Monarchist churches were scattered, but were usually in fairly large towns, and often close to or on the sea. A list found by Secretary Thurloe probably dating from 1656, showed agents in Bristol, Dartmouth, Portsmouth, Newport (Isle of Wight), Lewes and Sandwich, besides the Hull and Manchester/Liverpool groups.[1] Another group existed at Southampton.[2] Of those in East Anglia, Ipswich and Woodbridge were on river estuaries. Most of the inland churches were also in towns, such as Abingdon, Devizes, Canterbury, Reading, Oxford, Warwick, Lincoln, Sheffield, Bedford and Exeter.[3] In East Anglia the saints avoided the villages and congregated in the towns, at Norwich, North Walsham, Ipswich, Bury and Woodbridge.[4] The village groups that did exist, as at Skegby (Notts.) and Chalfont St. Giles (Bucks.), were unimportant, apparently taking no part in the national movement.[5] Where a Fifth Monarchist minister was beneficed in a village, as in the case of Tillinghast at Trunch (Norfolk) or Thomas Palmer at Aston-on-Trent (Derbyshire), his real interests were elsewhere. Palmer spent much of his time in Nottingham and London, and Tillinghast eventually left Trunch and moved to London. Similarly John Rogers left and ultimately forfeited his rich living at Purleigh (Essex) and settled in the capital.[6]

The areas of Fifth Monarchist strength show few common characteristics. London and East Anglia were relatively prosperous, with Parliamentarian and Puritan traditions. Wales was poor, royalist and Anglican. East Anglia, London and Devon were all important as cloth-producing areas, and an analysis of the social composition of the saints shows a high proportion of cloth-workers.[7] But there is no total correspondence, for other clothing centres, such as Essex, Yorkshire and the south-west midlands, supported few or no Fifth Monarchist groups.

Most of the Fifth Monarchist centres, being lowland towns,

---

[1] *Thurloe State Papers*, vi. 187.
[2] G. L. Turner, *Original Records of Early Nonconformity* (1911–14), i. 143.
[3] *Thurloe*, vi. 187; Turner, *Orig. Recs.*, i. 118; Public Record Office, S.P. 29/136, f. 65: A. Corley to Williamson, 4 Nov. 1665; A. G. Matthews, *Calamy Revised* (Oxford, 1934), p. 199; Bodl. MS. Clar. 81, f. 199: Sir W. Armorer to (Clarendon), 12 April 1664.
[4] *Thurloe*, iv. 687, vi. 187; anon., *Certain Quaeres* (1649), tit. pag.; *The Complaining Testimony* (1656), sig. A2.   [5] Turner, *Orig. Recs.*, i. 155, 78.
[6] *D.N.B.*, T. Palmer, Rogers, Tillinghast; Matthews, *Cal. Rev.*, p. 380; J. Tillinghast, *Mr. Tillinghasts Eight Last Sermons* (1655), preface by Feake, *sig.* A3v–4. See Biog. App. for Palmer and Tillinghast.
[7] See below, pp. 84–5.

possessed good road and river communications. Reading, Abingdon and Oxford were all on the Thames, one of the major commercial routes, and most centres were within fairly easy reach of navigable water. But North Wales, the central parts of northern England, important after 1660, and Devizes formed notable exceptions.[1] Some of the smaller towns were situated on important roads. In Cheshire, for example, Nantwich was on the London to Holyhead road, and Great Budworth on the London–Carlisle route. Ipswich and Wymondham were on the main routes from Norwich and Yarmouth to London.[2] But other East Anglian centres, such as North Walsham and Syleham, were not on any major roads. Road and river communications provide on the whole very little explanation of Fifth Monarchist distribution.

A more important circumstance was the influence of a strong local leader in a particular area. Powell and Llwyd were responsible for the whole movement in North Wales, created despite hostile traditions. Some of Powell's followers did not accept his Fifth Monarchist beliefs, and tried to minimize them. After the Restoration, when Llwyd was dead and Powell in prison and moderating his views, no Fifth Monarchist activities were reported in Wales. Powell's fiercest disciples were prepared to accept licences from the government in 1672.[3] In South Wales, where social and economic conditions were similar to those further north, the Puritan movement was dominated by Cromwellian supporters, Cradock and Philip Jones, and Fifth Monarchism did not appear.[4] John Wigan alone was responsible for bringing Baptist and Fifth Monarchist ideas to Cheshire and the Manchester area, and the churches at Budworth and Nantwich reflect his work. John Canne established the congregation at Hull, where he was chaplain to the garrison under Overton, and it survived after his removal.[5]

---

[1] T. S. Willan, *River Navigation in England, 1600–1750* (1936), pp. vi, 32.

[2] G. Scott Thomson, 'Roads in England and Wales in 1603', *Eng. Hist. Rev.*, xxxiii (1918), p. 242; J. Ogilby, *Britannia* (1675), maps facing pp. 44–5, 72–3, 90–1, 106–7.

[3] *Thurloe*, iv. 359; T. Richards, *Wales under the Indulgence (1672–1675)* (1928), pp. 1ff., 221–2; Turner, *Orig. Recs.*, ii. 1201/4; V. Powell, *The Bird in the Cage* (1661), p. 35; anon., *Vavasoris Examen et Purgamen* (1654), pp. 18–19.

[4] A. H. Dodd, 'A Remonstrance from Wales, 1655', *Bull. Bd. Celtic Studies*, xvii (1956–8), p. 283.

[5] W. T. Whitley, *Baptists of North-West England, 1649–1913* (London and Preston, 1913), pp. 41–7; *Thurloe*, vi. 187. For Wigan, Canne and Overton see Biog. App.; W. Whitaker, *One Line of the Puritan Tradition in Hull* (1910), pp. 22–3, 35; Bodl. MS. Rawl. A 57, f. 312: H. Smith to O. Cromwell, 11 Feb. 1658.

The importance of East Anglia to the movement largely reflected the dominating influence of William Bridge, the millenarian Independent minister of Great Yarmouth. Nearly all the Fifth Monarchist ministers there began their careers under him, were influenced by him, and continued to seek his advice after becoming Fifth Monarchists.[1] In the west the Baptist, Thomas Collier, played a similar role, creating a passively millenarian movement, many of the members of which later became Fifth Monarchists, such as Glasse and Nathaniel Strange.[2]

As an urban movement (except in Wales) the Fifth Monarchists provide no opportunity of testing Professor Everitt's recent hypothesis that the wood-pasture areas of England were the sources of religious dissent. There seems to be no correlation between these areas and such few rural groups as did exist.[3] The Quakers proved that sectarianism could flourish in the country, but the towns were more immediately promising. They constituted large assemblies of people of differing social and regional origins, accustomed to fresh ideas brought by immigrants and visiting traders. Literacy was higher in the towns, so that new ideas could be obtained from books and pamphlets, and since there were several clergy in the larger towns, there was some measure of freedom of choice in religion even before 1640. The traditional social controls of squire and parson, still dominant in the manorial areas of the country, were totally absent in the town. The control of the master over his servants was considerable, but during the interregnum his displeasure sometimes failed to prevent his servants from joining a radical sect.[4]

[1] J. Browne, *History of Congregationalism in Norfolk and Suffolk* (1877), *passim*; E. Calamy, *An Account of the Ministers . . . Ejected* (1713), p. 647; Norfolk Record Office, 'Church Book of Gt. Yarmouth, 1642–1664', pp. 51–2, 54; anon., *The Failing & Perishing of Good Men* (1663), sig. A3.
[2] G. F. Nuttall, 'The Baptist Western Association 1653–1658', *Journ. Eccles. Hist.*, xi (1960), pp. 213–18; for Glasse and Strange, see Biog. App.
[3] J. Thirsk, *The Agrarian History of England and Wales*, iv (Cambridge, 1967), p. 464; Prof. Everitt has documented the theory in his chapter, 'Nonconformity in Country Parishes', in *Land, Church and People: Essays Presented to Professor H. P. R. Finberg*, ed. J. Thirsk, *Agricultural Hist. Rev.*, 18 (1970), Supplement, pp. 178–99, basing his evidence largely on the Compton Census of 1676 in Kent. But though the reasons suggested for this phenomenon certainly seem valid, the absence of earlier documentation leaves an element of doubt as to the relative importance of forest areas as the source of dissent, or as a refuge for it after the Restoration. George Fox spoke of Baptists moving to the forest areas of Leicestershire after 1660 to avoid persecution: G. Fox, *Journal*, ed. J. Nickalls (Cambridge, 1952), pp. 428–9.
[4] MS. Rawl. A 47, fos. 26–7v.: A. de Samand to . . ., no date; P. Chamberlen, *The Disputes between Mr. Cranford and Dr. Chamberlen* (1652), sig. A2v. For a later example see C. Doe, *A Collection of Experiences* (1700), p. 30.

The Distribution and Composition of the Fifth Monarchy Men

The preoccupation of the Fifth Monarchists with political power probably also contributed to the movement's urban nature. Expecting to take part in the work of establishing Christ's kingdom, Fifth Monarchist ministers tended to move to the towns, especially London.[1] Ejected ministers converging on London more than filled the gaps in the leadership caused by the Restoration.[2]

Apart from the towns, the major source of Fifth Monarchist recruitment was the army, where millenarian excitement was intense in the later 1640s and early '50s. Like the large town, the New Model was a very different social organization from that with which most of its members were familiar. Traditional patterns of deference did not exist; birth was not of paramount importance, and the ordinary soldier could see himself not as a mere servant, but as a citizen and saint. Some thirty-four Fifth Monarchists appear to have been officers, and at least fifty-six are identifiable as common soldiers. The true total of the latter was probably far higher.[3] Many of the Fifth Monarchist ministers had been officers, including Wigan, Thomas Palmer, Simpson and Skinner, and Powell and Llwyd had raised troops and fought under Harrison. Helme had fought either as a soldier or officer, and Rogers, Canne and Marsden had all served as chaplains.[4]

Fifth Monarchism was brought to Hull by the army garrison, and many other churches probably originated in this way. The navy, too, was important. It was another new social form, and was another centre of millenarian enthusiasm. At the highest level, the millenarian Sir Henry Vane was chairman of the Admiralty Committee for a time, and the Fifth Monarchists Carew and Rich were among the Navy Commissioners.[5] During the First Dutch War (1652–4), Admiral Deane wrote of his hope that 'Christ alone may be exalted, which is the end of these terrible shakings'. Admiral Lawson wrote

[1] For examples see above, p. 77.
[2] See below, pp. 202–3.
[3] C. H. Firth and G. Davies, *The Regimental History of Cromwell's Army* (Oxford, 1940), *passim*; SP. 28/121b, 123–5, *passim* (muster-rolls); SP. 28/142, i–iii, *passim* (regimental lists).
[4] C. H. Firth, *Cromwell's Army* (1902), p. 328; Matthews, *Cal. Rev.*, pp. 339, 380, 529; E. Calamy, *A Continuation of the Account* (1727), p. 501; SP. 29/88, f. 128: information, ?1663; *A Perfect Diurnall of Some Passages*, 216 (23–30 Jan. 1654), p. 3092; *D.N.B.*, Canne, Llwyd, Palmer, Powell, Rogers. See Biog. App. for Helme, Skinner and Marsden.
[5] *Letters and Papers Relating to the First Dutch War 1652–1654*, ed. S. R. Gardiner and C. T. Atkinson (Navy Records Soc., xiii, xvii, xxx, xxxvii, xli, lxvi, 1899–1930), i. 53, vi. 106, 189.

that the war was 'in order to the design of God in the exaltation of Jesus Christ'.[1] John Portman, deputy treasurer to the fleet and secretary to the generals at sea, was a Fifth Monarchist, and so was his brother Edmund, clerk to the Treasurer of the Navy.[2] The celebrated captain, Owen Cox, was a Fifth Monarchist. William Pestell, captain of the *Satisfaction*, and at Hull in 1653, was a government informer against the Fifth Monarchists after the Restoration, and was probably a renegade saint. Capt. Henry Hatsell, the Plymouth agent of the Navy Commissioners between 1652–8, was arrested at Exeter in 1661 as a leader in an alleged Fifth Monarchist plot.[3] There were certainly close connections between the saints and the navy. In 1653 John Simpson and the Baptist Henry Jessey held a service on board Blake's flagship. The same year, John Rogers held a meeting of several congregations in London, and called on God to bless 'our friends in the Fleet'.[4] Woodbridge was a naval ship-building centre, and Ipswich was also a naval base: Fifth Monarchist groups existed at both, and at many other important ports.[5]

The actual numbers of Fifth Monarchists are highly elusive. The saints wished to impress and their enemies were alarmist, so that both gave inflated figures. The highest estimate, by Feake in 1655, was 40,000.[6] In 1659, a peak period, a royalist thought they numbered 20,000–30,000 armed men, and that 5,000 had assembled recently at Horsham (Sussex).[7] There were rumours that year of a secret list of 7,000 saints.[8] Venner's risings led people to speculate on the strength of the saints. It was alleged in 1657 that the 'gang' numbered 10,000–15,000. In 1661 there were said to be 5,000 Fifth Monarchists in London, and 30,000 in the rest of the country.[9] Vavasor Powell boasted in 1655 that he could produce 20,000 armed supporters in Wales.[10]

All these figures were merely guesses, and are totally unreliable. Despite Powell's boast, for example, he was able to secure only 322

---

[1] *Letters and Papers Relating to the First Dutch War 1652–1654*, iv. 369, 46.
[2] *Ibid.*, iii. 324, v. 106–7. See Biog. App. for the Portman brothers.
[3] *Ibid.*, i. 18–20, 23, 26, 65, iii. 131–3, v. 53–4, 63, 251–2. See Biog. App. for Cox and Hatsell.
[4] *Ibid.*, v. 411; *Severall Proceedings in Parliament*, 177 (10–17 Feb. 1653), p. 2790.
[5] *Letters and Papers*, iv. 39, v. 249, 260, 268, 270, 399, vi. 115; see above, p. 77.
[6] MS. Rawl. A 26, f. 242: Col. Whichcote to (?Cromwell), 18 May 1655.
[7] MS. Clar. 61, f. 103: J. Hopebetter (= Major Wood) to H. Simpson (?Hyde), 3 June 1659.   [8] *Thurloe*, vii. 687.
[9] Hist. MSS. Comm., 4, *Appendix to 5th Report*, p. 163; *Diary of Henry Townshend*, ed. J. W. Willis-Bund (1920), i. 66.   [10] *Thurloe*, iii. 137.

signatures for his petition, *A Word for God*. Admittedly, local authorities put pressure on people not to sign, but the petition had been phrased to attract the widest possible support.[1] The size of congregations varied enormously, from the 57 at Woodbridge over thirty years to the seven hundred at Danvers's London church in 1682.[2] The Fifth Monarchists were an elitist movement, and called for a high level of political commitment, and it seems probable that their numbers never exceeded ten thousand. This is obviously very small in terms of the national population, but the numbers of genuine Levellers and Commonwealthsmen were probably no greater. In any case the rising of 1661 was to remind contemporaries that numbers were less important than determination.[3]

The membership of the Fifth Monarchist movement consisted of three distinct groups. There was a number of army officers, some from the gentry, some risen from the ranks, who had not lost their millenarian zeal. There was a number of clergy, some from the universities, many having connections with the army.[4] These two groups were small in number but provided much of the leadership and produced most of the pamphlets. But they were far from typical. Contemporaries described the saints as 'the worst of men, the Scum, and very froth of baseness'; 'very inconsiderable, and indeed despicable'; the 'Scum, the very raf of Billingsgate'. Their meetings were said to be full of journeymen and women.[5] These were hostile accounts, but even Feake remarked that the saints were a 'company of illiterate men, and silly women', and Venner's manifesto in 1661 did not dispute the fact that the saints were a 'poor, obscure, illiterate' group.[6] In the church lists which survived, women easily outnumbered men.[7]

An analysis of the occupations of 233 Fifth Monarchists produces the following results.[8]

---

[1] *Thurloe*, iv. 383–4.

[2] 'Churchbook of Woodbridge', Dr. Williams's Lib., Harmer MSS. 76.5, fos. 2–3; SP. 29/419, f. 102: information, 1 June 1682.

[3] For Venner's rising see below, p. 199–200.

[4] See above, p. 80, and below, pp. 93–4.

[5] Anon., *Londons Glory, or, The Riot and Ruine of the Fifth Monarchy Men* (1661), p. 5; *Thurloe*, vi. 185, iii. 136–7, v. 759.

[6] M. Cary, *The Little Horns Doom* (1651), sig. a6; anon., *A Door of Hope*, p. 4.

[7] 'Churchbook of Lothbury Square', MS. Rawl. D 828, f. 17; 'Mill Yard Minutes', Dr. Williams's Lib., MSS. 533 B.1, index of members; 'Woodbridge Churchbook', fos. 2–3.

[8] Entries in brackets are not included in the totals and refer to the subsidiary occupations of persons counted elsewhere, e.g. artisans who practised several trades. Servants have been counted under their trades where known. Classes 1–2 are

The Distribution and Composition of the Fifth Monarchy Men

1. GENTRY/ESQUIRES   20

2. BENEFICED MINISTERS, PROFESSIONAL/OFFICIAL

ministers 34	physicians 4 (+ 1)	'medical man'
teachers 3 (+ 4)	navy officials 2	gaoler
publisher	(recorder)	(sequestrator)
ship-owner/ capt.	receiver-general (of taxes, in Devon)	48

3. AGRICULTURE

yeomen 7 (+ 1)	husbandmen 2 + 2 wives	cow-keeper		
labourers 7 + 2 wives			21	13%

4. (SHIP-)BUILDING AND ALLIED

bricklayers 2	glaziers 2	millwright		
plasterer	shipwrights 2		8	5%

5. WOODWORK, METAL

basketmaker	carpenter	clock-maker		
cooper	cutlers 2	goldsmiths 2		
gunsmith	ironmonger	joiners 2		
silver-refiners 2	silversmith	silver-spinner		
smiths 3	watchmaker		20	12%

6. MANUFACTURE/DISTRIBUTION OF FOOD, DRINK AND OTHER CONSUMABLES

apothecaries 2	bakers 2	brewers 2
brewer's clerk	butcher	chandler
cheesemonger	(coalman)	(coffee-house-keeper)
coffee and liquor seller	(distiller)	grocers 2
liquor-shop-keeper	maltsters 4 (+ 1)	mealman + a wife of

probably almost complete totals; classes 3–11 are only a small sample. To avoid distortion, percentages are therefore based on the totals of 3–11 only. All sources are given in the Biographical Appendix. It is not certain how long the Abingdon church remained Fifth Monarchist after Pendarves's death; only members up to 1664 have been included.

merchants 3	miller (+ 1)	oilman		
shopkeeper	tobacco-cutter	(tobacco- merchant)		
tobacco-pipe- maker + wife	tallow-chandler	victualler	31	19%

7. MANUFACTURE/DISTRIBUTION OF CLOTH AND LEATHER

button-sellers 2	cap-maker	clothworker		
cobbler	collar-maker	cordwainers 3		
draper	feltmaker	girdler		
haberdasher	hat-makers 2	hot-presser		
linen-drapers 2	milliner	ribbon-weaver		
shoe-makers 2 + wife	silk-dyer	silk-man		
silk-stocking- maker	silk-throwsters 3	silk-weavers 2		
tailors 16	weavers 2 (+ 1)	woolbroker		
woolcomber	woollen-drapers 3 + wife		55	33%

8. TRANSPORT

coachman	waterman	2	1%

9. MISCELLANEOUS

bag-mender	book-binder	book-seller		
bottle-maker/ brush-maker	broom-man	rope-maker		
scriveners 2	upholsterer	yeomen of Lon- don 4 ('yeoman' in this context was probably a term of status not occupation, which is un- known)	13	8%

10. LABOURERS | | | 7 | 4% |

11. APPRENTICES/SERVANTS OF UNKNOWN TRADES

apprentices 4   servants

(+ 1)	(i.e. apprentices or journeymen)		
	4 (+ 3)	8	5%

TOTAL, professional or above	68
TOTAL, below professional	165
TOTAL	233

The first two classes of this table are probably nearly complete, and their members are relatively well-known. The later ones are only a small sample, and though probably roughly representative, are weighted towards the London area.

The Welsh membership is almost completely omitted, because of the impossibility of establishing which of Powell's followers were genuine Fifth Monarchists. Professor Dodd ventured to ascribe occupations to only sixteen of the signatories of the *Word for God*, and these were not necessarily Fifth Monarchy men. They were:[1]

yeomen 5	husbandman	weavers 2	glovers 2
dyer	tanner	tailor	shopkeeper
mason	surgeon		

The table shows clearly how few Fifth Monarchists were engaged in agriculture at any level—only about one-seventh. Since many in this category were from Middlesex or Abingdon, the real proportion may be still smaller, for it is at least possible that the term yeoman referred to status not occupation, and a labourer was not necessarily engaged in agriculture.

The movement was able to attract persons in most of the 'mechanic' occupations, both small producers and retailers, but there were no big producers and only three 'merchants', which was in any case a flexible term. The clothing industry and trade was dominant, involving about a third of the total. The church at Exeter established by John Carew was said to consist largely of weavers and worsted-combers.[2] Overall, more saints were engaged in making than selling. None were capitalist clothiers.

The figures and other sources show that the Fifth Monarchists did attract the very bottom strata of society (excluding paupers), the labourers and servants, that is, apprentices and journeymen. Although some apprentices would later become masters, and many

[1] Dodd, 'Remonstrance', pp. 286–92.
[2] A. Brockett, *Nonconformity in Exeter, 1650–1875* (Manchester, 1962), p. 15.

came probably from a fairly substantial background, they lacked both money and personal freedom in their current situation. With no family commitments, they were an obvious source of militancy. It is not possible to reconstruct the age-structure of the movement, but Venner's congregation at Swan Alley in 1656 apparently consisted of 'divers young men, apprentices and others', and the preacher did 'much encourage youth, that they should be firm'.[1] Added together, these groups comprise about a sixth of the total, and perhaps more since many who were described by their trade only may well have been servants rather than masters. The importance of this group is the greatest contrast with the composition of the early Quakers, who attracted few (but rather more) professional men and substantial producers, large numbers of artisans and small retailers, but almost no labourers or servants. In the country their support came from yeomen and husbandmen.[2] Very recently, however, Professor R. T. Vann has argued that the early Quakers were drawn from a very wide social range, but with a high proportion of gentry, prosperous yeomen and rich tradesmen. If these findings are accepted, the contrast with the Fifth Monarchists is of course far greater. The Fifth Monarchists seem to have been the only movement to appeal to these groups, treat them as equals and include them within their projected franchise. Several active and important saints belonged to these groups. John More was forbidden to join Chamberlen's church by William Webb, his master, but did so after a public disputation, and soon played a leading part in the congregation, venturing to criticize Chamberlen as well as publishing several tracts.[3] John Clements, perhaps identical with the servant of that name, was present at the Fifth Monarchist rally at Abingdon in 1656, and was prominent in the group which seceded from John Simpson's church.[4] Another servant, Alexander de Samand, was ordered to stop attending the services of Powell, Feake and Simpson, whom his master thought 'Mad men'. But he refused to go to the preachers whom his master named, and forced a disputation to debate the issue. Since his master disallowed Feake and Powell as disputants, de Samand rejected Seaman and Preston, 'for I count

---

[1] *Thurloe*, iv. 650.

[2] A. Cole, 'Social Origins of the Early Friends', *J. Friends' Hist. Soc.*, xlviii (1957), pp. 99–118; R. T. Vann, 'Quakerism and the Social Structure in the Interregnum', *Past and Present*, xliii (1969), pp. 71–91; *The Social Development of English Quakerism, 1655–1755*, (Cambridge, Mass., 1969).

[3] See Biog. App. for More.   [4] See Biog. App. for Clements.

not them Ministers', and also ventured to prophesy judgement against Cromwell and all who opposed the Fifth Monarchy.[1] Samuel Clarke, a member of the Bell Lane church till 1673, later became assistant minister of the Baptist congregation at Mill Yard, despite being a mere labourer.[2]

The table suggests that Dr. Hill's description of the Fifth Monarchist movement as the 'victims of early industrial society' is largely but not entirely true.[3] It obtained support from the food industry and from other mechanics who, though humble, retained their independence in this period. It seems to have attracted little support from the soap-boiling, ship-building, sugar-refining or tobacco-making industries which employed the largest concentrations of labour. But it was strong in the brewing industry, where labour was also concentrated, and it was strongest in the clothing industry which was passing into the control of mercantile capitalists.

The English cloth industry was still carried on by the small master craftsman in his own workshop, assisted by a few journeymen or apprentices belonging to the household. But his materials were supplied and his products collected by one or more clothiers who were, in effect, his employers. Masters and journeymen alike were becoming mere wage-earners, and the gilds passed into the control of mercantile oligarchies. During the period 1640–60 the tailors, weavers and other craftsmen made a last but unsuccessful attempt to win back control.[4]

At the same time the cloth industry was undergoing another upheaval. In some areas, for example Suffolk and the west, the old, heavy cloth had been driven out by foreign, mainly Dutch, competition, and the industry was in steep decline. In Essex, part of Norfolk, and elsewhere new cheaper textiles, the 'New Draperies', had been introduced, and prosperity restored.[5] Lower costs and freedom from

[1] MS. Rawl. A 47, f. 26–7: A. de Samand to . . ., no date.
[2] (W. T. Whitley), 'The Bell Lane Church', *Trans. Baptist Hist. Soc.*, iv (1914–15), p. 128. See Biog. App. for Clarke.
[3] Review in *Eng. Hist. Rev.*, lxxxiii (1968), p. 397.
[4] G. Unwin, *Industrial Organization in the 16th and 17th Centuries* (Oxford, 1904), *passim*; E. Lipson, *The History of the Woollen and Worsted Industries* (1921), pp. 36, 44–5; M. James, *Social Problems and Policy during the Puritan Revolution 1640–60* (1932), pp. 193–240; F. Consitt, *The London Weavers' Company* (Oxford, 1933), esp. pp. 146–50.
[5] B. E. Supple, *Commercial Crisis and Change in England 1600–1642* (Cambridge, 1964), chap. 7; K. J. Allison, 'The Norfolk Worsted Industry in the 16th and 17th Centuries', *Yorkshire Bull. of Econ. and Social Research*, xii (1960), pp. 73–83, xiii (1961), pp. 61–77.

restrictions in these latter areas made entry to the rank of master easier, and the unit of production in Norfolk, for example, was very small. But the very small producer was all the more dependent on the middleman for his materials and on the London merchant for the distribution of his products. Moreover, freedom from restrictions permitted the rise of some big producers, and the employment of labour on a piecemeal basis instead of for a fixed term. In a depression the producer could simply lay off his workers.[1] In the Old Draperies a master was obliged to retain his assistants even during a depression, though this gave little protection when a clothier chose to run down his stocks and provided no new work.[2] Much of the London cloth industry, especially the silk industry, was situated in any case in the outer suburbs, beyond the reach of gild protection, and it was here that many of the Fifth Monarchist groups were to be found, in Shoreditch, Stepney, Bermondsey, Morefields and Southwark.[3] These changes took place over a period of two centuries or more, though the civil wars intensified the industry's troubles, disrupting the good communications vital for supplies and distribution. Stockpiles of wool and cloth were easy plunder for both sides.[4] A recovery at the end of the wars was checked by the renewal of Dutch competition with the end of the Thirty Years' War. Other major industries, such as food or building, were much more local in character, and less prone to sudden fluctuations. Rural artisans were usually also husbandmen, so that in bad times they still had subsistence.[5] But the urban worker was made destitute. Textile workers in densely populated areas, wholly dependent on wages, were the most important elements in most of the mediaeval European millenarian outbreaks.[6]

Large numbers of saints thus were drawn from occupations with a high level of social and economic insecurity. But economic crisis was not responsible for producing the movement. The years of greatest disruption in the cloth industry were during the war. Cloth exports were high during the Dutch war of 1652–4, although they were hit by Cromwell's later war with Spain. The years when prices rose

[1] Supple, *Commercial Crisis*, pp. 153–62.
[2] G. Unwin, 'Industries', *Victoria County Hist., Suffolk*, ii. 255–66: C. Wilson, *England's Apprenticeship 1603–1763* (1965), pp. 66–7.
[3] See Appendices I and II.
[4] James, *Social Problems*, pp. 56–61, 159–66.
[5] Allison, *art. cit.*, xii. 74, xiii. 70.
[6] N. Cohn, *The Pursuit of the Millennium* (1962), pp. 220–2, 250/4, 266, 280–1.

most steeply were 1646–50, and the army, where millenarianism was strongest, was sheltered from this inflation by a rise in wages in 1649.[1] The millenarian wave of the 1640s sprang rather from political and religious upheavals. Only after 1649 was this wave transformed into an organized, lower-class movement, stimulated by the king's execution and then by the realization that the Grandees were betraying the millennium.[2]

The rise of the Fifth Monarchists followed soon after the decline of the Levellers. Both were strong in the army and in London, and they shared certain important objectives such as the abolition of tithes and the reform of the law. These circumstances have led naturally to the suggestion that the two movements may have been connected. This idea has been developed by Perez Zagorin, who argues that the Fifth Monarchist movement owed its existence to the disillusion of Levellers with secular, political methods. Henceforth they came to seek the same objectives through supernatural intervention. Zagorin indicates the parallels between the objectives of the two groups, and argues that the rise of Fifth Monarchism was the 'inevitable product of the failure of the left-democratic revolution': only after the Levellers' defeat 'did enthusiasm for the thousand-year reign of Christ and his saints begin to spread'.[3] This last claim, however, is certainly unfounded, and this throws in doubt the whole thesis. Millenarian ideas were probably more widely spread in the 1640s than in the following decade, when they first took an organized form. Thomas Collier, preaching to the soldiers at Putney in September 1647, when Leveller influence in the army was still at its height, could preface a description of the New Jerusalem with the remark, 'I question not but that you have heard of the personal reign of Christ . . .'[4] It could perhaps be argued that the early millenarian tracts were of a general, spiritual character, and that millenarianism only later synthesized with radical political and social demands. But this too would be hard to substantiate. The early tracts were indeed generalized, but their radical tone was clear. Archer had attacked the 'tyranny and oppression of Kings', who would be destroyed and

[1] E. H. Phelps Brown and S. V. Hopkins, 'Seven Centuries of the Prices of Consumables . . .', *Economica*, new ser., xxiii (1956), p. 313; C. H. Firth, *Cromwell's Army* (1902), p. 186; James, *Social Problems*, pp. 159–66.
[2] See above, pp. 50–9.
[3] P. Zagorin, *A History of Political Thought in the English Revolution* (1954), p. 105. Cf. H. N. Brailsford, *The Levellers and the English Revolution* (1961), pp. 631–7.
[4] T. Collier, *A Discovery of the New Creation* (1647), in A. S. P. Woodhouse, *Puritanism and Liberty* (1938), p. 394.

followed by the rule of the elect over the reprobate. *A Glimpse of Sions Glory* proclaimed that '*blessed is he that dasheth the Brats of* Babylon *against the* Stones', and appealed directly to 'you that are of the meaner rank, common People'.[1] There were few detailed schemes for political and social reconstruction by any radical group until the approaching end of the war made them feasible. Millenarian and Leveller proposals then appeared quite closely together. At Putney in September 1647, Collier prophesied an imminent millennium in which there would be liberty of conscience, reform of the law and law-courts, the removal of tithes and the payment of the soldiers' arrears. The army itself was to implement the millennium: 'God calls for it at your hands.' Hugh Peter, also a millenarian army chaplain, called for a similar programme in his *Word for the Army* (October 1647), specifying law reform, the reform of tithes, tolera-tion and a godly magistracy.[2] Discontent with tithes and the law had a long tradition and became the common property of almost all the radical movements of the Interregnum. The Fifth Monarchists did borrow some ideas from radical secular ideologies—for example, the Norman Yoke theme—but it is surely unnecessary to suggest that millenarians needed to borrow their programme from the Levellers.

Though there were certainly similarities between the two move-ments, the differences were equally great. The Levellers had egali-tarian tendencies, whereas the Fifth Monarchists were an elitist movement. The Fifth Monarchists proposed to establish the Mosaic Laws, a suggestion which had no parallel amongst the Levellers. The case for a vital and close connection between the movements thus depends largely on the assumption that the areas of similarity were more important to radicals of the period than the areas of difference, and that the Fifth Monarchists' religious doctrines were merely an ideological superstructure of little real significance. This is difficult to reconcile with the rigid and repressive moral code advocated by the Fifth Monarchists (like many Puritan groups, but unlike the Levellers). Fifth Monarchist tracts, even Venner's manifestos, show a deep and committed religiosity.

Only detailed and comparative biographical information could ultimately prove or disprove Zagorin's thesis, and this information is

---

[1] J. Archer, *The Personall Reigne of Christ* (1642 edn.), pp. 32, 53; T. Goodwin, *A Glimpse of Sions Glory*, pp. 2, 5.
[2] Woodhouse, *Puritanism and Liberty*, pp. 394–6; H. Peter, 'A Word for the Army', in *The Harleian Miscellany*, (1744–6), v. 572–4.

for the most part, unobtainable. But in general terms, though the Fifth Monarchists and Levellers were both strong in the London area, the Fifth Monarchist strongholds in East Anglia and North Wales had not been Leveller centres—whereas East Anglia did have Puritan and sectarian traditions. A few individuals do seem to have connected the movements, such as Thomas Dafferne, a friend of Lilburne, whose London house later became a Fifth Monarchist rendezvous.[1] The only important figures who seem to have taken the same course were Adjutant-General Allen and Capt. Edmund Chillenden. Both were prominent Agitators in 1647, and both became Fifth Monarchists. Neither, however, represents a simple switch from secular to sectarian activity produced by the failure of the Levellers. Chillenden had been arrested as early as 1641 for attending a conventicle, and Allen was noted as preaching 'sweetly and spiritually' in the presence of Fairfax in December 1647. There is little evidence that either was very committed to Leveller doctrines. Chillenden was certainly active as an Agitator, but he was an unstable character. A friend of Lilburne in the 1630s, he had nevertheless betrayed Lilburne to the officials of the Star Chamber. Despite his radicalism in 1647, he co-operated with the officers in suppressing the Leveller mutiny at Ware in November of that year. He proved equally volatile as a Fifth Monarchist. Allen was a prominent Agitator, but at Putney he appealed not to the Leveller *Case of the Army* as a whole, but to the earlier army declarations which it contained, such as that of 14 June—the work of Ireton. He also supported the retention of the monarchy, in opposition to Rainborough and Sexby. Though Allen strongly supported the army's stand against Parliament in 1647, there is little to associate him with the political ideology of the Leveller leaders. Nothing is known of the attitudes at that time of Lt. Consolation Fox, an Agitator in Ingoldsby's regiment, and later a member of the Baptist/Fifth Monarchist congregation at Abingdon led by John Pendarves.[2]

Many of the leading Fifth Monarchists were certainly hostile to the Levellers. Col. Rich had attacked a widening of the franchise at the Putney debates, and Harrison criticized the Levellers and was distrusted by them as a 'gilded' hypocrite. Harrison and Courtney

---

[1] For Dafferne see Biog. App.
[2] For Chillenden, Allen and Fox see Biog. App.; for Allen see also *The Clarke Papers*, ed. C. H. Firth (Camden Soc., new series, xlix, liv, lxi–ii, 1891–1901), i. 372, 376–7, ii. 247.

each received an honorary M.A. at Oxford after suppressing the
Leveller mutiny at Burford in 1649.[1] Overton was very cautious,
stating that 'if a leveller be one, who bears affection to anarchy,
destroying propriety or government, then I am none. But if upon the
account of New-market and other engagements, for the setling of a
well-grounded government, redress of grievances . . . &c . . . I was
and am a leveller.'[2] Fifth Monarchist writers showed no sympathy.
John Canne attacked the Levellers as atheists who denied heaven
and hell, and defended the execution of Trooper Arnold after the
Ware mutiny.[3] Morgan Llwyd criticized the Levellers as 'ye sharp
people' who deserved to 'suffer as malefactors'.[4] Spittlehouse asserted
that the saints 'abominate any wicked action under the notion of
Leveling', and Chillenden claimed that when Leveller petitions were
introduced at religious services, he always 'caused them to be
throwne by'.[5]

The rank and file do not always share the ideas of their leaders,
and the antecedents of the ordinary Fifth Monarchist are mostly
unknown. But such evidence as does exist suggests that they, like
their pastors, often had an earlier sectarian background. Thus
Capt. Buttevant had belonged to Knollys's congregation in 1646.
John Joplin, a northern Fifth Monarchist in the 1660s, had earlier
belonged to Tillam's church at Hexham, and William Wainford had
belonged to the Norwich Congregationalist church since 1644.[6] Still
more important, in the declining years of the movement after the
Restoration, many of the Fifth Monarchists reverted to the 'orthodox' Congregationalist or Baptist position, when it was apparent
that this was no longer a path to radical political or social change.[7]

The discussion so far has tried to show why certain groups might
be attracted to Fifth Monarchism. Two further problems remain:
why any gentlemen or ministers should have supported a movement
so antipathetic to the existing social order, and why, among the
artisans, some individuals became saints whilst others did not.

Millenarians, including Fifth Monarchists, were not explicit as to

---

[1] *Clarke Papers*, i. 315, ii. 185; J. Lilburne, *The Legall Fundamentall Liberties* (1649),
p. 31; Biog. App., under Harrison and Courtney.
[2] *Thurloe*, iii. 110–11.
[3] J. Canne, *The Discoverer* (1649), p. 9; *The Discoverer*, 2nd part (1649), p. 52.
[4] M. Llwyd, *Gweithiau*, ed. T. E. Ellis and J. H. Davies (Bangor and London,
1899, 1908), ii. 237.
[5] J. Spittlehouse, *An Answer to one part of the Lord Protector's Speech* (1654), p. 1;
Thurloe, iv. 365.
[6] For all these, see Biog. App.   [7] See chap. 9, below.

why they had adopted their creed, beyond listing Biblical references. Arguing that the early Church had been millenarian, they accused their opponents of being the innovators. Aspinwall even claimed King David as an early Fifth Monarchy man.[1] In the political sphere they claimed to represent the 'Good Old Cause', the 'very same things being contended for by us yt were then' by Cromwell and others who had 'turned yr backs upon yr own practises, principles & ingagements'.[2]

Explaining why some millenarians did not become Fifth Monarchists, or rapidly fell away, Feake observed that 'the *spirit of the world* carried . . . them away'.[3] The hostility of property-owning millenarians to the social doctrines of the saints does explain why most avoided the movement. Contemporaries expressed surprise that any gentleman should become a saint.[4] The few who did, such as Rich and Overton, had often served in the army for almost all their adult lives, and thought as soldiers not gentry. Even then they repudiated the more radical social programmes that were suggested.[5] Among the early leaders who deserted rather than oppose the Protectorate were Major William Packer and Capt. John Spencer, both of whom had enriched themselves and bought crown lands.[6]

Similar considerations appear to have influenced the behaviour of ministers. Large numbers had served in the army, as chaplains or soldiers.[7] Those who had business interests on a large scale, or had close connections with the government, or accepted places from it, avoided Fifth Monarchism, however zealous their millenarianism. Owen, Thomas Goodwin, Sterry, Peter, Kiffin and Knollys fell in this category, condemning Fifth Monarchism as a threat to order.[8] Feake in 1653 attacked the 'gaping professors of those times' who sought to serve Mammon as well as God.[9]

Educational levels were also important. Twenty-one Fifth Monarchists had had a university education, nineteen ministers and two

---

[1] W. Aspinwall, *The Legislative Power* (1656), p. 12; N. Homes, *The Resurrection Revealed* (1654), pp. 4ff.
[2] MS. Rawl. A 29, f. 628: Rogers to T. Brookes, 29 Aug. 1655.
[3] C. Feake, *A Beam of Light* (1659), p. 44.
[4] SP. 29/375, f. 208: Sir Brian Broughton to Williamson, 27 Nov. 1675.
[5] See below, pp. 144-5.
[6] *D.N.B.*, Packer; (W. T. Whitley), 'Theobalds and Colonel Packer', *Trans. Bapt. Hist. Soc.*, iv (1914-15), pp. 58-63.
[7] See above, p. 80.
[8] *D.N.B.*, under each name; Bodl. MS. Carte 81, fos. 16-17*v*.: letter of Owen and others, 9 Jan. 1654; J. Nickolls, *Originall Letters* (1743), p. 160; *Thurloe*, i. 621.
[9] Brit. Mus. Add. MS. 39942, f. 13*v*.: sermon by Feake, 10 July 1653.

gentlemen, Carew and Danvers.[1] But the movement attracted no theologians, although several Doctors of Divinity, such as Goodwin, Owen and Homes, were enthusiastic millenarians. The saints' lack of academic ability is manifest in their pamphlets, and only one, Tillinghast, was able to produce a systematic study of the prophetic texts.[2] Moreover the educated ministers, like the gentry, were not to be found amongst the most radical and violent of the saints.

Amongst artisans, place, property and education were not important influences, but membership of the army was important, and there was a close relationship between military service and sainthood.[3]

Membership of a Fifth Monarchist or any gathered church answered two needs. It provided assurance of salvation, and a small, close-knit society offering company and assistance to its members. The need for certainty of salvation was not new in the period 1640–1660. The break-up of the universal church had raised the problem of which was the true path to salvation, and the doctrine of predestination probably increased anxiety by denying the possibility of earning a place in heaven. Two collections of 'experiences of grace' (spiritual autobiographies given by persons wishing to join a gathered church) were published by John Rogers and by the Independent Henry Walker, with a preface by Vavasor Powell, and show prolonged attempts to obtain certainty. Several people had been seeking assurance for twenty, thirty-four and forty years, and many confessed to lingering doubts even after becoming church-members.[4] Such doubts were self-generating. Ann Megson feared that because she could doubt her election she must be damned, since the true elect were beyond doubt.[5] Another woman was comforted when William Perkins told her that 'a desire to believe was faith it selfe', and so brought salvation. But she soon reflected that a desire to be rich was not the same as wealth itself, and relapsed into her former despair.[6]

---

[1] The ministers are Baylie, Browne, Chamberlen, Cockayne, Feake, Habergham, Helme, Marsden, A. and T. Palmer, Pendarves, Postlethwaite, Powell (?), Rogers, Stoneham, Taylor, Tillinghast, Woodall. Danvers is not certain, but the words 'of Trin. Col. Ox' are on the title page of the copy of his *Mystery of Magistracy* in the Congregationalists' Library, London.

[2] See below, p. 192–3.

[3] See above, p. 80.

[4] H. Walker, *Spirituall Experiences, Of sundry Beleevers* (2nd. edn., 1653), pp. 4, 7, 33, 217, 233, 275, 376, 382; pp. 1–408 contain 61 cases, and J. Rogers, *Ohel* (1653), pp. 393–439 contain a further 38.

[5] Rogers, *Ohel*, p. 416.

[6] Walker, *Spirituall Experiences*, pp. 115–18.

The Distribution and Composition of the Fifth Monarchy Men

What was new in the 1640s and '50s was the degree of religious liberty which enabled people to try various religious movements in their search for assurance. Tabitha Kelsall had been a Baptist and a Ranter before joining Rogers.[1] Even acceptance by a gathered church was not a guarantee of salvation: the only guarantee was a subjective feeling of certainty.[2] Consequently ministers found it hard to create any stability. John Simpson condemned men's frenetic search for new rites 'to get solid comfort to their soules, apprehending that they are undone creatures, and cannot be true Saints, unless they be under the true practise of all Ordinances'.[3] Thomas Mall, Independent minister at Exeter, asked the saints of Devon whether they were 'troubled with a *Vertigo* in your *Heads*, and *giddiness* in your *understandings*? . . . Have not you been *up* and *down*; now of *this* mind, then of *that*, embracing and following those opinions, and ways, which the times have smiled upon?'[4]

The fear of hell and damnation, implanted deliberately by the preachers, increased anxiety over salvation, and was described in vivid terms by many of the saints. Terrified at the age of ten by preachers 'thundring' on the agonies of the damned, John Rogers expected every night to be seized by the devil, brooded on the '*endlesse, easlesse* and *remedilesse* torments' in store, cursed 'that ever I was born', and thought he 'heard the *damned* roaring and *raving*, and saw them . . . *roasting*, and their frisking and frying in everlasting torments'. Before long he lost his reason.[5] Edward Wayman dreamed that he was seized and torn by a great black dog (the devil). One woman was terrified when her dog jumped on her bed one night, thinking the devil had come to take her away.[6] A girl of eleven dreamed of 'fire . . . shreeking' and a 'burning lake', and saw the 'Devill with his chaines' waiting for her.[7] Sarah Barnwell related how a preacher used an outbreak of plague in Dublin to dwell 'on the sad *condition* of some (even *Professors*) that were in *Hell* howling! Oh! this sad doctrine struck deep to the heart.'[8] Nine members of these

---

[1] Rogers, *Ohel*, p. 2 (pagination erratic: p. 412 is followed by pp. 1–12, then 413ff).

[2] Tillinghast, *Mr. Tillinghasts Eight Last Sermons*, p. 155.

[3] J. Simpson, *The Great Joy of Saints* (1654), 2nd pagin., p. 47; cf. J. Pendarves, *The Fear of God: What it is* (1657), pp. 2–3.

[4] T. Mall, *The Axe at the Root* (1668), p. 13.

[5] Rogers, *Ohel*, pp. 419–20, 426, 429–30.

[6] *Ibid.*, p. 409; Walker, *op. cit.*, p. 175.

[7] Walker, *op. cit.*, pp. 362–4.

[8] Rogers, *Ohel*, p. 415.

two churches were tempted or did attempt to commit suicide, to end at least the torments of this life. Rogers tried to kill himself several times. One small girl tried to choke herself by swallowing feathers from her pillow. Powell too had once tried to take his life.[1]

The saints often described the events which started them on their search for God. Bereavement was mentioned by ten of the group. Elizabeth Avery lost three children, and with them all meaning in life. Mary Turrant lost her husband through the plague and her children were murdered by the Irish rebels. Another woman was driven to distraction by the (mistaken) belief that her daughter had committed suicide. One lost her husband and found their business ruined; yet another lost her children by smallpox.[2] The terrors of warfare were also emphasized. Francis Bishop, a conscript, told of his panic under fire, and how he was court-martialled and sentenced to death. Terrified of imminent hell, he experienced a vision in his cell during the night and found faith and hope.[3] Major Andrew Manwaring was reminded of sin and hell when his father was killed by the Irish rebels and he himself was wounded fifteen times on the field at Tredagh.[4] One woman confessed her indifference to religion during the 'fulnesse of outward enjoyments', but sought assurance of salvation after seeing her husband and child killed by the royalists at the siege of Liverpool.[5] A sailor told of his capture by the Turks, French and Dutch, and of his near ship-wreck, which moved him first to a fear of hell and then to a sense of God's grace.[6] Other saints told of illnesses, unhappy marriages and desertion.[7] John Bywater was struck with terror as a small child when he saw a public execution and visualized his own torments in hell.[8]

Sometimes a person sought a new status in a church when economic disaster had undermined his place in society. Such disasters, he reflected, 'did not make us low in the sight of God, though before men' they might.[9] Humphrey Mills was the son of a High Sheriff, but when his father died the family broke up and he

[1] *Ibid.*, pp. 9, 427, 435; Walker, *op. cit.*, pp. 6, 25–6, 230, 235, 273, 354, 358; (E. Bagshaw), *The Life and Death of Mr. Vavasor Powell* (1671), p. 12.
[2] Rogers, *Ohel*, pp. 403–4, 11, 12, 413, 415; Walker, *op. cit.*, pp. 26, 43, 60, 68–9, 164–5.
[3] Rogers, *Ohel*, pp. 398–9. [4] *Ibid.*, pp. 2–3.
[5] Walker, *op. cit.*, pp. 8–13. [6] *Ibid.*, pp. 385–94.
[7] *Ibid.*, pp. 34, 140–3, 168–70; Rogers, *Ohel*, p. 413.
[8] Rogers, *Ohel*, p. 395.
[9] Walker, *op. cit.*, p. 74.

was sent to London as an apprentice, a change which he resented bitterly. He was also a failure at business and told how he had lost £1,400 even since his conversion, but being 'confident in Christ' he could 'over-look the World'. Adrian Strong observed that he had lost his money but found in Christ a better alternative. One saint brushed aside 'all things in the world as vaine, muck, and trifles'. Another said he faced adversity with the same spirit as Job: 'the Lord giveth, and the Lord taketh, blessed be the name of the Lord'.[1] When economic circumstances were mentioned, church membership always appeared not as a justification of profit but as a compensation for loss. But two women testified to the belief that God rewarded the godly with economic success. One admitted that she was often 'pondering how to be rich', but without success. Eventually she began to fear that this failure was a sign of damnation. Seeing her 'neighbours . . . flourish and prosper in the world more then I, I began to doubt that I did but play the hypo-crite, and that perhaps they did pray at home more then I'. Brought thus to a state of despair, she found assurance only after a vision.[2]

These autobiographies show how the saints themselves explained their conversion, but they seem to relate more to the occasion than the cause. Bereavement and personal setbacks were universal, but only a small minority reacted by becoming sectarians. Only a knowledge of the hereditary and environmental background of each individual would provide a partial explanation, and little informa-tion of this kind exists. Professor Walzer has suggested that im-migrants to the large towns, lost and uprooted from the society they knew, were attracted to Puritanism because it offered them a place in a new social group.[3] This theory, though unsupported, seems quite plausible. After returning from New England, Raphael Swinfield asked to join Rogers's church because he was '*walking alone, and very desolate* for want of such a society as this'. But only seven of the sixty-one saints in Walker's book appear to have moved from the provinces to London, and the move does not seem to have influenced their spiritual development.[4]

The family background of the saints seems a more fruitful line of approach. Only a minority mentioned such details, but eight,

[1] Rogers, *Ohel*, pp. 410, 9; Walker, *op. cit.*, pp. 8–18, 58, 246.
[2] Walker, *op. cit.*, pp. 78–84; cf. p. 34.
[3] M. Walzer, 'Puritanism as a Revolutionary Ideology', *History and Theory*, iii (1963–4), p. 78.
[4] Rogers, *Ohel*, p. 398; Walker, *op. cit.*, pp. 8–9, 35, 54, 166, 298, 359, 399.

including Rogers, said they were from Puritan or 'godly' families. Eight more said they had been seeking assurance of salvation since childhood or adolescence which probably means they were from Puritan homes where such a subject would be familiar from an early age. Three more had been in quest of salvation for between twenty and forty years, which probably took them back to their childhood. So nineteen of the group of 99 may well have been influenced by Puritan backgrounds, whilst only one, Col. Hewson, stated that he was from a profane family.[1]

The two congregations were Independent not Fifth Monarchist, but numerous later Fifth Monarchists were mentioned in the autobiographies, and the membership was probably fairly similar. London and East Anglia, traditionally Puritan areas, were Fifth Monarchist and sectarian strongholds. The isolated church at Skegby, Notts., was no doubt planted by the Fifth Monarchist minister Thomas Palmer of Aston, but the fact that the village had a Puritan minister in the 1630s may have prepared the way.[2] It is likely that there was a common (though not total) correlation between sectarianism and second-generation Puritanism.

[1] Rogers, *Ohel*, pp. 393–6, 403, 409–11, 414, 419–26; Walker, *op. cit.*, pp. 5, 33, 77, 88, 140, 161, 217, 357, 376, 382.
[2] R. A. Marchant, *The Puritans and the Church Courts in the Diocese of York, 1560–1642* (1960), p. 316.

CHAPTER FIVE

The Fifth Monarchists in Opposition, 1653–60

✠✦✠

In accepting the resignation of Barebones and establishing the Protectorate, Cromwell removed the fear of an attack on law and property, but exposed himself to the threat of a major breach in the army. Besides many staunchly republican officers, the army contained a number of high-ranking Fifth Monarchists, including Major-Generals Harrison and Overton, and Rich, Courtney and Wigan, with Allen and Vernon on the fringe of the movement.[1] The royalists believed that 'Harrison will have a strong party against the protector, and that we shall suddenly hear of an army on foot against him'.[2] But the expected clash did not materialize. On 21 December Harrison was asked 'if he could own and act under this present power, and declaring, that he could not, had his commission taken from him'.[3] He never showed powers of political leadership, but in any case there was little he could have done. The regiments most likely to give support, his own and those of Rich and Overton, were far distant in Scotland and at Hull. When details of the new regime eventually reached the north, a number of Harrison's troops deserted and returned to England, including the quarter-master and chaplain, and many of the Welsh contingent.[4] Major Wigan of Cromwell's regiment resigned his commission and returned to his former occupation as a minister in Manchester. Cornet Caithness, of Cromwell's Life-Guards, also resigned.[5] Overton came to London and told Cromwell of his discontents, but he promised to continue

---

[1] See Biog. App. for all these.
[2] *Thurloe State Papers*, i. 650.
[3] *Ibid.*, i. 641.
[4] *The Faithfull Scout*, 129 (27 Jan.–3 Feb. 1654), p. 1267; *A Perfect Diurnall*, 215 (30 Jan.–6 Feb.), p. 3098 (misprint for 3312).
[5] Sir C. H. Firth and G. Davies, *The Regimental History of Cromwell's Army* (Oxford, 1940), pp. 484–5; *Thurloe*, ii. 215.

to serve against the common enemy, the royalists in Scotland, and not to act against the government.[1] Col. Rich remained in the army for some time. Perhaps he hoped, like the author of *The Cause of God* (1659), that even after the fall of Barebones, Cromwell was still only deceiving the moderates, and would soon 'throw off this Mantle and come forth in his own true Spirit, . . . to exalt Jesus Christ'.[2] But resentment was certainly strong. Hugh Courtney wrote that the 'people of God are highly dissatisfied', especially as the solemnities with which the regime was inaugurated were 'too much after the old fashion'. Allen wrote from Ireland that ' 'Tis a day of darkness and confusion, very unlike that day of the glorious reign of Christ.'[3] After seeing Cromwell as hero and saint for many years, the millenarian officers found it impossible to recast him abruptly as the agent of Antichrist. Allen admitted, after airing his discontents, 'I love and honour him still', and decided to retain his commission. He remarked that it was for God to establish the millennium 'in his due time, and in the meane time it will concern his poor people not to be dreaming of reigning like kings hear on earth, but rather to prepare for that which was their maisters portion'.[4]

Of the Fifth Monarchist members of Barebones, Arthur Squibb lost or resigned his place on the Committee for Compounding, and disposed of his reversion to a Tellership at the Exchequer.[5] John Browne remained hostile but some of the others, John James, Richard Price and John Williams, even continued for a time to serve on county committees.[6] Early in February 1654 Harrison was ordered to retire to his father's house in Staffordshire, and after some delay he complied, having 'declared to live peaceably'. By May he was thought to be 'already forgotten, and totally layd aside'.[7]

The London preachers reacted far more violently to the fall of

---

[1] *D.N.B.*, Overton; J.R., *The sad Suffering Case of Major General Rob. Overton* (1659), pp. 4–5; *Thurloe*, iii. 67, 110–12.
[2] Anon., *The Cause of God*, p. 22.   [3] *Thurloe*, i. 639–40, ii. 215.
[4] *Thurloe*, ii. 214; Bodl. MS. Rawl. A 13, f. 26: Allen to Hart, 5 April 1654.
[5] Squibb was missing from the list of Commissioners for Compounding on 10 Feb. 1654: C. H. Firth and R. S. Rait, *Acts and Ordinances of the Interregnum, 1642–1660* (1911), ii. 839; *Cal. S.P. Dom., 1654*, p. 272.
[6] MS. Rawl. A 47, f. 30: J. Browne to J. Wright, n.d.; Firth and Rait, *Acts and Ord.*, ii. 971, 976–7, 1070, 1085, 1087.
[7] *Cal. S.P. Dom., 1653–4*, p. 386; *The Moderate Intelligencer*, 168 (8–14 March 1654), p. 1333; Bodl. MS. Clar. 48, f. 57: Hyde to Bellings, 10/20 March 1654; MS. Clar. 48, f. 227: same to same, 19/29 May.

Barebones, and poured out a torrent of invective against the apostate. At Christ Church on 19 December 1653 Feake and Vavasor Powell described him as 'the dissemblingest perjured villaine in the world'. The next day Feake discoursed on the little horn of Dan. vii. 8, and by denying that it was Charles I implied that it was Cromwell. Powell prophesied that the government would soon fall, and demanded 'Lord, wilt Thou have Oliver Cromwell or Jesus Christ to reign over us?' Both preachers were arrested on the following day, and the Blackfriars meetings were banned. Feake and Powell were released after a few days and promptly resumed their attacks. Feake was rearrested, along with John Simpson who had announced a vision that Cromwell would fall within six months, and on 28 January they were ordered to be imprisoned at Windsor. Powell escaped to Wales.[1] Col. Danvers was urging all the churches to join in a general attack on Cromwell, but nothing materialized at this time.[2]

Having silenced the three leading critics, the government and its supporters launched a campaign of counter-propaganda. Cromwell ordered a day of fasting and humiliation for 24 March, suggesting that people should ask forgiveness for seeking more 'for Saints having rule in the world, then over their own hearts'.[3] The General Baptists issued a declaration asserting their faith in the millennium, but arguing that until Christ appeared the saints were rather 'patiently to suffer from the world, as the Scriptures direct them, . . . than any wise to attain the Rule and Government therof'.[4] Early in January, the leading Independent ministers, Owen, Thomas Goodwin, Nye and Sidrach Simpson, composed a circular letter condemning the Fifth Monarchists by whom 'the Gospell hath bin dishonored, the way of Christ evil spoken of, the power of Magistracy weakened, and the Civil peace of the Nation endangered'. This paper was sent to other parts of the country, including East Anglia.[5] Kiffin and other Particular Baptists wrote a similar letter on 20 January, accusing the Fifth Monarchists of

---

[1] *Thurloe*, i. 641; *Cal. S.P. Dom., 1653–4*, pp. 308–9, 449; *Cal. S.P. Venetian, 1653–1654*, p. 169; Hist. MSS. Comm., lv, *Var. Coll. II*, p. 270; Public Record Office, P.R.O. 31/3/92, fos. 107–8: Bordeaux to Servien or Brienne, 19/29 Dec. 1653; *ibid.*, fos. 115, 117–v.: Bordeaux to Mazarin, same to Brienne, both 22 Dec./1 Jan. 1653/4; *Severall Proceedings*, 222 (22–29 Dec.), p. 3512; *Faithfull Scout*, 129 (27 Jan.– 3 Feb. 1654), p. 1269. [2] *Thurloe*, iv. 365.

[3] *Mercurius Politicus*, 197 (16–23 March 1654), pp. 3353–4.

[4] *The Humble Representation* (1654), reprinted in W. T. Whitley, *Minutes of the General Assembly* (1909–10), i. 4.

[5] Bodl. MS. Carte 81, f. 16v.: circular letter, 9 Jan. 1654; *ibid.*, f. 214v.: defence of ?Nye, 1663/4.

bringing 'shame and contempt to the whole nation', and recalling the tyranny of others who had claimed a divine right to rule, such as the late king.[1] The Independent minister, John Goodwin, denied the right of the saints to accelerate God's plans, and reprinted to good effect the *Declaration of divers Elders and Brethren* (1651), in which Feake and Simpson had argued the duty of all Christians to obey even infidel rulers.[2]

The government's most immediate problem was to silence Feake and Simpson, who continued to lead the movement from their prison at Windsor and were confident that God would bring them a speedy release.[3] Feake's congregation published fourteen letters he had sent them, attacking the apostasy of eminent men and urging the faithful to be ready 'to make a standing Army for the King of Saints, in the time appointed of the Father'.[4] Simpson wrote similar letters to his congregation at Allhallows the Great, urging them to 'help Christ to the throne of *England*'.[5]

As part of their propaganda, Simpson and other Fifth Monarchists recounted visions they had had of the imminent destruction of Cromwell.[6] The most celebrated visionary was Anna Trapnel, daughter of a shipwright of Stepney, a member of Simpson's congregation at Allhallows, and subject to visions since 1647.[7] In January 1654 she went to Whitehall to attend the examination of Powell and fell into a trance lasting many days, during which she uttered a torrent of divinely-inspired verse, prophesying that the Lord would 'batter' Cromwell and his friends.[8] Shortly afterwards the Lord directed her to visit Cornwall, which she did after taking leave of Feake and Simpson. She stayed at the house of Capt. Langden, one of the Fifth Monarchist members of Barebones, and met another former member, Major Bawden. The local clergy were openly hostile and soon procured a warrant for her arrest on the grounds that she was a second Holy Maid of Kent, spreading subversion. Langden

---

[1] J. Nickolls, *Original Letters* (1743), p. 160.
[2] J. Goodwin, Συγκρητισμός or *Dis-satisfaction Satisfied* (1654), pp. 10–11; *The Loyal Intelligencer*, 73 (23–30 Jan. 1654), pp. 132–3.
[3] *The Grand Politique Post*, 164 (7–15 Feb. 1654), p. 1304; *Certain Passages*, 8 (3–10 March), p. 62; *ibid.*, 15 (28 April–5 May), p. 123.
[4] C. Feake, *The New Non-conformist* (1654), esp. sig. A3.
[5] Anon., *The Old Leaven Purged out* (1658), 2nd pagin., p. 9.
[6] For Fifth Monarchist attitudes to visions, see below pp. 185–6.
[7] A. Trapnel, *The Cry of a Stone* (1654), pp. 7, 10–11.
[8] *Ibid.*, pp. 19, 61; Trapnel, *Strange and Wonderful Newes* (1654), *passim*; *Severall Proceedings*, 225 (12–19 Jan.), pp. 3562–4; cf. C. Burrage, 'Anna Trapnel's Prophecies', *Eng. Hist. Rev.*, xxvi (1911), pp. 526–35. See Biog. App.

and Bawden stood surety and she was bound over. But the case was attracting considerable notoriety. One Ensign Randall was cashiered for visiting her, and the government was persuaded in April to have her re-arrested and taken to London. She was kept in Bridewell during June and July, receiving many visitors.[1]

On 13 July the government released John Simpson, with orders not to come within ten miles of London. There seemed to be some hope that his views had moderated, and it was reported that he 'prays for the present power'.[2] But this change was of limited value since Simpson proved unable to carry his followers with him. Many condemned his apostasy, and though he broke the order and went to London in December to plead 'his Sameness to what he ever was', his audience decided he was not 'fully enlightened about the Kingdome of Christ'. Even a stormy interview with Cromwell, whom Simpson accused of breaking his word over tithes, committing treason by becoming sole head of state, and persecuting the saints, failed to convince his congregation.[3]

Moreover, Simpson's new and questionable moderation was offset by the growing extremism of John Rogers. Rogers had been a devoted admirer of Cromwell, but in December 1653 he sent a private letter to the Protector, and published an open letter, both calling for action against the '*Antichristian Clergy*' and the '*Heathenish Lawes*', and warning Cromwell that if he rejected God, God would reject him, which would 'make our *souls* mourne'. In the published letter he advised Cromwell to rely on those members who were 'faithful to Christ' in Barebones. 'When the *Wise men* (of the *world*) . . . faile you,' he urged, 'then send for the *Daniels*, . . . to confer with you upon the *Prophecies*.'[4] By January he was criticizing Cromwell as a dissembler, accused him in February of breaking promises, and launched a comprehensive attack in March, lamenting the apostasy of the great.[5] In May he prayed to have 'no lord

[1] *Anna Trapnel's Report and Plea* (1654), pp. 1–10, 13, 19ff; Trapnel, *A Legacy for Saints* (1654), pp. 49ff; *Cal. S.P. Dom., 1654*, pp. 86, 134, 436, 438; *Certain Passages*, 14 (14–21 April), p. 111; *The Weekly Intelligencer*, 328 (18–25 April), pp. 229–30; *Merc. Pol.*, 201 (13–20 March), pp. 3429–30; *A Perfect Account*, 179 (7–14 June), p. 1425.   [2] *Cal. S.P. Dom., 1654*, pp. 253, 256, 438.
[3] *Severall Procs.*, 253 (27 July–3 Aug.), p. 4003; *ibid.*, 255 (10–17 Aug.), p. 4034; *Clarke Papers*, ii. xxxiv–vii, iii. 13–15.
[4] J. Rogers, *To His Highnesse Lord General Cromwel . . . The humble Cautionary Proposals* (1653), brs.; MS. Rawl. A 47, fos. 32–5: Rogers to Cromwell, no date, probably Dec. 1653.
[5] W. Erbery, *An Olive Leaf* (1654), p. 2; *Certain Passages*, 5 (10–17 Feb.), p. 38; *ibid.*, 6, pp. 41–2; *Thurloe*, ii. 196.

protector but our Lord Jesus', and accused the government of having broken all the Ten Commandments. 'O thou black Whitehal! thou black Whitehal!' he exclaimed. 'Fah, fah, it stinks of the brimstone of Sodome, and the smoke of the bottomlesse pit.'[1] His house had already been searched for seditious papers, and he cannot have been surprised when he was arrested, in bed, on 27 July: in fact he said 'he did much desire to have been in prison'. He was lodged in Lambeth Palace and preached daily to a large number of visitors including Simpson.[2] Before his arrest he had taken care to put his views into print, comparing the regime and its probable fate with that of Charles I.[3]

With the leading Fifth Monarchists thus removed, lesser figures carried on the campaign. Among them was Col. Edward Lane, who compared Cromwell to Jehu, and accused him of gilding old idolatry with 'specious pretence'. Rogers added a fiery preface from his cell, declaring that the millennium was dawning, and comparing his lot with that of Christ—'Welcome *Cross*! welcome *Crown*!'[4] Thomas Higgenson argued that God would shortly destroy all rulers. William Aspinwall warned of the 'sad . . . calamities' about to sweep the world.[5] A delegation from Chamberlen's church visited Cromwell in February 1654 to plead for Christ's Kingdom, and to attack the lawyers and the national ministry.[6] John More, a member of the church, published a letter to Cromwell, denouncing him as the little horn (Dan. vii. 8) and the Beast of Revelation.[7] The saints also furthered the cause by pirating old millenarian sermons by Thomas Goodwin, now seen as a great apostate. Additional support for millenarianism, though not for the Fifth Monarchists' political position, was provided by Nathaniel Homes's *Resurrection Revealed*. This large and erudite 'proof' of the coming millennium won Homes the title '*Chiliastorum Achilles*'.[8] Fifth Monarchist zeal was also

---

[1] *Thurloe*, iii. 483–5.
[2] *Cal. S.P. Dom., 1654*, pp. 434, 438; *Mercurius Jocosus*, 4 (28 July–4 Aug.), p. 19; *Severall Proc.*, 253 (27 July–3 Aug.), p. 4003; *ibid.*, 255 (10–17 Aug.), pp. 4033–4; Rogers, *Jegar-Sahadutha* (1657), introd., p. 6.
[3] Rogers, *Mene, Tekel, Perez* (1654), p. 8 and *passim*.
[4] E. Lane, *An Image of our Reforming Times* (1654), sig. A1v–2v., p. 17.
[5] T. Higgenson, *Sighs for Righteousness* (1654), *passim*; W. Aspinwall, *A Premonition of Sundry Sad Calamities* (1654), p. 2 and *passim*. See Biog. App. for Higgenson.
[6] MS. Rawl. D 828, f. 339–v.: Lothbury Church Book, 7 Feb. 1654.
[7] J. More, *A Trumpet sounded* (1654), *passim*. See Biog. App. for More.
[8] T. Goodwin, *A Sermon of the Fifth Monarchy* (1654), and *The World to Come* (1655); Homes, *The Resurrection Revealed* (1654); T. Hall, *Chiliasto-mastix redivivus* (1657), p. 2.

sustained by hopes of great events in 1656. It was calculated that 1656 years passed from the Creation to the Great Flood, and since a similar length of time had passed since the birth of Christ, comparable wonders were anticipated. Morgan Llwyd held this view, as did John Tillinghast, who expected the fulfilment of the prophecies and the beginning of the millennium in 1656.[1]

Attacks on the regime in sermons and pamphlets brought notoriety to the saints, but were unlikely to shake the government. The Fifth Monarchists saw an opportunity for more effective opposition when a Parliament was summoned for 3 September 1654. Spittlehouse published a tract on 1 September, setting out the benefits of the Fifth Monarchy and accusing Cromwell of high treason for breaking the act of 1649 against government by a single person.[2] The London Fifth Monarchists produced a joint manifesto to coincide with the meeting of the new Parliament. They recalled the army declarations of St. Albans and Musselburgh and lamented that the government was 'so fully gorged with the flesh of Kings, Captains, and Nobles, &c. (i.e. with their Lands, Mannors, Estates, Parks, and Palaces) so as to sit at ease, and comply with Antichrist'. Regular meetings were established to settle the details of the Fifth Monarchy. The manifesto was signed by 150 people from ten congregations, representing the whole churches of Rogers and Chamberlen, and part of those of Feake, Raworth, Knollys, Simpson, Jessey, Barbon, Fenton and Highland. Signatures from other churches were omitted, as were those from outside London, including 'hundreds out of Kent', since it was hoped that these saints would draw up separate representations.[3]

The main Fifth Monarchist plan was for a petition to be circulated in the army and then presented to Parliament by Harrison (who was said to have been elected in eight different constituencies). The petition stated that the regime was worse than that of Charles I, and urged Parliament to extirpate this new tyranny and restore a 'state of perfect liberty'.[4] Cromwell countered this challenge

[1] M. Llwyd, *Gweithiau*, ed. T. E. Ellis and J. H. Davies (Bangor and London, 1899, 1908), i. 79–80; J. Tillinghast, *Generation Worke*, 3rd part (1654), pp. 171ff. For Fifth Monarchist beliefs relating to Biblical prophecies, see below, pp. 191–4.

[2] Spittlehouse, *Certaine Queries* (1654), *passim*.

[3] Anon., *A Declaration of Several of the Churches of Christ* (1654), *passim*, reprinted in *Trans. Baptist Hist. Soc.*, iii (1911–12), pp. 129–53; MS. Clar. 49, f. 58v.: G. Greene to . . ., 23 Sept. 1654.

[4] MS. Clar. 49, fos. 58v., 59: G. Greene to . . ., 23 Sept., 25 Sept.; Hist. MSS. Comm., lxiii, *Egmont MSS.*, i, p. 546.

firstly by attacking the 'mistaken notion' of Fifth Monarchism in his opening speech, claiming it threatened law, liberty and property.[1] Spittlehouse published a prompt vindication, for which he and his publisher, Livewell Chapman, were sent to join Rogers in prison at Lambeth.[2] Cromwell had Harrison arrested on 9 September, to be released a few days later after a friendly warning. The more dangerous members of Parliament were excluded by the imposition of the Recognition on 12 September, by which only those who swore to be loyal to the regime were allowed to enter the House.[3]

By the end of the year the cause had suffered further setbacks. Col. Rich had been removed from the army, possibly in connection with the petition which three colonels, Okey, Saunders and Alured, had drawn up against the Protector and circulated in the army.[4] Overton was also removed. He was accused of being privy to a plot by his subordinates to seize Monk and put himself at the head of a bid to destroy the government. Overton denied the charge, but captured papers showed the strength of his disaffection, and the government took the opportunity to silence a dangerous critic. He was brought to London in January 1655 and gaoled first in the Tower and then in Jersey. His regiment was purged.[5]

The government was naturally alarmed at the possibility of an alliance between the various disaffected groups and critics within the army. In the spring of 1654 one of Chamberlen's congregation, a French physician named Naudin, was arrested for plotting with M. de Baas of the French embassy to turn the army against Cromwell and to persuade Harrison to lead an Anabaptist rising. The affair caused a crisis in Anglo-French relations.[6] In the latter half of the year there were constant rumours of a massive conspiracy of the Levellers, Commonwealthsmen, Royalists and Fifth Monarchists. Overton was to hand over Hull to the king. Harrison and Rich were to lead a Fifth Monarchist rising. William Allen and Hugh Courtney were said to be stirring up sedition already in the west. The govern-

---

[1] Abbott, *Writings and Speeches*, iii. 437.

[2] J. Spittlehouse, *An Answer to one part of The Lord Protector's Speech* (1654); *Cal. S.P. Dom., 1654*, pp. 378, 389; J. Rogers, *Jegar-Sahadutha* (1657), introd., p. 15. For Chapman, see Biog. App.

[3] Gardiner, *Comm. and Protect.*, iii. 187 and note.

[4] *Thurloe*, iii. 55; Gardiner, *Comm. and Protect.*, iii. 211, 217.

[5] Gardiner, *Comm. and Protect.*, iii. 228–32.

[6] *Ibid.*, iii. 125–6, 136; *Cal. S.P. Dom., 1654*, pp. 289, 372; *Severall Proceedings*, 243 (18–25 May 1654), p. 3866; P.R.O. 31/3/95, f. 100: de Baas to Mazarin, 25 June; *ibid.*, fos. 105v.–6, 166v.: Bordeaux to Brienne, 28 and 30 June.

ment responded by arresting Wildman, the Leveller, in February 1655 and placing Allen under arrest at the same time.[1] A chance to dispose of the leading Fifth Monarchists was soon presented through Feake and Rogers.

Feake and ten of his followers were summoned before the Protector after the publication in December 1654 of his *Oppressed Close Prisoner*, accepting Cromwell as the *de facto* but not the *de iure* ruler, but Feake was not released.[2] Requests for the release of Rogers in January 1655 were turned down with the comment that 'if hee was at liberty, he would offend so high' that none could save him.[3] However Cromwell did grant him an interview on 6 February in the presence of twelve followers. A crowd of 250 which tried to follow was turned back. Rogers accused the Protector of being an apostate and persecutor, and was accused in turn of seeking confusion and bloodshed: 'you long to be at it; you want but an opportunity.' Cromwell argued, somewhat facetiously, that 'A Prisoner is a free man, as Christ hath made you free, and so you are a Free man', and when Rogers began to discourse of the reign of the Beast, he cut him short, remarking 'they are things I understand not.'[4] As Rogers was led away, another deputation arrived to demand the release of the prisoners. It consisted of Harrison, Rich, Carew, Courtney, Clement Ireton (brother of the late general) and Arthur Squibb. Cromwell told them that Feake and Rogers were gaoled for sedition, not religion, and dismissed them.[5] But on 13 February an informer told the government that Harrison, Feake and Rogers were involved in a plot, and that one plotter had said of Cromwell, 'would I had his flesh between my teeth'.[6] Next day Cromwell summoned the Fifth Monarchist deputation to answer for 'divers Printed treasonous Papers . . . to promote designs of Insurrection'. The saints ignored this summons since an illegal government had no authority to issue orders, but they were fetched next day and examined by Cromwell, with the Fifth Monarchist preachers Simpson, John Pendarves of Abingdon and one Bankes also present. Carew attacked Cromwell because he 'took the Crown from the

---

[1] Gardiner, *op. cit.*, iii. 228–32, 269–70; *Thurloe*, iii. 140, 147–8, 194; Ralph Josselin, *Diary, 1616–1683*, ed. E. Hockliffe (Camden Soc., 3rd ser., xv, 1908), p. 109; R. Vaughan, *The Protectorate of Oliver Cromwell* (1839), i. 136, 155.
[2] *Oppressed Close Prisoner*, p. 60; *Clarke Papers*, iii. 15.
[3] *Severall Proceedings*, 279 (25 Jan.–1 Feb. 1655), p. 4426; anon., *The Faithful Narrative of the late Testimony* (1655), pp. 2–3.
[4] *Faithful Narrative*, pp. 4–9, 12, 35.
[5] *Ibid.*, p. 41.   [6] *Thurloe*, iii. 160.

head of Christ, and put it on his own'. They all criticized the Parliament, 'whereby power is derived from the people, whereas all power belongs to Christ'. Far from pledging not to attack the government, they asserted that 'arms may be taken up against it'. In reply, Cromwell accused Harrison of preaching sedition, Carew of trying to subvert army officers, Rich of hindering tax collection, and Courtney of inciting men to arms in London, Norfolk and the west. The four saints were placed under house arrest for a few days, and ultimately Harrison and Courtney were lodged in Carisbrook Castle, Carew in Pendennis Castle in Cornwall and Rich at Windsor.[1]

Feake and Rogers remained in prison, but their spirit was far from broken. Rogers complained of his treatment and of the high prison fees at Lambeth. His gaoler replied that he had tried to stir up trouble, and that by arguing over the amount of fees he had contrived to pay nothing. Rogers preached through the prison windows every Sunday to a 'great concourse of People', and at the end of March he was moved to join Feake at Windsor.[2] Feake managed one day to seize the chapel pulpit, and railed against the government until he was pulled down. He abused the Protector as an 'Apostate, Covenant breaker, Jugler, Usurper, Tyrant, and Persecutor'. He taught his small son to run round singing 'The Protector is a foole', and Rogers taught his maid to rail. When locked in his cell, Feake preached all day through the windows until 'he could scarce speake for hoarsenesse', and the governor ordered his troops to beat on their drums for hours to drown the preacher. But Feake managed to subvert discipline, and one serjeant said he would 'suffer his head to be cut off' before he would touch the prisoners.[3] The prisoners sent letters to their congregations which were read out at Allhallows.[4] Rogers also tried to 'convert' ministers who supported the Protectorate. 'It is good for us to bee poore,' he wrote to Thomas Brookes, 'who must possesse all things.'[5]

[1] *Clarke Papers*, ii. 242–6, iii. 23–4; *Merc. Pol.*, 245 (15–22 Feb. 1655), p. 5147, *ibid.*, 246 (22 Feb.–1 March), p. 5163; Gardiner, *Comm. and Protect.*, iii. 266–8. For Pendarves see Biog. App.

[2] *Thurloe*, iii. 136, 485–6; Rogers, *Jegar*, introd., pp. 9–14; *Mercurius Fumigosus*, 43 (21–28 March), p. 338; *Perfect Proceedings*, 288 (29 March–5 April), p. 4565; *Cal. S.P. Dom., 1655*, p. 579; *Clarke Papers*, iii. 32.

[3] MS. Rawl. A 26, fos. 239–51: account by Col. Whichcote, 18 May 1655; *ibid.* fos. 252–4: 'A true relation of the . . . dealings exersised by ye Governor of Windsor Castelle . . . towards . . . ffeacke & John Rogers'; Rogers, *Jegar*, pp. 5–9; *Perfect Account*, 226 (2–9 May), p. 1808.

[4] *Perfect Account*, 217 (28 Feb.–7 March), p. 1736; *Weekly Post*, 124 (24 April–1 May), p. 1792.

[5] MS. Rawl. A 29, f. 629: Rogers to Brookes, 29 Aug. 1655.

Late in September the government moved the prisoners to the Isle of Wight, where at Carisbrook they joined Harrison and Court-ney.[1] Feake soon secured a removal to the mainland, whereupon he broke an order and went to London where he was placed under armed guard again.[2] Carew and Courtney were freed finally in October 1656, Rogers and Feake in December. Harrison was re-leased but restricted to his house at Highgate in March 1656, and Rich was freed probably about the same time.[3]

The government had removed the leading saints for a consider-able period, but this failed to remove all the danger. In 1655 the Fifth Monarchists adopted the policy which the government feared—of seeking alliances with other disaffected groups, and trying to subvert the army.

Vavasor Powell had been spreading disaffection in Wales since the beginning of the Protectorate. Morgan Llwyd was said to have preached that God had chosen Harrison, not Cromwell, as His lieutenant on earth. John Williams, a former member of Barebones, called Cromwell a king in all but name, and 'as great a tirant as the former'. The Welsh saints were rumoured to be repairing pistols, listing troops and riding round in armed parties; Powell was not above threatening to send a party of soldiers against a tenant who fell behind with the rent. Powell and others were indicted, but no trial followed, and all the sheriffs and justices were said to be his friends, appointed through Harrison during the Propagation period, and they listened to his seditious sermons with approval.[4]

By February 1654 Powell was said to be drawing up a remon-strance against the government, but nothing further was heard of this for some time. This was partly because Powell's militancy provoked opposition among the 'richer sort' of his followers, who threatened to arrest him to avert trouble.[5] One of John Williams's harangues was interrupted by the crowd demanding the return of the king.[6] One of Powell's enemies published a violently abusive pamphlet, alleging that he had misappropriated public money, and that his followers, such as Williams, claimed to have seen Christ on earth, and compared Him to '*old* Rice Williams *of* Newport' with

---

[1] *Cal. S. P. Dom., 1655*, pp. 374, 598; *Clarke Papers*, iii. 53; Rogers, *Jegar*, pp. 18 (misprint for 22)–33.
[2] *Clarke Papers*, iii. 61; *Thurloe*, v. 755–9; anon., *The Prophets Malachy and Isaiah* (1656) preface by Feake, p. 17; *Publick Intelligencer*, 6 (5–12 Nov. 1655), p. 94.
[3] *Cal. S.P. Dom., 1656–7*, pp. 130, 194; Rogers, *Jegar*, p. 113.
[4] *Thurloe*, ii. 93, 114 (misprint for 120), 124, 128–9, 174, 226.
[5] *Ibid.*, ii. 116, 124.   [6] *Ibid.*, ii. 46.

'a large grey beard'.[1] The elders of Powell's church published a vindication of their pastor, but instead of defending his millenarian ideas, they tried to minimize them, claiming that he 'doth very seldom, and then sparingly touch upon' them.[2] Powell's rumoured 20,000 supporters, 'ready to hazard their blood in defence of their cause', did not materialize.[3] It was in fact against the royalist rising of March 1655 that Powell did take up arms. He raised a force from the church and 'charging himself in the Van' was wounded in a successful engagement. Llwyd too supplied the government with information of royalist plans.[4]

But trouble recommenced when the royalist scare had been replaced by the hated rule of the Major-Generals. Major-General Berry met Powell who assured him that he was only drawing up a private petition.[5] But when in December 1655 the petition appeared, entitled *A Word for God*, with 322 signatures, it appeared far from innocuous. Seeking to attract all discontented forces, it accused the government of betraying the 'Good Old Cause' (defined as both the 'Advancement of Christ's Kingdom' and 'the Privileges of Parliament'), and attacked tithes and the heavy rate of taxation. A copy was handed to Cromwell by Richard Price, the former member of Barebones.[6] The *Word for God* was proof of the danger of a union of the Fifth Monarchists with other malcontents. At a mass meeting of five hundred at Allhallows on 3 December it was read out by Cornet Day (of Harrison's former regiment) and John Simpson. Day and Livewell Chapman, thought to be Powell's publisher, were arrested and Powell himself went into hiding, though he did later express some repentance to Berry over the petition.[7]

The paper had spread far outside London, and the government was alarmed at the likely consequences. It retaliated by distributing loyal replies to Powell, such as Richardson's *Plain Dealing*, the *Animadversions upon a letter and Paper*, and a profession of loyalty by about nine hundred saints in South Wales.[8] But discontents were

[1] A. Griffith, *Strena Vavasoriensis* (1654), esp. p. 6.
[2] Anon., *Vavasoris Examen, & Purgamen* (1654), p. 19 and *passim*.
[3] *Thurloe*, iii. 136, 291.
[4] *Ibid.*, iii. 207, 252; *Weekly Post*, 218 (13–20 March), p. 1746; *Faithful Scout*, 219 (16–23 March), p. 1744.
[5] *Thurloe*, iv. 228; *Merc. Pol.*, 285 (22–29 Nov. 1655), p. 5788.
[6] *Thurloe*, iv. 380–4; A. H. Dodd, 'A Remonstrance from Wales, 1655', *Bull. Board Celtic Studies*, xvii (1956–8), pp. 279–92; anon., *A True Catalogue* (1659), p. 10.
[7] *Clarke Papers*, iii. 62; *Thurloe*, iv. 321, 343, 359, 379, 394; *Cal. S.P. Dom., 1655–6*, pp. 109, 576; *Pub. Intelligencer*, 12 (17–24 Dec.), p. 192. For Day see Biog. App.
[8] S. Richardson, *Plain Dealing* (1656); anon., *Animadversions* (1656); anon., *The*

reported all round the country. Anna Trapnel had returned to Cornwall to visit Carew, and though her success was limited, there were ominous rumours of joint assemblies of Fifth Monarchists and Quakers. When questioned by a party of soldiers, Trapnel declared 'thou art of the Army of the Beast'.[1] At Lewes in Sussex there was trouble involving Walter Postlethwaite, a Fifth Monarchist minister who feared that God would abandon this apostate nation and go to America and thence to the East Indies to 'set up the Government of Jesus Christ amongst the Barbarous Places'. In the autumn of 1655 many of the sectaries in Lewes prepared a petition to Cromwell calling for the release of Feake and other saints, the abolition of Chancery and tithes, and the disbanding of the army. But the Fifth Monarchist group refused to participate on the grounds that a petition implied recognition of the government.[2]

Rather more serious was the trouble in East Anglia. The establishment of the Protectorate made little initial impact, apart from an attack by Tillinghast and by Richard Breviter's church at North Walsham.[3] In October 1654 about fifteen churches met to discuss the duty of the saints, perhaps through the influence of Courtney and of Tillinghast, whose preaching tours covered East Anglia and reached to London and Lewes.[4] But the arrest of Harrison and Rich destroyed any lingering hopes of the Protector, and discontent spread rapidly round Norwich and North Walsham.[5] The government warned the militia to be vigilant and distributed a letter from Cromwell against the Fifth Monarchists thoughout the eastern part of the country.[6] New attempts to stir up agitation after the *Word for God* met with some success. On 12 March 1656 messengers from twelve churches in Norfolk and Suffolk met at Norwich to debate the coming millennium and the duty of the saints towards the present government. The majority felt that though the millennium was at hand, they should accept the present powers, and they

Humble Representation . . . of several Churches . . . in South Wales (1656); *Thurloe*, iv. 445, 531.

[1] *Merc. Pol.*, 312 (29 May–5 June 1656), pp. 6997–8; *Pub. Intelligencer*, 13 (24–31 Dec. 1655), pp. 193–4.

[2] W. Postlethwaite, *A Voice from Heaven* (1655), sig. A6v.–7; *Thurloe*, iv. 151, 161. For Postlethwaite see Biog. App.

[3] J. Tillinghast, *Generation Worke*, 3rd part (1654), epistle from Breviter's church, and *passim*.

[4] *Clarke Papers*, ii. xxxiii–iv; J. Manning's epistle in Tillinghast, *Elijah's Mantle* (1658), sig. A2; Feake's preface in *Mr. Tillinghasts Eight Last Sermons* (1655), sig. A7v.

[5] *Thurloe*, iii. 328, iv. 472–3; Josselin, *Diary*, p. 115.   [6] *Thurloe*, iii. 311, iv. 170.

would regard trouble-makers with 'great sorrow and grief of heart'. But the dissatisfied minority held a rally in April, led by Stoneham of Ipswich, Habergham of Syleham, Woodhall of Woodbridge and Taylor of Bury St. Edmunds, when they planned a petition based on Powell's, calling on Cromwell to resign. They claimed, however, to be 'free from designe or intendment of trouble', although a few saints around North Walsham were 'tending to blood', led by Pooley, a shop-keeper named Rudduck and Buttevant of the Lifeguard. Major-General Haynes kept a close watch and assured them they would find no friends in the army if they attempted a rising.[1]

Opposition to the government diminished in Wales after the *Word for God*. A number of the signatories apostatized and accepted livings in the national ministry they had condemned.[2] Moreover, Morgan Llwyd was moving away from Powell's position. Long influenced by the mystic ideas of Jacob Boehme and William Erbery, and disappointed by the failings of the saints, he began to turn towards a kingdom within.[3] He seemed to sympathize with Cromwell's policy towards men such as Feake, remarking that 'if a good man be in a wild fit . . . it's kindness to him . . . to keep him alone a while.' Llwyd soon developed doubts after signing the *Word for God*, and wrote to Powell, 'Is this the Doore out of Babilon? or do ye Knocke at a wrong gate? . . . Lett us . . . without private mutterings tend our own work and waite within ourselves on God.'[4] He accepted a government salary in October 1656, became estranged from Powell, and began to consider non-Calvinist ideas on salvation. The Welsh movement was deprived of one of its two pillars.[5] Henceforth there were only occasional reminders of Welsh militancy. Powell was said to have presided over a suspicious meeting of four hundred people from seven or eight counties in June 1656.[6] He was

[1] *Thurloe*, iv. 329–30, 472–3, 581, 687, 698, v. 166–7, 187, 219, 220; *Merc. Pol.*, 301 (13–20 March 1656), pp. 6029–30; T. Carte, *A Collection of Original Letters* (1739), ii. 104.
[2] R. T. Jones, 'The Life, Work, and Thought of Vavasor Powell (1617–1670), (Oxford D. Phil. thesis, 1947), p. 158; T. Richards, *Religious Developments* (1923), pp. 224–5.
[3] E. Lewis Evans, 'Morgan Llwyd and Jacob Boehme', *Jacob Boehme Soc. Quart.*, I. iv (1953), pp. 11–16; W. Erbery, *A Call to the Churches* (1653), p. 22; Llwyd, *Gweithiau*, i. 89–90. For Fifth Monarchist attitudes to mystic ideas, see below, pp. 185–6.
[4] Llwyd, *Gweithiau*, ii. 222–3; Jones, 'Vavasor Powell', pp. 146–7.
[5] *Cal. S.P. Dom., 1656–7*, pp. 132, 167; Nat. Lib. Wales MS. 11, 439 D: Powell to Llwyd, 23 April 1657, transcribed in Jones, *op. cit.*, pp. 391–2.
[6] *Thurloe*, v. 112.

on a list of Fifth Monarchist agents found in April 1657, but denied any connection with Venner's rising.[1] In March 1658 John Williams was predicting that blood would be spilled that summer, but nothing materialized.[2]

Llwyd was not alone in changing course. The removal of the ablest leaders and the failure of the saints' expectations sapped enthusiasm. Thurloe claimed that 'their own party desert them every day'. As early as 1654 Tillinghast reflected how 'godly Ministers and people not many years past, did provoke one another from *Christs second coming*, and harp upon it, as neer; and how at present few speak of that'. The Quaker, George Whitehead, toured East Anglia in February 1657 and found the cause even at North Walsham 'of late somewhat shattered'.[3] John Simpson began to preach against the Fifth Monarchists, condemning plots, and advocating passive obedience to the government. This provoked a breach between militant and moderate elements at Allhallows, and the former eventually seceded under John Portman.[4] Simpson also launched another internal controversy over the seventh-day Sabbath against Spittlehouse and other Fifth Monarchists who had adopted it.[5] William Aspinwall put forward a very moderate new proposal, that the Fifth Monarchists, 'the best and truest friends unto Government', might even hold office under the Fourth Monarchy, if they discharged it in a godly manner.[6]

But there was no universal movement towards moderation. Indeed, from 1655 there were deliberate attempts by the Fifth Monarchists to subvert the army. A paper circulated in August 1655, entitled *A Short Discovery of his Highness's Intentions concerning Anabaptists in the Army*, accused Cromwell of planning a purge of Baptist officers, argued that Barebones had represented the spirit of the 'Good Old Cause', and urged the army to fight for their 'liberties and civil properties'. At least a thousand copies were printed, and many sent to Wales. It was found to have originated in the circle of Spittlehouse, and the authorship was traced to John

---

[1] *Thurloe*, vi. 187; Jones, *op. cit.*, pp. 391–2.
[2] MS. Rawl. A 61, f. 29: information, no date (? March 1658).
[3] Carte, *Orig. Letters*, ii. 104; *Thurloe*, iv. 698; Tillinghast, *Generation-Work*, 2nd part (1654), p. 161; G. Nuttall, *Early Quaker Letters* (typescript 1952), p. 221.
[4] *Thurloe*, iv. 545; anon., *The Old Leaven Purged out* (1658), *passim*. See Appendix III.
[5] J. Spittlehouse, *A Manifestation of sundry gross absurdities*, and *A Return to some Expressions* (both 1656). On the seventh-day Sabbath see below, pp. 175, 224.
[6] W. Aspinwall, *The Legislative Power* (1656), pp. 36–7.

Sturgeon, one of Cromwell's Lifeguard and a Baptist pastor, with both Leveller and royalist links. He was arrested late in August. Two similar tracts appeared in the next two months, reproaching Baptists who remained passively in the army with 'retaining the mark of the Beast'.[1] A paper in November 1655 launched a more comprehensive attack on the government for high taxes, failures in foreign and commercial policy, and for gaoling the saints, (a category widened to include Ludlow and Okey). It ended with a vision of Feake and Rogers judging the world.[2]

The campaign continued in 1656. In September a tract addressed to the soldiers of Hull, following Canne's expulsion, claimed that God was punishing the apostate army, citing its defeat in the West Indies by 'fifty Cow-killers'. The garrison should return to God's duty and disobey the officers. Otherwise they would be 'the most monstruous wretches that ever trampled on the ground throughout the Globe of all the Earth'.[3] *A Looking-Glasse* in October reprinted speeches and army declarations of the period 1647–53 to demonstrate the apostasy of the age. More important was *England's Remembrancers,* a tract distributed during the Parliamentary elections of 1656 urging voters to choose godly men to revive the 'Good Old Cause' and establish Christ's kingdom. It was spread round the north, in London, round Norfolk and Suffolk by Buttevant, and at the Fifth Monarchist meetings of Thomas Venner in Swan Alley, Coleman Street.[4] Despite the pressure of the Major-Generals, both Harrison and Rich were apparently elected to Parliament.[5]

This vigorous propaganda campaign failed to shake the government's control over the army. Rather more successful, at least at first, were the Fifth Monarchists' negotiations during the winter of 1655–6 with the Commonwealthsmen, led by Vice-Admiral Lawson, Capt. Lyons and Col. Okey. The Fifth Monarchists were represented by Portman, Squibb, Clement Ireton and Thomas Venner, a cooper who had returned from New England, and had been

---

[1] *A Short Discovery* is reprinted in *Thurloe*, iii. 150–1; *Clarke Papers*, iii. 51; *Thurloe*, iii. 149, 738–9; anon., *The Protector (So called) In Part Unvailed, passim*; anon., *A Ground Voice*, p. 5 and *passim*. For Sturgeon see Biog. App.

[2] Ro. Bl., *A Letter from a Christian Friend* (1655), pp. 2, 5, 6, 8. The author may have been Robert Blackborne, a naval official and friend of Portman, or Cornet Blackwell, a friend of Allen.

[3] Anon., *To the Honest Souldiers of the Garrison of Hull* (1656), brs. On the West Indian incident see Gardiner, *Comm. and Protect.*, iv. 139–40.

[4] Reprinted in *Thurloe*, v. 268–71; *Thurloe*, v. 272–3, 297, 342.

[5] P.R.O. 31/3/100, f. 20: Bordeaux to Brienne, 23 Aug./2 Sept. 1656; *Cal. S.P. Dom., 1656–7*, p. 67.

removed from his post at the Tower on a charge of plotting to blow it up.[1] A list of Fifth Monarchist contacts, found in 1657 but probably dating from the time of the negotiations, listed agents throughout the country, including the well-known names of Vavasor Powell, Stoneham and Taylor, Wigan and Capt. Langden.[2] The basis of the alliance was to be the *Healing Question* of Sir Henry Vane, which had called for a new government on a mixed republican and theocratic basis. Harrison and Rich had refused to take part in these talks, and the meetings broke down altogether when the Fifth Monarchists refused to agree to any form of government in advance, and certainly not to the suggested government of forty ex-Rumpers. Thurloe was fully aware of the proceedings, and in the summer of 1656 arrested Lawson, Lyons, Okey, Rich, Venner and Portman, as well as Ludlow and Bradshaw. Portman lost his naval post, Rich was detained in Windsor Castle and Harrison, whose house at Highgate was a Fifth Monarchist rendezvous, was sent to Pendennis.[3] Wentworth Day, released in July, was rearrested in September for spreading seditious papers and, as has been mentioned, John Canne was banished from Hull where Fifth Monarchist ideas were infecting the fleet and garrison.[4] Rich and probably Harrison were freed in October along with Carew and Courtney, when the elections were safely over.[5]

Not all the Fifth Monarchists were cowed by the government's intervention. Nathaniel Bunch, a cobbler's apprentice who attended Venner's meetings, claimed there were six thousand armed men ready to destroy the regime and determined 'to have the protector suffer at Whitehall gate as the late king did'. John Jones preached to the congregation in March 1656 that it was not murder 'to destroy such as are enemies against Michael your prince'.[6] Thurloe was convinced that their 'intention is to trye for it with the sword, if they can get any convenient number together'. Several Baptist assemblies had been held in March, and Danvers, who 'would faine

---

[1] *Thurloe*, v. 197, vi. 185; on Venner see *ibid.*, iii. 520 and Biog. App.
[2] *Thurloe*, vi. 187.
[3] *Thurloe*, iv. 698, v. 197, 248, 407, vi. 185–6; Gardiner, *Comm. and Protect.*, iv. 259–61, 264–6; Vane, *A Healing Question* (1656), reprinted in *Somers Tracts*, vi. 304–15; Carte, *Orig. Letters*, ii. 104, 111–12; *Clarke Papers*, iii. 68–9; *Cal. S.P. Dom.*, *1656–7*, pp. 71, 112, 581; E. Ludlow, *Memoirs*, ed. C. H. Firth (Oxford, 1894), ii. 10.
[4] *Cal. S.P. Dom.*, *1656–7*, pp. 41, 52, 116, 431.
[5] *Ibid.*, p. 130; *Merc. Pol.*, 331 (9–16 Oct. 1656), pp. 7333–4.
[6] *Thurloe*, iv. 621, 650. For Jones, see Biog. App.

be in armes' and Buttevant had tried to stir them to a rebellion, though in vain.[1] At Swan Alley, John Gardiner and others were preaching on such texts as Deut. xxxii. 42, 'I will make mine arrowes drunk with blood . . .' The congregation 'wept, that the tears ran down their faces, sighed, and groaned' during the service.[2]

When John Pendarves died in September 1656 of 'plague in ye gutts', his funeral at Abingdon provided an opportunity for a massive Fifth Monarchist rally.[3] Representatives came from all over the country, Buttevant, Portman and John Jones from London, Rudduck and others from East Anglia, Langden from Cornwall and one 'Thom. Cann' (probably a mistake for John) from Hull. Joining with the Abingdon Fifth Monarchists, the saints debated their duty for two days. The question was put, '*whether Gods people must be a bloody people* (in an active sense)', and was carried with enthusiasm. On the third day a party of fifty soldiers dispersed the saints by force, the saints crying 'Lord appeare, now or never for confounding of these, thine and our Enemies', whilst the women shouted 'Hold on, ye Sons of Syon'. Five saints, including Rudduck, were arrested and sent to Windsor Castle, and John Canne claimed 'the Souldiers were more *wilde* and *savage*, then the Beasts they rid upon'. Thurloe claimed that but for this action there would have been a rising at Abingdon, but the Fifth Monarchists were probably correct in denying this.[4]

A few days before the funeral, the militant resolutions were published of a series of Fifth Monarchist meetings, probably in London. Praising the work of John of Leyden as a worthy precedent, the saints condemned Cromwell as the little horn, and decided that their duty was a 'smiting work', to 'visibly appeare in a millitary posture for Christ' and throw down 'Nations, Provinces, Universities, Corporations, Cities, Towns, Kings, Rulers, Chief Captains', and so on.[5] Other saints gave proof of their resolution. In Ireland, Allen, Vernon and other Baptist officers resigned in November 1656 rather than appear any longer to accept the regime.[6] Feake

[1] *Thurloe*, iv. 191, 629, 698.
[2] *Thurloe*, v. 60–1.
[3] MS. Rawl. D 859, f. 162: note on death of Pendarves.
[4] Anon., *The Complaining Testimony of . . . Sions Children* (1656), sig. A2–v; W. Ley, 'Ὑπεραδπιδτὴς, or, A Buckler for the Church of England* (Oxford, 1656), p. 15; W. Hughes, *Munster and Abingdon* (Oxford, 1657), pp. 88–9, 92–4; anon., *True Catalogue*, pp. 12–13; J. Canne, *The Time of the End* (1657), p. 80; *Thurloe*, vi. 185; anon., *A Witness to the Saints* (1657), pp. 5–6.
[5] Anon., *The Banner of Truth Displayed* (1656), pp. 26, 28, 48–9, 71.
[6] *Thurloe*, v. 670.

had announced in July 1656, whilst still under armed guard, that Cromwell's *'Counsells* are *evill,* that his *government is evill* . . . that his *workes* are *evill'.* As soon as he was released in December, he went to the Allhallows meeting, declaring that the 'government is as Babylonish as ever', and that 'the churches are gathering corruption', and called for a purge: 'I am for rending and dividing yet more.' Simpson, Jessey and Kiffin, who were present and urged moderation, were taunted by the crowd with cries of 'courtier' and 'apostate'.[1]

By the beginning of 1657 the militant saints of Venner's congregation were planning a rising. They had created a secret organization in London, with five groups of twenty-five members, only one member in each cell knowing details of the others. They obtained maps and telescopes, and studied the disposition of the government's troops. Attempts to win over other Fifth Monarchist groups, however, met with little success. Feake and Chapman were excluded for some unknown reason. Harrison and Carew refused to join them, Carew saying they 'were not of a Gospell spiritt'. John Rogers had been warned against them by the Abingdon and Ipswich churches and declared 'he would be hanged before he would goe out with this spiritt'.[2] Most Fifth Monarchists refused to take up arms unless God had given a clear signal. Otherwise they would be 'more capable of being cut down with the grass, then of cutting down the grass'.[3] The conspirators had no such sign, and were themselves divided over timing. Feuds with other groups forced them to break off contacts to avoid betrayal, and there was friction even with Portman's militant saints. A manifesto was printed, declaring that the kingdom was Christ's, that it would be ruled by a sanhedrin chosen by the saints, that laws would be derived from the Bible, and that there would be a reform of all land tenures. It was planned to attack a troop of horse, and then proceed through Epping Forest towards East Anglia, where they hoped to gain most recruits. Spoil was to be held in common, and it was resolved that for the time being the army was to be the chief enemy, rather than the priests and lawyers. About eighty saints were to assemble at Mile End Green in Shoreditch on the evening of 9 April 1657. But the rebellion was

---

[1] Anon., *Prophets Malachy and Isaiah,* epistle by Feake, p. 14; *Thurloe,* v. 755; *Publick Intelligencer,* 64 (29 Dec. 1656–5 Jan. 1657), p. 1099.
[2] *Thurloe,* vi. 185; C. Burrage, 'The Fifth Monarchy Insurrections', *Eng. Hist. Rev.,* xxv (1910), pp. 726, 729, 731–3.
[3] J. Canne, *The Time of the End* (1657), epistle by J. Rogers, sig. A7v. For Fifth Monarchist ideas on rebellion see below, pp. 131–6.

a fiasco. Government troops arrived whilst the saints were still gathering, arrested twenty rebels, and seized arms, five hundred copies of the manifesto, and (according to one unlikely report) five or six thousand pounds. Venner was sent to the Tower, remaining there until 1659, and Cornet Day and other prisoners were lodged in the Gatehouse and at Lambeth. Harrison, Rich, Danvers, Courtney, Lawson and Okey were detained briefly, but were soon found not to have been implicated.[1] The Venetian Resident asserted that the plotters had arms for 25,000 and proposed to slaughter all the nobility, and that similar plots had been unearthed in other parts of the country. Forces were certainly sent to other regions, and Thurloe probably treated as suspects all the agents named in the captured list.[2] But the only other known attempt at a rising was when a group of sixty was broken up and captured one night near Epping. The prisoners were produced at Whitehall at six o'clock the next morning.[3]

Predictably, Venner's plot brought down a heap of abuse on the saints. The Protector condemned them in Parliament, and Henry Cromwell thought that only a final settlement, a new monarchy, would solve the problem. They were accused of carrying out the Devil's policy, and of preaching communism.[4] With the failure of the prophecies, and perhaps of the plot, the movement seemed to be in decline. Rogers noted in the summer of that year that the saints' 'Coldness, Cowardliness, and Carelessness is (almost) *incredible*', and that many were drifting away, convinced that there would be no millennium, or that it was far off, or that it would be set up in Germany or elsewhere.[5]

The next challenge to the regime came not from a major group but from John Sturgeon, recently cashiered over his *Short Discovery*. In May 1656 he had been preaching against the government at

---

[1] Burrage, 'Fifth Monarchy Insurrections', pp. 722–47; C. H. Firth, *Last Years of the Protectorate* (1909), i. 213–18; *Thurloe*, vi. 163, 184–8, 194, 291, vii. 622; *Clarke Papers*, iii. 105–6; *Cal. S.P. Dom., 1656–7*, pp. 344, 351; Hist. MSS. Comm., iv, *App. to the 5th Report, Sutherland MSS.*, p. 163; *Pub. Intelligencer*, 78 (6–13 April 1657), pp. 1291–2; *ibid.*, 71 (misprint for 80), p. 1312; *Merc. Pol.*, 357 (9–16 April), pp. 7726–7; *ibid.*, 358, pp. 7742–3.

[2] *Cal. S.P. Venetian, 1657–9*, pp. 45–6, 53; Hist. MSS. Comm., iv, *App. to the 5th Rep., Sutherland MSS.*, p. 163.

[3] Lord John Russell, *The Life of William Lord Russell* (1819), pp. 13–14; Firth, *Last Years*, p. 218n.

[4] Abbott, *Writings and Speeches*, iv. 489; *Thurloe*, vi. 222; anon., *The Downfall of the Fifth Monarchy* (1657), p. 10; T. Hall, *Chiliasto-mastix redivivus* (1657), p. 53.

[5] Rogers, *Jegar*, introd., pp. 3, 37.

Reading, and drawing vast crowds. Shortly afterwards he was one of a group of Baptists and Levellers who offered their support to Charles II on condition that the king should restore the Long Parliament, establish liberty of conscience and abolish tithes.[1] Although this offer was rejected, Sturgeon crossed to the continent and continued to intrigue. In May 1657 he was arrested in London trying to smuggle in copies of *Killing No Murder*, a tract which appeared falsely in William Allen's name and urged Cromwell's assassination.[2]

During the first half of 1657, a scheme to make Cromwell king was being canvassed.[3] This was opposed by the Fifth Monarchists, who held that the crown belonged only to Christ. But since they already saw Cromwell as the arch-enemy, it is unlikely that Venner's plot sprang from this cause, as a royalist asserted. The claim that 'because they have sworn against kingship the name of emperor will content them' is equally implausible.[4] The saints pointed out that at Musselburgh monarchy had been seen as one of the ten horns of the Beast. Saul had been punished for accepting a crown against the will of God, and God 'did never institute or approve the office of a King, or Kingly government'. From Hull came a report that the Fifth Monarchists were 'very high' whilst the issue was open, and Feake declared that God's favourites, Moses, Gideon and Nehemiah, had refused the crown and that 'we Fifth-monarchy-men cannot justify the present proceedings'.[5] Anna Trapnel published her visions on the subject:

> *Spirit and Voice hath made a league*
> *Against Cromwel and his Crown*
> *The which I am confident the Lord*
> *Will ere long so strike down . . .*
> *. . . And his posterity*
> *They shall not sit upon his throne.*[6]

Before long the London Fifth Monarchists showed signs of reviving confidence. In June 1657 a vindication appeared of Venner's

[1] *Thurloe*, iv. 752; T. Crosby, *The History of the English Baptists* (1738–40), i, appendix, pp. 72–86.
[2] Firth, *Last Years*, i. 225–33.
[3] *Ibid.*, i. 128–200.
[4] *Cal. S.P. Dom.*, 1656–7, p. 344.
[5] Anon., *English Liberty and Property Asserted* (1657), pp. 3, 6, 7, 8; MS. Rawl. A 57, f. 312: H. Smith to Cromwell, 11 Feb. 1658; *Thurloe*, vii. 57–8.
[6] Trapnel, unitled book of verse in Bodleian, S.1.42 Th., p. 273.

attempted rising. The saints appeared indignant that the government had interrupted their 'smiting work', and justified rebellion by claiming that 'in this Dispensation, a Sword is as really the appointment of Christ, as any other Ordinance in the Church'.[1] Many leading saints appeared to be adopting a militant position, partly through the belief that the 42 months of the Beast's dominion (Rev. xi. 2), calculated from the beginning of the Protectorate, would expire in June 1657. Rogers was said to have preached that Venner's cause was good, but 'they did not time it well; however they would not desist till they had the Tyrants head from his shoulders'. Canne published a tract arguing that the saints would unite and destroy Cromwell at the end of the $3\frac{1}{2}$ years, and Feake added a preface comparing Cromwell to Barabbas.[2] There was a report in June that Harrison, Canne, Feake and Rogers 'professe themselves ready for an insurrection; the time being now come, as they say, wherein the three yeares and halfe is at an end, in which the witnesses have lyen dead, and that there will be a resurrection of them'. However their inactivity in April 1657 made it unlikely that they would stir unless there was a sign from heaven, and Cromwell felt sufficiently confident to free Harrison, Rich and Lawson in July from all remaining restrictions.[3]

Although the end of the $3\frac{1}{2}$ years passed without incident, Rogers set about raising the spirit of the saints by instituting a series of weekly meetings to promote the coming kingdom, and invited Presbyterians, Independents, Baptists, Seekers and Seventh-Day Sabbatarians to participate. He produced a declaration, entitled *A Reviving Word*, with 120 signatures, and members can be identified from the churches of Rogers, Venner, Chamberlen, Simpson, and Barbone.[4] But in February 1658 Rogers was seized along with Courtney and Portman on a charge of possessing seditious books designed to create dissaffection in the army. Numerous copies of the pamphlet, probably *Some Considerations by way of Proposal*, were seized in Courtney's room. It defended Venner's manifesto, and urged that the saints should be Christ's 'Battle-axe' in setting up the new kingdom.[5] The prisoners were kept in the Tower, where

---

[1] Anon., *A Witnes to the Saints* (1657), pp. 2, 6–7, 8.
[2] T. Hall, *Chiliasto-mastix*, p. 54; Canne, *Time of the End*, sig. A5, pp. 185, 198.
[3] *Thurloe*, vi. 349; *Clarke Papers*, iii. 113.
[4] Rogers, *A Reviving Word for the Quick and the Dead* (1657), pp. 22–4, 59, 66–8.
[5] *Thurloe*, vi. 775; anon., *Some Considerations* (1658), sig. A2v., C1; *Publick Intell.*, 120 (1–8 Feb. 1658), p. 286; *ibid.*, 121, pp. 299–301, 321 (pagination erratic).

Portman handed out to the soldiers copies of the Musselburgh Declaration of 1650. This pamphlet, commended by Cromwell at the time as a 'simple spiritual one', was now condemned as 'seditious' by his officials. Courtney was not released until September, and Portman not until February 1659.[1] Feake and Cornet Day preached in support of the prisoners, but soon afterwards Day was arrested with Canne, John Belcher (a bricklayer who was a Fifth Monarchist and Seventh-Day Baptist) and others at a meeting in Swan Alley on 1 April 1658. Feake attacked these arrests too, and was therefore put in the Tower for a few days to silence him. But he and Rogers were both released on 16 April, in time to attend Day's trial on 22 April.[2] Day and another defendant, John Clark, both refused to plead, denied the legality of the government, produced the Act of 1649 against the rule of a single person, and asserted that not they but the magistrates were guilty of treason. Day also asked for twelve witnesses to be called to prove his claim that the Protector was a 'jugler'. Ignoring these issues, the magistrates imposed a heavy fine and imprisonment of twelve and six months respectively. Canne and the other prisoners found there were no charges against them, but when Canne demanded an apology for his arrest, he was sent to Newgate for contempt and for handing out copies of the Musselburgh Declaration in court.[3]

During these clashes with the authorities, the Fifth Monarchists did not lose sight of their main objective of winning over the army, the Baptists and the Commonwealthsmen. Canne hoped that at the end of the $3\frac{1}{2}$ years the 'wise shall understand', and the Commonwealthsmen, though 'not enlightned further' than in civil matters, would join against the little horn.[4] John Rogers, still a millenarian, but now, since his imprisonment with Sir Henry Vane, an advocate of Vane's principle of government by all who supported the Good Old Cause rather than by the saints alone, also pressed for a union with the 'upright' Commonwealth party.[5] The most important bid

---

[1] Abbott, *Writings and Speeches*, ii. 302; *Publick Intell.*, 122 (15–22 Feb.), pp. 333–4; *Merc. Pol.*, 404 (18–25 Feb.), pp. 339–40; *Cal. S.P. Dom., 1658–9*, p. 145; *Thurloe*, vii. 619, 620, 623.

[2] *Thurloe*, vii. 18, 58–9; anon., *A Narrative; Wherin is faithfully set forth the sufferings of John Canne* (1658), *passim*; *Clarke Papers*, iii. 146; *Merc. Pol.*, 409 (25 March–1 April), p. 430; *ibid.*, 411, p. 453; *Publick Intell.*, 119 (5–12 April), p. 446. For Belcher, see Biog. App.

[3] *A Narrative, passim*; *A True Catalogue*, p. 13. For Clark see Biog. App.

[4] Canne, *Time of the End*, pp. 166–7, 195; Canne, *The Time of Finding* (1658), sig. A1.

[5] Rogers, *Jegar*, p. 19; Rogers, Διαπυλιτεία. *A Christian Concertation* (1659), p. 22.

to win over the Baptists was in May 1658. A conference of the Western Baptists was being held at Dorchester, led by Thomas Collier; and other prominent Baptists, such as Kiffin, were also present. During the proceedings, Carew, Allen and Vernon arrived and urged that the Fifth Monarchists and Baptists should combine. But Kiffin and Collier opposed this with determination, and eventually carried the day.[1]

In June the Fifth Monarchists almost had a taste of power when the government, feeling its unpopularity, apparently contemplated bringing Rich, Vane and Ludlow on to the Council.[2] This scheme was dropped, but in the eighteen months after Cromwell's death on 3 September 1658 the saints were rarely far from the centre of the nation's turbulent affairs as the Revolution disintegrated.

On Oliver's death, his son Richard succeeded peacefully, but without his father's power or prestige the Protectorate was a much weaker structure. The Fifth Monarchists, like other dissident groups, realized that their prospects were more encouraging. There was a surge in morale and strength, and Rogers wrote that their 'hopes are the highest throughout *England* (to see such a *Reviving in the midst of the years*, of the *Old Cause*)'.[3] Several hours before Oliver's death they sent emissaries round the country to spread the good news, and were reported, surprisingly, to have chosen Lambert as well as Harrison as their leader, and earlier they had also been negotiating with Fleetwood.[4] Within a few days they were inveighing openly against the government. Feake preached that 'if they had brought a Devil out of Whitehall in the shape of a man' he would have been made Protector.[5] Chillenden had hitherto adopted a quietist position, probably in gratitude for the Protector's leniency when he was cashiered from the army after an affair with his maid, but now he too launched a violent attack on Richard.[6]

As respect for Oliver's memory faded, his work began to be undone. The cases of political prisoners detained without trial were reviewed. John Portman had remained in the public view by

---

[1] *Thurloe*, vii. 138–40; B. R. White, 'The Organisation of the Particular Baptists, 1644–1660', *J. Eccles. Hist.*, xvii (1966), p. 222.

[2] *Thurloe*, vii. 154.

[3] Rogers, *The Plain Case of the Common-weal* (1659), p. 8.

[4] *Thurloe*, vii. 415; MS. Clar. 53, f. 234*v*.: F. Hancock (i.e. Sir A. Broderick) to ?Hyde, 20 Jan. 1657.   [5] *Clarke Papers*, iii. 163.

[6] E. Chillenden, *Nathans Parable* (1653), sig. D2; *The Phanatique Intelligencer*, 1 (21 March 1660), p. 8; MS. Rawl. A 8, f. 127: Otes to Jeffes, 15 Nov. 1653; *Clarke Papers*, iii. 162.

escaping briefly from the Tower in December 1658. His case was debated in Parliament in February 1659, and he was released.[1] Courtney was freed about the same time. Overton too pressed for a review, and an apologia for him was published. In March he made a triumphant return to London, and was released.[2] Sturgeon, however, was being sought on a charge of high treason, probably because of his royalist intrigues.[3]

Richard's Parliament on the whole had little more sympathy for the sects or the 'Good Old Cause' than its predecessors, and the Fifth Monarchy Men must have viewed with relief the growing hostility of critics in the army, and their intrigues with republicans in the Parliament. Baxter noted that the Fifth Monarchists 'followed Sir *Henry Vane*, and raised a great and violent clamorous Party against him [Richard], among the Sectaries in the City: *Rogers* and *Feake* . . . preach them into Fury.'[4] The crisis came on 22 April 1659 when Fleetwood and the officers forced Richard to dissolve his assembly, a manoeuvre in which Harrison was said to be involved.[5] All the opponents of the Protectorate hastened to offer their ideas as to how the 'Good Old Cause' might best be restored. Two clear strands of Fifth Monarchist thought became apparent. One group looked back to Barebones as the highest attainment of the Cause, and advised Fleetwood to use it as his guide.[6] Chamberlen called for a Parliament not to be elected 'by a confused Rabble, nor yet returned by a more Corrupt Sheriff; but to be chosen, or at least approved by the several Congregations'. Feake published a history of the Fifth Monarchists, emphasizing Musselburgh and Barebones, and recalling the apostasy of the Rump.[7] Meetings of the junior officers and saints pressed for a new sanhedrin of seventy members, 'butt the cry was great against itt, as a thinge the people of England would nott be bound by', and all these pleas were unheeded.[8]

[1] *Merc. Pol.*, 548 (30 Dec. 1658–6 Jan. 1659), pp. 134–5; *Publick Intell.*, 157 (27 Dec.–3 Jan.), pp. 127–8; *Thurloe*, vii. 619, 620, 623; *Cal. S.P. Dom.*, *1658–9*, p. 284; *Diary of Thomas Burton, Esq.*, ed. J. T. Rutt (1828), ii. 494; *C.J.*, vii. 607.
[2] *Perfect Diurnall*, 1 (21 Feb.), 9. 7; *Cal. S.P. Ven.*, *1657–9*, pp. 292, 298, 300; J. R., *Sad Suffering Case*; *D.N.B.*, Overton.
[3] *Cal. S.P. Dom.*, *1658–9*, p. 582.
[4] R. Baxter, *Reliquiae Baxterianae*, ed. M. Sylvester (1696), i. 101.
[5] G. Davies, *The Restoration of Charles II* (San Marino, California, 1955), p. 84; MS. Clar. 60, f. 323v.: Mordaunt to Hyde, 10 April 1659.
[6] Anon., *A true Copie of a Paper delivered to Lt. G. Fleetwood* (1659) *passim; The Cause of God, And of these Nations* (1659), p. 21.
[7] P. Chamberlen, *The Declaration and Proclamation of the Army of God* (2nd edn., 1659), p. 5; C. Feake, *A Beam of Light* (1659), pp. 23, 29, 48ff.
[8] *Clarke Papers*, iv. 21.

Many Fifth Monarchists, however, supported a different and much more widely popular view of the 'Good Old Cause', in calling for the return of the Rump. In April 1653 the saints had greeted its fall with joy, but Rogers had come to see the saints as not only the sectarians but all supporters of Parliament against the rule of a single person. He had even hoped that Richard's Parliament would assume sovereignty.[1] William Allen urged the army to find where it had apostatized by seeing when God's providence had deserted it, and suggested it was when the Rump was expelled.[2] Many other pamphlets were urging the same course, and the Grandees eventually adopted it.[3]

Under the restored Rump the Fifth Monarchists' fortunes continued to rise. They were recognized as uncorrupted opponents of the Protectorate and rewarded accordingly. From May to August Canne was made editor of the government press, *Mercurius Politicus* and *The Publick Intelligencer*.[4] He utilized the opportunity to publish a declaration by himself, Jessey and others thanking God for His 'never-to-be-forgotten shaking and overturning providence', and declaring that '*the day of Redemption draweth nigh*'.[5] Rich and Allen were given regiments, as was Overton, with Wigan as his Lieut.-Col., Vernon was made Quarter-Master-General, and Courtney was discussed (though not chosen) as Governor of Beaumaris. Chillenden was recommissioned, and Cornet Day was released.[6] Richard Price, Powell's supporter, was given the command of all the militia forces in North Wales, and John Bawden was made a major in the Cornish militia. Courtney, Carew, Danvers, Clement Ireton, Col. John James, Rich and John Williams all became Commissioners for the Militia in one or more counties.[7]

These changes represented a great accession of strength to the Fifth Monarchists, whose morale was now high. Canne called for a national day of 'Holy Rejoycing in the Lord, . . . for his late Salvation begun'. He claimed that the fall of Richard '*strengthens me*

---

[1] Rogers, *Plain Case*, pp. 10, 14, 20–2.
[2] W. Allen, *A Faithful Memorial* (1659), reprinted in *Somers Tracts*, vi. 498–504.
[3] Davies, *Restoration*, pp. 87–90.
[4] *C.J.*, vii. 652, 758; *Clarke Papers*, iv. 43.
[5] *Publick Intelligencer*, 176 (9–16 May), p. 426.
[6] *Clarke Papers*, iv. 19, 25, 60; *Cal. S.P. Dom.*, *1658–9*, pp. 375, 382, 387; *ibid.*, *1659–60*, pp. 13, 45, 47, 296, 562; *Merc. Pol.*, 278 (misprint for 575) (7–14 July), p. 582.
[7] *Cal. S.P. Dom.*, *1659–60*, pp. 16, 50, 93, 565; Firth and Rait, *Acts and Ords.*, ii. 1290, 1294, 1312, 1322, 1324–8, 1331, 1334–5.

in my former opinion, viz. That the Earth-quake is begun'.[1] Rogers welcomed the Rump, and outlined his new ideal (borrowed, he admitted, from Vane) of 'a holy, Christian, and *Theocratick Commonwealth*' which protected '*fundamental Rights*', especially the people's '*power of chusing their own Rulers unto the Supreme Trust*'. He condemned the 'rigid fifth Mon. man' who denied this right.[2]

The success of the Fifth Monarchists in achieving a position of considerable importance in the state provoked a torrent of attacks from critics who realized that the saints were now dangerous as well as irritating. On 6 June 1659 a paper was scattered in the London streets claiming that the Fifth Monarchists were 'Arm'd, officer'd, and every way in a Readiness' to attack the army on the following Tuesday, burn the city, and massacre 'all considerable People of all sorts'. Vane and Feake were said to be the leaders.[3] Another tract warned Londoners that the saints would deprive them of religion, laws, property, liberties and life.[4] In 1660 a satirical catalogue was published of pseudo-Fifth Monarchist books, with titles such as the following:

> The Saints shall possess the Earth; proving, That it is lawful for the brethren to stab, cut the throats of, or any way make an end of the Wicked of this World, if so be there will thereby any profit accrue to themselves.[5]

Canne's editorial post enabled him to retaliate to some extent. In July he printed an accusation that the malignants of Tiverton, in order to win popular support to oppress the saints, had aroused the whole town at dead of night with an invented story that the Fifth Monarchists, Quakers and Baptists were murdering the citizens.[6]

Although they had won a stronger position, the Fifth Monarchists soon became dissatisfied when they saw that the Rump, as before, was failing to reform the law or the church or in any way hasten

---

[1] *Publick Intell.*, 176 (9–16 May), pp. 426–9; J. Osborne, *An Indictment against Tythes* (1659), epistle by Canne, sig. A3.
[2] Rogers, *Mr. Pryn's Good Old Cause Stated and Stunted* (1659), pp. 10, 20; Rogers, *Christian Concertation*, pp. 17, 45, 59; Rogers, *Mr. Harrington's Parallel Unparallel'd* (1659), p. 6.
[3] Anon., *An Alarum to the city and Souldiery* (1659); Bodl. MS. Tanner 51, f. 74: J. Ireton to Fleetwood, 6 June 1659.
[4] Anon., *The Londoners Last Warning* (1659), *passim*.
[5] Anon., *Bibliotheca Fanatica* (1660), p. 7.
[6] *Merc. Pol.*, 580 (21–8 July), pp. 617–18; *Loyall Scout*, 13 (22–9 July), pp. 108–9; *Weekly Post*, 13 (26 July–2 Aug.), pp. 106–7.

Christ's kingdom. In August they thought it necessary to reprint extracts from old millenarian sermons, army declarations and speeches, warning those who had 'warped aside' to 'Remember Lots Wife' (Luke xvii. 32). They condemned the Rump for its inactivity, and for containing so many 'Mercenary Lawyers' and supporters of the Protectorate.[1] The following month a group of Fifth Monarchists, Baptists and Levellers, including Jessey, Powell, Allen, Vernon, Courtney, Portman, Clement Ireton, Price, Wigan, Danvers, Overton and Day, demanded that all former supporters of the Protectorate should be removed from office, and that the law and ministry should be reformed on biblical lines.[2] Even Canne, when giving encouragement to the Rump as early as May, had thought it necessary to warn the members of God's wrath if they ignored His work.[3] The Rump caused specific irritation by barring Harrison from office, being unable to forgive his part in their fall in 1653, by keeping Feake and Simpson out of their former livings at Christ Church and St. Botolph's, Bishopsgate, and by removing Canne.[4] Members in the army had their own grievances. Wigan complained that Fifth Monarchists were discriminated against, and Ludlow stated that the Grandees had only agreed with the greatest reluctance to reinstate Overton and Rich.[5]

There was widespread discontent with the Rump, especially in the army, since arrears had still not been paid. Moreover the Grandees were disenchanted when their creation tried to assert its independence. Some toyed with the idea of a military junto, with Richard restored as a nominal Protector, some remained loyal to the Rump, and others, like Lambert, intrigued with the Fifth Monarchists. By July the situation was being described accurately as one of 'universal confusion'.[6] Edward Hyde had long thought the Fifth Monarchists were 'like to make madd worke, and will be the first who must begin the worke' of creating an anarchy which would produce the Restoration.[7] The royalists listened hopefully to reports

---

[1] Anon., *The Fifth Monarchy or Kingdom of Christ . . . Asserted* (1659), pp. 51–2 and *passim*.

[2] Anon., *An Essay towards Settlement* (1659), brs.; answered by E. Johnson, *An Examination of the Essay* (1659).

[3] J. Canne, *A Seasonable Word* (1659), p. 6.

[4] Anon., *A Faithfull Searching Home Word* (1659), pp. 8, 9, 10.

[5] *Cal. S.P. Dom., 1659–60*, pp. 45–6; Ludlow, *Memoirs*, ii. 82, 95.

[6] Davies, *Restoration*, pp. 144–50; MS. Clar. 66, f. 74*v*.: R. Bramble (i.e. Col. Phillips) to (Hyde), 28 Oct. 1659; *Thurloe*, vii. 704.

[7] MS. Clar. 55, f. 4: Hyde to the king, 24 May/3 June 1657.

that the Fifth Monarchists were arming apace, and ignored the suggestion that the saints were 'like Weomen whose tongue is their best weapon'. News of Harrison was sought after eagerly, and since the saints were 'the fittest instruments to promote the confusion', they would if necessary have to be 'cajoled' into a rising. Royalist news-writers speculated on a rumoured secret list of seven thousand Fifth Monarchists preparing for action, and on a rumoured rally of five thousand saints at Horsham on 1 June. They concluded hopefully that 'Wee dayly expect a Massaker'.[1]

The second dissolution of the Rump, if predictable, occurred quite suddenly. The Rump attempted to assert its authority by revoking the commissions of the most hostile officers, including Lambert, Desborough and Packer. Unwilling to be destroyed by their own creation, the Grandees expelled the assembly on the next day, 13 October, and removed those army officers who remained faithful to the Rump.[2] Some of the saints rejoiced at the fall of the Rump, which had done little to satisfy them. A tract by Stoneham and his church rejoiced that the army could now set up Christ's kingdom, and Feake added a preface reviling the Rump as 'several broken pieces of those Governments that have lately suffered shipwrack.'[3] Chamberlen had been very critical of Parliamentary pretensions, asking 'Whether it were not far more honourable for Parliaments to have their Authority from God, . . . then derived . . . from the People, who themselves never had it?'[4] In November a paper, entitled *A Claim for Christ and his Laws*, was handed in by the saints to the Committee of the Army, urging it to recognize that only Christ and His Laws could stand when all other foundations were collapsing.[5]

But the Fifth Monarchists were now hopelessly fragmented. Some were still loyal to the Rump, whilst others attacked both the Rump and the Grandees. A manifesto appeared in October, signed by many of the instigators of the *Essay towards a Settlement*, regretting that they expected '*no more reformation or liberty from* Wallingford

[1] MS. Clar. 57, f. 132v.: Sir G. Crowe to Mr. Ro. (i.e. ?Roots), Feb. 1658; MS. Clar. 61, f. 173v.: Roberts (i.e. Cooper) to G. Coles (i.e. Hyde), 10 June 1659; MS. Clar. 63, f. 40: the king to ?Hyde, 24 June 1659; MS. Clar. 67, fos. 250v–251: A. Graves (i.e. Phillips) to (Hyde), 16 Dec. 1659; MS. Clar. 61, f. 320: H. (i.e. Broderick) to (Hyde), 24 June 1659; Hist. MSS. Comm., xv, *Braye MSS.*, pp. 204, 208; *Thurloe*, vii. 687; MS. Clar. 61, f. 103: J. Hopebetter (i.e. Wood) to H. Simpson (i.e. ?Hyde), 3 June 1659.
[2] Davies, *Restoration*, pp. 151–2; Ludlow, *Memoirs*, ii. 148–9.
[3] B. Stoneham, *A Serious Proposal* (1659), pp. 5, 11.
[4] P. Chamberlen, *Legislative Power in Problemes* (1659), p. 2.
[5] *Occurrences From Forraign Parts*, 42 (22–9 Nov. 1659), p. 488.

house', the Grandees' headquarters, '*than we had these last seven years from* Whitehall'. A number of Baptist churches in the midlands and south-west also subscribed, including Abingdon.[1] A similar tract in December demanded the recall of the godly members of Barebones, supplemented by other men of the same nature.[2]

The Grandees were as suspicious of the Fifth Monarchists as the Rump had been. Harrison was still excluded from any office, and Carew was barred from the Committee of Safety, though Rich retained his commission.[3] The position of the Grandees was weakened, however, by the fact that both General Monk in Scotland and the navy refused to accept their coup. Moreover, Overton fortified Hull, where he was Governor, and held out for the Fifth Monarchy, condemning the Grandees, Monk, and even the Rump, which he had supported against the Grandees as recently as 11 October.[4]

Overshadowed by the threat from Monk, the regime of the Grandees lacked any stability. Attempts to win over the navy, at a meeting at which Courtney was present, proved unsuccessful, and Lawson remained loyal to the Rump.[5] The General Council of Officers resolved on 10 December to call a new Parliament, despite Rich's pleas for the Rump. In the meantime they created a new body called the 'Conservators' or 'keepers of Fundamentals', nominating Harrison, Carew, Overton and Lawson among others.[6] But this move failed to widen their support. Many regiments refused to accept their authority. When Rich's regiment was sent, without its colonel, to reduce the garrison at Portsmouth which supported the Rump, Rich joined his forces and the whole regiment declared for Parliament and joined the garrison.[7] The Grandees eventually despaired of controlling the situation, and allowed the Rump to reassemble on 26 December. Rich and Overton were thanked by the House, and Rich was given a new commission. Arthur Squibb was released from the Isle of Man.[8]

[1] Anon., *A Warning-Piece to the General Council* (1659), pp. 6, 9, 10.
[2] Anon., *A Faithfull Searching Home Word* (1659), pp. 38–9.
[3] C. H. Firth, *The Life of Thomas Harrison* (Worcester, Mass., 1893), p. 51; Ludlow, *Memoirs*, ii. 148–9; Davies, *Restoration*, p. 157.
[4] R. Overton, *The Humble and Healing Advice* (1659), p. 5 and *passim*; *A Letter from Ma. Gen. Overton* (1659), brs; MS. Clar. 67, f. 220v.: J.S. (i.e. Shaw) to Hyde, 15/25 Dec. 1659; *Weekly Post*, 26 (25 Oct.–1 Nov. 1659), p. 201.
[5] M.H. (probably Mark Harrison), *A Narrative of the Proceedings of the Fleet* (1659), *passim*; Davies, *Restoration*, pp. 183–4.
[6] Davies, *Restoration*, pp. 185–6; Ludlow, *Memoirs*, ii. 163, 165, 173–4.
[7] Ludlow, *Memoirs*, ii. 183–4.
[8] *Merc. Pol.*, 604 (19–26 Jan. 1660), p. 1049; *C.J.*, vii. 799; Davies, *Restoration*, pp. 187–9, 256; *Publick Intell.*, 209 (26 Dec.–2 Jan. 1660), p. 976.

The return of the Rump proved a hollow victory for the 'Good Old Cause'. Monk was alone in having financial security and therefore dependable troops, and when he marched into London in February 1660 and recalled the Presbyterians excluded from the Long Parliament in 1648, the Restoration became inevitable. There were only a few last efforts to uphold the old cause. William Allen, now colonel of an Irish regiment, made a new appeal to the army, but without result.[1] Colonel Rich was deprived of his command for filling his regiment with fanatics, abusing the Rump for spurning Harrison, and seeking 'to break all civil authority to make way for the Fifth Monarchy'. But he rejoined his regiment near Beccles, and tried to stir up his troops to make another stand. The gathered churches of East Anglia were said to be planning to raise forces to help him. But when government troops advanced, the plan collapsed, and Rich was imprisoned until May.[2]

Overton made an equally short-lived attempt. He regarded Monk as 'imbargued with that Spirit . . . which . . . Diametrically opposes the designe of God', and in January 1660 he wrote to Monk in support of the Rump, opposing the return of the secluded members and any government by a single person. In February he condemned those who sought to restore the king, and when he was dismissed by Parliament on 6 March, he boldly 'declared for Jesus Christ'. The Council of State, however, sent to Hull a former Governor, Major Henry Smith, who proceeded to borrow money from friends in the town, which he used to buy off Overton's troops. Finding his soldiers unreliable, Overton was forced to submit.[3]

The saints were now silent. Livewell Chapman, the major Fifth Monarchist publisher since 1653, was in hiding from March and in prison from May. John Rogers, who had gone to Ireland, was arrested as early as January.[4] Huge plots were invented involving the Fifth Monarchists, and served as a pretext for the arrest of

---

[1] W. Allen, *A Word to the Army* (1660), *passim*; *Clarke Papers*, iv. 165, 252.
[2] Hist. MSS. Comm., li, *Leyborne–Popham MSS.*, pp. 157–8, 162–6, 168–9; Ludlow, *Memoirs*, ii, 238; *Cal. S.P. Dom., 1659–60*, p. 571; *Merc. Pol.*, 609 (23 Feb.–1 March 1660), p. 1134; *ibid.*, 610, p. 1157; *C.J.*, vii. 866; *Parliamentary Intelligencer*, 10 (20–7 Feb.), p. 144; Nuttall, *Early Quaker Letters*, p. 279; MS. Clar. 70, f. 110v.: ?Seymour to Hyde, 9 March 1660.
[3] Overton, *Humble . . . Advice*, p. 5; *Publick Intell.*, 213 (23–30 Jan.), pp. 1038–9; *Clarke Papers*, iv. 245–6; *Parl. Intell.*, 12 (5–12 March), pp. 182–3; *Merc. Pol.*, 610 (1–8 March), p. 1155; Ludlow, *Memoirs*, ii. 246–7; MS. Clar. 70, f. 110v.; J. Price, *The Mystery and Method of His Majesty's Happy Restauration* (1680), p. 126.
[4] *Cal. S.P. Dom., 1659–60*, pp. 572, 575, 328; *Merc. Pol.*, 19 (3–10 May), p. 292.

Courtney, Allen and Vernon.[1] Vavasor Powell had been seized, without a charge, in February, and by April the royalists were already raiding the houses of prominent Independent and Baptist ministers.[2]

Charles II was proclaimed on 8 May, and entered London on 29 May. The saints, of course, were not solely responsible for the Restoration. But their vociferous demands for political, social and religious revolution discredited the republican governments which proved unable to contain them. In 1653 they had been partly responsible for the conservative reaction which led to the Protectorate. Their activities, and the rumours of imminent massacres and spoliation, helped to lead in 1660 to the general belief that there could be no settled order until the king returned.

[1] 'Copy of a Notable Letter', Brit. Mus. MS. Stowe 185, fos. 168–70: 8 April 1660; SP. 18/220, f. 65–v.: R. Jones to T. Taylor, 4 April 1660; *Cal. S.P. Dom.*, *1659–60*, p. 573; MS. Clar. 71, f. 250: Hall (i.e. Halsall) to Hyde, 13 April 1660; *ibid.*, f. 343: (Wood) to G. Coles (i.e. Hyde), 20 April 1660.
[2] H. Jessey, *The Lords Loud Call to England* (1660), pp. 13, 18 and *passim*.

CHAPTER SIX

The Political, Social and Economic Ideas
of the Fifth Monarchy Men

▸◆◂

The Fifth Monarchists saw existing society as the creation of the antichristian Fourth Monarchy. In looking forward to the millennium, they demanded that its whole structure should be remodelled in accordance with the pattern laid down in the Bible, especially in the prophecies of Daniel and Revelation. The essence of their beliefs was a declared readiness to destroy by force the kingdoms of the world, to invert the social order, and thereafter to be the rulers of the earth. Fifth Monarchism was a loosely co-ordinated movement and never possessed a common programme. But though there were a number of important differences dividing the saints, there was also a considerable measure of agreement over fundamental ideas.

It was the saints' professed readiness to take up arms to implement the kingdom of heaven that brought them most into disrepute. Many groups had preached the millennium without calling upon their adherents to do anything more than purify themselves and wait. The Fifth Monarchists, however, justified their more aggressive attitude by citing favourable scriptural passages. Harrison quoted Daniel vii. 18 to the sceptical Ludlow: 'the saints . . . shall *take* the kingdom . . .' But Ludlow was able to quote in reply from Daniel vii. 22, that 'judgment was *given* to the saints'.[1] The Bible presumably justified rather than determined the saints' attitude. This attitude sprang partly from the political-religious situation in Europe in the century since the Reformation. The continental wars and the English civil wars were seen as the struggles of Christ's champions against the disciples of the Devil. When the Grandees, the Rump and Cromwell all apostatized, the Fifth Monarchists

---

[1] E. Ludlow, *Memoirs*, ed. C. H. Firth (Oxford, 1894), ii. 7–8. My italics.

could claim to represent God's cause in its true form, pursuing the activist approach which had been followed since 1642.[1]

The saints asserted their belief in violence in nearly all their pamphlets, and even face to face with the Protector.[2] Naturally, their opponents portrayed them as a bloodthirsty band forever scheming massacres. In fact the Fifth Monarchists staged only two minor risings in the whole course of the movement, and the problem is thus raised of how militant they really were.

Cromwell himself asserted that the saints were eager to spill blood. 'You long to be at it; you want but an opportunity,' he told them. Thurloe believed the saints had a 'constant meeting to put us into blood'.[3] Alarmist propaganda was spread to increase public hostility. There were rumours in June 1659 that the Fifth Monarchists were about to fire London. In July the town of Tiverton was in uproar over an alleged plot by the saints to massacre the inhabitants.[4] William Prynne asserted that the saints wished to throw down all governments 'and set up a *popular Anarchy*'.[5]

The Fifth Monarchists were insistent that they must bear witness, as Rogers put it, '*praedicando, praecando,* or *praeliando*'.[6] Over preaching and praying there was unanimity. They were to 'denounce the wrath of God against *Rulers*, for their Apostacies and abhominable hypocrisies; yea, and to deale particularly with them, laying the finger on the sore, pointing unto the Abhominations by name'.[7] Tillinghast declared the fact that God's plans were unchangeable was no excuse 'for us . . . to *sit still and do nothing . . . to the effecting these glorious things*'. They lived in the time of the fulfilment of the prophecies and 'of necessity must the Witnesses of Christ in this Age bear forth such a testimony of truth as may lay a foundation' for Christ's kingdom.[8] The saints agreed that they had a military duty. Rogers stressed that they 'must be at it, when they have the *Call*'. Such prominent saints as Harrison, Courtney, Simpson and Pendarves argued that the Protectorate was illegal, and that arms could be

---

[1] C. Feake, *A Beam of Light* (1659), *passim*; Bodl. MS. Rawl. A 29, f. 628: J. Rogers to T. Brookes, 26 Aug. 1655; anon., *The Fifth Monarchy, . . . Asserted* (1659), p. 36 (misprint for 48). See above, chapters 2 and 3, and p. 93.
[2] For example, anon., *The Faithfull Narrative of the late Testimony* (1655), p. 34.
[3] Anon., *Faithfull Narrative*, p. 35; *Thurloe*, v. 122.
[4] Above, p. 125.
[5] W. Prynne, *A true and perfect Narrative* (1659), p. 20.
[6] Anon., *Faithfull Narrative*, p. 34.
[7] W. Llanvaedonon, *A Brief Exposition upon the Second Psalme* (1655), p. 23.
[8] J. Tillinghast, *Generation-Worke*, 3rd part (1654), p. 221; Tillinghast, *Knowledge of the Times* (1654), p. 345.

taken up against it without sin.[1] John James, a Fifth Monarchist preacher executed in 1661, said that Christ would 'use his people in his hand as his *Battle-ax . . . and Weapons of War*'; the same phrase was used by other saints.[2] It was asserted that 'a Sword is as really the appointment of Christ, as any other Ordinance in the Church . . . And a man may as well go into the harvest without his Sickle, as to this work without . . . his Sword.'[3] Mary Cary thought it lawful for the saints 'to fight against such as would murther, and destroy them (as the Associates of the Beast would)'.[4] At the funeral of Pendarves in 1656 the gathered saints resolved that 'Gods people must be a bloody people (in an active sense)'.[5]

Besides threatening violence, the Fifth Monarchists rejected altogether the legality of the Protectorate. Anna Trapnel bluntly told a soldier who questioned her: 'The Lord Protector we own not; Thou art of the Army of the Beast.' Postlethwaite refused to sign a petition to the Protector lest he be thought to have accepted the legality of the regime. Feake and Spittlehouse accepted it only as a *de facto* regime.[6] Several asserted their right to rebel. Rogers argued that only godly governments need be obeyed, and that if Cromwell disagreed, he should not have fought against Charles I. William Llanvaedonon thought it '*No Treason against the Royall Law of King Jesus*, whatever it may be against the Lawes of men, *to seeke to draw men from their obedience to these . . . perverse Rulers*.' Carew and Courtney were accused of trying to subvert officials and stir up resistance, and a pamphleteer attacking Cromwell asserted that he would as soon 'pluck out my right eye, as yeild to pay him Taxes'.[7] After 1660, many Fifth Monarchists accepted that God had restored the Stuarts to punish the people for their sins, and accordingly recognized the validity of the monarchy as long as God appeared to support it. But Henry Danvers and Thomas Palmer argued the

---

[1] *Clarke Papers*, ii. 242–6.
[2] Anon., *A Narrative of the Apprehending . . . of John James* (1662), p. 34; anon., *Some Considerations by way of Proposall* (1658), sig. C1v. Cf. Jer. li. 20. For James, see Biog. App.
[3] Anon., *A Witnes to the Saints* (1657), p. 6.
[4] M. Cary, *The Little Horns Doom & Downfall* (1651), p. 125.
[5] W. Hughes, *Munster and Abingdon* (Oxford, 1657), pp. 88–9.
[6] *Publick Intelligencer*, 13 (24–31 Dec. 1655), pp. 193–4; *Thurloe*, iv. 151; C. Feake, *The Oppressed Close Prisoner* (1655), pp. 54, 60; J. Spittlehouse, *The Royall Advocate* (1655), p. 19.
[7] MS. Rawl. A 47, f. 35: J. Rogers to Cromwell, no date; Llanvaedonon, *Brief Exposition*, p. 47; *Clarke Papers*, ii. 245; anon., *The Protector (So called,) In Part Unvailed* (1655), p. 76.

right and duty of the saints to overthrow the regime, and there were numerous plots and attempted risings seeking to do this.[1]

These militant statements provided ready material for critics, but they represent only one aspect of the Fifth Monarchist position. The majority of saints were not ready to spring to arms as soon as opportunity arose. They wanted to be convinced by some clear divine signal that Christ Himself was calling them. John Canne explained that though the saints would smash the powers of the world, they '*do abhor all secret Designes and Plots*', and that it was '*belowe their Principles, to provide Pikes and Muskets, or any such Ammunition*'. Their own inclinations and the ending of the prophetic periods were '*no ground for action*'. The saints would '*remain in their Chambers*' until God gave the call. Then, 'so clear and certain will the thing bee (they having the word of God and his spirit for it, providence likewise leading the way) that they shall publikely declare, what they intend to do', and the government's support would wither away.[2] This meant in practice that the violence of most of the saints was strictly verbal, for the majority never did feel that God had called them to arms. Rogers warned that if the saints stirred before 'the Time and the Season', they were 'more capable of being cut down with the grass, then of cutting down the grass'.[3] Simpson, Chillenden, Chamberlen and Morgan Llwyd all repudiated violence.[4] William Allen reflected that 'we Have had many years of blood, and warr enough to make good men desire an End'. His friend Vernon urged the saints to 'wait still in weeping, in supplication until the times of refreshment' should come.[5] Aspinwall even claimed that the saints, 'the best and truest friends unto Government', could hold office under the Fourth Monarchy, though more often saints felt that this would be to contaminate themselves.[6] After the Restoration, Vavasor Powell saw no scriptural warrant 'to affirm, that there are no *Magistrates* now in being in the World,

---

[1] Below, chapter 9, p. 208 and *passim*. For Palmer, see Biog. App.

[2] J. Canne, *Truth with Time* (1656), sig. B1v, B2; Canne, *The Time of the End* (1657), p. 206; Canne, *The Time of Finding* (1658), sig. A2v–A3.

[3] Canne, *Time of the End*, epistle by Rogers, sig. a7v.

[4] *Thurloe*, iv. 365, 545; J. Ives, *Saturday no Sabbath* (1659), p. 59; M. Llwyd, *Gweithiau*, ed. T. E. Ellis and J. H. Davies (Bangor and London, 1899, 1908), ii. 237.

[5] MS. Rawl. A 13, f. 26: Allen to T. Hart, 5 April 1654; W. Allen, *The Captive Taken from the Strong* (1658), epistle by Vernon, sig. A8.

[6] W. Aspinwall, *Legislative Power* (1656), p. 36; Feake, *Oppressed Close Prisoner*, p. 76; anon., *A Ground Voice* (1655), p. 7; Bury and West Suffolk Record Office, 'Church Book of Bury St. Edmunds', transcribed by J. Duncan, p. 16.

or that the *Magistrates*, under and belonging to the fourth *Monarchy*, are not to be obey'd'. Even in the great prophetic year 1666 the saints refused to rise without a clear sign from heaven.[1] All these expressions of moderation sprang probably from the reflection, voiced in 1655 by Feake, that '*Tyranny* it self is not so ugly a monster by many Degrees . . . as is *Anarchy*.'[2]

Fifth Monarchism, however, was a heterogeneous movement. Many pamphleteers were army officers or educated ministers who provided much of the leadership but formed only a small proportion of the total membership. Their views on violence, and some other issues, were significantly different from those of the masses, who represented different social groups. All the saints believed in the imminence of the millennium, but the leaders were hesitant to produce anarchy in seeking to establish Christ's kingdom. There was sometimes conflict and tension between the groups. Rogers opposed Venner's plot in 1657, and when a delegation from Venner's church visited him, his wife told them that 'he durst not speake with us, . . . for ought she knew, wee came to murther her husband.' Despite his opposition, some of his followers joined both Venner's risings, and one of them declared 'wee did not live in an age to expect miracles; that Babilon cannot bee destroyed, . . . by only faith and prayer; but you must be of courage, . . . and proceed by force.'[3] Though Simpson preached caution, his more radical followers split off, formed their own congregation and negotiated with Venner.[4] One of the London saints, John Jones, preached that it was not murder to kill Cromwell, and Venner's risings were a natural result of this attitude. The plotters were determined to go ahead although Harrison, Carew, Feake and Rogers refused to join them, and despite so many setbacks that they 'began to thinke that surely the Lord had not a purpose that wee should now begin the worke'.[5] This attitude outlived Venner. In 1661 William James, preaching in Whitechapel, 'prayed yt God would putt an Axe into ye hand of

[1] V. Powell, *The Bird in the Cage, Chirping* (1661), p. 35; on 1666 see below, pp. 213–14.
[2] Feake, *Oppressed Close Prisoner*, p. 11; H. Danvers, *The Mystery of Magistracy* (1663), p. 18.
[3] C. Burrage, 'The Fifth Monarchy Insurrections', *Eng. Hist. Rev.*, xxv (1910), pp. 729, 733; *Thurloe*, iii. 136; compare the list of Rogers's followers in his *A Reviving Word* (1657), pp. 66–8, and anon., *A Declaration of several of the Churches of Christ* (1654), with the plotters listed by Burrage, p. 738. Atwood, Gardner, Gregson, Grove, Hancock, Medley, Rutter and Simmons were involved.
[4] Anon., *The Old Leaven Purged* (1658), *passim*; Burrage, *art. cit.*, p. 731.
[5] *Thurloe*, iv. 650; Burrage, *art. cit.*, pp. 726, 732.

some of his servants' to cut down king and bishops. Nathaniel Strange, a preacher and former officer, had urged the saints in 1664 to attack Whitehall and seize Charles II and the Duke of Albemarle, and two years later one Captain Harris was trying to stir up the saints to arms.[1]

The governments under Cromwell and Charles II certainly failed to appreciate that the violent language of the leading saints clothed relatively moderate codes of behaviour. But vigilance was justified by the very different principles held by some at least amongst the masses, and for some years there was a real possibility of violence.

A second feature dividing the Fifth Monarchists from contemporary millenarians, besides their declared readiness to use violence when God commanded, was a willingness to elaborate the political, social and economic structure of the kingdom of Christ. Mede and Alsted had not envisaged political or social changes in the millennium. Alsted thought it would consist not in 'bodily pleasures . . . but . . . Spirituall joyes'. Presbyterian millenarians envisaged a godly king and an established Presbyterian church-system in an unchanged society.[2] John Archer prophesied long life, health and riches, but did not discuss the structure of society in detail.[3] Thomas Goodwin and Nathaniel Homes, Independent pastors but also academics, discussed millenarian society with great caution. Homes thought there would be peace, prosperity and long life and 'No *superiority of persons*' but he confessed also that his 'heart trembles to think of a *popular parity; a levilling Anarchie*, to which these times, to my terrour, much incline among the multitude'.[4] Goodwin asserted that the saints would 'eat, and drink, and build houses' in the millennium, and that 'God intends to make use of the Common People in the great Worke of proclaiming the Kingdome.' But he added hastily that its establishment must be the work 'of Great ones, of Noble, of Learned ones'.[5] The Fifth Monarchists proved to be much bolder and more specific in their predictions.

In describing the government in the millennium, the Fifth

---

[1] See below, pp. 208–9.
[2] J. H. Alsted, *The Beloved City* (1643), p. 70; see above, pp. 28, 45.
[3] J. Archer, *The Personall Reigne of Christ* (1642), pp. 27–30.
[4] N. Homes, *The Resurrection Revealed* (1654), pp. 507, 523; Homes, *A Sermon, Preached Before . . . Thomas Foote* (1650), p. 32.
[5] T. Goodwin, *A Sermon of the Fifth Monarchy* (1654), p. 31; Goodwin, *A Glimpse of Sions Glory* (1641), pp. 5, 7.

Monarchists were unanimous that the saints would reign with Christ their king. They were somewhat hesitant to usurp the divine prerogative of settling constitutional details, feeling they ought rather to 'wait for such issue as the providence of God should bring things to'.[1] But many did venture to make speculative arrangements.

The first problem, over which there was considerable disagreement, was to decide whether Christ intended to appear and reign in person. Mary Cary, John Rogers and Thomas Tillam thought that Christ would be present.[2] John Archer had thought that Christ would come at first and then withdraw, whereas Danvers believed that He would not appear until the end of the thousand years.[3] Aspinwall doubted whether Christ would appear at all, but the most popular position was that of Tillinghast, who divided the millennium into an evening and a morning kingdom. The first would be founded and run by the saints, and Christ would only appear in the second, when perfection had been attained.[4] This theory both justified the Fifth Monarchists' activist approach, and gave them liberty to organize the first part of the millennium as they thought best.

Many Fifth Monarchists described the characteristics of the ideal rulers, as depicted in the Old Testament. Danvers said they should be wise, godly, well-known, just, and haters of covetousness, citing appropriate texts, and this formula was used often.[5] All suggestions concerning the government were based on the Bible. Up to 1653 several saints saw Cromwell in the light of an Old Testament Judge, and were ready to concede him absolute power.[6] If Christ did appear in person, the government would of course be monarchical, and in 1659 the saints were alleged to have refused to swear against a Single Person lest this should exclude Christ.[7] They were resolute, however, in attacking any earthly monarchy, except perhaps for Harrison's cryptic reference in 1653 to a godly monarchy.[8] Feake had preached as early as 1646 that monarchy was

---

[1] *Thurloe*, vi. 186; anon., *Some Considerations* (1658), sig. A2v–B1.
[2] M. Cary, *Little Horns Doom*, p. 213; J. Rogers, *Ohel* (1653), p. 24; T. Tillam, *The Two Witnesses* (1651), pp. 109–10. For Tillam, see Biog. App.
[3] Archer, *Personall Reigne*, pp. 16, 22; H. Danvers, *Theopolis* (1672), p. 89.
[4] W. Aspinwall, *A Brief Description of the Fifth Monarchy* (1653), p. 4; J. Tillinghast, *Mr. Tillinghasts Eight Last Sermons* (1655), p. 62.
[5] Danvers, *Mystery of Magistracy*, p. 3. See also anon., *An Essay towards Settlement* (1659), brs.; J. Rogers, *To his Excellency* (1653), brs.; anon., *Some Considerations*, pp. 15–16. Most texts were from Deut. and Exodus.
[6] See above, pp. 62–3.
[7] Anon., *Certain Quaeres* (1649), p. 6; T. Carte, *Original Letters* (1739), ii. 203.
[8] See above, p. 66.

by nature antichristian, and the saints were unanimous in 1657–8 in opposing the scheme to make Cromwell king. Camshaw Helme and Anthony Palmer, two ministers who became notable Fifth Monarchists after the Restoration, had joined in a petition against the proposal.[1] Rogers and Carew were hostile to the rule of any single person, and when accused of seeking to oust Cromwell to instal Harrison in his place, Rogers denied that he had the 'least . . . thought . . . of throwing down one man to set up another'.[2]

Until Christ arrived, the government was to be by the small minority who formed the elect, organized into a church-parliament based on the Jewish sanhedrin. Even Rogers, who for a time saw Cromwell as a second Moses, accepted this as the ideal government.[3] The tyranny of the godly over the unregenerate was one logical result of Calvinist elitism, and there was certainly nothing democratic in the Fifth Monarchists' programme. The Norfolk petition of 1649 demanded 'what right or claim meer natural and worldly men have to Rule and Government', asking 'How can the kingdom be the Saints' when the ungodly are electors, and elected to Govern?' Carew, Harrison, Courtney and Rich objected to the Protectorate because 'it had a Parliament in it, whereby power is derived from the people, whereas all power belongs to Christ'. In 1659 the Ipswich congregation condemned popular elections altogether.[4]

Instead of the ungodly, only church-members were to vote, with each congregation nominating representatives to a sanhedrin.[5] In 1651 a number of ministers, including Feake and Simpson, published a slightly more liberal proposal, opening the franchise to all the 'visible saints', that is, God's elect, and thus including those who belonged voluntarily to Presbyterian churches.[6] Barebones Parliament in 1653 was not chosen in this manner, but a number of gathered churches, including Fifth Monarchist ones, did press their nominees on Cromwell.[7] Venner's group in 1657 urged that the elect,

[1] T. Edwards, *Gangraena* (1646), iii. 147–8; J. Nickolls, *Original Letters* (1743), p. 121; see above, p. 119. For Helme and Palmer, see Biog. App.
[2] MS. Rawl. A 47, fos. 33–4: Rogers to Cromwell, ?Dec. 1653/Jan. 1654; J. Cornubiensis (i.e. J. Carew), *The Grand Catastrophe* (1654), pp. 11–12; Rogers, *Jegar-Sahadutha* (1657), p. 39.
[3] Anon., *Certain Quaeres*, p. 6; Rogers, *To his Excellency*, brs.
[4] Anon., *Certain Quaeres*, p. 8; *Clarke Papers*, ii. 244; B. Stoneham, *A Serious Proposal* (1659), p. 3.
[5] Anon., *Certain Quaeres*, pp. 6–7; anon., *A Cry for a Right Improvement* (1652, misprint for 1651), p. 9; anon., *A Model of a New Representative* (1651), pp. 3–4; D. T., *Certain Queries* (1651), p. 8.
[6] Anon., *A Declaration of divers Elders* (1651), pp. 5, 8.
[7] J. Nickolls, *Original Letters*, pp. 94, 124–6.

the 'Lord's Freemen', should choose a supreme council, to last one year.[1] In 1659 some of the saints called for a sanhedrin of seventy members, and Chamberlen called for rulers to 'be chosen, or at least approved by the several Congregations'.[2] Government by the visible saints was the system adopted in Massachusetts and New Haven, where Aspinwall and Venner had lived for many years, and the English saints must have been encouraged by this example.[3]

Some Fifth Monarchists showed traces of the more democratic tendencies in radical political thought in the interregnum. Aspinwall asserted that the rulers must be chosen by the 'suffrage of the people', though he emphasized that they must then be approved by the gathered churches, and that candidates must be church-members.[4] Recognizing that the number of the godly was small, Mary Cary was prepared to allow 'civil and blamelesse' men to supplement them.[5] John Rogers came near to Sir Henry Vane's position in the later years of the Protectorate, urging that not only saints but all supporters of the (republican, oligarchic) 'Good Old Cause' should be electors, but by this time Rogers was not an orthodox Fifth Monarchist.[6] Rogers seems to have been alone in referring to the radical new concept of 'natural Rights' and *'fundamental Rights'*, which the Levellers had adopted, and to which the Quakers occasionally referred. Rogers, however, thought that such rights could be forfeited, for example by those who had not supported Parliament.[7] A similar concept may have been behind the phrase affirming the 'just Civill Liberties of English men' which appeared in Powell's *Word for God*, though this was a deliberate attempt to win support from outside the Fifth Monarchist movement.[8] Venner's second manifesto made a passing reference to 'our Birth-rights', and expressed the hope that all would become saints in the millennium, which would begin with a 'great and general conversion'.

---

[1] W. Medley, *A Standard Set Up* (1657), p. 18.

[2] *Clarke Papers*, iv. 21; P. Chamberlen, *The Declaration and Proclamation of the Army of God* (1659), p. 5.

[3] G. L. Haskins, *Law and Authority in Early Massachusetts* (New York, 1960), pp. 45ff, 63; W. Aspinwall, *Legislative Power* (1656), p. 25.

[4] Aspinwall, *Legislative Power*, pp. 22–4.

[5] M. Cary, *Twelve New Proposals* (1653), p. 12.

[6] J. Rogers, *Christian Concertation*, (1659), pp. 59–60; Rogers, *The Plain Case of the Common-weal* (1659), p. 10.

[7] Rogers, *Christian Concertation*, pp. 42–3, 59–60; Rogers, *Mr. Pryn's Good Old Cause* (1659), p. 10; Rogers, *Sagrir* (1653), sig. A2; C. Hill, *Puritanism and Revolution* (1962), p. 79; H. N. Brailsford, *The Levellers and the English Revolution* (1961), p. 262; H. Barbour, *The Quakers in Puritan England* (New Haven and London, 1964), p. 245; E. Burrough, *Good Counsel* (1659), p. 23.   [8] *Thurloe*, iv. 382.

But this tract too was a deliberate attempt to appeal to all who 'own at least the negative part of our cause'.[1]

The Fifth Monarchists' wish was to restrict choice to the godly, and their ideal was to leave it to God alone. Similarly, Vane looked forward to when God and men would choose magistrates together.[2] In 1653 the saints' wish took the form of urging Cromwell alone, as God's instrument, to choose all the members of Barebones.[3] It also found expression in the importance which the Fifth Monarchists attached to the system of lot, 'wherein', said Danvers, 'the Lord also was called into the choice'. He cited numerous Old Testament parallels, including the choice of King Saul and the Jewish sanhedrin by lot.[4] Thomas Tillam condemned playing cards and dice because they profaned a method by which God made known His wishes to men, and were thus 'the highest abuse of this glorious appeal by way of lot'.[5] In 1653, Chillenden's congregation had suggested that Barebones be composed of men chosen out of a larger number 'by lot, after solemn prayer (a way much owned by God . . .)'.[6] Though the idea that God's will could be ascertained by this practice was coming under attack in the seventeenth century, lots were also used for this purpose by the Baptists, by the Moravians and later by the Methodists.[7]

The aim of the Fifth Monarchists was to use power to enforce godly discipline on the masses. Far from withering away in the millennium, the duties of the magistrate would expand into new spheres. John Eliot, a New England minister whose vision of the millennium was published by Livewell Chapman, visualized officials over every ten, fifty, hundred and thousand people, with a separate law court for each group of fifty.[8] Danvers wrote that the magistrates were to study the Mosaic laws and then punish the ungodly, and Aspinwall affirmed that they would bring 'terrour to them that do evil'.[9] Mary Cary advised them to sponsor evangelism and punish

---

[1] Anon., *A Door of Hope* (1661), pp. 7, 11.
[2] Anon., *The Tryall of Sir Henry Vane* (1662), p. 121.   [3] See above, pp. 63–4.
[4] Danvers, *Mystery of Magistracy*, pp. 4–5.
[5] T. Tillam, *The Temple of Lively Stones* (1660), p. 357.
[6] Nickolls, *Original Letters*, p. 122.
[7] W. E. H. Lecky, *History of the Rise and Influence of the Spirit of Rationalism* (1865), i. 307 and note; J. J. Goadby, *Bye-Paths in Baptist History* (1871), pp. 298–301; W. H. G. Armytage, *Heavens Below* (1961), pp. 49–50; cf. K. V. Thomas, *Religion and the Decline of Magic* (1971), pp. 118–24.
[8] J. Eliot, *The Christian Commonwealth* (1659), pp. 4, 12, 7 (misprint for 15); cf. Exod. xviii. 21.
[9] Danvers, *Mystery of Magistracy*, pp. 6–7; Aspinwall, *Legislative Power*, p. 28.

drunkards, whoremasters and swearers. Those guilty of such vices were condemned fiercely.[1] The saints were to behave with purity and sobriety, uncorrupted in a sinful world. *The Banner of Truth* said they would be 'a pure and chaste people', not defiled by women.[2] Hostile propagandists were of course delighted when Chillenden was expelled from the army and his church after an affair with his maid had come to light.[3] A similar charge was made against Harrison, and Spittlehouse was accused of drunkenness, but apparently without evidence.[4] Behaviour was to be grave. Aspinwall said that in the millennium the saints would not 'break jests, to make the carnal multitude merry'.[5] John More argued that laughter itself was a sin, though 'When the Anchant of dayes shall sit downe . . . Upon a burning fiery throne . . . Then the godly shall Laugh it amaine.' Chamberlen, his more moderate pastor, replied that some laughter sprang from joy, not unbelief.[6] The saints insisted on sobriety in dress. Distinctions in dress, enforced by a series of sumptuary acts, served to indicate and perpetuate social differentiation. To attack the finery of the upper classes, as did the Fifth Monarchists and Quakers, was to attack the social structure.[7] John Pendarves called on the saints to dress plainly as a sign, '*a light amidst a crooked generation*', symbolizing that the saints were 'not of this world' but were 'crucifying the lusts of the flesh, the lusts of the eyes, and pride of life'. He also emphasized the needs of the poor, and asserted that the 'clothing of Christ in his poore members' was 'to be preferr'd before providing such needlesse trimmings'.[8] Rogers condemned lawyers for their long, powdered hair. Trapnel criticized saints who followed the latest French and Spanish fashions, and Tillam attacked effeminate men who wore long hair and shaved off their beards.[9] Mary Cary condem-

[1] M. Cary, *Twelve New Proposals, passim*; Cary, *A Word in Season* (1647), pp. 1–2; anon., *The Failing and Perishing of Good Men* (1663), p. 13; Llwyd, *Gweithiau*, i. 89; Brit. Mus. Add. MS. 38856, f. 79: 'A doore of hope opened into the valley of Achan', ?1663.

[2] *Banner of Truth* (1656), p. 37.

[3] Anon., *The Phanatique Intelligencer* (1660), p. 8; MS. Rawl. A 8, f. 127: S. Otes to R. Jeffes, 15 Nov. 1653; E. Chillenden, *Nathans Parable* (1653), *passim*.

[4] Anon., *A Pair of Spectacles for the Citie* (1648), p. 5; Thurloe, iii. 136.

[5] Aspinwall, *Legislative Power*, p. 25.

[6] MS. Rawl. D 828, f. 39: Church Book of Lothbury Square.

[7] Q. Bell, *Of Human Finery* (1947), *passim*; Barbour, *Quakers*, pp. 167–8.

[8] J. Pendarves, *Arrowes against Babylon* (1656), suffix entitled *Endeavours for Reformation in Apparrel*, pp. 19–20, 21, 25.

[9] E. Rogers, *The Life and Opinions of a Fifth Monarchy man* (1867), p. 91; A. Trapnel, untitled book of verse in Bodleian (1658), p. 553; Tillam, *Temple*, pp. 292–3.

ned people, especially saints, who followed 'fickle, nice, phantastical, and foolish' fashions, remarking 'how unsuitable to their high calling! as if they had not things of a higher nature to minde.' But she thought that in the millennium the saints would appear in 'rich apparel'.[1] Harrison and Chamberlen were from a higher position in society, and showed different ideas. Both wore their hair long. Harrison appeared in Parliament in 'a scarlet coat and cloak, both laden with gold and silver lace', and even went to his execution *'accoutred in a velvet coat and things very compleat'*.[2]

The Fifth Monarchists recognized that both the elect and the reprobate might belong to any social group, and their programme cannot be defined wholly in terms of class. Rogers prophesied doom to 'all that are involved with the Beast', to the beggar as well as the Lord Protector.[3] Nevertheless, the saints did see the millennium as a social revolution, and their enemies accused them of seeking to annihilate the upper levels of society. Feake had indeed taught in 1646 that there was in aristocracy 'an enmity against Christ'. In 1660 he was accused of wanting to destroy the aristocracy and gentry and make the 'Rulers of the Earth . . . sit bare-breeched upon Hawthorn-Bushes'.[4] The onslaught in the *Door of Hope* against the 'old bloody, Popish, wicked Gentry of the Nation' was apparently aimed at the whole of that class.[5]

The demand for social revolution sprang from two sources. The first was a desire for vengeance by people feeling oppressed or humiliated by their social superiors. The saints often showed more enthusiasm for uprooting Babylon than for planting Jerusalem, and their favourite text was Psalm cxlix. 8, with its promise of binding kings with chains and nobles with fetters of iron. Anna Trapnel waited hopefully for the Lord to 'batter' the great men of the earth, praying

> *O come with vengeance, come dear Lord,*
> *That there bloude may drop out,*
> *That do now rob and steal from thee.*[6]

---

[1] Cary, *Little Horns Doom*, pp. 268–9.
[2] Portrait of Harrison in P. G. Rogers, *The Fifth Monarchy Men* (1966), p. 108, and of Chamberlen in *Seventh Day Baptists in Europe and America*, vol. i, ed. C. H. Greene and J. L. Gamble (Plainford, New Jersey, 1910), p. 72; L. Hutchinson, *Memoirs of the Life of Colonel Hutchinson*, ed. C. H. Firth (1906), p. 281; anon., *Observations Upon the Last Actions . . . of . . . Harrison* (1660), p. 4.
[3] Canne, *Time of the End*, epistle by Rogers, *sig.* a8.
[4] Edwards, *Gangraena*, iii. 148; J. Feak, pseud., *A Funeral Sermon* (1660), p. 15; anon., *Bibliotheca Fanatica* (1659), p. 7.   [5] *Door of Hope*, p. 8.
[6] A. Trapnel, *The Cry of a Stone* (1654), p. 19; Trapnel, *Voice for the King of Saints* (1658), p. 19.

Morgan Llwyd anticipated with relish 'plague, flame, sword, and hailestones great' falling on the proud and mighty. Venner's rebels thought themselves chosen by God to 'Thrash the Mountains', and John Simpson preached of his vision of when the 'wicked, ungodly, and unbelieving men shall be raised as slaves, and vassals, and be brought forth in chaines and fetters, before the dreadfull tribunall'.[1] Belcher and Squibb anticipated the ruin of existing rulers and a state of 'dignity and prosperity' for the saints.[2]

A second source of the demand for social revolution was the belief, common to many believers in predestination, that secular aristocracy was as nothing compared to the aristocracy of the elect. 'A Nation', it was said, 'is more beholding to the meanest Kitchin maid in it, that hath in her a spirit of prayer, than to a thousand of her profane swaggering Gentry.'[3] John Rogers condemned the 'corrupt Naughty Nobles' and derided nobility as 'but a fancy for children and fools'. True nobility consisted 'not in *outward pompe* and *vanity*, but in *inward grace* and *piety*. I forget (says honest old *Fox*) *Lords*, and *ladies*, for *society* of his *Saints* . . . And as *Christ* . . . with his *Nobility* (*viz. Saints*) arises *bigward*; Earthly Kings and their *Nobilities* doe fall backward.'[4] Foxe used this concept to disregard the social hierarchy, but for the Fifth Monarchists it was a justification for destroying the social structure. The Barebones Parliament was said to have considered a plan to abolish all titles of honour.[5] Feake preached that in the millennium there would be 'no difference betwixt high and low, the greatest, and the poorest beggar'. Another pamphleteer predicted that 'the Commoner shall be a Freeman, and no longer remain in bondage'.[6] The saints showed their scorn for the existing social order by sometimes refusing hat-honour and using the 'thee' form, like the Quakers. When Venner and his companions were brought before Cromwell in 1657, it was noted that they would 'not put off their hats to the Protector, and *thou* him at every word'. Officials had to pull off Wentworth Day's hat at his trial in 1658, whereupon Day retorted that he was no Quaker but that he kept on his hat

[1] Llwyd, *Gweithiau*, i. 79; Medley, *Standard Set Up*, pp. 11, 23; J. Simpson, *The Great Joy of Saints* (1654), p. 118.
[2] E. A. Payne, 'More about the Sabbatarian Baptists', *Bapt. Quart.*, xiv (1951–2), pp. 162–3.
[3] Anon., *Failing and Perishing*, p. 13.
[4] Rogers, *Ohel*, pp. 11, 22–3.
[5] MS. Clar. 46, f. 71: newsletter, 8 July 1653.
[6] *Thurloe*, v. 755; anon., *The Year of Wonders* (1652), p. 16.

because 'he could not own their authority'.[1] Similarly, Feake and his supporters kept on their hats as a protest when psalms were sung at Christ Church in 1654.[2]

Feake's reference to the end of inequality raises the question of whether millenarian society (as distinct from government) would have been egalitarian. Certainly the Fifth Monarchists felt that even men who were not visible saints would benefit in the millennium. The *Certain Quaeres* of 1649 emphasized that 'natural men (enjoying their Estates) will be at rest also and much satisfied.'[3] The attributes of the future magistrates, specified in the Old Testament and repeated by the Fifth Monarchists, committed the millennial state to a policy of social justice: they included the love of truth, impartiality, mercy, a willingness to help the oppressed and be 'Easers of the people'.[4] The projected reforms in the law, land tenure and the treatment of the poor applied to all, not merely the saints. The Fifth Monarchists advocated social equality, as well as justice, in so far as they rejected the validity of existing distinctions by birth between natural (i.e. unregenerate) men. They attacked the status of the gentry and aristocracy as a whole. But the saints clearly saw themselves as a social as well as a political elite, justified by their divine election. Although the social structure of the millennium was never described in detail, this assumption was often revealed. Simpson expected the saints to appear as kings, and another author saw them as nobles and princes.[5] Spittlehouse spoke of '*our new built* Arrastocracy'. He thought the nobility could be 'excellent ornaments', but the existing nobleman, who cared little for God's work, was 'the foulest fiend the Devill hath upon earth'. Echoing Münster, where John of Leyden had reigned as a messianic king with twelve 'dukes', formerly artisans, Anna Trapnel prophesied that God would make the saints earls and potentates.[6] Society would have been far from egalitarian.

The Fifth Monarchists' hope of a social revolution in the millennium sprang from their dissatisfaction with both existing society and their place within that society. Not all the saints, however,

---

[1] Hist. MSS. Comm., iv., *App. to 5th Report, Sutherland MSS*, p. 163; anon., *A Narrative; Wherein is faithfully set forth* (1658), p. 7; Barbour, *Quakers*, pp. 163–6.
[2] J.N., *Proh Tempora! Proh Mores!* (1654), p. 6.
[3] *Certain Quaeres*, p. 4.
[4] Cf. Rogers, *To his Excellency*, brs.
[5] Simpson, *Great Joy*, p. 118; anon., *Some Considerations*, p. 121.
[6] Spittlehouse, *Rome Ruin'd by Whitehall* (1650), pp. 327, 342; N. Cohn, *The Pursuit of the Millennium* (1962), p. 305; A. Trapnel, *Cry of a Stone*, p. 40.

were social revolutionaries. The few, but important, high-ranking officers and the educated ministers adopted a more conservative position. One defended social differences by arguing that 'Variety *is the* beauty *of the universe, and an exercise of* Vertue. *Where would* bounty, *and* humility *be, if there were not* Rich?'[1] Suggesting in 1653 that the army should elect the new assembly, Spittlehouse wanted to restrict the franchise to the officers, as 'a meanes to keep the private Souldiery at quiet', and because the soldiers had dangerous ideas. He also noted that the 'distinctions of *Masters* and *Servants* are not taken away but maintained' in the New Testament.[2] Peter Chamberlen sought to exclude the 'confused Rabble', and hoped that by his schemes for the poor, they would accept their social status without complaint and become 'more tractable to all duties and commands', for there were 'none more untractable, then idle Beggars'. Many years after the Restoration he wrote to Archbishop Sheldon, expressing his scorn for 'Mechanick Church Wardens'.[3] Some of the saints were themselves alarmed at the threat to property. At the Putney debates in 1647, Colonel Rich pointed out that 'You have five to one in this Kingdom that have no permanent interest' who would 'make it their interest to chuse those that have no interest. It may happen, that the majority may by law . . . destroy propertie.'[4] Despite the saints' preoccupation with sexual offences, Frederick Woodall declared that he 'that affirms a community of persons and things, is more abominably wicked then he that commits the act of Adultery'.[5]

The different attitudes of the saints was shown clearly in the contrasting views they held concerning the Münster Anabaptists. Throughout the 1640s and '50s, critics asserted that all sectarians, especially the Fifth Monarchists, wished to repeat the atrocities which had occurred at Münster.[6] Aspinwall and Canne condemned the Münster Anabaptists, and denied there was any similarity between the movements. Danvers took a middle course, condemning the atrocities, but arguing that the only histories were written by

[1] Anon., *The Cause of God* (1659), sig. B2.
[2] Spittlehouse, *The Army Vindicated* (1653), p. 11; Spittlehouse, *Rome Ruin'd*, p. 171.
[3] P. Chamberlen, *The Poore Mans Advocate* (1649), p. 9; Bodl. MS. Tanner 160, f. 71: Chamberlen to Sheldon, 21 July 1680.
[4] *Clarke Papers*, i. 315.
[5] F. Woodall, *Natural and Spiritual Light* (1655), p. 5.
[6] For example, anon., *A Short History of the Anabaptists of High and Low Germany* (1642); W. Hughes, *Munster and Abingdon* (Oxford, 1657).

the Anabaptists' enemies, and were probably false.[1] John More and
Spittlehouse, however, accepted the Münster Anabaptists as their
greatest inspiration. They spoke of Lutherans as '*no other then Romish
Sectaries*', referred to Catholic, Episcopal and Presbyterian churches
as the 'old Strumpet and her . . . daughters', and described
Müntzer, Storch and Becold as '*Champions of the Truth*'.[2] Militant
saints meeting in 1656 declared boldly that their duty was 'the
same with the work . . . which . . . is reputed a monster and called
Munster' by the unenlightened.[3]

To make permanent their social revolution, the saints needed
to alter the economic structure of society, especially land ownership.
As early as 1645 the millenarians were said to preach that 'the
wicked have no property in their estates. That the promise might
be fulfilled, that the meek must inherit the earth.'[4] The Fifth
Monarchists were often accused of advocating common ownership,
and of planning to confiscate the lands of the gentry and 'ungodly'.
Cromwell claimed that 'if one man had twelve cows, they held
another that wanted cows ought to take a share with his neighbour.[5]
Because of such rumours, many saw the attack on tithes in the
Barebones assembly as the beginning of a total attack on property.[6]

In fact, none of the Fifth Monarchists preached common ownership, and many declared their support for private property.[7]
Nevertheless, many of the saints did have radical plans. Morgan
Llwyd visualized a great redistribution of land so that 'no poor
men shall have too little, nor the rich too much.'[8] Venner's rebels
promised to respect private property, but made no promise concerning the property of those who opposed them. They visualized
seizing great spoils in battle, and massive forfeitures afterwards
through treason and rebellions. In 1657 they proposed to put part

[1] Aspinwall, *Legislative Power*, p. 37; Canne, *A Voice From the Temple* (1653), p. 6;
H. Danvers, *A Treatise of Baptism* (1675), p. 326.
[2] J. Spittlehouse and J. More, *A Vindication of the Continued Succession* (1652),
pp. 14–15.
[3] Anon., *Banner of Truth*, pp. 48–9.
[4] E. Pagitt, *Heresiography* (2nd edn., 1645), p. 126.
[5] Anon., *An Alarum to Corporations* (1659), p. 8; anon., *The Londoners Last Warning*
(1659), p. 5; MS. Rawl. A 61, f. 29: information, ? March 1658; Abbott, *Writings
and Speeches of Oliver Cromwell*, iv. 417.
[6] J. Hall, *Confusion Confounded* (1654), pp. 4–5; anon., *An Answer to a Paper*
(1653), p. 2.
[7] For example, anon., *Certain Quaeres*, p. 4; *The Speeches and Prayers . . . of the
late King's Judges* (1660), p. 19; *Thurloe*, iii. 110–11.
[8] Llwyd, *Gweithiau*, ii. 237.

of it in a common treasury for the 'work of the Lord', with the rest shared out equally between the saints. In 1661 they again planned a treasury to pay for a permanent crusading army.[1]

Although the Fifth Monarchists were a largely urban group they made a number of proposals concerning agrarian conditions. The only detailed suggestions came from groups in East Anglia, or were contained in the manifestos of Venner's two risings, when the saints were seeking the widest possible support. Like the Quakers and the Levellers, they proposed the abolition of all copyhold and customary tenures, and such feudal relics as heriots, fines and amercements. They attacked also the system of primogeniture, which served to perpetuate the inequalities of the social structure.[2] John Rogers condemned fines and homage to lords, and Stoneham's congregation called for the abolition of all 'enslaving' tenures. A petition from Norfolk in 1649 attacked arbitrary fines and 'that unparallel'd Oath of Fealty and Homage', advocating a maximum entry fine of one year's rent, and a maximum rent of 4d–6d *per* acre *per annum*.[3]

To the Fifth Monarchists, the whole social structure was unjust, and they therefore approached the problem of the poor without the common assumption that the poor were '(for the most part) a cursed generation', and without the indifference commonly accompanying it.[4] They did not see the problem as a moral one, nor its solution as either punishment or indiscriminate alms-giving. In 1654 Chamberlen's church urged Cromwell to tackle the problem, and Chamberlen himself described the poor as worthy men, adding 'Who art thou, that despisest the poore? saith the Lord.'[5] Mary Cary was an exception, arguing that able-bodied beggars were idle and should be made to work in the work-house to encourage them to seek better jobs outside. Vavasor Powell, too, thought it shameful that there should be so many beggars who 'may be counterfeits'. But even Cary was concerned about the sick or helpless poor, urging a rate of 3d on all letters to raise funds for them, and Powell helped

---

[1] Burrage, 'Fifth Monarchy Insurrections', p. 731; Medley, *Standard Set Up*, p. 19; anon, *A Door of Hope* (1661), p. 10; *Thurloe*, vi. 163.
[2] Medley, *Standard Set Up*, p. 20; anon., *Door of Hope*, p. 10; Barbour, *Quakers*, pp. 170–1; Brailsford, *Levellers*, pp. 191, 437–43.
[3] Rogers, *Sagrir*, pp. 57–8; Stoneham, *Serious Proposal*, p. 4; *A Perfect Diurnall*, 294 (12–19 March 1649), pp. 2326, 1349 (pagination hopelessly erratic).
[4] C. Hill, *Society and Puritanism in Pre-Revolutionary England* (1966), p. 283; cf. *ibid.*, pp. 259–97.
[5] MS. Rawl. D 828, f. 33a–*v*; Chamberlen, *Poore Mans Advocate*, p. 11.

the local poor with clothing and hospitality, and was said to spend one-fifth of his income on charity.[1]

The saints emphasized the duty of the magistrate to provide work for the poor, a neglected aspect of the Elizabethan legislation, and argued that *'there should be no beggar in Israel,* and in wel-govern'd Common-wealths' there were none. Venner's rebels urged that the poor be set to work, that 'we might have no beggars'.[2] The saints' writings often reflected the growing importance of the commercial and industrial section of society, for which the poor formed a huge pool of cheap captive labour, of immense potential value. The Fifth Monarchists, of course, were far from being capital-ists, yet even Venner's followers, the 'very scum' of society, grasped clearly the importance of production and trade, and advocated mercantilist policies.[3] The most elaborate scheme for the poor came from Chamberlen. He sought to build up a public stock from the lands and goods of the king, bishops and deans and chapters, using also tithes, commons and disused mines. This would provide sufficient agricultural and industrial work to employ the poor, and the profits would enable taxation to be abolished within a year. Ten years later, in 1659, he was still enthusiastic about the scheme. It would need £500,000 to float, and he was confident he could raise this sum from five hundred 'noble, well-intentioned, godly' men. His plan was borrowed and advocated by Lilburne.[4] The idea of using confiscated lands to set up stocks for the poor was also put forward by some Quakers, by Hugh Peter and by William Erbery.[5]

Many of the economic ideas and predictions of the saints reflected the interests and prejudices of the artisan and small trader. The Fifth Monarchists attacked monopolies and the great merchants, predicting 'doleful howling, and mourning among the Merchants of Babilon'. Rogers prophesied the downfall of merchants in Christ's

---

[1] Cary, *Twelve New Proposals,* p. 9; V. Powell, *God the Father Glorified* (1649), p. 60; (E. Bagshaw), *The Life and Death of Mr. Vavasor Powell* (1671), pp. 111, 117.
[2] Chamberlen, *Legislative Power* (1659), p. 5 (misprint for 4); Powell, *God the Father,* p. 60; anon., *Door of Hope,* p. 5; cf. H. Peter, *Good Work for a Good Magistrate* (1651), pp. 20ff; R. H. Tawney, *Religion and the Rise of Capitalism* (1938), pp. 251–70.
[3] See below, pp. 149–50.
[4] Chamberlen, *Poore Mans Advocate,* esp. sig. A4, pp. 3, 17, 24, 43; Chamberlen, *A Scourge for a Denn of Thieves* (1659), pp. 5, 8; *idem., Plus Ultra* (1651), brs; *idem, Declaration and Proclamation,* pp. 4–5; Brailsford, *Levellers,* pp. 613–14.
[5] Barbour, *Quakers,* p. 171; Peter, *Good Work,* pp. 17–18; Nickolls, *Original Letters,* pp. 88–9.

kingdom, and Aspinwall predicted that the 'despicable ones' would lose their 'forreign Trade and Shipping'.[1] Surprisingly, there are no references to the contemporary struggles of the small masters and journeymen to overthrow the oligarchic control of the gilds, except for a general promise in the *Door of Hope* that 'Monarchy and Lordship' would be destroyed in 'Cities, Societies' and elsewhere.[2] Sometimes the viewpoint of the wage-earner found expression, as when Mary Cary looked forward to a time when men would not 'labour and toyl day and night . . . to maintain others that live . . . in idleness'. In the millennium men would 'comfortably enjoy the work of their hands'. This viewpoint was expressed more forcibly in 1675 when a Fifth Monarchist named John Mason took a prominent part in riots by the London weavers.[3]

But many of the saints were engaged in the cloth industry, and they realized that foreign trade was of great importance, and was indeed an essential part of the millennium itself. After the Restoration the saints bewailed 'the lamentable crye of the poore of the lande for wante, through the decay of tradeing'.[4] Chamberlen suggested a national bank to finance the increase of trade, and a fleet permanently at sea to protect merchantmen, and he was echoed by Rogers.[5] The saints often condemned customs duties, but they sought strict protection, not free trade. One pamphleteer condemned Cromwell for 'letting the French upon our Merchants and Manufactors, that the French by having a free-trade may reduce the English to like poverty; and . . . vassellage'.[6] Chamberlen demanded high tolls on all imports of finished goods and exports of raw materials, and complete freedom for the import of raw materials and the export of finished goods.[7] Venner's manifesto in 1661 explained that in the millennium there would be a complete ban on the export of unwrought leather, of fuller's earth, used in the cleansing of cloth, and of other raw materials. Another saint wished to ban the export

[1] Anon., *Banner of Truth*, p. 71; Canne, *Time of the End*, epistle by Rogers, sig. a8; Aspinwall, *A Premonition of Sundry Sad Calamities* (1655), p. 15; anon., *Some Considerations*, p. 2; *Thurloe*, iv. 381; Spittlehouse, *Rome Ruin'd*, sig. a1v.

[2] *Door of Hope*, p. 10.

[3] M. Cary, *Little Horns Doom*, pp. 307–8, 310; *Cal. S.P. Dom.*, *1675–6*, pp. 258–9.

[4] Chamberlen, *Legislative Power*, p. 6 (misprint for 7); Add. MS. 38856, f. 79: 'Doore of hope opened'.

[5] Chamberlen, *Poore Mans Advocate*, p. 24; Chamberlen, *Legislative Power*, p. 7 (misprint for 6); Rogers, *Plain Case*, pp. 20–1.

[6] J.S. (?J. Spittlehouse), *The Picture of a New Courtier* (1656), p. 12.

[7] Chamberlen, *Poore Mans Advocate*, p. 24; Chamberlen, *Declaration and Proclamation*, p. 4.

of fuller's earth to Holland, since it was strengthening England's competitor.[1]

Despite the Fifth Monarchists' concern for production, they had little to say on the important question of usury. They attacked covetousness and 'covetous oppression', and Rogers once widened this to a general attack on trade and production, on *'the Cities and Corporations . . . where every man is . . . seeking himself, . . . buying, selling, building, planting, &c. as in the days of* Noah, *but doth not regard the Day of the Lord! O London! . . . Seat of the second Beast! next to Rome mayst thou look for the Wrath upon thee!'*[2] Rogers attacked usurers, the 'Mony-Merchants', and Chamberlen referred to them disparagingly, but no saint condemned the practice of usury itself.[3] John Brayne, a millenarian minister admired by the Fifth Monarchists, asserted that 'God . . . is expressly against usury', but the saints ignored this passage, perhaps seeing the system as an indispensable evil.[4]

The saints were promised that by the increase of trade and production a golden age of wealth would dawn. Chamberlen was sure that the state would be able to end taxation and pay off the army's arrears, and 'Peace and safety, plenty and prosperity should overflow the Land.'[5] There would be no taxes in the millennium. Venner promised to remove customs, excise and, indeed, all taxes, and Aspinwall promised *'No Custom or Excize in the days of the Messiah.'* Spittlehouse, Stoneham and Powell did the same, and John Williams preached inflammatory sermons against taxes.[6] The saints attacked the heavy rate of taxation under both the Protectorate and the restored Stuarts. Feake claimed, rather disingenuously, that a godly magistrate 'never layd tax upon ye people, but they unasked for gave him what they thought he had need of'. Cromwell and his officials were accused of appropriating state revenues, till they were 'choked with lands, parks, and manors'.[7]

---

[1] Anon., *Door of Hope*, p. 5; D.T., *Certain Queries* (1651), p. 16.
[2] Above, p. 137; Llwyd, *Gweithiau*, ii. 237; Feake, *The New Non-conformist* (1654), p. 10; Canne, *Time of the End*, epistle by Rogers, sig. a6v.
[3] Rogers, *Mene, Tekel* (1654), p. 10; Chamberlen, *Scourge for a Denn*, p. 7.
[4] J. Brayne, *The New Earth* (1653), p. 70. For Brayne see Biog. App.
[5] Chamberlen, *Scourge for a Denn*, p. 4; *Poore Mans Advocate*, pp. 23–4; *Plus Ultra*, brs; *Legislative Power*, p. 6 (misprint for 7).
[6] Anon., *Door of Hope*, p. 10; Aspinwall, *Legislative Power*, p. 12; Spittlehouse, *Royall Advocate*, sig. A3v; Stoneham, *Serious Proposal*, p. 4; Thurloe, ii. 46, iv. 382.
[7] Thurloe, v. 60, vii. 58; Add. MS. 38856, f. 79: 'Doore of hope opened'; *Cal. S.P. Dom., 1653–4*, p. 306; anon., *The Prophets Malachy and Isaiah* (1656), epistle by Feake, p. 14.

The mercantilist approach of the Fifth Monarchists makes it necessary to examine their position on foreign policy. The application of the prophetic texts of the Bible to the contemporary European situation made the saints inevitably outward-looking. Such an interpretation was not restricted to the Fifth Monarchists. The Scottish general, Leslie, had urged a crusade to throw down Rome and the Catholic monarchies. In 1644 this plan was said to be popular amongst the leading politicians and officers in London, and Cromwell once remarked that 'if he were ten years younger, there was not a king in Europe he would not make tremble.' The Quakers called for an attack on Rome. In addition to the religious crusade, John Goodwin, Hugh Peter and the Levellers urged a political crusade against monarchs.[1]

England, according to the Fifth Monarchists, represented a precedent of what God intended to do elsewhere.[2] They showed a strong interest in the cause abroad at all times, and even at his execution Carew could hope that his death would help the cause overseas.[3] The saints wanted a military crusade, firstly on behalf of oppressed Protestants, and secondly to overthrow the popish powers of Antichrist. Venner's group proposed to send help to the Waldensians. Morgan Llwyd advocated a league of Protestant crusaders, and thought 'there were many of them in Holland, some in France, and a few in Spain'.[4] John Rogers demanded 'how durst our *Army* to be still, now the *work* is to do *abroad*? Are there no *Protestants* in *France* and *Germany* (even) now under persecution?'[5] Venner's men called for an invasion of France, Spain, Germany and Rome. Llwyd, Feake, Rogers, Tillinghast and Trapnel all promised that the saints' army would overthrow the Turks and the Pope and his helpers, especially the Habsburgs and the French.[6] On occasion the Fifth Monarchists showed traces of the republican ideology of world revolution. Feake in 1646 thought 'there was in *Monarchie* . . . an enmity against Christ', and that by 'raising combustions in

---

[1] C. Hill, *Puritanism and Revolution*, pp. 130ff; R. Baillie, *Letters and Journals* (Edinburgh, 1775), ii. 24; E. Burrough, *Good Counsel*, p. 26.

[2] Spittlehouse, *The first Addresses* (1653), p. 5.

[3] Anon., *Speeches and Prayers*, p. 14.

[4] Anon., *Door of Hope*, p. 3; M. Llwyd, 'The Book of the Three Birds', trans. L. J. Parry, *Trans. Nat. Eisteddfod of Wales, 1896* (Liverpool, 1898), p. 207.

[5] Rogers, *Sagrir*, p. 14.

[6] Anon., *Door of Hope*, p. 3; Llwyd, 'Book of the Three Birds', p. 207; J.N., *Proh Tempora!*, p. 7; Rogers, *Sagrir*, p. 134; Tillinghast, *Generation-Worke*, 2nd part (1654), pp. 38–41, 57, 69–70, 81–2; Trapnel, untitled book of verse, p. 153.

the bowells' of France, Spain and Holland, Christ would destroy them. John Rogers wanted an alliance with Venice and thought the army should be sent to Bordeaux in 1653 not only because the rebels were Protestants but because they were '*Subjects . . . that lie under the Iron yoke of Tyranny*'.[1]

The wish to crusade against Catholics and tyrants should have led logically to a policy of allying with the Protestant, republican Dutch against Spain, widely regarded as the chief prop of the Papacy. Robert Parker, an earlier apocalyptic writer, had urged an alliance with the Dutch and German Protestant princes against the Habsburgs and the Pope.[2] Chamberlen advised Cromwell to make peace with the Dutch and go to war against France and Spain. But apart from Chamberlen, who admired his 'Neighbours blessed Bee-hive', all the Fifth Monarchist commentators were vociferous advocates of the Dutch war.[3] Even more surprisingly, they opposed the later war with Spain.

Religious, political and economic considerations all led the saints to this unexpected policy. Feake in 1646 had justified his prediction of divine wrath against the Dutch by referring to their sin of 'Tolerating Arminianisme'. Another author condemned them for giving help to the king of Scots.[4] More common was a feeling of anger that instead of joining in a religious alliance, the Dutch had been motivated by '*Covetousness* and *Greediness*, *Ingratitude* and *Unthankfulness*' for English help in the previous century.[5] Rogers pressed for war against the Dutch as a 'treacherous! self-seeking! and ungrateful people!' In similar vein, Powell denounced the Dutch ambassadors as drunkards.[6] The saints, however, made it clear that they did not seek revenge against the Dutch as an end in itself. Feake explained that he would 'never believe that this Navy was made on purpose for the breaking of our Neighbours in pieces; and there an end. We shall at last joyn together, and do such work for God as was never done in the world.' The purpose was to secure an offensive alliance by force. Rogers urged war, but only that a peace might be made 'upon the *account* of Christ, to

[1] Edwards, *Gangraena*, iii. 147–8; Rogers, *Sagrir*, pp. 14, 134.
[2] R. Parker, *The Mystery of the Vialls Opened* (1651), pp. 13–14.
[3] Chamberlen, *Legislative Power*, pp. 7, 6 (misprints for 6, 7).
[4] Edwards, *Gangraena*, iii. 147; anon., *Year of Wonders*, p. 12.
[5] Anon., *The Examiner defended* (1652), p. 18.
[6] Rogers, *Ohel*, introduction, p. 12; A. Griffith, *Mercurius Cambro-Britannicus* (1652), p. 13.

engage together against *Antichrist, Rome, Prelates*'. Morgan Llwyd expressed the same idea in his doggerel verse:

> *Fight not the Dutch but on Christs score . . .*
> *Holland by sea shall be pulld downe . . .*
> *and with us give to Christ their crowne,*
> *and joyne hand in hand . . .*
> *With them wee quarter but one night,*
> *and so to Ffrance and Spaine.*[1]

The Dutch alliance was thought to be essential, not only because of their naval resources, but because the Netherlands were thought to be the best landing place for an English invasion of the continent. At Blackfriars in 1653 a 'great rabble of the rout' was asked where, if peace were made, 'should they have a landing-place, when they went to do the great work of the Lord?' A remonstrance was presented to Barebones, urging the same strategy. The 'most facile' way to conquer Rome, it was claimed, was 'by invading France and Holland'.[2]

The apostasy of the Dutch from the divine crusade was for many Fifth Monarchists the reason for supporting the war of 1652–4, with a zeal expressed in terms of 'fire, murther and flame!'[3] But it appears that the London saints, at least, also recognized the clash between the commercial interests of the English and the Dutch, and hoped by the war to crush their rivals. Venner's rebels feared the competition of the Dutch cloth industry, and the war had brought great benefits to the weavers. The Dutch were cut off from their Spanish source of raw wool, and the English gained a monopoly of the sale of finished cloth to Spain. Moreover the English could hope to end and even usurp the virtual monopoly of trade in the Baltic (a major vent for cloth), which the Dutch had acquired since 1650 by an agreement with Denmark. The war was accordingly popular with the clothworkers, and with the sects in which they were well-represented.[4] Harrison 'choaked the poore Cittizens' with

[1] R. L'Estrange, *The Dissenter's Sayings, The Second Part* (1681), p. 61; Rogers, *Ohel*, introd., p. 13; Llwyd, *Gweithiau*, i. 77.
[2] *Thurloe*, i. 534; cf. *ibid.*, pp. 442, 574, 612; *Moderate Intelligencer*, 10 (4–11 July 1653), p. 110.
[3] *Thurloe*, i. 442.
[4] R. W. K. Hinton, *The Eastland Trade and the Common Weal* (1959), esp. pp. 84ff; J. E. Farnell, 'The Navigation Act of 1651, the First Dutch War, and the London Community', *Econ. Hist. Rev.*, xvi (1963–4), pp. 450–2; *idem*, 'The Usurpation of Honest London Householders: Barebone's Parliament', *Eng. Hist. Rev.*, lxxxii

propaganda, preaching that 'when we have beaten the Dutch, . . . the whole world should saile into this Commonwealth; . . . the Dutch must be destroyed; and we shall have an heaven upon earth.'[1] Mary Cary urged the vigorous prosecution of the war, claiming that God would destroy the Dutch and Danes if they opposed England's interests.[2] Cromwell's peace with the Dutch in 1654, which failed to secure an English monopoly in the Baltic and ended the monopoly in Spain, was received with dismay by the Fifth Monarchists. Chillenden accused him of selling English trade to the Dutch, and Venner's congregation thought the terms not only dishonourable but 'Unsafe'.[3] But on this point, as on others, there was no uniformity within the movement. John Canne specifically condemned the wish to make economic gains from the war, arguing that 'our proper worke is, . . . not to look after Merchants, as to grow great and rich by the wealth of other Nations.' He claimed that 'it is not prizes, or the Enemies Goods, our hearts or hands should desireously be upon; But to destroy *Babylon*, stain the glory of Kings and Kingdom, and lay low the high and great mountains of the earth.'[4]

Spain was regarded as the main support of the Papacy, yet the saints condemned Cromwell's war against Spain, and rejoiced in the failure of the Hispaniola expedition. The reasons they gave were that Cromwell was motivated by greed and ambition, not godliness, and that his failure showed that God's providence was against him.[5] But on other occasions they recognized that God could use ungodly men to accomplish the divine purpose. Since the war involved abandoning to the Dutch the Spanish sources of raw wool, and the market for finished cloth, it seems likely that the real or potential economic effects of the war on the cloth-workers were also a decisive consideration.

The Restoration produced a rapid change in the Fifth Monarchists' outlook on foreign affairs. They viewed with alarm the king's Catholic marriage, and feared the return of popery to England.[6]

(1967), p. 44; *idem.*, 'The Politics of the City of London (1649–57)' (Chicago Univ. Ph.D. thesis, 1963; microfilm in Bodleian), pp. 270–307.
[1] MS. Clar. 45, f. 380v.: newsletter, 13 May 1653.
[2] M. Cary, *The Resurrection of the Witnesses* (1653), p. 133.
[3] *Thurloe*, v. 286; Medley, *Standard Set Up*, p. 7.
[4] J. Canne, *A Voice from the Temple* (1653), p. 39.
[5] Anon., *Some Considerations*, p. 2; Canne, *Time of the End*, p. 88; *Thurloe*, iv. 650.
[6] Add. MS. 38856, f. 79v.: 'Doore of hope opened'.

The Dutch government, despite its failings, was more genuinely Protestant than the Stuart regime. Henceforth the Fifth Monarchists hoped for Dutch support in their intrigues. In 1665 they refused to rise until they saw whether the Dutch would win the naval war and send them help, and Vavasor Powell anticipated a Dutch victory.[1] The economic considerations of the saints had not changed, but they were submerged now that the most immediate problem was that of survival.

The policy of protection had an obvious economic appeal to some of the saints. But many of them can have found little cause for enthusiasm in the detailed social and economic proposals of the preachers and pamphleteers. The strength of millenarianism, however, was the flexibility of the idea. Whatever an individual disliked, he was free to believe would be removed in the kingdom of heaven. Venner's manifesto did particularize, but the saints left their plans open-ended, noting that 'whatsoever can be named of a common or publick good, we meane by the Kingdome of Christ.'[2]

It is likely that many saints derived their enthusiasm more from generalized biblical promises than from detailed programmes, and the most common descriptions of the millennium were in simple and timeless terms. The saints were promised long life and immunity from sickness. *The Banner of Truth* guaranteed them immortality, and Aspinwall and Danvers predicted perfect health. Mary Cary thought the saints 'shall live till they come to a good old age'. In addition, there would be peace and plenty, and prosperity without hard work.[3] Taxation would cease.[4] To achieve such a glorious condition, human nature, and indeed all nature, would be transformed miraculously at the beginning of the millennium. As for the wolf and the leopard, Christ would 'chaine up their devouring nature'.[5] Henceforth the saints would enjoy a 'store of provisions, . . . and treasure'.[6]

[1] *Cal. S.P. Dom., 1663–4*, p. 405; ibid., '64–5, p. 514; ibid., '65–6, p. 270; ibid., '66–7, p. 427; SP. 29/114, fos. 19–20v.: information, ? March 1665; SP. 29/129, f. 187: A. Newport to Williamson, 22 Aug. 1665. See also below, p. 212–13.
[2] Anon., *Door of Hope*, p. 5.
[3] Anon., *Banner of Truth*, p. 20; Aspinwall, *Brief Description*, p. 13; Aspinwall, *Legislative Power*, p. 35; Danvers, *Theopolis*, pp. 39, 77; Cary, *Little Horns Doom*, p. 71.
[4] See above, p. 150.
[5] N. Homes, *The Resurrection Revealed* (1654), p. 507; anon., *Banner of Truth*, p. 20; R. Tichborne, *The Rest of Faith* (1649), p. 46.
[6] Aspinwall, *Brief Description*, p. 13.

As a result of these changes, the Fifth Monarchists guaranteed everlasting happiness. God would fill the saints 'with joy and rejoycing and turn their mourning into joy, so that they shall not sorrow any more at all'. Aspinwall promised 'glory and happines', and Danvers spoke of 'when *Jerusalem* shall be a rejoycing and her people a joy'.[1] John Bunyan, a millenarian though not a Fifth Monarchist, looked forward to when it would be 'always summer, always sunshine, always pleasant, green, fruitful, and beautiful'. 'All the spiders, and dragons, and owls and foul spirits of Antichrist' would be destroyed, whilst the 'pretty robins' would 'most sweetly send forth their pleasant notes'.[2]

Several contemporaries realized that it was these general and sweeping promises that attracted mass support. Thurloe reflected cynically that though the Fifth Monarchists 'speake great words of . . . the beautifull kingdom of holies, which they would erect . . . yet the baits they lay to catch men with are taking away of taxes, excise, customs, and tithes'. Another critic observed that to stir up men to sedition thay made 'large promises . . . of Health, Wealth, Peace, Protection'.[3] A more sympathetic commentator appreciated that 'Men variously impoverished by the long troubles, full of discontents, and tired by long expectation of amendment must needs have great propensions to hearken to those that proclaim times of refreshing—a golden age—at hand.'[4] It seems probable that the appeal of Fifth Monarchism to the rank and file was based on the three considerations of vengeance on their social superiors, the end of all taxation, and a generalized vision of future bliss.

[1] Cary, *Little Horns Doom*, p. 74; Aspinwall, *Brief Description*, p. 13; Danvers, *Theopolis*, p. 39.

[2] J. Bunyan, *The Holy City*, in *Works*, ed. G. Offor (1862), iii. 409, 459.

[3] *Thurloe*, vi. 185; T. Hall, *Chiliasto-mastix redivivus* (1657), p. 53.

[4] R. Vaughan, *The Protectorate of Oliver Cromwell* (1839), i. 156.

CHAPTER SEVEN

Fifth Monarchists and the Reform of the Law

A demand for drastic reforms in the law was one of the most frequent items in Fifth Monarchist programmes. The saints' concern was shared not merely by the radical movements of the interregnum but since the early sixteenth century and throughout society. This preoccupation represented the convergence of several sources of discontent. There was firstly a long tradition of resentment at the corruption of the lawyers. Secondly there was a belief among lower social classes that the organization and content of the law made it an instrument of social oppression. More recently, the rapid movement of parts of society towards commerce and industry convinced more influential groups that traditional law was unsatisfactory.[1]

The Fifth Monarchists were concerned with the administration, organization and content of the law. Complaints at the lawyers' greed and corruption were traditional. There were often long delays in deciding suits, which were seen as a device to increase fees. The court of Chancery was said to have a back-log of 23,000 cases.[2] Fees and 'gifts' were payable to the lawyer, the judge, the prison-officer and, as a Fifth Monarchist condemned to death discovered, even to the hangman to secure a speedy departure from the world.[3] Another major grievance was the centralization of justice, which produced further delays and compelled the poor to travel to London on trivial matters. John Jones of Neath, Glamorgan, complained that poor men were brought from Yorkshire and Cornwall to appear in cases involving no more than five shillings,

---

[1] For a summary see E. W. Ives, ed., *The English Revolution, 1600–1660* (1968), pp. 115–30.
[2] L.D., 'An exact relation' (1654) in *Somers Tracts*, vi. 275.
[3] Anon., *A Narrative of the Apprehending . . . of John James* (1662), p. 26.

on pain of outlawry.[1] These abuses made it difficult for anyone
to obtain justice, and put the law entirely out of the reach of the
poor. The popular legends of Gamelyn and Robin Hood, dating
from the fourteenth century, embodied the belief that justice could
only be found outside the law: the climax of Gamelyn's tale shows
the hero executing corrupt justices, sheriff and jury.[2] There could
be little hope of justice against the gentleman who was also the
local Justice of the Peace. There was equally little justice in the
system whereby punishment was made to fit the status of the
criminal rather than the crime. Whipping and mutilation were confined to the lower classes, and the outcry when Prynne lost his
ears sprang from the fact that he was a gentleman, not from the
brutality of the sentence in itself.[3] The poor would probably have
agreed with the assertion of the German Anabaptist, Thomas
Müntzer, that the nobility were guilty of colossal robbery in sharing
out the land between themselves, and yet dared to hang the poor for
petty theft.[4] Oliver Cromwell conceded that the law, 'as it is now
constituted, serves only to maintain the lawyers, and to encourage
the rich to oppress the poor'.[5]

In this sphere, the complaints of the Fifth Monarchists were
very similar to those of other groups. John Rogers, for example,
condemned the 'Norman' language of the laws, and complained of
the centralization which made suitors come to London, 'to wait
there for *justice* four, five, six, eight, or ten *years* in Law, till the
Norman Lawyers have made themselves rich by removing *suits* out of
one *Court* into another, and by retarding of *justice*, to the *ruine* of
the *Client*'.[6]

Something was done during the interregnum to meet these complaints. The Rump ordered that all legal proceedings and records
should be in English, and established a committee which considered
more far-reaching plans. The Barebones assembly produced more
radical, though abortive, proposals, and the first Protectorate
Parliament made some short-lived modifications to Chancery. But
most plans were obstructed by the unwavering opposition of almost
all lawyers. 'We cannot mention the reformation of the law,'

[1] J. Jones, *Works* (1650), pp. 104–5. (Not to be confused with the Fifth Monarchist John Jones.)
[2] M. Keen, *The Outlaws of Medieval Legend* (1961), pp. 78–173.
[3] C. Hill, *Society and Puritanism in Pre-Revolutionary England* (1966 edn.), pp. 385–7.
[4] N. Cohn, *The Pursuit of the Millennium* (1962 edn.), pp. 262–3.
[5] E. Ludlow, *Memoirs*, ed. C. H. Firth (Oxford, 1894), i. 246.
[6] J. Rogers, *Sagrir* (1653), pp. 49–51. On the 'Norman Yoke' see below, p. 167.

Cromwell complained, 'but they presently cry out, we design to destroy propriety.'[1]

These minor changes did not appease the radicals. The Fifth Monarchists sought the total abolition of the legal profession and of all existing law courts. They called for the total abolition of fees, and for the layman's right to plead his own cause.[2] It was claimed that the Barebones Parliament, in which they had an active group, had defeated by only one vote a motion to banish all lawyers from London, as no longer necessary.[3] Merely to adopt the English language in law was not a sufficient defence against the lawyers. '*Are not the* Lawyers *as compleat* Knaves *in plaine* English *as they are in their* other language?' asked John Rogers. The whole legal profession must be abolished and not replaced.[4] Rogers also suggested a land register in each county to record mortgages and land transactions, which would reduce litigation.[5]

Other radical groups, including the Levellers and Quakers, produced similar proposals, calling for the reduction of fees, the simplification of procedure, the right of laymen to plead their own causes and the codification of the law.[6]

Nothing was done to alter the organization of the courts, though this was one of the radicals' chief concerns. The Levellers called for the abolition of all central courts, including Chancery, and of central judges on circuit. They argued that all cases should be tried locally before elected judges and juries.[7] The Independent minister Hugh Peter suggested that each hundred should choose three peacemakers each year to settle small disputes. Legal offices should be elective, and there should be no appeal outside the county where the case originated.[8] John Brayne, minister of the Soke, Winchester, derived from the Bible a plan for permanent judges in each city, with a supreme sanhedrin of 72 judges as the highest appeal.[9] The

---

[1] G. B. Nourse, 'Law Reforms under the Commonwealth and Protectorate', *Law Quart. Rev.*, lxxv (1959), pp. 512–29; M. Cotterell, 'Interregnum law reform: the Hale Commission of 1652', *Eng. Hist. Rev.*, lxxxiii (1968), pp. 689–704; Ludlow, *Memoirs*, i. 246.

[2] Rogers, *Sagrir*, p. 139; J. Spittlehouse, *The Royall Advocate* (1655), sig. A4.

[3] Bodl. MS. Clar. 47, f. 43: newsletter, 4 Nov. 1653.

[4] Rogers, *Ohel* (1653), pp. 222–3; Rogers, *Sagrir*, p. 62.

[5] Bodl. MS. Rawl. A 47, f. 34: Rogers to Cromwell, ?Dec. 1653/Jan. 1654.

[6] S. Prall, *The Agitation for Law Reform* (The Hague, 1966), *passim*; H. N. Brailsford, *The Levellers and the English Revolution* (1961), pp. 531, 535; W. Schenk, *The Concern for Social Justice* (1948), p. 124.   [7] Brailsford, *Levellers*, pp. 531–2.

[8] H. Peter, *Good Work for a Good Magistrate* (1651), pp. 29, 38–42.

[9] J. Brayne, *The New Earth* (1653), p. 5, citing 2 Chron. xix. 5 and Deut. xvi. 18. For Brayne see Biog. App.

Fifth Monarchists Rogers, Spittlehouse and Chamberlen called for judges to be elected in each city. Rogers also urged that each shire should choose six men to settle causes over land, trespass, or assault and battery, before a jury.[1] The manifesto of Venner's rising in 1657 elaborated a scheme by which a court was to meet each month in every market town for minor cases, and in each county town every three months for major cases, with a supreme council for appeals. The judges and officials were not to be chosen by all the free men, as the Levellers proposed, but by the 'Lord's Freemen', the members of the gathered churches.[2]

The Fifth Monarchists were unanimous in seeking not to reform but to abolish Chancery, and they found widespread support when they attempted in the Barebones Parliament to abolish it.[3] They intended to abolish all existing courts, and attacked Chancery first probably because it was so widely unpopular. But it was felt too that the distinction of a court of equity and an ordinary court proved that there was no equity in common law.[4] In the millennium, Chancery would be unnecessary. 'Was there ever sutes for Title of Land heard of in all the worst of Kings of Israel?' asked Peter Chamberlen. The adoption of God's laws would 'end all sutes in a day, and payes all Debts without Arrests or Imprisonments'.[5]

Decentralization and the abolition of the lawyers' privileges would go far towards ending the role of the law as an instrument of social oppression. This objective was stressed repeatedly. Venner's manifesto emphasized that justice must be 'without respect of Persons, or taking of gifts and bribes' and demanded that 'no person of what Ranck, Degree, or Qualities soever be priviledged from law'. 'What do Priviledges signifie,' Chamberlen asked, 'saving thou shalt not Steal, but I may.'[6] John More took offence at the Protector's right to pardon offences other than murder and treason, for it *'made void'* God's law, which 'appointeth death in other cases'.[7]

---

[1] Rogers, *Sagrir*, p. 139; Spittlehouse, *Royall Advocate*, sig. A3v.; Chamberlen, *The Declaration and Proclamation of the Army of God* (1659), p. 4; MS. Rawl. A 47, f. 34: Rogers to Cromwell.
[2] W. Medley, *A Standard Set Up* (1657), pp. 17–18.
[3] See above, pp. 70, 73.
[4] A. Boon, *Examen Legum Angliae* (1656), p. 45.
[5] P. Chamberlen, *Legislative Power in Problemes* (1659), p. 5 (misprint for 4).
[6] Medley, *Standard Set Up*, pp. 16, 17, 19; Chamberlen, *Legislative Power*, p. 5; T. Higgenson, *Sighs for Righteousness* (1654), p. 10.
[7] J. More, *A Trumpet sounded* (1654), p. 17.

Fifth Monarchists and the Reform of the Law

The Fifth Monarchists, like many others, wanted to change the content as well as the administration of the law. The growth of commerce and industry rendered old laws inadequate and obstructive. It has been argued that L.C.J. Coke tried to by-pass the problem by giving judgements favourable to the business community on the basis of a single precedent, even against the whole stream of tradition, although recently this has been disputed.[1] Others thought that the laws would have to be altered by Parliament. James I in 1607 spoke of 'the obscuritie . . . want of fulnesse and variation' of the laws, and called for the 'clearing and the sweeping off' of most of them. Francis Bacon urged the codification of the law, with the repeal of obsolete laws and the enactment of new statutes where necessary.[2]

Further pressure for reforms derived from the humanists' realization that crime was produced by the failings of society as well as those of the criminal. Sir Thomas More pointed out that society first created thieves and then hanged them. Thomas Starkey ascribed to Cardinal Pole the view that the laws were unjustifiably barbarous as well as ineffective.[3] Oliver Cromwell accepted this reasoning, and declared that 'to hang a man for sixpence, threepence, I know not what; . . . This is a thing God will reckon for.'[4]

Material interests were involved as well as humanitarian ones. In early capitalist society criminals were seen as potential cheap labourers. Existing practices seemed irrational, for executing a thief did not restore stolen goods, and gaoling a debtor did not help the creditor. Both More and Starkey urged that the thief should be spared, but should be put to work by the state, and made to repay the goods stolen.[5] Most of the radical reformers of the interregnum wanted to abolish the death penalty for theft and the

---

[1] Hill, *Society and Puritanism*, pp. 153–9; R. H. Tawney, *Religion and the Rise of Capitalism* (1938 edn.), pp. 165–8, 236; D. O. Wagner, 'Coke and the Rise of Economic Liberalism', *Econ. Hist. Rev.*, vi (1935–6), pp. 30–44; B. Malament, 'The "Economic Liberalism" of Sir Edward Coke', *Yale Law Journal*, lxxvi (1966–7), pp. 1321–58.

[2] James I, *The Political Works*, ed. C. H. McIlwain (New York, 1965), pp. 292–3; F. Bacon, *Works*, ed. J. Spedding, R. L. Ellis, D. D. Heath (1857–74), v. 98–100, xii. 41, 84–6, xiii. 57–71, xiv. 181, 358–64.

[3] A. B. Ferguson, *The Articulate Citizen and the English Renaissance* (Durham, N. Carolina, 1965), esp. chap. 7; T. More, *The Complete Works*, ed. E. Surtz and J. H. Hexter (New Haven and London, 1965), iv. 71; T. Starkey, *A Dialogue between . . . Pole . . . and Lupset*, ed. K. M. Burton (1948), pp. 114–15, 174.

[4] W. C. Abbott, *Writings and Speeches of Oliver Cromwell*, iv. 274.

[5] More, *Works*, iv. 77; Starkey, *Dialogue*, p. 177; G. Rusche and O. Kirchheimer, *Punishment and Social Structure* (New York, 1939), esp. pp. 24–52.

imprisonment of debtors, ten thousand of whom were said to be languishing in prison.[1]

There seems to be little connection between these rational and humanitarian proposals, and the Fifth Monarchists' demand for the restoration of the Mosaic Code, which brought them abuse and ridicule. Marchamont Needham, journalist and government propagandist, mocked the saints for wishing to bring in the 'whole Catalogue of old dreaming Rabbies, to justle out *Coke* and *Littleton*'. The saints were stung by the allegations of 'that blasphemous *Rabshakeh*, *Needham*' that everyone would have to be 'seven years apprentice to *Moses*'.[2] Cromwell feared the effect of the Mosaic laws, open to the subjective interpretation of anyone, however ignorant, would be 'the confusion of all things'. A member of Barebones feared it would 'shortly have introduced the bitterest and sorest persecution'. A number of Presbyterian ministers expressed the fear in 1654 that the Mosaic laws would lead not to the kingdom of Christ but a new Egyptian bondage.[3]

The Fifth Monarchists were not prepared to accept partial alterations within the existing laws. 'It is not enough to change some of these *Lawes*, and so to *reforme* them (as is intended by most of you),' John Rogers told the members of Barebones. 'O no: that wil be to poor *purpose*, and it is not *your worke* now, which is to provide for the *Fifth* [Monarchy] . . . by bringing in the *Lawes* of *God* given by *Moses*.'[4] Almost every Fifth Monarchist pamphlet demanded the establishment of the Law of God, though many did not particularize beyond that. When on trial for treason, Harrison and several of Venner's followers demanded to be tried by the Law of God, and so did John James, 'at which the lawyers gave a great hiss'.[5] Though Rogers asserted that law should be based on reason and the will of the people, he argued that God's law represented pure reason and the real popular will.[6]

It is necessary to examine what the saints meant by 'God's law'. It was generally agreed that the term covered three separate

---

[1] Brailsford, *Levellers*, pp. 127–8, 531, 649; Schenk, *Concern for Social Justice*, p. 124.
[2] *The Observator*, 1 (24–31 Oct. 1654), p. 8; Spittlehouse, *Royall Advocate*, sig. A4.
[3] Abbott, *Writings and Speeches*, iv. 489; anon., *An Answer to a Paper* (1653), p. 3; H. Chambers *et al.*, *An Apology for the Ministers of the County of Wilts.* (1654), p. 16.
[4] Rogers, *Sagrir*, sig. A4–v.
[5] H. Finch, earl of Nottingham, *An Exact and most Impartial Accompt of the . . . Trial . . . of Twenty nine Regicides* (1660), pp. 21, 30; *Somers Tracts*, vii. 470; T. B. Howell, *A Complete Collection of State Trials*, vi (1816), p. 75.
[6] Rogers, *Sagrir*, pp. 32ff, 45, 137, 139.

branches. First there was the moral law, that is, the Ten Commandments and the Sermon on the Mount.[1] Secondly there was the
judicial law, the various judgements for infringing these rules,
contained mostly in the five Books of Moses. Lastly there was the
ceremonial law, the rules and statutes of Aaron governing the Jewish
church, its feasts, rituals and sacrifices. Christian churches had pre-
served a large degree of unity concerning these laws. In seventeenth-century England all (except the Ranters and other antinomian and perfectionist sects) agreed that the moral laws were still in
force, as a moral guide. All agreed that with the coming of Christ's
church the ceremonial law was 'utterly abolished'.[2] Until the rise
of the Fifth Monarchists it was also generally agreed that the
judicial laws had applied only to the ancient state of Israel, and
were now irrelevant. As long as a nation's laws were generally in
accord with the moral law, theologians were willing to accept the
right of the magistrate to alter details as times and circumstances
demanded. Calvin taught that laws might vary from place to place
as long as they did not infringe equity, which was the basis of
the moral law. Bishop Hooper thought it sufficient that laws did
not actually contradict God's law.[3] The Puritan, Richard Sibbes,
thought the Old Testament laws were full of 'difficulty and obscurity', and when William Gouge noted the difference between
Jewish and current penalties for breaching the Sabbath, he seemed
to feel that it was the Old Testament penalty for which excuses
needed to be found.[4] The fact that thieves were now executed
instead of making multiple restitution, as in Israel, was justified
because 'the necessitie is greater amongst us', and, by William
Perkins, because the Jews were richer than the English so that
property had been of relatively less importance.[5]

The Fifth Monarchists were prepared to accept that the ceremonial laws were defunct. But they demanded the full implementa-
tion of the judicial laws. The fact that these would be wholly

[1] Exod. xx.; Deut. v.; Matt. v–vii.

[2] Spittlehouse, *Royall Advocate*, p. 6; though see below, p. 202.

[3] C. D. Cremeans, *The Reception of Calvinistic Thought in England* (Urbana, 1949),
pp. 12, 13, 106; *The Later Writings of Bishop Hooper*, ed. C. Nevinson, Parker
Society, xlvi (1852), p. 77.

[4] R. Sibbes, *Complete Works*, ed. A. B. Grosart (Edinburgh, 1862–4), iv. 204; W.
Gouge, *Annotations Upon all the Books of the Old and New Testament* (2nd edn., 1651),
note on Numb. xv. 35 (unpaginated).

[5] J. Weemse, *An Explication of the Iudiciall Lawes of Moses* (1632), p. 148; W.
Perkins, *Works* (1612–13), i. 64; cf. C. H. and K. George, *The Protestant Mind of
the English Reformation* (Princeton, New Jersey, 1961), pp. 225ff.

inadequate for regulating disputes over property or commercial matters was hardly noticed. Chamberlen said simply that such disputes would not exist in the millennium. Rogers, who alone faced the problem, was compelled to abandon the Bible and suggest a land register.[1]

None of the Fifth Monarchist pamphleteers gave a full account of the projected code, and there is no sign that any made a systematic study of the Old Testament references. Aspinwall observed merely that they 'lye scattered up and down in the holy Scriptures'. Though he published a list of crimes and their biblical penalties, this was taken from the projected Mosaic law-code for Massachus-etts, drawn up by the New England minister, John Cotton.[2] Otherwise the saints were content to refer to the works of John Brayne and of A. Boon, otherwise unknown, which set out the commandments, statutes and judgements. Neither Brayne nor Boon was a Fifth Monarchist.[3]

The saints' pamphlets suggest that they were interested in two specific areas of the law rather than with the problem as a whole. They were preoccupied firstly with the laws relating to theft and debt, and secondly with those regulating personal morality, mainly sexual but also covering observance of the Sabbath and obedience to parents. Many writers stressed the judicial laws concerning theft and debt, by which the restitution of stolen goods and the repayment of the debt would replace the existing penalties of death and imprisonment respectively. Most urged severer penalties for sexual offences, though often in vague terms. Rogers claimed it was '*manslaughter* to put any to death for *mere theft*', and wicked and cruel to gaol debtors. He suggested that thieves should be sold into hard labour, or otherwise put to work to pay back what they had stolen.[4] The manifestos of Venner's risings called for God's law in its entirety, but ignoring moral offences specified only that thieves should be set to work to restore the value of what they had taken, and that there should be relief for the 'abuses and oppressions' afflicting both creditors and debtors. Chamberlen called for debtors to be freed and set to work to pay back what they owed. He urged

---

[1] Above, pp. 159–60.
[2] W. Aspinwall, *A Brief Description of the Fifth Monarchy* (1653), p. 9; Aspinwall, *The Legislative Power* (1656), pp. 30–2; J. Cotton, *An Abstract of Laws* (1655), *passim*.
[3] Brayne, *New Earth*, pp. 12–78: cited by Rogers, *Sagrir*, p. 114; Spittlehouse *Royall Advocate*, p. 29. A. Boon, *Examen Legum*, *passim*: cited by anon. *The Fifth Monarchy . . . Asserted* (1659), p. 51; anon., *The Old Leaven Purged* (1658), p. 11.
[4] Rogers, *Sagrir*, pp. 81, 109.

also strict penalties against sexual offenders, though without giving details.[1] Spittlehouse considered that in condemning thieves, judges were condemning themselves to eternal damnation.[2] Of all the Fifth Monarchist writers, only Aspinwall and Spittlehouse said specifically that all moral offences should be punished by death if they had been in Israel, though More also implied this.[3] When the saints' general demands are broken down into detailed proposals, they seem for the most part quite closely in line with other contemporary suggestions. It was the justification they gave for their legal proposals which was most exceptional.

Two problems surround the Fifth Monarchist attitude to law: why the pamphleteers believed that the judicial laws of Moses were still valid, and why the Mosaic laws proved a popular part of the saints' programme. The Fifth Monarchists themselves explained their support for the judicial laws by arguing that God had commanded them and had never revoked this command. They cited Christ's words, 'Think not that I am come to destroy the Law', and those of the Apostles: 'Do we then make void the law . . . ? God forbid: . . . we establish the law.'[4] Though Christ had rejected death for adultery, Spittlehouse explained that this was only because the true law could not be enforced, owing to the Roman occupation of Israel.[5] The Norfolk petitioners argued that since God had supplied the law, it would be a 'sin, . . . to set up the dim light of nature for our law'. The law was already complete and 'practicable within one Moneth', and Thomas Higgenson argued that 'nothing might be diminished, because it was one, nor anything added thereto, because it was perfect'. 'Can men make Lawes better than God?' Rogers asked the Barebones Parliament. 'Then if *Moses* dare not set up any other *Lawes*, . . . how dare you?'[6] Chamberlen insisted that law came only from God, and not 'from Kings (as some would have it) or (as others say) from the People, who themselves never had it'. He argued that the judicial laws were eternal, asking 'Whether Time or Place, Nation or Sex alter that Law? or whether God be altered

---

1 Medley, *Standard Set Up*, p. 15; anon., *A Door of Hope* (1661), p. 5; Chamberlen, *Declaration and Proclamation*, p. 5; Chamberlen, *Legislative Power*, p. 3.
2 J. Spittlehouse, *The first Addresses to . . . the Lord General* (1653), p. 17.
3 Aspinwall, *Legislative Power*, pp. 30–1; Spittlehouse, *First Addresses*, p. 21; J. More, *Trumpet Sounded*, p. 17.
4 Matt. v. 17; Romans iii. 31, both quoted by Spittlehouse, *Royall Advocate*, p. 5.
5 Spittlehouse, *First Addresses*, p. 23.
6 Anon., *Certain Quaeres* (1649), p. 8; Chamberlen, *Legislative Power*, p. 2; T. Higgenson, *Sighs for Righteousness* (1654), p. 19; Rogers, *Sagrir*, sig. A4v.

that made it? so that, what was Idolatry, Blasphemy, Murther, Adultery, Theft, or Fals Witness so long agoe in *Palestine* among the Jewes; is it not so now in *England* among the Gentiles?' To those who said that law should be based on reason and precedent, he replied that there could be no one more rational than God, and no precedent older than the Books of Moses.[1]

The saints thus rested their position on an objective interpretation of the biblical texts, and it would be impossible to doubt their great reliance on the letter of Scripture. The institutions and laws of the Jews, the first chosen people, had a special appeal to the builders of the New Jerusalem. The call for the laws of the Jews was consistent with the Fifth Monarchists' demand for the Old Testament political institutions, and their interest in Jewish religious practices, such as the Seventh-Day Sabbath. Nevertheless, the disproportionate importance they gave to the problems of theft and debt suggests that they were attracted to specific doctrines which earlier teachers, equally bibliocentric, had found less appealing or unacceptable. Moreover, their omission of the judicial law's condemnation of usury, which Brayne did include, suggests they were not wholly dispassionate.[2] It is, then, worth seeking a social basis for their demands. Their programme seems to have been one attractive to the small producers, sharing the aspirations of mercantilist society. Usury was accepted tacitly. The relief of debtors meant also the security of the creditors, and the reprieve of the thief meant the return of the value of the goods stolen. Humanitarianism coincided with the better protection of property. Only one of the Fifth Monarchist writers was sufficiently impartial to include a biblical teaching which protected debtors at the expense of creditors, namely, the Old Testament law that debts were quashed after seven years.[3] The other pamphleteers failed to notice the point. The demand that 'manstealers be punished with death' according to the Mosaic law may well have been connected with the practice of kidnapping children and apprentices and 'spiriting' them to Virginia and elsewhere as forced labour. This practice was common in London by the 1650s, and mob riots against such 'Spirits' had already led to several deaths.[4]

[1] Chamberlen, *Legislative Power*, pp. 2, 3, 5 (misprint for 4).
[2] Brayne, *New Earth*, p. 70; see above, p. 150.
[3] Aspinwall, *Legislative Power*, pp. 30–2.
[4] *Door of Hope*, p. 5; J. C. Jeaffreson, ed., *Middlesex County Records*, iii (1888) esp. pp. 182, 254–5, 278. I owe this suggestion to Dr. R. Clifton.

Fifth Monarchists and the Reform of the Law

Many of the saints were not independent producers but journey-men, labourers and apprentices, who would not have had the same interest in changing the laws on theft and debt. But equally they would have had no reason to support the ferocious and repressive laws which defended the privileges of the property-owning classes. Lord Burghley had been informed in 1596 that 'the simple country man or woman' would not help to convict even vagabonds known to be thieves because 'they would not procure any man's death for all the goods in the world'. Probably many shared the opinion of Major William Rainborough, voiced at Putney, that the 'cheif end' of government was 'to preserve persons as well as estates'.[1] Perhaps still more important, the Fifth Monarchist preachers were able to stir up popular hatred against the lawyers by portraying them as an integral part of the antichristian Fourth Monarchy and of an alien tyranny. The saints fitted the lawyers into the popular myth of the 'Norman Yoke'. Chamberlen claimed that the lawyer 'enslaves us to the Norman Tyranny', and Spittlehouse alleged that existing laws were derived from the 'corrupt reason of *William the Conqueror*'.[2] Rogers's work *Sagrir* suggested there was a vast conspiracy of lawyers and landowners to oppress the nation, and he called for the '*Peoples Liberties* from the *Norman* and *Babylonian Yokes*'. He ascribed all the abuses in the content and administration of the law to the Norman Conquest, and also cited Domesday Book to prove that heavy taxation was a Norman innovation. By denouncing King William and all his successors as the little horn of Daniel vii. 8, Rogers contrived to blend Norman and biblical propaganda. He placed the whole civil war in the Norman context, arguing that '*Oliver* the *Conquerer* went out to War, and ingaged against the *Normans*, . . . for the people, to free them from *tyranny*'.[3] So the lawyer ceased to be a remote, irrelevant figure; as a vital prop of the existing social structure, he became a natural target for popular hatred.

The Fifth Monarchists' extreme penalties for immoral behaviour, especially sexual offences, were largely in line with general Puritan thinking. The Rump actually passed measures establishing the death penalty for adultery, incest and blasphemy, and severe penalties for

---

[1] C. Hill, *Puritanism and Revolution* (1962), p. 233n.; *The Clarke Papers*, ed. C. H. Firth (Camden Soc., new series, xlix, liv, lxi–ii, 1891–1901), i. 320.
[2] Chamberlen, *Legislative Power*, p. 6 (misprint for 5); Spittlehouse, *First Addresses*, p. 17; see on the Norman Yoke, Hill, *Puritanism and Revolution*, pp. 50–122.
[3] Rogers, *Sagrir*, title page, pp. 39, 47, 49, 51, 56–8, 81, 89, 110, 125.

swearing and for profanation of the Sabbath.[1] The literal implications of the saints' programme were, of course, even more bloodthirsty, though few writers actually specified the extensive use of the death penalty.[2] Edward Stennet, on the fringe of the movement, called for the judicial laws, but added that many Old Testament magistrates had used leniency.[3] It is possible that some saints knew only the outlines, not the details of the Mosaic Code. John Cowell declared that he left Stennet's church in horror when he discovered, after at least thirteen years' membership, that the judicial law laid down the death penalty for profanation of the Sabbath.[4]

The exact beliefs of most members are unobtainable, but it is clear that they supported rigorous discipline. Perhaps in part this can be traced back to the taste of urban craftsmen for the productive virtues of sobriety and discipline. Perhaps too it represents the common sectarian rejection of conventional moral behaviour.[5] Their emphasis on the godly life, like their belief in themselves as the elect, served to justify their self-appointed role as God's true magistracy commissioned to wreak divine vengeance on the 'swaggering gentry' and 'naughty Nobles'.[6]

But the saints' call for the whole law of Moses cannot be explained adequately solely in social terms. It has to be fitted into a tradition of advocacy of the Mosaic Code which went back far beyond the interregnum. The saints were fond of citing the tradition that the mythical British king, Lucius, and Alfred the Great had modelled their laws on the Ten Commandments.[7] The Lollards had held a number of views similar to the Fifth Monarchists'. Wyclif attacked the profiteering lawyers and argued that men were not bound to obey laws not based on scripture. He condemned the view that 'sinful men's laws, full of error, be more needful than the gospel'. William Swynderby condemned the imprisonment of debtors.[8]

---

[1] Nourse, 'Law Reform', p. 517.
[2] See above, p. 165.
[3] E. Stennet, *The Royall Law Contended for* (2nd edn., 1667), pp. 26–7. For Stennet see Biog. App.
[4] J. Cowell, *The Snare Broken* (1677), pp. 46–51.
[5] W. Stark, *The Sociology of Religion* (1966–7), ii. 184–97.
[6] Anon., *The Failing and Perishing of Good Men* (1663), p. 13; Rogers, *Ohel*, introd., p. 11.
[7] For example, Chamberlen, *Legislative Power*, p. 5 (misprint for 4).
[8] *The English Works of Wyclif Hitherto Unpublished*, ed. F. D. Mathew, E.E.T.S., lxxiv (1880), pp. 184–5; *Chronicon Angliae*, ed. E. M. Thompson, Rolls Series, xliiv (1874), pp. 321, 340; Wyclif, *Select English Works*, ed. T. Arnold (Oxford, 1869–71), i. 96, ii. 230–1, iii. 153. (Spelling modernized.)

Walter Brute, preaching in 1392, declared it was 'to be wondered at, why thieves are, among Christians, for theft put to death, when after the law of Moses they were not put to death. Christians suffer adulterers to live, Sodomites, and they who curse father and mother, and many other horrible sinners; . . . So we neither keep the law of righteousness given by God, nor the law of mercy taught by Christ.' This sermon was printed by Foxe, and was thus readily available in the seventeenth century.[1] The chronicler, Henry of Knighton, claimed that the cry 'Legem dei, Goddis lawe', was the watchword of the Lollard movement.[2]

The orthodox position did not change after the Reformation, but there was a revived interest in the judicial law. When attacking sexual immorality, Bishop Latimer declared, 'I would wish that Moses's law were restored for punishment of lechery.'[3] Thomas Cartwright denied that 'any magistrate can save the life of blasphemers, contemptuous and stubborn idolaters, murderers, adulterers, incestuous persons, and such like.' Archbishop Whitgift complained in 1574 that 'it is now disputed at every table, whether the magistrate be of necessity bound to the judicials of Moses, so that he may not punish otherwise than is there prescribed . . .; which is most absurd, . . . and . . . seditious.'[4] Philip Stubbes demanded death for blasphemy following the Mosaic Code, 'which law judicial standeth in force to the world's end'. The Brownists were convinced that the judicial laws were 'not made for the Jewes' state only (as Mr. Calvine hath taught) but for all mankind'.[5] Amongst some Puritans there was a feeling of uncertainty. William Perkins stated that some judicial laws applied only to Israel, but that others dealing with such matters as murder and adultery were of universal application. Archbishop Ussher held a similar view.[6]

There was also interest in the judicial laws on the continent. In 1534 the Anabaptists of Münster drew up a legal code which restored the capital offences of the Bible, such as blasphemy,

---

[1] J. Foxe, *Acts and Monuments*, ed. J. Pratt (1877), iii. 160.
[2] *Chronicon Henrici Knighton*, ed. J. R. Lumby, Rolls Series, xcii–b (1895), p. 186.
[3] J. W. Blench, *Preaching in England in the late Fifteenth and Sixteenth Centuries* (Oxford, 1964), p. 274.
[4] J. Whitgift, *Works*, ed. J. Ayre, Parker Soc., xliv, xlviii, l(1851–3), i. 270, 272, iii. 576.
[5] T. Rogers, *The Catholic Doctrine of the Church of England*, ed. J. J. S. Perowne, Parker Soc., lii (1854), pp. 90–1; *The Writings of Henry Barrow, 1587–90*, ed. L. H. Carlson (1962), p. 414.
[6] Perkins, *Works*, i. 520–1; J. Ussher, *A Body of Divinitie* (1645), p. 204.

adultery and disobedience to parents, as well as imposing death for theft, begging, and even greed.[1] The radical German reformers Müntzer and Carlstadt were in favour of restoring the judicial laws. Martin Bucer, a more moderate reformer, envisaged a religious utopia in England in which no law would be valid unless derived immediately from Christ's laws and the Ten Commandments.[2]

It is difficult to assess how far the Fifth Monarchists were influenced by these precedents. But they certainly knew Foxe's works, which incorporated Lollard beliefs, they knew something of Münster, and John Rogers referred to Carlstadt's statement that '*he would have all Magistrates to rule by the Judicials of* Moses.'[3] They were definitely influenced by more recent precedents, especially in America. In 1636 John Cotton had drawn up a body of laws for Massachusetts, based almost wholly on the Mosaic Code, and demanding death for blasphemy and adultery, and restitution for theft. This proposal was not accepted, but the code adopted in 1648 adopted these features. It also served as a model for the laws of New Haven, where in 1644 the General Court declared that the judicial laws of Moses should be the colony's code.[4] Disappointed with New England, Cotton's followers looked towards the mother country at the approach of the civil war. His code was published in London in 1641 with the inaccurate but hopefully persuasive title *An Abstract of the Lawes of New England, As they are now established*. The following year Cotton urged all states to reintroduce the Mosaic laws and penalties.[5] Aspinwall returned from New England, republished Cotton's code, and, as mentioned above, based his own skeletal law system upon it.[6] John Eliot, the New England 'Apostle to the Indians', also demanded the restoration of the judicial laws. So did Hugh Peter, another returning colonist, who claimed that 'the Moral Law is doubtless best: to which *Moses's* judicials added, with *Solomon's* Rules and experiments, will bee compleat'. Existing legal records, including

[1] H. von Kerssenbroch, *Anabaptistici Furoris . . . Narratio*, ed. D. H. Detmer (Münster, 1899–1900), pp. 579–81.
[2] G. H. Williams, ed., *Spiritual and Anabaptist Writers* (1957), pp. 47–8; C. Hopf, *Martin Bucer and the English Reformation* (Oxford, 1946), pp. 101–6; W. Pauck, *Das Reich Gottes auf Erden* (Berlin, 1928), pp. 23, 45–6; Pauck, 'Martin Bucer's Conception of a Christian State', *Princeton Theolog. Rev.*, xxvi (1928), pp. 80–8.
[3] J. Rogers, *Jegar-Sahadutha* (1657), epistle to the Reader.
[4] G. L. Haskins, *Law and Authority in Early Massachusetts* (New York, 1960), pp. 125ff; I. M. Calder, 'John Cotton and the New Haven Colony', *New England Quart.*, iii (1930), pp. 82–4.
[5] J. Cotton, *The Powring out of the Seven Vials* (1642), 3rd vial, p. 21.
[6] Above, p. 164.

those in the Tower, should then be burnt.[1] The tradition of advocacy for the Mosaic laws thus survived into the 1640s and '50s. Even Richard Overton, the Leveller, called for the abolition of the death penalty for theft 'according to the Law of God' as well as to 'the old law of the land'. Thomas Gilbert, a Congregationalist who was chaplain of Magdalen College, Oxford, from 1656 to 1660, argued at the Whitehall debates of December 1648 that so far as the judicial law 'was a fence and out worke to the Morall law, itt stands with the Morall law, and that still bindes upon men . . . Soe . . . the Judiciall law . . . is still the duty of Magistrates.'[2] It is at least possible that the Rump's moral legislation was prompted by considerations of this kind.

The Fifth Monarchists' proposals to alter the content and structure of the law were ridiculed at the time (and since) as unique and bizarre, though in fact they owed much to both secular and religious traditions of suggested reforms. The especial degree of hostility the Fifth Monarchists aroused sprang probably from their success in publicizing their ideology, and from the fact that, unlike their precursors, they appeared in 1653 to come close to an opportunity to implement their programme.

[1] J. Eliot, *The Christian Commonwealth* (1659), *sig.* B3, p. 35; Peter, *Good Work*, pp. 32–3.
[2] R. Overton, *An Appeal from the Commons* (1647), in A. S. P. Woodhouse, *Puritanism and Liberty* (1938), p. 338; *Clarke Papers*, ii. 124–5; A. G. Matthews, *Calamy Revised* (Oxford, 1934), pp. 221–2.

CHAPTER EIGHT

The Religious and Intellectual Attitudes
of the Fifth Monarchists

The Fifth Monarchists were hated and feared by their contemporaries as a social and political threat, and their religious beliefs were often dismissed as hypocrisy. But the religious convictions of the saints were an integral part of their outlook. The manifesto of Venner's rising in 1657 proclaimed the saints' trust in the love of God, so that 'to us to die is gain, and to live is gain; so that tribulation, nor distresse, or persecution, or Famine, or nakednesse, or peril, or sword; neither Death nor Life, nor Angels, nor Principalities, . . . shall be able to separate us, from the love of God.'[1]

The Fifth Monarchists, however, are not easy to classify in religious terms. They never matched the common declarations of faith and practice which contemporary sects, such as the General and Particular Baptists and the Congregationalists achieved quite quickly, nor their degree of organization.[2] There was nothing unique in their faith or worship. They differed from the Baptists and Congregationalists only in certain details of eschatology and in their political attitude. But they saw themselves as a distinct group, and possessed some rudimentary form of organization, and their meetings had a religious as well as political function. The Fifth Monarchists were a sect, albeit an amorphous one, though their genesis was political rather than religious.

The Fifth Monarchists were drawn largely from the ranks of existing Baptists and Congregationalists, from whom they derived their concept of the Church and worship. The true church was a 'gathered

---

[1] W. Medley, *A Standard Set Up* (1657), p. 24.
[2] Anon., *The Confession of Faith, of those Churches . . . called Anabaptists* (1644); *Declaration of the Faith and Order . . . in the Congregational Churches* (1658); W. T. Whitley, ed., *Minutes of the General Assembly of the General Baptist Churches*, i (1909); B. R. White, 'The Organization of the Particular Baptists, 1644–1660', *J. Eccles. Hist.*, xvii (1966), pp. 209–26.

172

congregation', a voluntary body of those who were convinced they had been saved by God's grace, and were thus the 'elect', and who separated themselves from society. The elect were an unspecified but small proportion of the population, Spittlehouse apparently thinking in terms of one-quarter.[1] The unregenerate were excluded from the gathered church, though where a minister of these ideas held a parochial living during the interregnum, a compromise was sometimes reached by which most services were public, but only the elect were allowed communion. Thomas Palmer was prosecuted in 1658 for refusing communion to his parishioners.[2] Each gathered church was a sovereign body, and every member had the right to speak and to choose officers.[3] Spittlehouse argued that it was not essential to have officers at all, and congregations sometimes went for several years without a pastor.[4] The Fifth Monarchists retained the traditional three regular officers, the pastor, elders and deacons. In some congregations, such as that of Pendarves, some of the pastor's functions were given to a separate officer, the 'teacher'. Woodall, however, called this unscriptural, and Chamberlen held both offices at once, though this caused some resentment.[5] Many writers insisted that preaching should be restricted to ordained ministers, but it was conceded generally that anyone with an 'immediate infallible revelation' from God could preach. Claims to such revelation were not always scrutinized closely, and the church at Abingdon had at least four regular preachers besides its pastor.[6] More radical saints argued that true ordination came only from God, and not from men at all.[7]

The rights of the inspired raised the problem of the role of women

[1] C. Feake, *The Oppressed Close Prisoner* (1655), p. 96; J. Spittlehouse, *Rome Ruin'd* (1650), p. 250. On the gathered churches, see G. F. Nuttall, *Visible Saints* (Oxford, 1957) and *The Holy Spirit in Puritan Faith and Experience* (2nd edn. Oxford, 1947); J. Browne, *History of Congregationalism in Norfolk and Suffolk* (1877); R. Barclay, *The Inner Life of the Religious Societies* (1876).
[2] A. Palmer, *A Scripture-Rale* (1654), *passim*; A. G. Matthews, *Calamy Revised* (Oxford, 1934), p. 380.
[3] Anon., *Some Considerations* (1658), p. 17.
[4] Spittlehouse, *Rome Ruin'd*, pp. 291–2; Browne, *Congregationalism*, pp. 398, 461.
[5] J. Atherton, *The Pastor Turn'd Pope* (1654), sig. A4; T. Harmer, *Miscellaneous Works* (1823), pp. 194, 197; Bodl. MS. Rawlinson D 828, f. 75: Church Book of Lothbury Square.
[6] Anon., *The Disputes between Mr. Cranford and Dr. Chamberlen* (1652), p. 5; M. Cary, *A Word in Season* (1647), p. 4; C. Helme, *Life in Death* (1660), sig. A2v.; E. Chillenden, *Preaching without Ordination* (1647), *passim*; Atherton, *Pastor Turn'd Pope*, pp. 3–5.
[7] W. A. (?i.e. Aspinwall), *Certaine Queries touching the Ordination of Ministers* (1647), *passim*; T. Weld, *Mr. Tillam's Account Examined* (1657), appendix; Nuttall, *Holy Spirit*, p. 85.

in the sects, for women too claimed inspiration. Enormous respect was paid to women who appeared to be endowed with divine grace, such as Sarah Wight and the Fifth Monarchist prophetess Anna Trapnel. Mary Cary styled herself a 'Minister', though there is no evidence that she had a congregation. John Rogers's church in Dublin barred women from teaching or being elders, but allowed them to vote and speak on church matters, and to hold the office of deacon. Sister Harrison brought up the issue in Chamberlen's church by claiming equal rights of speech. After a fierce dispute, ordinary women were given no rights at all, but it was agreed that a prophetess might speak, prophesy and pray. Spittlehouse, a member, had argued in favour of women speaking on ordinary church matters.[1] Women also played a part in matters other than spiritual. A list captured by Thurloe in 1657 showed the Fifth Monarchist agent at Lincoln was a woman, Abigail Marshall. There seems to have been a distinct group of 'sisters that meet togeather' in Venner's congregation, and in 1657 they were entrusted with the task of spreading the rebels' manifesto. In the 1661 rising, a woman rebel was alleged to have been 'taken all in Armour'.[2] The Fifth Monarchists did not try to raise the status of women inside the family, except to place obedience to the church above that to the husband, despite accusations that they wished to emancipate wives from their husbands. Nevertheless, the weakening of masculine supremacy in the sect must have had some impact on the family.[3] The only radical change proposed by Fifth Monarchists on the subject of the family was a call for the abolition of primogeniture, by which the 'Monopolies of elder Brethren' would be destroyed.[4]

Membership of the gathered churches was confined to people who had given testimonies to prove their state of grace, and no further test seems to have been imposed when one of these 'visible saints' became a Fifth Monarchist. But some sort of rough orthodoxy was

[1] See K. V. Thomas, 'Women and the Civil War Sects', in T. Aston, ed., *Crisis in Europe, 1560–1660* (1965), pp. 317–40; G. F. Nuttall, *James Nayler: A Fresh Approach* (1954), *passim*; M. Cary, *The Resurrection of the Witnesses* (1648), title page; J. Rogers, *Ohel* (1653), pp. 463 (misprinted as 563)–75; MS. Rawl. D 828, fos. 30–2; Spittlehouse, *Rome Ruin'd*, p. 314. Fox, however, met a 'sort of people' who believed that women had no souls: G. Fox, *Journal*, ed. J. L. Nickalls (Cambridge, 1952), pp. 8–9.

[2] *Thurloe*, vi. 187; C. Burrage, 'The Fifth Monarchy Insurrections', *Eng. Hist. Rev.*, xxv (1910), p. 735; anon., *Londons Glory* (1661), p. 14.

[3] Anon., *The Holy Sisters Conspiracy against their Husbands* (1661), *passim*; Thomas, 'Women and the . . . Sects', p. 340.

[4] Anon., *A Door of Hope* (1661), p. 10.

envisaged. Feake declared his wish to purge the movement; Simpson was said to be 'not fully enlightened', and in 1653 Rogers was excluded from the Fifth Monarchists' meetings.[1]

The saints were preoccupied with the imminent world revolution, and probably for this reason failed to create any lasting national organization. They came closest to a regional organization in London, where in 1652 six congregations held regular meetings, and two years later groups from ten churches inaugurated weekly meetings. In 1657 Rogers organized a series of weekly gatherings of saints from at least five churches.[2] In East Anglia there were close links between the Congregationalist churches, in which the Fifth Monarchists shared, but occasionally the Fifth Monarchists held their own assemblies.[3] The supremacy of Vavasor Powell gave some unity to the movement in Wales. Llwyd moved towards quietism, and the next leaders, John Williams and Richard Price, were both disciples of Powell.[4]

There was also a shadowy organization on a national scale. The Fifth Monarchist group in Barebones sent letters to sympathetic churches throughout the country. At the funeral of Pendarves in 1656 representatives came from many parts of the country, and the list of Fifth Monarchist contacts which was seized in 1657 showed agents in places as distant as Cornwall and Hull. In 1661 there was a report that Medley was acting as a secretary in charge of the national correspondence of the movement.[5] Nevertheless, there were internal divisions among the saints on such matters as infant baptism, the true Sabbath and predestination, and Rogers was probably right when he told Cromwell in 1655 that the Fifth Monarchists were only 'driven by your Sword to love one another'.[6]

The saints naturally regarded national, hierarchical churches, such as the Anglican and attempted Presbyterian systems, as antichristian.[7] Rogers argued that any national church was insufferable, because unbiblical, even if it offered toleration. Feake denied that the clergy of a national church, 'from the highest Archbishop . . . to the

---

[1] *Thurloe*, v. 759; *Clarke Papers*, ii. p. xxxv; Rogers, *Ohel*, introduction, p. 69.
[2] See above, pp. 59–60, 105, 120.
[3] Browne, *Congregationalism, passim*; above, pp. 111–12.
[4] T. Richards, *Religious Developments in Wales, 1654–62* (1923), p. 228.
[5] See above, pp. 72, 77, 116; SP. 29/44, f. 267.
[6] Anon., *The Faithfull Narrative* (1655), p. 37.
[7] Spittlehouse, *An Explanation of the Commission* (1653), p. 6 (misprint for 12); V. Powell, *God the Father* (1649), pp. 57–8; anon., *A Door of Hope* (1661), p. 4.

meanest Curate', were true ministers at all.[1] Accordingly, the saints looked with great suspicion upon the Triers, established by Cromwell in 1654 to examine and approve ministers. They saw them as the first step towards a new national church, and compared 'Lord Triers' to 'Lord Bishops'. Only Simpson, currying favour, defended the Triers, and it was partly on this account that many of his followers seceded.[2]

Several relics of the national church survived in the Protectorate period, notably parochial livings, lay patronage, and tithes. The saints were consistent in condemning lay patrons.[3] Parochial livings were also contrary to the voluntary principle, as the basic unit of the national church, and they were attacked by Feake and Powell. They were said to derive 'their Rise and Authority from *Antichrist*, supported by the *Beast*, and for which there is not the least footing in the Word of God'.[4]

But a number of Fifth Monarchists, like some Congregationalists and a few Baptists, failed to act in accordance with this principle. Habergham, Stoneham, Postlethwaite, Thomas Palmer and Marsden all held parochial livings until ejected at the Restoration. If less well-known saints are included, and men whose Fifth Monarchy activity was mainly after 1660, the names must be added of Richard Astley, Thomas Baylie, Robert Browne, Camshaw Helme, Anthony Palmer, Timothy Roberts, John Skinner, Richard Swift and Richard Whitehurst. Moreover, John Simpson was rector of St. Botolph's, Bishopsgate (1652–5, '59–62), and several other saints held lectureships.[5]

As the interregnum advanced, however, many Fifth Monarchists did reconcile their actions with their principles by resigning their livings. Feake held no living after he was removed from Christ Church, Newgate, in 1655, and he attacked parochial clergy. Rogers held nothing more than a lectureship after he lost the living at Purleigh, Essex, in 1653. Breviter, vicar of North Walsham, resigned his living in 1656, and John Wigan held no further position after resigning as curate of Birch Chapel, Manchester. Powell was prob-

[1] Rogers, *Christian Concertation* (1659), p. 79; Feake, *Oppressed Close Prisoner*, p. 93.
[2] Anon., *The Prophets Malachy and Isaiah Prophesying* (1656), epistle by Feake, p. 7; anon., *Some Considerations*, p. 1; W. Postlethwaite, *A Voice from Heaven* (1655), p. 85; *Thurloe*, iv. 382; anon., *The Old Leaven Purged* (1658), 2nd pagination, p. 2.
[3] Rogers, *Ohel*, introd., p. 29; Medley, *Standard Set Up*, p. 5; anon., *Old Leaven Purged*, 1st pagin., p. 11; *Thurloe*, ii. 196.
[4] *Thurloe*, iv. 381, v. 756; anon., *The Fifth Monarchy . . . Asserted* (1659), p. 52.
[5] For all these, see Biog. App., and Matthews, *Cal. Rev., passim*.

ably minister of Dartford, Kent, in 1644, but held no later livings.[1] The 'mechanic' preachers, like Venner, never held livings.

During the interregnum there was strong pressure, especially from the sectarians, for the abolition of the system of tithes, hated because they were oppressive and because they maintained the antichristian church. Such criticisms were not novel, and had been made earlier by the Lollards and the German Anabaptists, amongst others.[2] Most Fifth Monarchists lived in urban areas where tithes had been commuted to a fixed cash payment which had, through inflation, become quite small. But they shared the hatred of tithes. Mary Cary complained that they burdened the consciences and estates of the saints. Others condemned them as belonging to the Levitical, not Christian priesthood. Canne declared that Christ would not descend until tithes were removed.[3] Several saints emphasized the connection between tithes and the loss of independence. Canne said he opposed them not because they were a burden but because they were the basis of a national church. Feake argued that any true minister must abandon his living, tithes, glebe and any other state maintenance to preserve his independence.[4] The Fifth Monarchists in Barebones joined in the effort to destroy tithes, and Rogers attended the Parliamentary committee to press the case.[5]

One Fifth Monarchist proposal was that ministers should maintain themselves; Chamberlen, a physician, James, a weaver, and Venner, a cooper, all did so.[6] Others held that a congregation should support its pastor with voluntary gifts.[7] Realists recognized that many of the elect were poor or parsimonious, and would provide for the maintenance of a relatively small number of ministers. But Spittlehouse reflected that as three-quarters of the people were not

[1] Matthews, *Cal. Rev.*, pp. 71, 529; *J. Friends' Hist. Soc.*, xiv (1917), pp. 171–2; Feake, *Oppressed Close Prisoner*, p. 96; E. Rogers, *The Life and Opinions of a Fifth Monarchy Man* (1867), pp. 33–4; A. G. Matthews, *Walker Revised* (Oxford, 1948), p. 215.
[2] M. James, 'The Political Importance of the Tithes Controversy in the English Revolution, 1640–60', *History*, n.s., xxvi (1941–2), pp. 1–18; *Chronicon Angliae*, ed. E. M. Thompson (Rolls Series, lxiv, 1874), p. 340; J. Wyclif, *Select English Works*, ed. T. Arnold (Oxford, 1869–71), iii. 176, 312; G. H. Williams, *The Radical Reformation* (1962), pp. 30, 68, 80, 98, 184.
[3] M. Cary, *Twelve New Proposals* (1653), p. 5; anon., *Old Leaven Purged*, p. 30; *Door of Hope*, p. 10; Thurloe, iv. 382; Canne, *The Time of Finding* (1658), p. 5.
[4] Canne, *A Second Voyce from the Temple* (1653), p. 11; Feake, *Oppressed Close Prisoner*, p. 112.
[5] See above, pp. 70, 73–4.
[6] Anon., *Fifth Monarchy . . . Asserted*, p. 52.
[7] Spittlehouse, *Certaine Queries* (1654), p. 10; anon., *Some Considerations*, p. 18.

'*fit materials* for the building of the new *Jerusalem* . . . so they will stand in need of the fewer Shepheards'.[1]

The problem was most serious for those Fifth Monarchists who had trained at the universities for the ministry, and had no other profession. They responded to it in a variety of ways. Woodall actually defended tithes, whilst Rogers accepted a post in Ireland partly because it freed him from the dilemma. Simpson simultaneously condemned tithes and accepted them.[2] Powell's views changed constantly over several years, before ending in total condemnation.[3] Quite often a minister rejected tithes but accepted augmentations, state grants which were derived from the tithes of sequestered clergy and similar sources, and were equally incompatible with the principle of independence. Thus Powell, Wigan, Helme, Woodall, Stoneham, Swift and Taylor received tithes indirectly, whilst Pendarves and Postlethwaite received state money from the sale of confiscated church lands. Courtney, Powell and Llwyd were connected under Harrison's leadership with the Propagation scheme in Wales, the finances of which were based on tithes. Danvers was a Trustee for the use of sequestered tithes during the Commonwealth. John Canne accepted a state salary as chaplain of the garrison at Hull.[4] Mary Cary, Chamberlen and Llwyd were among several who condemned tithes but hoped the state would provide some alternative maintenance for the clergy.[5] This would have freed them from the onus of collecting a levy which they thought unjustified, but would not have provided total independence.

In the sphere of worship, the Fifth Monarchists envisaged revolutionary changes when the millennium arrived. The ministry and the church would be swept away, for Christ would be present in person. All ordinances would be abolished. John Archer had even thought

---

[1] Spittlehouse, *Rome Ruin'd*, p. 250.

[2] F. Woodall, *Natural and Spiritual Light* (1655), p. 6; Rogers, *Ohel*, introd., p. 28; anon., *Old Leaven Purged*, p. 30; *Cal. S.P. Dom., 1655*, p. 226; *Clarke Papers*, ii. pp. xxxv–vi.

[3] R. T. Jones, 'The Life, Work, and Thought of Vavasor Powell, 1617–1670' (Oxford Univ. D.Phil. thesis, 1947), pp. 295–6.

[4] W. A. Shaw, *A History of the English Church During the Civil Wars and Under the Commonwealth* (1900), ii. 536, 561, 544, 589, 595, 508, 512; C. H. Firth and R. S. Rait, *Acts and Ordinances of the Interregnum, 1642–1660* (1911), ii. 144, 209, 343, 345; *Cal. S.P. Dom., 1651–2*, p. 211.

[5] M. Cary, *Twelve New Proposals*, pp. 7–8; Chamberlen, *The Declaration and Proclamation of the Army of God* (1659), p. 6; T. Richards, *Wales under the Indulgence (1672–1675)*, p. 7.

that faith would be unnecessary, since the truth would be manifest. The saints would serve Christ with praise and prayer alone.[1]

Until the millennium arrived, however, the faith and practice of the saints differed little from that of the other gathered churches. Although there were some General Baptists among them, most Fifth Monarchists believed that the elect were a predestined group saved by grace alone.[2] They accepted a Sabbath, though there were fierce disputes as to whether it was on the first or seventh day.[3] They accepted the ordinances of baptism and communion, though there was further dispute as to whether the laying on of hands (after ordination, baptism, communion) was a lost ordinance which should be revived. The latter was urged most strongly by those saints who had adopted the Jewish sabbath.[4]

Fifth Monarchist services were held variously in parish churches, houses, taverns, cellars, warehouses and in the open.[5] Only one instance is known of them actually building a meeting-house.[6] Like other sectarians they avoided the pagan names of days and months, referring to the 'first day' and 'second month'.[7] They condemned all liturgies and set prayers, and regarded the Lord's Prayer only as a model for their own prayers.[8] Choirs and organs were condemned because they appealed to the 'carnal senses', but hymns and psalms were accepted as scriptural, and the saints composed their own hymns. Feake and his followers, however, laughed aloud at the 'howling' of psalms during public services at Christ Church, Newgate, and kept on their hats as a mark of protest. The services, which

[1] M. Cary, *The Little Horns Doom* (1651), pp. 255–60; H. Danvers, *Theopolis* (1672), pp. 172–5; T. Edwards, *Gangraena* (1646), i. 23; J. Archer, *The Personall Reigne of Christ* (1642), pp. 17, 27.

[2] E.g., V. Powell, *God the Father*, p. 29; J. Simpson, *The Great Joy of Saints* (1654), 2nd pagin., pp. 54–227.

[3] W. Aspinwall, *The Abrogation of the Jewish Sabbath* (1657); Spittlehouse, *A Return to some Expressions* (1656); T. Tillam, *The Seventh-day Sabbath Sought out* (1657), all *passim*. Simpson apparently held a mystical view of Christ as an eternal Sabbath: Spittlehouse, *A Manifestation of sundry gross absurdities* (1656), p. 2.

[4] Anon., *A Discourse Between Cap. Kiffin, and Dr. Chamberlen* (1654), *passim*; J. More, *A Lost Ordinance Restored* (1654), *passim*; (E. Bagshaw), *The Life and Death of Mr. Vavasor Powell* (1671), p. 41.

[5] For an example of each: W. J. Harte, 'Ecclesiastical and Religious Affairs in Exeter, 1640–62', *Reports and Trans. Devon. Assoc.*, lxix (1937), p. 55; G. Lyon Turner, *Original Records of Early Nonconformity* (1911–14), i. 155; SP. 29/71, f. 147: information, 9 April 1663; SP. 29/421, f. 324: J. Harris to Jenkins, 13 Nov. 1682; Turner, *op. cit.*, i. 144; T. Crosby, *The History of the English Baptists* (1738–40), i. 377.

[6] Atherton, *Pastor Turn'd Pope*, sig. A4.

[7] For example, Feake, *The New Non-conformist* (1654), *passim*.

[8] Powell, *Common-Prayer-Book no Divine Service* (1660), *passim*; anon., *Door of Hope*, p. 4; Spittlehouse, *Rome Ruin'd*, pp. 186–7.

were often highly emotional, consisted mainly of extempore prayer and preaching, though not rhetorical preaching aimed at the senses. The sermons, which could last up to six or seven hours and were often semi-political, were liable to frequent interruptions by the congregation, and the whole service sometimes ended in chaos. When there was no pulpit, the preacher might stand on a bench or table to address the saints.[1] A later critic reflected that the Fifth Monarchist 'so hates a Gentleman, as he can't endure God shud be serv'd like one'.[2]

Fifth Monarchists were generally opposed to taking oaths, as a misuse of God's name. But Fox alleged that they gave way under pressure, and told a magistrate after the Restoration that this was one method of distinguishing a Fifth Monarchist from a Quaker. Spittlehouse thought that oaths were '*to God's glory*' in ending strife, but Stuart magistrates would not have found Fox's advice of much help, for most Fifth Monarchists refused to take the oaths required after 1660. Indeed, Sir William Armorer wrote to Clarendon in 1664 that the difference between Fifth Monarchists and Baptists was that only the former refused to take the oaths.[3]

The greatest dispute dividing the early sects was whether baptism should be administered to infants or to believers alone. The Fifth Monarchists contained saints of both persuasions, but there was probably a majority in favour of infant baptism.[4] The affiliations of the movement in East Anglia and Wales were almost wholly with the Congregationalists. Vavasor Powell seems to have been rebaptized in 1655, but there is no evidence that his disciples followed his example.[5] Feake and John Canne are often described as Baptists, but were not so.[6] More importantly, though several leading saints were rebaptized in the later 1650s, namely Harrison, Carew, Courtney and probably Powell, none of the saints thought the matter of

---

[1] Spittlehouse, *Rome Ruin'd*, p. 204; J.N., *Proh Tempora!* (1654), p. 6; T. Tillam, *The Temple of Lively Stones* (1660), p. 273; (Bagshaw), *Life . . . of . . . Vavasor Powell*, p. 108; anon., *Three Hymnes* (1650), pp. 6–8; Simpson, *Great Joy*, p. 94; Nuttall, *Holy Spirit*, p. 68; *Thurloe*, iv. 650, v. 60–1, 759.

[2] R. Flecknoe, *Enigmatical Characters* (1665), p. 28.

[3] *Thurloe*, iv. 151; Fox, *Journal*, p. 531; Spittlehouse, *Rome Ruin'd*, p. 171; Bodl. MS. Clar. 81, f. 199: Sir W. Armorer to (Clarendon), 12 April 1664.

[4] L. F. Brown, *The Political Activities of the Baptists and Fifth Monarchy Men* (1911), pp. 203–4, was mistaken in thinking that Baptists predominated.

[5] *Thurloe*, v. 220; Nuttall, *Visible Saints*, pp. 119–20; Richards, *Religious Developments*, pp. 214–17.

[6] *Certain Passages*, 28 (21–8 July 1654), p. 220; C. Burrage, 'Was John Canne a Baptist?', *Trans. Bapt. Hist. Soc.*, iii. (1912–13), pp. 212–46; J. F. Wilson, 'Another Look at John Canne', *Church Hist.*, xxxiii (1964), pp. 34–48.

sufficient importance to exclude members of different judgements. They condemned as 'abominable Popery' disputes over such 'controversial' matters. If a man was one of the elect, it did not matter what ordinances he observed, or whether, indeed, he belonged to a church at all.[1] There was even some latitude in theology, with General Baptists, who accepted some degree of free will, joining in assemblies of strict predestinarians.[2] Simpson was exceptional in consigning to hell all who held free will.[3]

The sense of the imminence of the millennium gave the Fifth Monarchists an ecumenical aspect. Pendarves criticized saints for arguing over ordinances when they should have been studying the prophecies. Rogers denied that the Fifth Monarchists were a sect at all, saying they were 'of such a *latitude* as takes in *all Saints*, all such as are *sanctified in Christ Jesus*, without respect of what *Form* or *Judgement* he is'.[4] The saints accepted that godly persons were to be found among several denominations, even among Presbyterians and occasionally Quakers. Morgan Llwyd explained that

> *Out of all these will Christ compound*
> *An army for himselfe;*
> *so satan getts of all these sects*
> *the parings and the pelfe.*[5]

Accordingly Mary Cary and Rogers, declared that meeting houses should be open to all. Chamberlen even placed a notice in a newspaper announcing that 'All Christians may meet at Dr. *Chamberlains* in White Friers every third day called Tuesday.' In later years he made attempts to unite all the churches in Christendom.[6]

In practice the only sects with whom the Fifth Monarchists had close contacts were the Baptists and Congregationalists. In East Anglia, for example, several Congregationalists were prepared to

---

[1] *Publick Intelligencer*, 120 (1–8 Feb. 1658), p. 286; *Thurloe*, iv. 373; Simpson, *Great Joy*, 2nd pagin., pp. 36, 47; Rogers, *A Reviving Word* (1657), p. 40; V. Powell, עדפד בפה *Or the Bird in the Cage* (1661), p. 22; Nuttall, *Holy Spirit*, p. 96.

[2] As in the *Declaration of . . . the Churches of Christ* (1654): above, p. 105.

[3] Anon., *Truths Conflict with Error* (1650), p. 70.

[4] J. Pendarves, *The Fear of God* (1657), pp. 2, 4; anon., *Faithfull Narrative*, p. 37.

[5] Anon., *A Declaration of Divers Elders* (1651), p. 5; Cary, *Little Horns Doom*, p. 22; M. Llwyd, *Gweithiau*, ed. T. E. Ellis and J. H. Davies (Bangor and London, 1899, 1908), i. 25, ii. 270–1.

[6] M. Cary, *Twelve New Proposals*, p. 5; Rogers, *Ohel*, p. 311; *Perfect Diurnall*, 217 (13–19 Feb. 1654), p. 3116 (misprint for 3344); Bodl. MS. Tanner 35, fos. 2, 95, 104, 133: Chamberlen to Archbishop Sheldon, 1682.

publish posthumously some of Tillinghast's sermons, and others published a work jointly with Woodall.[1] The mass services at Allhallows the Great, in London, were attended by Baptists such as Kiffin, Jessey and Highland as well as the Fifth Monarchists. After the Restoration, Simpson and Anthony Palmer preached at services together with Kiffin, Knollys, Jessey and Wise.[2] Frequently in London, Fifth Monarchist groups existed within Baptist or Congregationalist churches, apparently amicably. At Allhallows however, the arrangement ended in disaster, and the church broke up.[3] At St. Botolph's, Aldgate, the saints met together with the Presbyterians, but almost came to blows with them. Even Feake's group was prepared to worship with the main congregation at Christ Church, though the saints disrupted 'popish' parts of the services.[4] Fifth Monarchists were admitted to the Baptist assembly at Dorchester in 1658, and after the Restoration there are several instances of Fifth Monarchists and other sects meeting together regularly.[5]

With other religious groups, however, the Fifth Monarchists' connections were very weak. Finding common cause against the Anglican enemy, they occasionally joined with Presbyterians after 1660.[6] But the usual attitude towards Presbyterians was one of fierce hostility. Chamberlen described them as ministers of Antichrist, because their ordination was derived from bishops and so ultimately from Rome, and Spittlehouse also denounced them as 'Daughters of that grand Harlot'.[7] For other saints, the Presbyterians' 'pure' theology was outweighed by their wish to form a national church.[8]

Towards Antinomianism the saints were equally hostile, although several had held Antinomian principles in earlier years, especially Simpson. The Fifth Monarchists stressed the contrary principle, of literalism, and their devotion to the Mosaic Code led them to condemn Antinomians and even more the Ranters, and Simpson was

[1] Tillinghast, *Elijah's Mantle* (1658), sig. A5, A7; J. Martin, S. Petto and F. Woodall, *The Preacher Sent* (1658); see above, p. 175.

[2] *Thurloe*, v. 755; *Cal. S.P. Dom.*, *1653–4*, p. 393; SP. 29/41, f. 106: information, 11 Sept. 1661; SP. 29/43, fos. 105–7: E. Potter to Nicholas, 13 Oct. 1661.

[3] E.g., anon., *A Declaration of the Churches of Christ* (1654); anon., *Old Leaven Purged*, *passim*; cf. Appendix III.

[4] J. A. Dodd, 'Troubles in a City Parish Under the Protectorate', *Eng. Hist. Rev.*, x (1895), pp. 41–54; J.N., *Proh Tempora!*, p. 6.

[5] *Thurloe*, vii. 140; Turner, *Original Records*, i. 144, 155, 169.

[6] For example, SP. 29/42, f. 69: W. Pestell to Nicholas, 26 Sept. 1661.

[7] Anon., *Disputes between Cranford and Chamberlen*, pp. 8–9; Spittlehouse, *A Vindication of the Continued Succession* (1652), p. 15.

[8] Postlethwaite, *Voice from Heaven*, pp. 33, 47; Powell, *God the Father*, p. 57; Feake, *A Beam of Light* (1659), sig. A3–v.

as hostile as any.[1] They condemned also the Familists, and the
Socinian doctrines of John Biddle, although Chillenden showed a
rare ecumenical spirit in allowing Biddle to preach in his chapel.[2]

Relations were more complex with the Quakers, who used very
similar millenarian language, and were often confused with the
Fifth Monarchists by contemporaries. Moreover, some Fifth Monarchists did become Quakers.[3] Several showed sympathy or interest,
especially Morgan Llwyd, Colonel Overton and, on occasion,
Powell. Anna Trapnel was said to have addressed joint meetings of
Fifth Monarchists and Quakers.[4] But again the usual attitude was
one of hostility, because of the Quakers' allegorizing of fundamentals,
especially the millennium. Spittlehouse declared that the '*Quakers
Tenent is the Devils last game he hath to play*'. Canne, John James,
Trapnel, Wigan and Woodall, representing all strands of Fifth
Monarchist thought, were among many more who rejected the
Quakers because of this 'spiritualization'.[5] Fox, in return, thought
the Fifth Monarchists 'none of Christ's servants, but the beast's and
whore's'.[6]

Despite an ecumenical approach, the Fifth Monarchists thus
found little of which to approve in other religious groups, and this
raises the problem of how far they believed in toleration. Their
pamphleteers called for a complete end of control and interference
by the magistrate, who had no special knowledge of divine truth.[7]
Some even urged that non-Christians and blasphemers should be
tolerated, and Simpson urged toleration for the Familists, to follow

[1] T. Gataker, *Gods Eye on his Israel* (1645), sig. A3*v.*, C2*v*; G. Huehns, *Antinomianism in English History* (1951), esp. p. 130; Simpson, *Great Joy*, 2nd pagin.,
pp. 248, 273; Spittlehouse, *The Royall Advocate* (1655), p. 7; Aspinwall, *Abrogation*,
p. 14; Trapnel, *The Cry of a Stone* (1654), p. 57.

[2] Anon., *Some Considerations*, p. 3; Simpson, *Great Joy*, pp. 55ff; C. H. Firth and
G. Davies, *The Regimental History of Cromwell's Army* (Oxford, 1940), p. 214.

[3] H. Barbour, *The Quakers in Puritan England* (New Haven and London, 1964),
pp. 182–8; anon., *Observations Upon the Last Actions . . . of . . . Harrison* (1661), p. 17;
see below, pp. 223–4.

[4] Fox, *Journal*, pp. 93, 172; *Mercurius Politicus*, 312 (29 May–5 June 1656), p.
6998; R. Davies, *An Account of the Convincement . . . of . . . Richard Davies* (3rd edn.,
1771), p. 69.

[5] Spittlehouse, *Royall Advocate*, p. 34; Canne, *Truth with Time* (1656), sig. B3;
G. Fox, *John James, I hearing* (1658), *passim*; Trapnel, Untitled book of verse
(1658; Bodl. shelfmark S.1.42 Th.), esp. pp. 48–9; J. Wigan, *Antichrist's strongest
Hold overturned* (1665), *passim*; Woodall, *Natural . . . Light, passim*. For an analysis
of early Quaker millenarianism, simultaneously literal and allegorical in its
approach, see T. L. Underwood, 'Early Quaker Eschatology' in P. Toon, ed.,
Puritans, the Millennium and the Future of Israel (1970), pp. 90–103.

[6] Fox, *Journal*, p. 420.

[7] Anon., *Fifth Monarchy . . . Asserted*, p. 53; Medley, *Standard Set Up*, p. 16;
Rogers, *Ohel*, pp. 172, 177.

Christ's example and because force could produce at the most only outward conformity.[1] Chamberlen later hoped that Charles II could be king 'of Papists and Protestants, . . . Anabaptists and Quakers, . . . Jews and Gentiles, Turks and Infidels'.[2]

It is not possible to know how far the saints would have put this enlightened programme into action. Cromwell was certainly not convinced of their tolerance.[3] During the Protectorate the Fifth Monarchists criticized the persecution of 'erring' sectaries such as Biddle and Naylor.[4] But after the fall of Richard Cromwell, Colonel Rich demanded that a soldier should be barred from the post of quarter-master because he was a Quaker, which suggests that toleration was envisaged but not equality in civil rights.[5] Mary Cary wished to tolerate papists and atheists, but this was condemned by Rogers, and by Canne, who also excluded 'Hereticks' from toleration, a very ambiguous loophole.[6] A more common attitude towards the Catholics was to revive the fear of popery which had swept the country in the early 1640s. Chamberlen hinted that the law and lawyers served to 'help on the work of the Jesuits'. John Williams preached in 1654 that Cromwell was a 'protector to protect you in slaverie and poperie'.[7] The *Door of Hope* was still more alarmist, recalling the massacres of St. Bartholomew and 1641, and claiming that the 'old cursed Popish Party . . . hath already laid the design of a Butchery and Massacre of the honest party in this Nation'. As proof it cited the favour of Irish lords at court, the return of Henrietta Maria, and the 'multitudes of the cruell bloody *Spaniards*, under the pretext of Attendants on the Prince and Ambassador of Spain . . . advantageously placed in the heart of . . . *London*'. The Fifth Monarchist declaration used in the 1663 rising similarly attacked the 'swarming of preists, Jesuits and outlandish papists' who would bring England under Roman or even Turkish jurisdiction.[8]

---

[1] J. Vernon, *The Swords Abuse Asserted* (1648), p. 4; H. Danvers, *Certain Quaeries* (1649), p. 4; Simpson, *Great Joy*, pp. 25–7.

[2] P. Chamberlen, *A Speech Visibly Spoken* (1662), p. 15.

[3] Anon., *Faithfull Narrative*, p. 37.

[4] Anon., *The Protector (So called,) In Part Unvailed* (1655), p. 233; *Some Considerations*, p. 3; *To the Officers and Souldiers of the Army, . . . a sober admonition* (1657), pp. 1–3.

[5] Richards, *Religious Developments*, p. 238.

[6] Cary, *Word in Season*, p. 10; Rogers, *Christian Concertation* (1659), p. 79; Canne, *The Discoverer* (1649), p. 11.

[7] P. Chamberlen, *Legislative Power* (1659), p. 7; *Thurloe*, ii. 128.

[8] *Door of Hope*, pp. 6–7; 'A doore of hope opened', B.M. Add. MS. 38856, f. 79*v*.

The saints showed little sympathy for supporters of the Anglican or Presbyterian state system. Canne urged the Barebones assembly to annul the old episcopal ministry to prevent services being held with the old prayer-book.[1] Feake hoped that the saints would establish a 'Glorious, Evangelical inquisition', and, like Spittlehouse, called for a purge not only of corrupt clergy but of all who favoured episcopal or Presbyterian church government.[2] A considerable number of Fifth Monarchist ministers were prepared in 1654 to act on local committees for ejecting 'scandalous' ministers.[3] Despite their ecumenical pretensions, it seems doubtful whether Fifth Monarchist toleration would have extended further than to the sects, and they would probably have allowed Presbyterianism only in the form of gathered churches of voluntary members.

One of the reasons for the saints' rejection of a national church was that it implied the validity of human authority in religious matters. The saints accepted only the authority of scripture, regarded reason as ungodly, and saw all precedents as popish.[4] But there was also a pronounced mystical element in Fifth Monarchist thought, shown by the saints' emphasis on inward illumination, usually through dreams and visions. The works of Paracelsus, the sixteenth-century scientist and mystic, and of Jacob Boehme, the German mystic and millenarian, found many admirers in England, especially after they were translated into English during the 1640s and 1650s.[5] Morgan Llwyd has been called a 'disciple of Jacob Boehme'. He translated some of Boehme's work into Welsh, and his *Book of the Three Birds* owed much to Boehme's *Mysterium Magnum*.[6] Great importance was placed on visions and dreams, sent by God or the Devil, in the process of conversion. In fifteen of the testimonies discussed earlier a vision or dream was the most important event in the conversion

---

[1] Canne, *Second Voyce*, p. 10.
[2] Feake, *Oppressed Close Prisoner*, p. 105; Feake, *Beam of Light*, p. 41; Spittlehouse, *The first Addresses* (1653), pp. 6–7.
[3] Firth and Rait, *Acts. and Ords.*, ii. 971–2, 975–7, 980, 984.
[4] Anon., *A Model of a New Representative* (1651), p. 5; Spittlehouse, *Return*, p. 10; C. Barksdale, *The Disputation at Winchcombe* (Oxford, 1653), pp. 10–11; anon., *Certain Quaeres* (1649), p. 8.
[5] S. Hutin, *Les disciples anglais de Jacob Boehme* (Paris, 1960), pp. 38–9, 48–53; M. L. Bailey, *Milton and Jakob Boehme* (New York, 1914), pp. 57–114; D. Hirst, *Hidden Riches* (1964), pp. 76–109; A. G. Debus, *The English Paracelsians* (1965), *passim*; P. M. Rattansi, 'Paracelsus and the Puritan Revolution', *Ambix*, xi ((1963), pp. 24–31.
[6] Richards, *Religious Developments*, p. 211; E. Lewis Evans, 'Morgan Llwyd and Jacob Boehme', *Jacob Boehme Soc. Quart.*, I. iv. (1953), pp. 11–16; Brit. Mus. Catalogue, *s.n.* Llwyd.

process.[1] Thomas Tillam believed that the only true ministers were those who had been called by God in 'Visions, Dreams, Revelations, or immediately from Heaven'. John Rogers said he had been called to the ministry by a dream. Vavasor Powell was a 'great observer of Dreams, and what God might speak to himself or others by them'.[2] When God did speak, it was often to pass judgement on contemporary political issues. The doggerel verse uttered by Anna Trapnel with divine inspiration included attacks on the Protectorate regime, on the proposal to make Cromwell king, and comments on foreign policy, education, and the Quaker movement.[3] Some of the visions were similar in character to those in Daniel, and much more transparent. John Simpson's vision was an undisguised prophecy of the downfall of Cromwell. He described four visions of a 'great O', who was seen running towards a crown, occupying the chair of state, sprouting horns and finally being cast down and destroyed.[4] Owen Lloyd, a follower of Morgan Llwyd, described a vision of a black panther, which by stealth was able to overcome the whole world until destroyed by God. Lloyd sent this vision to Rogers shortly after the fall of Barebones, and the panther was doubtless Cromwell. It was published in 1662, when the panther had probably come to represent Charles II, and republished in Dutch in 1688, when it was presumably aimed at James II.[5] In 1665 Helme and his congregation in London were interested in 'visions in the air at Honiton', which they saw as a sign that divine intervention was imminent.[6]

These visions had only a slight resemblance to biblical ones, and the Fifth Monarchists also accepted other irrational and totally non-biblical sources of knowledge. The congregation at Brickendenbury, near Hertford, where Skinner sometimes preached to a congregation of up to five hundred, had a prophecy in 1664 of a king sent by God for three years to perform certain tasks, after which he would be destroyed. This they applied to Charles II, although the allotted time was already past.[7] Perhaps following John Foxe, John Rogers

[1] Above, pp. 94–8, esp. 95. Rogers, *Ohel*, pp. 397–401, 404–6, 408–9, 1 (*sic*.), 413, 415, 430–1, 436; H. Walker, *Spiritual Experiences* (2nd edn., 1653), pp. 46, 82–4, 236–7, 364, 370–2.
[2] Weld, *Mr. Tillam's Account*, suffix; Rogers, *Ohel*, p. 436; (Bagshaw), *Life and Death of Mr. Vavasor Powell*, p. 114.
[3] Trapnel, Untitled book of verse, pp. 47–9, 153, 159, 266, 273.
[4] Anon., *Old Leaven Purged*, 2nd pagin., pp. 19–20.
[5] O. Lloyd, *The Panther Prophecy* (1662); *Het Gezigt van den Panther* (no place, 1688). [6] SP. 29/120, f. 57: P. (?Pestell) to Arlington, 3 May 1665.
[7] SP. 29/99, f. 16*v*.; information, 2 June 1664; SP. 29/88, f. 128: information, ?1663.

cited the Sibylline prophecies, and those of Nostradamus and Paracelsus, and other saints cited the prophecies of Merlin and Mother
Shipton.[1] Rogers mentioned that he had been tempted to take up
magic, and in later years appeared to believe that it was a genuine,
if diabolical art.[2] Simpson shared the common belief in alchemy, and
John Canne, whilst pastor of a separatist church at Amsterdam in the
1630s, was said to have controlled not only 'a Printers work-house'
and an 'Aqua-vitae shop' but also an 'Alchymists laboratory'. The
saints also seem to have believed in witchcraft, which both Aspinwall
and Higgenson included among the crimes to be punished only by
death.[3]

Another means of ascertaining the divine will, accepted by most
sectarians and many more, was by observing the workings of providence. Many believed that the great series of victories in the 1640s
proved that God favoured the Parliamentary cause. Cromwell believed firmly in providence as an indication of God's will. The Fifth
Monarchists shared this outlook. Spittlehouse believed that the
smaller numbers dying of the plague after the establishment of the
republic in 1649 proved that God favoured the new regime.[4] The
defeat of the government's forces at Hispaniola in 1656 was proof
that God was opposed to the Protectorate.[5] Many of the saints
accepted that the Restoration could only have happened because
God willed it, but they noted the deaths and misfortunes of individual persecutors as proof that ultimately God favoured their cause,
and they saw the Great Plague as divine vengeance on their enemies.[6]

The saints were less certain about the value of astrology. All seem
to have accepted that the stars under which a person was born influenced his life and fortunes. Morgan Llwyd thought that the
planets ruled the outward man, but had no influence over his
spiritual condition. Spittlehouse, who described astrology 'as the
Princess to the rest of the Sciences', thought it was 'the same to the outward . . . man, as Divinity to the inward'.[7] William Allen and Owen

[1] Rogers, *Sagrir* (1653), pp. 131–2; Spittlehouse, *Rome Ruin'd*, sig. A3; anon.,
The Year of Wonders (1652), p. 13. For Foxe, see above, p. 26.
[2] Rogers, *Ohel*, p. 433.
[3] Simpson, *Great Joy*, p. 31; Aspinwall, *The Legislative Power* (1656), p. 30; T.
Higgenson, *Sighs for Righteousness* (1654), p. 10; C. Burrage, *The Early English
Dissenters* (1912), i. 181.
[4] Spittlehouse, *Rome Ruin'd*, sig. b1.
[5] Anon., *Some Considerations*, p. 7; *Old Leaven Purged*, p. 4.
[6] See below, pp. 197–8, 206.
[7] A. N. Palmer, *A History of the Older Nonconformity of Wrexham* (Wrexham, 1889),
p. 16 and note; Spittlehouse, *Rome Ruin'd*, sig. b3–v.

Cox both had their horoscopes calculated, and Cox visited the astrologer John Gadbury, who called Cox his 'very good friend', to obtain an astrological prediction of the fortunes of a projected voyage, which was done by studying the state of the stars at the launching of the ship.[1]

The saints were less certain of the validity of astrological claims to predict future events. Mary Cary criticized 'Prophane men' who 'are apt to admire *Booker* and *Lilly*', and John Jones, a preacher at Swan Alley, Coleman Street, repudiated astrological predictions of the imminent downfall of Cromwell's government.[2] But the *Year of Wonders* used astrological predictions. Spittlehouse accepted Lilly's prophecies, and Allen even defended them in conversation with Charles I, arguing that Lilly was 'an honest man, and writes but what his art informs him'. Charles, surprisingly, was said to have concurred with this.[3] Cox was prepared to bring a gold chain to Lilly from the King of Sweden, about whom Lilly had published favourable predictions.[4] Chamberlen in 1662 accepted the forecast of astrologers that a plague was imminent, though a generation later the church to which he had belonged rebuked a member for the 'unbecomingness' of his belief in 'vulgar astrology'.[5] Spittlehouse, incidentally, defended the Seventh Day Sabbath partly on the ground '*that the seven Stars did preach the seventh day sabbath, and therefore the Heathen kept the Saturday, which is so called of* Saturn *the seventh Planet*'. Jeremiah Ives, with whom he was disputing the subject, thought this 'vain Philosophy indeed'.[6]

Like other sects emphasizing both biblical literalism and inward inspiration, the Fifth Monarchists found little place for learning and the universities. They stressed that ministers were made by God, not by education, and denied that university-trained men were true ministers unless also called by a congregation.[7] Spittlehouse denounced the universities as 'very fountains of Atheism, and Anti-

[1] Bodl. MS. Ashmole 210, f. 134v., 427, f. 59v.: horoscopes of Allen and Cox; J. Gadbury, *Nauticum Astrologicum: or, the Astrologicall Seaman* (1961), pp. 79–80, 118–19.

[2] M. Cary, *The Resurrection of the Witnesses* (1653 edn.), sig. B2; *Thurloe*, iv. 650.

[3] Anon., *Year of Wonders*, esp. pp. 9, 15; Spittlehouse, *Rome Ruin'd*, sig. b2v.; W. Lilly, *History of his Life and Times* (1826), p. 63.

[4] Lilly, *History*, p. 74.

[5] Chamberlen, *The Sober Man's Vindication* (1662), brs.; Dr. Williams's Library, London, MS. 533 B.1.: 'Mill Yard Minutes, being the Church Book of the Seventh Day General Baptist Congregation, 1673–1840', (Xerox copy, 1951), f. 56.

[6] J. Ives, *Saturday no Sabbath* (1659), p. 226.

[7] Feake, *Oppressed Close Prisoner*, p. 105; Feake, *Beam of Light*, p. 41; Spittlehouse, *First Addresses*, pp. 6–7.

christianism', breeding 'ravenous Rooks' to devour tithes. 'What are the Authors', he demanded, 'which their Libraries are stuffed withal other than Heathenish and Antichristian?' He attacked all 'vain Philosophy', and thought classical languages and all learning not to be found in the Bible were worthless.[1] One saint asserted that the universities were founded by the Pope.[2] Anna Trapnel considered human learning unnecessary since

> *Christs Scholars . . . are perfected*
> *with learning from above.*[3]

Chamberlen, Powell, Simpson and Rogers were among others who condemned 'heathen' learning, by which 'men learn to sing the whores songs, but not the *songs of Zyon*'.[4]

Only two writers elaborated schemes for university reform, using the colleges as a basis for world evangelization. Mary Cary wanted to use university revenues to train poor but godly youths for the propagation of the gospel and the service of the state. Spittlehouse suggested that each college should teach one language to poor and godly youths who would then be sent as missionaries to the appropriate country. Greek would be taught only to missionaries destined for Greece! Ministers to work in England would need no such training. Hugh Peter devised a similar scheme.[5]

In practice, Fifth Monarchist behaviour did not wholly correspond to these principles. Harrison and Courtney accepted honorary degrees from Oxford in 1649, Rogers took a degree in 1664, and Feake sent his son to university in 1660.[6] Instead of ignoring 'Heathen' languages, some Fifth Monarchists cited classical and mediaeval Greek and Latin authors, as well as Hebrew works, although opponents often derided the standards of their scholarship.[7]

As the schemes for university reform showed, the Fifth Monarchists were very concerned with evangelism. There was a deep desire to

---

[1] Spittlehouse, *First Addresses*, pp. 4, 10 (misprints for 10, 12), 13.
[2] *Thurloe*, iv. 625.   [3] Trapnel, *Cry of a Stone*, p. 42.
[4] Anon., *An Alarum to Corporations* (1659), p. 7; anon., *Old Leaven Purged*, 2nd pagin., p. 4; J. Canne, *The Time of the End* (1657), epistle by Rogers, sig. a4v.
[5] Cary, *Twelve New Proposals*, p. 7; Spittlehouse, *First Addresses*, pp. 14–15; H. Peter, *Good Work for a Good Magistrate* (1651), pp. 6–11.
[6] J. Foster, *Alumni Oxonienses: The Members of the University of Oxford, 1500–1714* (Oxford, 1891–2), i. 336, ii. 488, 662, iii. 1274.
[7] E.g., Danvers, *A Treatise of Baptism* (1675, 1st edn. 1673), *passim*; Rogers, *Christian Concertation*, p. 16 and *passim*; Simpson, *Great Joy*, p. 4; T. Curwen, *This is An Answer to John Wiggan's Book* (1665), MS. postscript in Brit. Mus. copy; J. Harrington, *A Parallel of the Spirit of the People* (1659), pp. 2–3.

spread the Gospel to the dark corners of England and overseas, to call all the saints to make ready the path of Christ. Anna Trapnel urged that preachers be sent to India and Africa, and Tillinghast wanted to send them to Turkey, India and Ireland, as well as Northumberland and Cumberland.[1] Unlike the Quakers, the Fifth Monarchists did not send any missionaries abroad, but they were interested and active in the Propagation Commission in Wales, Tillam undertook a mission in the north, and Rogers and Aspinwall undertook ministries in Ireland.[2]

The impetus for evangelism derived partly from the saints' emphasis on preaching, and their conviction that God's elect were scattered around the world waiting for the call. But it sprang also from the belief that the biblical prophecies speaking of the conversion of the Jews and Gentiles were about to be fulfilled.[3] The saints looked for the conversion and restoration of the Jews as a sign that the millennium was near, and though several dates were mentioned, 1655/6 was the most popular.[4] Mary Cary expected the Jews' conversion as soon as Christianity was cleansed from popery and prelatism. Aspinwall thought the Jews would have the chief part in setting up New Jerusalem, and John Archer expected them to have the highest place in it, as God's first chosen people.[5] Rogers, Llwyd, Danvers, Spittlehouse and Carew all expected their conversion and return.[6] The belief in a chosen people, the increased interest in the Old Testament and Biblical literalism, and the general apocalyptic mood all produced widespread interest in the Jews both in England and the continent. There were a number of instances in England in the sixteenth and early seventeenth centuries of people adopting Jewish customs and rites, including Richard Bruern, a theologian

[1] Trapnel, Untitled book of verse, pp. 13–14; Trapnel, *Voice for the King of Saints* (1658), p. 19; Tillinghast, *Six Several Treatises* (1663), p. 80; J. Canne, *The Improvement of Mercy* (1649), p. 4.

[2] Firth and Rait, *Acts and Ords.*, ii. 343, 345; Powell, *Bird in the Cage*, sig. A8–B3; Z. Grey, *An Impartial Examination of . . . Mr. Daniel Neal's History of the Puritans* (1736–9), iii. appendix, pp. 149–50; R. Howell, *Newcastle Upon Tyne and the Puritan Revolution* (Oxford, 1967), pp. 249–53; for Rogers and Aspinwall, see Biog. App.

[3] Anon., *Door of Hope*, p. 11 (citing Isaiah lx. 5).

[4] Tillinghast, *Generation-Worke*, 2nd part (1654), pp. 62–3; anon., *The Banner of Truth* (1656), p. 47; Canne, *A Voice from the Temple* (1653), pp. 27–31.

[5] Cary, *Little Horns Doom*, pp. 140–4; Aspinwall, *Legislative Power*, sig. A2v.; Archer, *Personall Reigne*, p. 26.

[6] Rogers, *Reviving Word*, pp. 17–18; Llwyd, 'The Book of the Three Birds', trans. L. J. Parry, *Trans. Nat. Eisteddfod of Wales, 1896* (Liverpool, 1898), p. 208; Danvers, *Theopolis*, p. 72; Spittlehouse, *Certaine Queries*, p. 11; anon., *The Speeches and Prayers of some of the late King's Judges* (1660), p. 21.

who became a canon of Windsor, and Provost of Eton under Elizabeth, John Traske, a minister, in James's reign, and Thomas Tany, the London goldsmith who during the interregnum claimed to be the High Priest of the Jews. Cromwell as Protector set up a committee to discuss the proposal that the Jews be re-admitted to England, but the interest in the Jews was shared by at least one royalist pamphleteer.[1] The Jews themselves were expecting a second coming, and in 1666 flocked after a self-proclaimed Messiah.[2]

Cromwell and many on his committee may have been interested in the Jews mainly for the benefits which their financial expertise would bring if they returned to England. The Fifth Monarchists were more concerned with the Jews' conversion and return to Israel, and none of the pamphlets advocated their readmission to England. But there was an alleged proposal in Barebones, possibly by a Fifth Monarchist, to allow the Jews to return and trade, which suggests that even the saints' interest may have been shaped to some small degree by economic considerations.[3]

The Jews played a considerable part in the general Fifth Monarchist scheme of eschatology. The saints' interpretation of the biblical prophecies deviated relatively little from what was accepted generally. The 'synchronisms' of Joseph Mede, 'famously known to most that read books', were accepted not only by Fifth Monarchists but by such diverse men as James Durham, the Presbyterian, Thomas Goodwin, the Independent, and Edward Waple, an Anglican who in 1693 called Mede 'the Ornament of our Church'.[4] In the 1690s Archbishop Sancroft and Bishop Lloyd of St. Asaph were praising Mede's system and calculating modifications about the date of the burning of Rome and the coming of the millennium.[5] The only

---

[1] C. Roth, *A History of the Jews in England* (Oxford, 1949), pp. 149–72; Roth, 'The Return of the Jews to England', *The Listener*, lvi (1956), pp. 20–1; Sir H. Finch, *The Worlds Great Restauration* (1621), *passim*; J. Alsted, *The Beloved City*, trans. W. Burton (1643), pp. 8–10; D.R. (a Frenchman), *The Morning Alarum*, trans. N. Johnson (1651), pp. 18–19; H. J. Schoeps, *Philosemitismus im Barock* (Tübingen, 1952), *passim*; J. Fines, ' "Judaising" in the Period of the English Reformation—the Case of Richard Bruern', *Trans. Jewish Hist. Soc. of England*, xxi (1962–7), pp. 323–6; J. Traske, *A Treatise of Libertie from Iudaisme* (1620), *passim*; T. Tany, *Hear, O Earth* (1653), brs.; anon., Κλεὶς Προφητείας, *Or, The Key of Prophecie* (1660), p. 24.

[2] Below, pp. 213–14.

[3] *Thurloe*, i. 387; MS. Clar. 46, f. 109: newsletter, 15 July 1653.

[4] J. Mede, *The Key of the Revelation*, trans. R. More (1643), *passim*; N. Homes, *The Revelation Revealed* (1654), p. 46; J. Durham, *A Commentarie Upon . . . Revelation* (3rd edn., Amsterdam, 1660), pp. 333ff; T. Goodwin, *The World to Come* (1655), p. 13; E. Waple, *The Book of the Revelation* (1693), *sig.* A2v.; see above, p. 46.

[5] J. Evelyn, *Diary*, ed. E. S. de Beer (Oxford, 1955), iv. 636, v. 26, 322.

confusion in the seventeenth century was over chronology, since there was, as Canne complained, no obvious starting-point from which to count the prophetic numbers.[1] Tillinghast was the only Fifth Monarchist to attempt to systematize the prophecies. Drawing widely on earlier expositions, he saw the prophecies in a wider historical perspective, ridiculing those who hastened to identify the Beast as Charles I or Cromwell, 'as if nothing from the time the *Roman* Monarchy began, were transacted or done worthy to bee noted, till King *Charles* arose'.[2] Tillinghast calculated the 1260 days (interpreted as years following Numb. xiv. 34) in which the witnesses lie dead (Rev. xi. 3) from A.D. 396, when the Popes began to assume political power. The 1290 days of the profanation of the temple (Dan. xii. 11) were calculated from the destruction of the Temple at Jerusalem in A.D. 366. Thus the collapse of the Beast—the Papacy —and also the restoration of the Jews could be expected in 1656. Daniel's reference to the total perfection beginning after 1335 days (Dan. xii. 12), beginning also in 366, was taken to mean that Christ would not appear in person until 1701. Christ's kingdom had, then, a twofold nature, a first part in which the saints use physical force to establish the millennium, with Christ appearing later at the moment of perfection.[3] Though not all Fifth Monarchists shared this belief as to the time of Christ's appearance,[4] Tillinghast's interpretation enabled the saints to reconcile their faith that God alone could establish His kingdom with their conviction that the saints must take direct action to set up the New Jerusalem. When Simpson ventured to suggest that the millennium might not begin until Christ appeared in person, his meeting broke up in disorder.[5] Tillinghast explained that God chose to act through the saints on earth, as revealed in Jerem. li. 20: 'Thou art my battle-axe and weapons of war: for with thee will I break in pieces the nations.' 'The present worke of God', he argued, 'is, to bring downe lofty men, . . . and to throwe down Antichrist.' God would reward all who discharged this duty: 'O, saith he, there's such a one, he speakes for me, and he appears and pleads for me against the sins of the times, O writt it down presently (saith God), I will not have that forgot.' Disobedience could not disrupt God's plans, for God was 'never at a loss for instruments', but

---

[1] Canne, *Truth with Time*, p. 6.
[2] J. Tillinghast, *Knowledge of the Times* (1654), p. 78.
[3] Tillinghast, *Knowledge, passim; Mr. Tillinghasts Eight Last Sermons* (1655), pp. 61–2.
[4] See p. 137, above.
[5] *Thurloe*, iv. 545.

Tillinghast thought God would probably choose then to set up His kingdom elsewhere.[1]

Tillinghast also analysed in detail the vials of wrath poured out by God's angel on the sinful world (Rev. xvi). The first vial was Luther's declaration of the truth; the second the destruction of episcopacy by the Long Parliament. The third represented the troubles of ungodly kings and governments, such as the fall of Charles I, and upheavals in France and the Netherlands. The others, still to come, would include the collapse of the Habsburg Empire, the fall of Rome, and the destruction of the Ottoman Empire by England.[2] Tillinghast was held in great esteem by other saints who for some years argued that events of apocalyptic importance had taken place in 1656/7, though not noticed by the ungodly.[3] Nevertheless, many other dates were mentioned, among them 1641, '45, '48, '49, 1650, '55-7, and 1660, '65.[4] Many of the Fifth Monarchists stressed that their dates were approximate, and prudently gave alternatives.[5] The date on which there was the greatest agreement was 1666, calculated from the Number of the Beast which was 666 (Rev. xiii. 18). Men had been looking forward to this year since the previous century, and its near approach brought intense and widespread excitement.[6] The failure of any great event to materialize in that year was a severe blow. Perhaps it was reflected in Henry Danvers's analysis of the prophecies in 1672 in which he declared it was impossible to specify exact years.[7] But the Glorious Revolution, replacing the papist James II with the Protestant William of Orange, sent the millenarians back to the sacred texts, and they quickly proved that all the prophecies referred to 1688-9.[8]

The most important innovation of the Fifth Monarchists was to relate the monsters and beasts of the prophecies to living figures in

[1] Tillinghast, *Eight Last Sermons*, pp. 219, 230-1; *Generatione-Work* (1653), sig. A6-v; *Knowledge*, sig. a5v.

[2] Tillinghast, *Generation-Work*, 2nd part (1654), pp. 1-82.

[3] Canne, *The Time of Finding*, pp. 273-9; anon., *Door of Hope*, pp. 12-13; anon., *The Protector (So called)*, p. 94.

[4] M. Cary, *Resurrection* (1653), sig. Div., p. 125; Llwyd, *Gweithiau*, i. 22; Canne, *Time of Finding*, p. 273; Canne, *Voice from the Temple*, pp. 13, 29-30; N. Homes, *A Sermon, Preached Before . . . Thomas Foote* (1650), p. 17; anon., *Door of Hope*, p. 16.

[5] Llwyd, *Gweithiau*, loc. cit.; Homes, *op. and loc. cit.*; T. Parker, *The Visions and Prophecies of Daniel Expounded* (1646), pp. 138, 141, prudently gave 1649 and 1859 as alternatives.

[6] See below, pp. 213-14.

[7] Danvers, *Theopolis*, p. 46.

[8] For example, B. Keach, *Antichrist Stormed* (1689), pp. 145, 188; H. Knollys, *An Exposition of the whole Book of the Revelation* (1689), pp. 130-1.

the English political scene. After stating that the Little Horn of Dan. vii. 8 was Charles I, or the whole series of English kings, they came to identify it with Cromwell during the Protectorate, and proved that the number of the Beast, 666, referred to him.[1]

Though these suggestions appeared bizarre even to contemporaries, they were no more implausible than some royalist suggestions. About 1646 an Anglican minister identified Cromwell, Essex, Fairfax and Waller as the four horns of the beast in Dan. viii. 8. Griffith Williams, bishop of Ossory, argued that the number 666 referred to Cromwell, or to the Long Parliament, which another writer 'proved' by claiming there had been in all 666 members of the Long Parliament. Another identified the Beast as the Solemn League and Covenant, which had 666 words. The future Charles II was even hailed as the Fifth Monarch.[2] The eschatological eccentricities of the period were by no means confined to the Fifth Monarchy Men.

[1] Aspinwall, *A Brief Description of the Fifth Monarchy* (1653), p. 1; Rogers, *Sagrir*, p. 125; Cary, *Little Horns Doom*, p. 6; anon., *A Ground Voice* (1655), p. 3; J. More, *A Trumpet Sounded* (1654), pp. 1, 7–8; anon., *Faithfull Narrative*, p. 35.
[2] Matthews, *Walker Revised*, p. 253; G. Williams, *The Great Antichrist Revealed* (1660), pp. 49, 52–3; anon., *Key of Prophecie*, p. 15; *Diary of Henry Townshend*, ed. J. W. Willis Bund, i (1920), p. 74; A. Evans, *Mr. Evans and Mr. Peningtons Prophesie* (1655), *passim*.

CHAPTER NINE

The Later Years of the Fifth Monarchy Men

❖❖❖

Charles II entered London in May 1660, amidst general rejoicing. But for the Fifth Monarchists, the Restoration was an unparalleled blow. The non-fulfilment of their prophecies in the 1650s had been a disappointment, but the central pillars of their faith, the providential triumphs of the civil war, the fall of the bishops, and the execution of the king, had remained intact. The Restoration shattered them all.

Strict censorship and a ban on religious meetings outside the Established Church returned not far behind the king. The Fifth Monarchists were driven underground, and the stream of their pamphlets dried up. The only subsequent information about them is provided by hostile sources, which are far from satisfactory. The government was interested only in details of plots and conventicles. Local justices branded all dissenters as 'fanatics' or 'conventiclers', making identification impossible. Church-wardens found it impossible in towns and large or scattered villages to 'bee so well acquainted one with another, . . . as to present dissenters by name'. Not all were zealous in enforcing ecclesiastical uniformity. The church-wardens of Amwell Magna, Herts., thought it worthy of note that 'severall of the Inhabitants come constantly to Church'. Those of Kensington presented no dissenters in 1669 because, they said, 'we have no more Schismaticks . . . than have been formerly presented, who (we doubt) are no changelings.'[1]

There was severe persecution under Charles II and James II, but it varied from time to time according to the fluctuations of royal policy, and from place to place according to the attitudes of local

[1] Guildhall Library, MS. 9583, London and Middx. church-wardens' presentments: box 2 (1677/8, 1685), Amwell Magna; box 1a (1669-75), Kensington.

officials. The parish constables of Suffolk did not prosecute non-conformists, and suppressed information against them. When John Williams and other followers of Vavasor Powell were arrested in Wales in 1664, they were released promptly by two friendly Deputy-Lieutenants, despite not having taken the Oaths of Allegiance and Supremacy.[1]

The new government had none of Cromwell's scruples in dealing with the Fifth Monarchists. Harrison and Carew were tried and executed as regicides in October 1660. They presented themselves as martyrs for the Fifth Monarchist cause, and even royalists admitted that the effect of the executions was to strengthen the determination of the saints, who 'mean all to die Martyrs'. A forged pamphlet asserting that many Fifth Monarchists were becoming ardent royalists, and Harrison's alleged belief that he would rise from the dead after his execution, were probably both attempts to weaken the saints' morale.[2]

Several other leading saints were removed by imprisonment. Overton, Courtney and William Allen were arrested in December 1660 on vague charges of plotting, and Rich and Vernon had followed by February.[3] Cornet Day, seized in September 1660 for abusing the king, was re-arrested in January.[4] Allen and Vernon were freed in June 1661 on the condition of permanent exile, which they ignored. Courtney was still in prison in 1663.[5] Three other leaders, Portman, Rye and Goodgroom were all gaoled in 1661–2, and were still in prison in 1667.[6] Overton was still a prisoner in 1671, and probably died soon afterwards.[7] Colonel Rich was more fortunate. He was detained, on very mild terms, in London and then

[1] G. R. Cragg, *Puritanism in the Period of the Great Persecution* (Cambridge, 1957), *passim*; Ipswich Rec. Office, Quarter-Sessions Order Book, 1665–76: 16 July 1669; P.R.O., State Papers, Charles II, SP. 29/97, f. 153: G. Gwynne to E. of Carbery, 30 April 1664.

[2] H. Finch, earl of Nottingham, *An Exact and most Impartial Accompt Of the . . . Trial . . . of . . . Twenty nine Regicides* (1660), pp. 26, 33–4, 76, 282; anon., *The Speeches and Prayers of Some of the late King's Judges* (1660), pp. 1–23; S. Pepys, *Diary*, ed. H. B. Wheatley (1893), i. 260; anon., *A Declaration of Maj. Gen. Harrison* (1660), p. 7; anon., *Observations Upon the Last Actions . . . of . . . Harrison* (1660), pp. 9, 17–18.

[3] *Cal. S.P. Dom., 1660–1*, pp. 424, 520; *ibid.*, *'61–2*, p. 12; *Mercurius Publicus*, 51 (13–20 Dec. 1660), p. 821; *ibid.*, 54 (27 Dec. '60–3 Jan. '61), p. 846.

[4] J. C. Jeaffreson, *Middlesex County Records*, iii. (1888), pp. 306–7; *Merc. Publicus*, 2 (10–17 Jan. '61), p. 22.

[5] *Cal. S.P. Dom., 1661–2*, p. 12; SP. 29/67, f. 103: list of prisoners, 14 Jan. 1663.

[6] Worcester Coll., Oxford, MS. 33, f. 111*v*.: list of prisoners, Aug. 1662; *Cal. S.P. Dom., 1661–2*, pp. 253, 552; SP. 29/34, f. 120: information, 18 April 1661; SP. 29/218, f. 142: list of prisoners, 1667. For Rye and Goodgroom see Biog. App.

[7] *D.N.B.*, Overton; *Cal. S.P. Dom., 1671–2*, p. 13.

at Southsea. He married the daughter of the earl of Ancrum and through these court connections he secured his release in 1665. Rich refused to take the oaths, but promised that 'he did freelie submitt to the providence of God, and . . . that he could & did pray heartilie' for the king.[1]

Much of the lay leadership of the movement was thus removed permanently in 1660–1, and much of the ministerial leadership also disappeared. Woodall, Taylor, Stoneham and Postlethwaite do not seem to have engaged in any Fifth Monarchist activities after the Restoration. John Rogers fled to the Netherlands, and though he later returned and resumed his activities, he avoided publicity and even dedicated a medical treatise in very hypocritical terms to the 'Praecellentissimo, Prudentissimo Amplissimoque' earl of Clarendon.[2] Christopher Feake abandoned his London congregation and went into hiding at Dorking, where he was discovered in 1663. He showed very little fighting spirit. On being told he must go to London, he declared in alarm, 'I feare I may be knocked on ye head in London, for I know I have many enemyes.' In July 1664 he was released, having given a bond to be of good behaviour.[3] John Canne retired to the Netherlands, and remained there until his death.[4] Vavasor Powell was arrested in July 1660, and sent to Southsea Castle in 1662. Apart from a few months' freedom in 1667–8 he remained a prisoner until his death in 1670. A dream, shortly before his death, in which he imagined himself 'with [St.] *Paul, Harrison,* . . . and others of the saints' showed that his beliefs were basically unchanged.[5]

Much of the Fifth Monarchists' position rested upon a belief in God's providences, and many of them reacted to the Restoration by seeing it as a divine punishment:

> *. . . we have sin'd; and therefore for our sin*
> *Frustrate was made that* Glorious Design;
> *And we are brought where first we did begin.*[6]

---

[1] *D.N.B.*, Rich; SP. 29/31, f. 78: petition of J. Holbrooke, Feb. 1661; SP. 29/84, f. 1: J. Tippett to Sir J. Lawson, 17 Nov. 1663; SP. 29/109, f. 115*v*.: information, ?1664; *Cal. S.P. Dom., 1661–2*, pp. 112, 463; *ibid.*, *'64–5*, p. 483.

[2] *D.N.B.*, Rogers; Rogers, *Analecta Inauguralia* (1664), sig. A3.

[3] SP. 29/90, fos. 24–8, 55, 57; SP. 29/100, f. 208: letters to and about Feake; *Cal. S.P. Dom., 1663–4*, pp. 394, 430–3.

[4] *D.N.B.*, Canne.

[5] *Cal. S.P. Dom., 1660–1*, pp. 123, 130, 135–6, 176, 484; *ibid.*, *'61–2*, p. 463; SP. 29/237, f. 222: H.H. to (Sir R. Carew), March 1668; (E. Bagshaw), *The Life and Death of Mr. Vavasor Powell* (1671), pp. 134, 189, 195.

[6] Anon., *A Memorial on the Death of . . . Nathaniel Strange* (1666), brs.

God had thrown down king and bishops but allowed their return 'for the sinnes of those yt carried on their private ends'.[1] 'Backsliding England' could expect great calamities, for her

> . . . *Oaths, base-crouchings, deep Apostacie,*
> *To sins and vengeance flood-gates opened hath,*

and the death of godly men signified God removing His saints from the imminent vengeance.[2] The great plague of 1665 was seen as part of this divine retribution.[3]

Most saints advised submission to God's providence, and a sanctification of life to restore His favour. They accepted the regime as imposed by God, but rejected the episcopal church as contrary to scripture. They should, wrote Henry Danvers, be 'humbled under God's mighty hand', and they should pray for the government, but only 'as enemies', owning 'subjection to them, only as a plague, judgment and curse'.[4]

The Restoration was a blow to millenarian hopes, but it did not destroy them. John Talbot still had the confidence in 1664 to keep a diary of acts of oppression against the saints, to be revenged when times changed.[5] Fifth Monarchists who did publish tracts after the Restoration revealed a millenarian faith, shaken but intact. Danvers in 1672 described New Jerusalem in detail, but gave no dates for its establishment. Stoneham proclaimed the millennium, but was not sure whether it was imminent or still far off. Thomas Taylor and Richard Breviter continued to speak of it, but in the most general terms. Vavasor Powell thought the Fifth Monarchy had been 'unanswerably proved', but stressed that the government must be obeyed and that 'It is a great *piece of prudence in an evil time to be silent.*'[6]

Not all the saints were prepared to be so submissive. Some saw the restored monarchy as even more antichristian than the Protectorate, and found grim comfort in the belief that 'a *Beast never bites more*

---

[1] SP. 29/43, f. 85*v.*: information of J. Crabb, 11 Oct. 1661.
[2] Anon., *Bochim. Sighs poured out* . . . [*for*] *John Vernon* (1667), brs.
[3] Brit. Mus. Add. MS. 15226, fos. 80–3*v.*: E.N., 'London's Plague-Sore Discovered'; anon., *A Mite from Three Mourners* (1666), brs.
[4] Danvers, *The Mystery of Magistracy* (1663), pp. 21–3.
[5] SP. 29/99, f. 17: information, 2 June 1664. For Talbot, see Biog. App.
[6] Danvers, *Theopolis* (1672), *passim*; B. Stoneham, *The Voice of a Cry at Midnight* (1664), p. 27; T. Taylor, *Jacob Wrestling with God* (1692, 1st publ. 1663), sig. A6–7; R. Breviter, *The Mighty Christ the Saints Help* (1662), pp. 8–9, 28, 90–3; V. Powell, *The Bird in the Cage* (1661), pp. 5–6, 8, 35, 38.

ferociously, and deadly, then when dying.[1] Several were eager to make it a quick death.

As early as 19 May 1660 a preacher in Coleman Street, perhaps of Venner's church, was 'vilifying' Charles II.[2] It was reported in November that 'a horrid intention of murdering the King and divers of the nobility by 5 Monarchy men' had been discovered.[3] In December, Overton and some other officers were arrested on a vague charge of plotting. This has sometimes been connected with Venner's rising, but it seems unlikely. In 1657 most of the Fifth Monarchists had refused to join Venner, and it is most improbable that republican Grandees would have done so. The assertion was probably an attempt to blacken the officers, who were never brought to trial, and to magnify the importance of Venner's band.[4]

On the evening of Sunday 6 January 1661 about fifty of Venner's followers left their meeting house and marched to St. Paul's. They had printed a manifesto, *A Door of Hope*, and had as their rallying-cry, 'King Jesus, and the heads upon the gate.' Apart from this objective, their plans seem to have been vague. They defeated an armed party sent against them and then retired to the woods near Highgate. Early on 9 January they reappeared in the city and fought with great ferocity against the Life Guards and a whole regiment. London was plunged into confusion. The rebels killed about twenty soldiers, and lost twenty-six of their own men. About twenty were captured, and others escaped. Contemporaries put their numbers at 300–400, but admitted that less than fifty were ever seen together. A woman was said to have been taken 'all in Armour'.[5] A wave of arrests followed, and many Quakers, Baptists and Congregationalists were seized. Though all three hastened to dissociate themselves from the rising, a royal ban on conventicles came a few days later.[6] Venner had destroyed any chance of toleration.

Twenty rebels, including Venner, were put on trial. Sixteen were

---

[1] Anon., *Antipharmacum Saluberrime* (1664), *sig.* A2.
[2] Bodl. MS. Clar. 72, f. 419: information, 19 May 1660.
[3] Hist. MSS. Comm., xlv, *Buccleuch MSS.*, i, p. 312.
[4] E. Pagitt, *Heresiography* (6th edn., 1662), pp. 525 (misprint for 285)–288; R. Baillie, *Letters and Journals* (Edinburgh, 1775), ii. 444; see above, pp. 117–18.
[5] C. Burrage, 'The Fifth Monarchy Insurrections', *Eng. Hist. Rev.*, xxv (1910), pp. 739–45; Sir W. Foster, 'Venner's Rebellion', *London Topog. Record*, xviii (1942), pp. 30–3; anon., *The Last farewel to the . . . Fifth Monarchy Men* (1661), *passim*; anon., *Londons Glory* (1661), *passim*.
[6] *A Renunciation and Declaration of the . . . Congregational Churches* (1661); *The Humble Apology of some . . . Anabaptists* (1661); *A Declaration from the . . . Quakers* (1661).

found guilty, and four acquitted; only two expressed regrets. Venner asserted that not he but Christ was their leader, but the popular belief that the rebels expected Christ to appear in person to lead them was ridiculed in their own manifesto. Venner and twelve others were executed, their heads being placed on London Bridge, and their meeting house was destroyed.[1]

Efforts were made to show that Venner had been the leader of a nation-wide plot. There were reports of a stir in Leicestershire on 6 January, and of 'declarations found for King Jesus' in Oxfordshire and Cheshire.[2] Better documented was a report from Exeter on 23 January that Venner had been there within the last five weeks, that large quantities of arms had been seized, and that a man had been arrested carrying two hundred Fifth Monarchist letters. A hundred suspects were under arrest, including Byfield, already known as a Fifth Monarchist, Thomas Mall and John Searl, two local ejected Congregationalist ministers, and Captain Henry Hatsell, the naval commissioner in the west. Another probably implicated was Colonel Francis Buffett, a prominent plotter for the next twenty years. Hatsell was soon released, and there seem to have been no further proceedings.[3]

Some violence continued in London after Venner's death. A plot due to take place on 15 April 1661 was discovered the previous day, and a search made in Newgate for seditious papers connected with it produced a riot among the prisoners. John Portman and one John Smith, condemned but reprieved for rebelling with Venner, were named as leaders, along with (implausibly) Hanserd Knollys. The same night a party of Fifth Monarchists was discovered in Fleet Street pulling down and burning the decorations erected for the coronation. Several were arrested, and the trained bands were ordered to keep guard every night.[4] A few days later, Portman was preaching in Newgate, demanding that the 'righteous blood' of Harrison be avenged.[5]

[1] *Somers Tracts*, vii. 469–72; T. B. Howell, *A Complete Collection of State Trials*, vi (1816), pp. 67–8, 106–17; Pepys, *Diary*, i. 323; SP. 29/28, fos. 130–2: list of prisoners; *Merc. Publicus*, 3 (17–24 Jan. 1661), pp. 38–9, 48; anon., *A Door of Hope* (1661), p. 4.
[2] *Merc. Publicus*, 2 (10–17 Jan.), pp. 17–18; *Diary of Henry Townshend*, ed. J. W. Willis Bund, vol. i (1920), p. 66.
[3] *Merc. Publicus*, 4 (24–31 Jan. 1661), p. 62; *Cal. S.P. Dom., 1660–1*, p. 516; *ibid.*, '61–2, p. 537. For Byfield and Hatsell see Biog. App.; for Mall and Searl see A. G. Matthews, *Calamy Revised* (Oxford, 1934), pp. 335, 430–1.
[4] Anon., *A true Discovery of a Bloody Plot* (1661), pp. 1–2; anon., *The Traytors Unvailed* (1661), *passim*.   [5] SP. 29/34, f. 120: information, 18 April 1661.

On 19 October 1661 a preacher named John James was arrested at his conventicle in Bullstake Alley, and charged with speaking and plotting treason. James denied these accusations, but the mere admission that he was a Fifth Monarchist was enough to secure his conviction, and he was executed at Tyburn on 26 November.[1] Indeed, any sectarian with millenarian ideas was liable to stand in some danger. Benjamin Keach, a Baptist minister in Buckinghamshire, was brought before the Aylesbury assizes in 1664 for publishing a child's primer containing passive millenarian beliefs. Lord Chief Justice Hyde told him bluntly: 'I know your religion, you are a Fifth Monarchy Man; . . . I shall take such order, as you shall do no more mischief.' Keach was accordingly put in the stocks twice, was fined, and had his books burnt in public.[2]

A few saints reacted to the Restoration in totally different ways. Two actually welcomed the king. One of them, John Sturgeon, was made a Messenger of the Exchequer, resigning the post in 1662 through ill health. The other was Peter Chamberlen, who regained the post of royal physician which he had held under Charles I. At first he refused the oaths, and attacked the whole idea of oath-taking, but in 1661 he took a modified form, accepting Charles as head of the church 'under the Lord Jesus Christ'. He even ventured to claim £50,000 which he pretended to have lost in the royalist cause. Sturgeon and Chamberlen seem to have welcomed the king because he offered religious toleration with stable government, but neither returned to opposition when this was seen to be an empty promise.[3]

Certain other saints rejected the new regime altogether. Thomas Tillam, brooding in his prison cell in 1660, soon decided that the saints must emigrate 'because ye sins of this kingdome are so great, yt ye Lord will destroy itt'. Christopher Pooley, one of the most militant of the East Anglian Fifth Monarchists, became his disciple.[4] By 1661 they already had a scheme for two hundred families to settle in the Palatinate, and though they were both arrested that year, the

---

[1] Anon., *A Narrative of the Apprehending . . . of John James* (1661), *passim*; Howell, *State Trials*, vi. 67–104. For James, see Biog. App.

[2] Howell, *State Trials*, vi. 701–10.

[3] Sturgeon, *A Plea for Tolleration* (1661), *passim*; Cal. S.P. Dom., *1660–1*, p. 144; ibid., '61–2, p. 513; Chamberlen, *A Speech Visibly Spoken* (1662), *passim*; *idem.*, 'A Case of Conscience', MS. Clar. 74, fos. 418–19; *idem, Non Inventus* (?1665), in SP. 29/142, fos. 41–3; SP. 29/31, fos. 141–2: petition of Chamberlen, ?Feb. 1661; SP. 29/237, f. 117: petition of Chamberlen, ?1667.

[4] Tillam, *The Temple of Lively Stones* (1660), epistle by Pooley, and p. 19; SP. 29/181, f. 193: C. Sanderson to Williamson, 14 Dec. 1666.

plan went ahead.[1] Pooley returned to England in 1664 to recruit new settlers, and spread reports of comfort and plenty. He was back in 1666 with one John Foxey, asserting that the Palgrave was not merely sympathetic but was a likely convert. They were reported in Northumberland, Yorkshire and Nottinghamshire, and Pooley was finally captured in Ipswich in 1667 and sent before Secretary Arlington.[2] By January 1668 Pooley and Foxey were active again, apparently in Durham, and in March a ship full of new emigrants sailed from Harwich.[3]

The beliefs and practices of this group differed considerably from the Fifth Monarchist norm. Tillam was accused of preaching Judaism in 1661, and the German settlement adopted all Jewish rites, including circumcision, the sacrifices and the ceremonial laws. They even wished to rebuild the Temple. They were also accused of practising communism, and of allowing polygamy and concubinage.[4]

In 1666 the government obtained a copy of the settlers' 'Solemn Covenant'. It rejected all antichristian rulers, and forbade saints to bear arms for them or take oaths. The saints recognized Christ as their only king, and vowed to 'advance his holy throne'. Coins bearing the image of antichristian kings were not legal tender. On property it was stated ambiguously that goods would be 'either in Community or propriety as providence shall order itt according to a persons freenes'.[5]

What became of the settlement is unknown. Tillam is thought to have died about 1676, and Pooley and some others were apparently restored to the orthodox Seventh Day Baptist fold by 1677, probably back in England.[6]

With so much of the leadership destroyed or scattered, the Fifth Monarchist cause was kept alive only by an influx of new leaders

[1] SP. 29/40, f. 157: information of J. Thedam, 27 Aug. 1661; SP. 29/41, f. 1–*v*.: information of Sir Wm. Killigrew, 1 Sept. 1661; SP. 29/446, f. 139: information, ?29 June 1661.
[2] SP. 29/106, fos. 17–18: W.N. to H. Muddiman, 5 Dec. 1664; SP. 29/181, . 193: C. Sanderson to Williamson, 14 Dec. 1666; SP. 29/190, f. 189: same to same, 5 Feb. 1667; SP. 29/207, f. 1: L. Jones and others to Albemarle, 25 June 1667; *Cal. S.P. Dom.*, *1667*, p. 235.
[3] *Cal. S.P. Dom.*, *1667–8*, p. 154; SP. 29/236, f. 28: S. Taylor to Williamson, 5 March 1668.
[4] SP. 29/41, f. 1; SP. 29/236, f. 28; J. Cowell, *Divine Oracles* (1664), pp. 30–3, chaps. 7–9; Cowell, *The Snare Broken* (1673), pp. 2–6.
[5] SP. 29/181, f. 195–*v*.: 'The Solemn Covenant'.
[6] E. A. Payne, 'Thomas Tillam', *Bapt. Quart.*, xvii (1957–8), p. 66; E. Stennet, *The Insnared Taken in the Work of his Hands* (1677/9), p. 7.

from outside London. Ejected ministers were prominent. Thomas Palmer from Aston, Derbyshire, was henceforth often in London, and Camshaw Helme and Anthony Palmer, ejected from Gloucestershire, also moved to the city. These latter were not previously known as Fifth Monarchists, and in January 1661 Helme declared he was a Congregationalist, not a 'rebellious Fifth-Monarchy-Man'. But he took over Feake's congregation, and he and Palmer were soon known as among the leading Fifth Monarchists. Nathaniel Strange and Thomas Glasse from Devon and John Skinner from Gloucestershire were all Baptist ministers who moved to London after 1660 and became Fifth Monarchists. It seems surprising that these men should be attracted to a movement which God appeared to have abandoned. Probably they were already enthusiastic millenarians who hitherto had simply not come into contact with the Fifth Monarchists. Palmer and Helme were also committed against monarchy, and the Restoration may have increased their radicalism.[1] Moreover the changing moral climate of the nation, especially of the court, aroused the fierce resentment of the sects. 'Severall thousands' of Fifth Monarchists condemned the blasphemy and wickedness of the times which the court encouraged. One Samuel Gardner joined Tong's plot in 1662 in disgust that 'any King should reigne haveing 2 bastards before he was marryed'. Christopher Crayle, a Vennerite, was 'very Cheerfull' because such wickedness meant that 'the King and his bishops were Riding post haste to their owne destruction.'[2]

In the face of persecution, the sects drew together to some degree. Secretary Nicholas noted Presbyterians, Baptists and Fifth Monarchists all meeting together, preaching that deliverance was near. Many Presbyterians probably disapproved of this, but in 1664 a group of Presbyterian ministers was lamenting that some of 'their leadeing men' had actually joined the Fifth Monarchists.[3] There were many meetings with Baptists and Congregationalists, and Simpson preached every week at Allhallows with Knollys and Jessey.[4] In

---

[1] See Biog. App. for all these; Matthews, *Cal. Rev.*, pp. 256, 380, 444, 478; C. Helme, *Life in Death* (1661), sig. A2v.; SP. 29/42, f. 69: W. Pestell to Nicholas, 26 Sept. 1661; SP. 29/99, f. 16–17: information, 2 June 1664; SP. 29/120, f. 57: P. to Arlington, 3 May 1665.

[2] Brit. Mus. Add. MS. 38856, f. 79: 'A doore of hope opened', ?1663; SP. 29/66, f. 73v.: list of prisoners, 1662; SP. 29/42, f. 69v.: Pestell to Nicholas, 26 Sept. 1661.

[3] MS. Clar. 75, f. 191: Nicholas to Clarendon, 13 Sept. 1661; SP. 29/42, f. 69; SP. 29/103, f. 262: information, 27 Oct. 1664.

[4] SP. 29/41, f. 106: information, 11 Sept. 1661.

October 1660 Simpson boldly defended the regicides, who he said were justified before God; he called on the saints to be 'ready and willing' to 'fight it out to the last Breth against the Enemys of the truth', knowing they 'must overcome, they shall overcome and they will overcome', and reign as judges with Christ.[1] Predictably the government arrested him, in November 1661, and though he was released later on taking the oaths, he remained quiet until his death in June 1662. His supporters were disappointed at this submission, and the sermon preached at his funeral was an attempt to defend him against this last charge of betrayal.[2]

Anthony Palmer, who sometimes preached with Simpson, thought the wickedness of the times proved that 'the beast was upon his last worke'. He and Helme, 'violent Proiecting men', acquired great influence over the gathered churches in London and elsewhere. A list of preachers, drawn up probably in the autumn of 1661, showed that Rogers and Feake were still sometimes active in London. Rogers, Helme and Palmer preached against the Court, and predicted that God would 'blast them'.[3] In 1662 the Fifth Monarchists held a day of fasting with other nonconformists to mark the trial of Vane and Lambert. Vane repaid them at his execution with a fervent millenarian prayer, anticipating the reign of the saints on earth with Christ.[4]

From 1663 the government began to receive reports of conventicles held by Glasse, Strange, Skinner, Danvers and Vernon, who, ignoring his sentence of exile, was practising medicine in Epsom, Ewell and then Newington. The group had some important contacts. In 1664 Sir John Vaughan and another Member of Parliament were attending it, and a clerk of the Commons was said to be passing on information to the fanatics. The group also met at the house of Alderman Pennoyer, and that of George Cockayne, an early saint who had apostatized but was in 1664 'now a 5t Monarchist' again.

---

[1] *Cal. S.P. Dom., 1660–1*, p. 320; SP. 29/34, f. 2: W. Williamson to Sir John Meanes, 1 April 1661; SP. 29/42, f. 66: information, 26 Sept. 1661; SP. 29/43, f. 106v.–7: E. Potter to Sir E. Broughton, 13 Oct. 1661; SP. 29/44, f. 270: same to same, n.d.

[2] *Cal. S.P. Dom., 1661–2*, p. 162; anon., *The Failing & Perishing of Good Men* (1663), pp. 18–20.

[3] SP. 29/34, f. 2: Williamson to Meanes; SP. 29/65, f. 17: R. Johnston to Sec. Bennet, ?17 Dec. 1662; SP. 29/47, f. 107: information, no date; SP. 29/42, f. 69: Pestell to Nicholas, 26 Sept. 1661.

[4] SP. 29/56, f. 15: O. Peck to Garrett, 2 June 1662; anon., *The Tryal of Sir Henry Vane, Kt.* (1662), pp. 90, 93, 121.

Cockayne's meetings attracted four or five knights and the countesses of Peterborough and Anglesey.[1]

Despite the fact that the group met in at least twenty different places in the course of two years, the government was kept informed of their activities. The Fifth Monarchist groups were riddled with saints who, through bribes or threats, had become government agents. William Pestell, who had given information against Venner, told how an unsuspecting saint came to his home and brought his wife the latest news. One agent, probably Pestell, was entrusted by Helme and his congregation to report on their behalf on rumoured apparitions in the west. Peter Crabb, another agent, was supplied with information by John Belcher, one of the foremost saints. At a meeting in 1665 one saint confessed he was an informer, and accused three others present of being the same. The congregation debated whether to murder them all, but decided against it. The incident was reported to the authorities by yet another agent, so that at least one-sixth of those present were informers.[2]

Many of the agents were acting under threats, not from choice, and the government could not be sure of their loyalty. William Ecring supplied information, but seems to have been still a genuine Fifth Monarchist.[3] Even the trained bands were not wholly reliable. In 1664 they surprised Vernon and Glasse at a conventicle in Cannon Street, but one of their officers, named Cox, contrived to create such confusion that all but one of the congregation escaped. Cox took the captive to a tavern and warned him about trepanners. Finally, on payment of a small bribe, the prisoner was allowed to leave 'to doe ye needes of nature', and naturally was seen no more.[4]

With the return of censorship it was difficult for the saints to print pamphlets to spread their cause. No clearly Fifth Monarchist work survives which was printed after 1661. The pamphlets that the Fifth Monarchists did produce were millenarian in tone but aimed at the

[1] SP. 29/71, f. 147: information, ?9 April 1663; SP. 29/99, f. 16: information, 2 June 1664; SP. 29/100, f. 17: information, ?1 July 1664; SP. 29/101, f. 201: information, 7 Aug. '64; SP. 29/103, f. 262: information, 27 Oct. '64; SP. 29/105, f. 75: information, 20 November '64; SP. 29/110, f. 216: information, Jan. '65; SP. 29/111, f. 140: information, Jan. '65; SP. 29/121, f. 64: information, May '65; J. Vernon, *The Compleat Scholler* (1666), pp. 6–8; on Vaughan see D. T. Witcombe; *Charles II and the Cavalier House of Commons* (Manchester, 1966), p. 209.

[2] SP. 29/42, f. 69v.: Pestell to Nicholas; *Cal. S.P. Dom., 1661–2*, p. 188; SP. 29/120, f. 57: P. to Arlington, 3 May 1665; SP. 29/80, f. 192: Crabb to Bennet, 22 Sept. 1663; SP. 29/116, f. 235: information, ?March '65.

[3] SP. 29/449, f. 61v.: information, 28 July 1664; SP. 29/99, f. 17: information, 2 June '64. [4] SP. 29/449, f. 61.

support of the whole nonconformist body. Powell attacked the new Book of Common Prayer. Tillam urged the saints not to attend Anglican services and Helme exhorted them to remain loyal to their gathered congregation.[1] The Fifth Monarchists also spread pamphlets in support of the 'Good Old Cause', such as *Mene Tekel* (most often ascribed to Roger Jones), the *Phoenix* and *Antipharmacum Saluberrime*. An apparently Fifth Monarchist tract, *The Judgement with those called 5t. Monarchy men*, was reported in 1669, but there is no known copy of it.[2]

The saints soon devised new interpretations of the prophecies to reconcile them with the unexpected course of events. In April 1661 they were spreading an account of the calamities to precede the Day of Judgement in 1670. Pepys reported a popular nonconformist belief that the world would end in 1662. Owen Lloyd's *Panther-Prophecy* was published in 1662, suggesting the approaching downfall of Charles II.[3]

Although providence seemed to have abandoned the saints, they sought desperately to prove that the ways of God, though obscure, were just. They argued that whilst God was using wicked men to punish them for their sins, He also destroyed their persecutors to reassure the saints that they were still the chosen people. A man who went to jeer at Harrison being taken to the gallows was said to have had a fit and fallen dead. Another who helped to drive Anthony Palmer from his parish was also struck dead. Collections of such episodes were published, and though the majority seem to have concerned Baptists and Congregationalists, many Fifth Monarchist centres were the scenes of the events. Danvers, Cockayne and Jessey were suspected of being responsible for these tracts, and Livewell Chapman helped in their publication.[4] Many involved in the trial of John James were also said to have met sudden and mysterious deaths.[5]

London seems to have played an even more dominant role after

---

[1] Powell, *Common-Prayer-Book no Divine Service* (1660), *passim*; Tillam, *The Temple*, pp. 187–92 and *passim*; C. Helme, *Life in Death*, pp. 5, 8.

[2] SP. 29/99, f. 17: information, 2 June 1664; SP. 29/449, f. 61: information, 28 July '64; *Cal. S.P. Dom.*, *1661–2*, p. 23; *ibid.*, *'68–9*, p. 342.

[3] Anon., *A true Discovery of a Bloody Plot*, p. 3; Pepys, *Diary*, ii. 401; see above, p. 186.

[4] Anon., *ΕΝΙΑΥΤΟΣ ΤΕΡΑΣΤΙΟΣ Mirabilis Annus, or the Year of Prodigies and Wonders* (1661), pp. 76 (misprint for 78), 79–80 and *passim*; *Mirabilis Annus Secundus* (1662); *Mirabilis Annus Secundus: or, the Second Part of the Second Years Prodigies* (1662); *Cal. S.P. Dom.*, *1661–2*, pp. 23, 87, 128, 173; *ibid.*, *'63–4*, p. 180.

[5] Anon., *A Narrative . . . of John James*, p. 47.

1660 than before. No Fifth Monarchy activities were reported in Wales after that year, though Powell's followers continued to hold meetings.[1] East Anglia also became quiet. Many of the leaders had moderated their views, some including Buttevant had moved to London, and Pooley had emigrated.[2]

Nevertheless the Fifth Monarchists did attempt to carry their cause outside the capital. In 1661 Pestell reported that they had sent agents to Yorkshire, Durham, Devon and Great Yarmouth. The leading missionaries were (Anthony) Palmer, Helme, Belcher, Feake, Canne and Rogers who 'travell from County to County and are hardly a month in a place'. Venner's son-in-law, Medley, kept the papers of the national correspondence and acted as accountant.[3] Thomas Palmer was another itinerant. He was arrested at Egerton, Kent, in 1662 by a Colonel Colepeper, who threatened to hang him at once. But finding the colonel to suffer from disturbing visions, Palmer persuaded him that these were the results of his sins, and in this way secured his release.[4]

The London meetings and sermons naturally irritated the authorities. As mentioned before, they arrested Simpson and nearly caught Glasse and Vernon. They also seized Chapman, Thimbleton and Cockayne, and searched for Strange, Danvers, Skinner and Anthony Palmer.[5] But when the preachers urged only passive defiance and patience, there seemed little real cause for alarm. The Duke of Albemarle thought in 1663 that the Fifth Monarchists were 'so weake and inconsiderable that I am confident they will nott be dangerous'.[6] Samuel Butler thought they might be licensed at £5 a year, paying extra for liberty to expound on Revelation, and Abraham Cowley also treated them as comical rather than dangerous.[7] There was also a proposal that they should be arrested, disarmed and shipped off to Venice as mercenaries.[8] The saints were

---

[1] SP. 29/97, f. 153: G. Gwynne to e. of Carbery, 30 April 1664.
[2] SP. 29/44, f. 265: information, 1661; see above, pp. 197–8, 201–2.
[3] SP. 29/44, f. 267: Pestell to Nicholas, 28 Nov. 1661; SP. 29/42, f. 69v.: same to same, 26 Sept. 1661.
[4] A. G. Matthews, 'A Censored Letter', *Trans. Congregationalist Hist. Soc.*, ix (1924–6), pp. 267–8; *D.N.B.*, T. Palmer.
[5] Above, pp. 204–5. *Cal. S.P. Dom., 1661–2*, pp. 124, 397–8, 434, 552; *ibid., '63–4*, pp. 349, 393, 494, 502, 581–2.
[6] Hist. MSS. Coll., lxxi, *Finch MSS.*, i, p. 299: d. of Albemarle to e. of Winchilsea, 28 Dec. 1663.
[7] S. Butler, *A Proposal Humbly Offered for the Farming of Liberty of Conscience* (1663), pp. 8, 10: A. Cowley, *Cutter of Coleman-Street* (1663), *passim*.
[8] SP. 29/143, f. 128: memorandum, ?1665.

far too weak to overthrow the government, but they were potentially dangerous in three ways. They might organize an assassination plot, they might join any other plotters to further their cause, or they might give assistance to a Dutch invasion.

Despite the common acceptance of God's providence, two saints did publish theories of resistance. Danvers accepted that God's will must be obeyed if He had restored the king, but he claimed that providence was 'indistinct . . . as Eccles. 8.14. It happeneth to the just according to the work of the wicked; and to the wicked, according to the work of the just. So that no Argument can be made from it.' He claimed the saints had a duty to resist antichristian rulers 'by open or secret resistance, when the providence of God makes way for the same'. The mere fact of not being caught proved God's support for the plotter.[1] Thomas Palmer, a less subtle casuist, rejected the biblical claim that all powers are of God, and asserted that no 'Antichristian Kings were called by God' and that it was a great sin to accept the monarchy which God had destroyed.[2]

There was from the time of Venner onwards an undercurrent of violence among the saints, though most of it was empty talk. The government was informed in 1661 of a house-to-house collection, possibly to raise money for rebellion. Captain Owen Cox caused alarm by mooring his ship, laden with powder and ammunition, at Sandwich, and was eventually seized on a charge of seditious language.[3] In September 1661 John Belcher, described as a dangerous man who had only held back from Venner's rising through a quarrel over tactics, reappeared in London, and was reported later to be holding a meeting to arrange a time 'to finish the Lords worke, as they call it'.[4] William James prayed at a meeting in Duke's Place, Westminster, that 'God would putt an Axe into ye hand of some of his servants, to hewe down Roote and branch of King and Bishopps.'[5] In 1665 Helme and his group were thought to be in the mood for a rising at any moment, and the following January one Captain Harris was reported to have been trying for two years to enlist the saints for a rising.[6] Nathaniel Strange had denounced the

---

[1] H. Danvers, *Mysterie of Magistracy*, pp. 20–5, 37.

[2] Palmer, *The Saints Freedom from Tyranny Vindicated* (1667), pp. 9, 11, 30.

[3] SP. 29/34, f. 2*v*.: W. Williamson to Meanes, 1 April 1661; SP. 29/44, f. 267*v*.: Pestell to Nicholas, 28 Nov. 1661.

[4] SP. 29/42, f. 69*v*.: Pestell to Nicholas, 26 Sept. 1661; SP. 29/80, f. 192: P. Crabb to Bennet, 22 Sept. 1663.

[5] SP. 29/43, f. 85–*v*.: information of J. Crabb, 11 Oct. 1661.

[6] SP. 29/120, f. 57: P. to Arlington, 3 May 1665; SP. 29/144, f. 49: G. Phillipps to Arlington, 3 Jan. 1666.

king as the Beast in 1662, and the government made repeated efforts to capture him. In 1665 Strange, a 'rash heady person', was trying to persuade the saints to attack Whitehall, and Timothy Roberts, ejected from Barton in Westmorland, assured them that the saints in the north were ready to rise at the first opportunity.[1]

None of these threats materialized, but the Fifth Monarchists were, as was feared, 'fitt to strike in with any that shall appeare in Rebellion'.[2] They were alleged to be in a plot in 1661 in which Portman was named and Harrington and Wildman were said to be prominent. The affair was highly nebulous, and probably largely fictitious, serving mainly as an excuse to gaol Harrington and prosecute Vane and Lambert.[3] In the autumn of 1662 the 'Tong Plot' was discovered. Ensign Tong and his associates had planned to surprise the king and Albemarle, and then bring over republican exiles from Holland. Though all the sects and republican interests were alleged to be involved, the Fifth Monarchists were 'to lead the van'. Two government agents, Hill and Riggs, fanned the plot and then betrayed it, trying to incriminate as many as possible. They named, among others, Strange, Danvers, Anthony Palmer, Helme and John Rogers, but these allegations were probably fictitious and the government took proceedings only against Tong and five others, who were executed. Among the prisoners were John Venner, an ivory-turner and apparently a Fifth Monarchist, James Webb, described as an Anabaptist or Fifth Monarchist, and one Goodwin of the Mill Yard Seventh Day church led by William Sellers, to which Chamberlen belonged. Sellers had earlier published a Seventh Day pamphlet with Spittlehouse.[4]

The most important plot of the post-Restoration period was the Yorkshire rising of 1663, led by a number of former republican officers, with most backing in Yorkshire, Durham and Westmorland.

---

[1] SP. 29/56, f. 12: information, 2 June 1662; *Cal. S.P. Dom., 1661–2*, pp. 124, 397, 434; *ibid., '63–4*, p. 2; SP. 29/114, fos. 19–20*v*.: information of A.W., March 1665. For Roberts see Biog. App.
[2] SP. 29/56, f. 195: W. Williamson to Sir W. Compton, 25 June 1662.
[3] W. C. Abbott, 'English Conspiracy and Dissent, 1660–1674', *American Hist. Rev.*, xiv (1908–9), pp. 508–10; Howell, *State Trials*, vi. 114–17.
[4] W. Hill, *A Brief Narrative of that Stupendious Tragedie* (1662), *passim*; Abbott, 'English Conspiracy', pp. 514–15; *Merc. Publicus*, 50 (11–18 Dec. '62), pp. 808–10; *ibid.*, 51, p. 838; *ibid.*, 3 (15–22 Jan. '63), pp. 33–4, 48; *ibid.*, 8 (19–26 Feb.), p. 124; *ibid.*, 9, p. 140; SP. 29/66, fos. 72–3*v*.: list of prisoners; on Sellers see J. W. Thirtle, 'Dr. Peter Chamberlen . . .', *Trans. Baptist Hist. Soc.*, iii (1912–13), pp. 186–7; cf. W. Saller and J. Spittlehouse, *An Appeal to the Consciences of the chief Magistrates* (1657).

Preparations were under way in the winter of 1662–3, with an attack on York planned for August. But like other plots, it was riddled with agents, and a hundred leading members were seized the day before the planned attack. The remaining plotters devised new plans, but most were captured on 10 October. The few who escaped attempted a rising on 12 October, but dispersed when they saw how small their numbers were. About twenty were executed in 1664.[1]

The north had not been a Fifth Monarchist stronghold, but the itinerants had apparently had some success, for the saints were certainly involved in the plot.[2] John Joplin, Gaoler of Durham under the Protectorate and a leading plotter, had become 'a furious Fifth-Monarchy fanatic', and wrote slogans in support of King Jesus on the prison walls.[3] There was a dispute between the Fifth Monarchists and the other rebels over the contents of their manifesto, which seems to have been 'A doore of hope opened into the valley of Achan'. It was wholly Fifth Monarchist in tone, attacking the swarming of the papists, the idolatry of the Church and the sad plight of the poor. It declared that the 'use of temporall weapons of warr is a lawfull meanes of Gods owne institucione' and promised that when the saints had set up Christ's kingdom in England, they would go on to destroy 'Gog and Magog, Pope and turks'.[4] The two agents sent to negotiate with dissident groups in London were both prominent Fifth Monarchists, Jeremiah Marsden and Thomas Palmer. Marsden also had contacts in Ireland and visited malcontents in the west. Palmer was the heart of the plot in Nottinghamshire, with Capt. Lockyer of Skegby, Notts. (where there was a Fifth Monarchist group in 1669). John Wigan and Nathaniel Strange were also involved, and one Hatfield was named as a plotter, former officer and Fifth Monarchist—probably Captain Anthony Hatfield, a squire of Hatfield near Doncaster. Two other saints in the plot were Captain Edward Cary, who was seized but escaped from prison in 1664 and became a notorious plotter, and John Patshall, a Vennerite acquitted in 1661, who was eventually captured in 1666 but promptly escaped.[5]

---

[1] J. Walker, 'The Yorkshire Plot, 1663', *Yorks. Arch. J.*, xxxi (1932–4) pp. 348–59.
[2] SP. 29/78, f. 12: Sir T. Gower to Bennet, 1 Aug. 1663; Hist. MSS. Comm., xxxiii, *Lonsdale MSS*, p. 93. [3] *Cal. S.P. Dom., 1666–7*, p. 318.
[4] SP. 29/80, f. 272: information, ?Sept. 1663; Brit. Mus. Add. MS. 38856, fos. 79–80: 'A doore of hope opened into the valley of Achan . . . out of the North'; E. Price, *Eye-Salve for England* (1667), pp. 4–6 and *passim*.
[5] SP. 29/80, f. 272v.; SP. 29/85, f. 103: information, ?16 Dec. 1663; SP. 29/92,

The name of Colonel Danvers was mentioned frequently in connection with plots, but there were two dissidents of that name, often confused.[1] Robert Danvers, grandson of Coke, claimed a seat in the Lords in 1660, but was expelled. It was probably Robert who was connected with Tong. He was arrested by the end of 1663, and whilst in the Tower gave information about the Yorkshire Plot. In July 1664 he escaped, but was in prison in the Isle of Wight in 1667. He later went abroad, and died at Calais in 1674.[2]

Henry Danvers was alleged to be planning a rising, with Clement Ireton, as early as June 1661.[3] A government correspondent who kept watch on him reported that the Fifth Monarchists were plotting to rise in December 1663. Attempts were made to seize Danvers, Strange and Skinner, but Danvers had already gone into hiding. He appeared briefly in 1664, touring Staffordshire, and was meeting plotters and preaching in London in June. In April 1665 he was captured in London, but rescued by the mob on his way to the Tower. Only one rescuer was caught, possibly Clement Ireton who was in the Tower in 1667 as an accomplice of Danvers.[4]

The 'Danvers Plot' of 1665 was an alleged attempt to seize the Tower, kill the king, fire the city, establish a republic and carry out a redistribution of property. It was planned for 3 September 1665, but several of the leaders were arrested, including Colonel Rathbone. Eight were found guilty and executed. They were not described as Fifth Monarchists at the time, and the plot may have been more broadly based. L'Estrange, writing later, called them Fifth Monarchists, though he claimed they were tools of the Jesuits, and his account is generally unreliable. But the beliefs of Danvers and Ireton are not open to doubt, and Rathbone had formerly associated with John Rogers.[5]

---

f. 112: information, 9 Feb. 1664; SP. 20/100, f. 89: . . . to Bennet, 11 July 1664; SP. 29/78, f. 12: Sir T. Gower to Bennet, 1 Aug. 1663; *Cal. S.P. Dom., 1663–4*, pp. 652–3; *ibid., '64–5*, p. 293; *ibid., '65–6*, pp. 400, 404, 416. For Hatfield, Cary and Patshall see Biog. App.

[1] Including by *D.N.B.* The attempt here to distinguish them is by no means definitive.

[2] *Cal. S.P. Dom., 1663–4*, pp. 51, 328, 461, 463, 608, 652–3; *D.N.B.*, R. Danvers.

[3] SP. 29/446, f. 139: information, ?29 June 1661.

[4] *Cal. S.P. Dom., 1663–4*, pp. 346, 393, 367, 565, 606; *ibid., '64–5*, pp. 506, 508, 542, 555; Pepys, *Diary*, v. 40; SP. 29/287, f. 48v.: list of prisoners.

[5] *London Gazette*, 48 (26–30 April 1666); Jeaffreson, *Middx. Recs.*, iii. 376, iv. 269–270; E. Hyde, earl of Clarendon, *The life of Edward, earl of Clarendon* (Dublin, 1759 edn.), iii. 550–1; J. Lingard, *A History of England* (1849 edn.), xi. 290–1; R. L'Estrange, *A Compendious History of the Most Remarkable Passages* (1680), pp. 4–6. For Rathbone see Biog. App.

London was full of likely rebels at the time of the plot, among
them Colonel Thomas Blood, the most notorious adventurer of the
period. Originally a royalist, Blood felt slighted after 1660. In 1663
he had attempted to seize Dublin Castle, and he was involved in the
Yorkshire plot. In 1667, in the company of Captain Lockyer, he
freed Captain John Mason from an armed escort taking him to York
to be tried for treason. Blood was not a Fifth Monarchist, but found
the more militant saints congenial companions.[1] Thomas Palmer
and Strange were in London, where the latter succumbed to the
plague. Marsden was playing a double role, negotiating with plotters
abroad but appearing at court as a favourite. John Wigan, released
on bail from Lancaster prison, also went to London, but died there of
plague in 1665.[2] In August 1666 Blood and Palmer went to Ireland,
and there were soon reports of a plot concerning them. Danvers,
Marsden, Edward Cary, Lockyer and Robert Perrott (formerly a
lieutenant in Harrison's regiment and a preacher in Danvers's
congregation) were also involved.[3]

In the west Colonel Buffett was still active. He was arrested in 1662
for planning disturbances in conjunction with London plotters, but
escaped in 1664 by breaking parole. The following year he was
alleged to have ten thousand supporters, and to be involved in a
plan to seize the Tower, which suggests he was in contact with
Danvers. He avoided arrest, and in 1666 his brother was proclaiming
the victory of the 'Good Old Cause' within a year.[4]

Plots and rumours were all the more alarming to the government
because of its fear that the saints would assist a possible Dutch invasion. The Fifth Monarchists' earlier scorn for the Dutch as apo-
states to Mammon gave way in the 1660s to a feeling of Protestant
and republican solidarity.[5] Some of them found refuge in the
Netherlands, and there was a considerable traffic in goods and propa-

---

[1] W. C. Abbott, *Colonel Thomas Blood, Crownstealer* (Oxford, 1911), *passim*; W. T.
Whitley, 'Colonel Thomas Blood', *Bapt. Quart.*, iv (1928-9), pp. 27-30; R.H.,
'Remarks on the Life and Death of the famed Mr. Blood', *Somers Tracts*, viii,
438-54.
[2] SP. 29/121, f. 247: information, 22 May 1665; *Cal. S.P. Dom., 1664-5*, pp.
246, 261; *ibid.*, '65-6, p. 24; T. Curwen, *This is an Answer to John Wiggan's Book*
(1665), p. 152; Matthews, *Cal. Rev.*, p. 529.
[3] SP. 29/168, f. 211: Capt. Grice to Williamson, 24 Aug. 1666; *Cal. S.P. Dom.,
1666-7*, pp. 537, 545; *ibid.*, '71-2, p. 65; R.H., 'Remarks on . . . Blood', p. 448;
SP. 29/437, f. 84: . . . to Jenkins, 22 March 1684. For Perrott see Biog. App.
[4] *Cal. S.P. Dom., 1661-2*, pp. 443-4, 537; *ibid.*, '64-5, pp. 19, 544; *ibid.*, '65-6
pp. 25, 340; *ibid.*, '66-7, p. 31.
[5] See above, pp. 152-5.

ganda. It was alleged that Hanserd Knollys would help the Dutch in any crisis. In 1665 the Fifth Monarchists were reported to be waiting to see how the Anglo-Dutch war would develop, and were hoping that the Dutch would supply enough aid to enable a rising to be attempted. Captain Owen Cox was urged to take command of a frigate and use it to bring over exiles.[1] With two major Anglo-Dutch wars in the 1660s and '70s, there was a real source of danger.

The Fifth Monarchists' greatest hopes lay not in Dutch help but in divine intervention, and they continued to scrutinize the prophetic texts. Attention was focused on 1666 as the year of apocalyptic wonders, proved by the fact that the Number of the Beast was 666. The year had been seen in this light since the previous century, and John Archer, John Rogers and John Canne all expected cataclysmic events to occur. George Fox ridiculed the Fifth Monarchists 'who looked for Christ's personal coming . . . in 1666,' noting that 'some of them did prepare themselves when it thundered and rained and thought Christ was coming to set up his kingdom.'[2] This excitement was not confined to the saints, or even to England. Hopes were shared, apparently arising independently, by the Russian dissenters (Raskolniki), by the German prophet Kotter, and by Placentinus, a professor at Brandenburg who expected a local millennium in which the elector would win the crown of Bohemia.[3] John Evelyn said the excitement spread to all Protestant nations, and that it affected the Jews, always looking for the Messiah, more than any. In 1647 there had been a report of the Jews gathering under one 'Josias Catzias (in Illyria, Bithinia and Cappadocia) for the conquering of the Holy Land'. The approach of 1666 brought still greater excitement. Rumours of the discovery of the lost tribes of Israel aroused hopes which naturally produced a self-appointed Messiah, one Sabbatai Sevi, son of a broker of Smyrna. Jews throughout the Ottoman Empire abandoned their work and indulged in extremes of mortification to prepare themselves for the return to

[1] SP. 29/42, f. 69: Pestell to Nicholas, 26 Sept. 1661; SP. 29/44, f. 267-*v*.: same to same, 28 Nov. 1661; SP. 29/80, f. 192: P. Crabb to Bennet, 22 Sept. '63; SP. 29/93, f. 167*v*.: information, Feb. '64; SP. 29/99, f. 17: information, 2 June 1664; SP. 29/114, fos. 19–20*v*.: information, of A.W., March 1665; *Cal. S.P. Dom.*, *1664–5*, pp. 6, 297, 514.
[2] See above, p. 26; J. Archer, *The Personall Reigne of Christ upon Earth* (1642), pp. 50–1; J. Rogers, *Ohel* (1653), introd., p. 24; J. Canne, *A Voice from the Temple* (1653), pp. 24–5; G. Fox, *Journal*, ed. J. L. Nickalls (Cambridge, 1952), p. 419.
[3] F. C. Conybeare, *Russian Dissenters* (New York, 1962), p. 64; anon., *Prophecies of Christopher Kotter* (2nd edn., 1664), p. 12; Matthews, 'Censored Letter', p. 278. For Kotter, see below, pp. 234–5.

Jerusalem. They congregated at Constantinople from as far away as Poland, Germany and the Netherlands. The movement collapsed only when Sabbatai admitted the fraud, on being arrested and told that arrows would be shot at him to test his immortality.[1]

The activities of Sevi were followed with interest in Europe. Nathaniel Homes was kept informed by the Flemish millenarian Serarius, who was secretary to Spinoza, and who accepted Sevi's claims. The literary circle of Oldenburg, Robert Boyle, Serarius and Spinoza exchanged information and discussed developments at length.[2] The Fifth Monarchists ascribed a large role to the Jews in the approach of the millennium. In 1661 they had circulated a letter purporting to be by the Vice-Consul of Aleppo to the Jews at Jerusalem, which claimed that two hundred old men, aged a thousand years, had been preaching repentance and predicting the Day of Judgement in 1670. The Fifth Monarchist Thomas Chappell seems to have accepted Sevi's divinity, and the stories of pillars of fire above his head.[3] The Fifth Monarchists saw the Great Plague and Great Fire as proof that God was beginning the destruction of Antichrist, though the plague inadvertently killed many saints too. Dryden felt it necessary to write his *Annus Mirabilis* (1667) to dispute the belief that God was taking vengeance on the English regime. Vavasor Powell was preaching on the imminent fall of the ungodly.[4]

But no attempt to establish the millennium took place in 1666. It was feared that the plague and Monk's absence at sea would encourage a rising in London, and Courtney and Thimbleton were reported to be active among the fanatics on the Essex–Herts. border in January.[5] But doubts about God's will were 'the great obstruc-

---

[1] J. Evelyn, *The History of the Three late famous Impostors* (1669), pp. 41–126; R. Knolles and Sir P. Rycaut, *The Turkish History*, . . . *with the Continuation to* . . . *MDCLXXXVIII* (1687), pp. 174–84; anon., *Doomes-day:* . . . *with the gathering together of the Jews* (1647), title page, p. 2.

[2] P. Serarius, *The Last Letters To the London Merchants* (1665), *passim*; *The Correspondence of Henry Oldenburg*, ed. A. Rupert Hall and Marie B. Hall (Madison, Milwaukee and London, 1965–6), iii. 23, 49–51, 59, 447, 637.

[3] Anon., *A true Discovery of a Bloody Plot*, p. 3; SP. 29/162, f. 157: T. Chappell to J. Fitten, 12 July 1666. For Chappell see Biog. App. For Fifth Monarchists and the Jews, see above, pp., 191–2.

[4] SP. 29/162, f. 157; *Cal. S.P. Dom.*, *1664–5*, p. 484; *ibid.*, '*65–6*, p. 24; *ibid.*, '*66–7*, p. 149; E. N. Hooker, 'The Purpose of Dryden's *Annus Mirabilis*', *Huntington Lib. Quart.*, x (1946–7), pp. 49–67; SP. 29/144, f. 81: Sir G. Southwell to Arlington, 5 Jan. 1666.

[5] SP. 29/144, f. 138: Eyton to ?F. Manley, 8 Jan. 1666; for Thimbleton see Biog. App.

tion'; the saints were resolved to wait patiently 'till there bee such a way opened that all yt feare God shall bee satisfied wth there call to ye worke'.[1] The Fire was apparently not enough. In March 1668 a Fifth Monarchist preacher from Herefordshire told the saints in London that their work was to listen to God, to be 'in a readiness to goe when he Calles and not before he Calles; and when he Calles, then to seek by prudentiall pollicy to avoyd danger is the only way to be involved in danger'. It was hardly a call to arms.[2]

In 1669 a report was compiled of nonconformist numbers, and in 1672 the king issued the Declaration of Indulgence, under which many nonconformists took out licences to hold religious meetings. Documents from these two episodes throw some light on the extent of the Fifth Monarchy movement after ten years of restored Stuart rule, and on how many were abandoning their militant views and accepting the regime. The 1669 records are far from comprehensive, and mention only seven Fifth Monarchist congregations. Groups were listed in a warehouse at Southwark and in a tailor's at St. Mary Overy's Dock. Thomas Okey held meetings at Devizes, James Wise taught at Southampton, Henry Cock was prominent in a meeting at Chalfont St. Giles, Bucks., followers of Palmer met at Skegby, Notts., and those of Wigan at Great Budworth, Cheshire.[3] Other Fifth Monarchist groups, not mentioned in the list, existed during the 1660s at Canterbury, Edgware, Reading, Chester and Sheffield.[4] Thirty-nine Fifth Monarchists were in prison in Surrey in 1661.[5] A millenarian minister preached to two thousand hearers at Oldbury, Worcs., in 1667, though there is no evidence to prove the assertion that he was a Fifth Monarchist.[6] One Nicholas Cox of Northamptonshire went to London in 1670 to declare his determination to 'be true to King Jesus'.[7]

The 1672 records show that many of the Fifth Monarchist

---

[1] SP. 29/144, f. 49: G. Phillips to Arlington, 3 Jan. 1666.

[2] SP. 29/237, f. 222: H.H. to ?Sir R. Carew, March 1668.

[3] G. L. Turner, *Original Records of Early Nonconformity* (1911–14), i. 78, 118, 143, 144, 155, 169.

[4] SP. 29/136, f. 65: A. Corley to Williamson, 4 Nov. 1665; Gter. London Rec. Office, Middx. Branch, convictions of conventiclers, MR/RC-1, no. 46; MS. Clar. 81, f. 199: Sir W. Armorer to (Clarendon), 12 April 1664; SP. 29/264, f. 206: M. Anderton to Williamson, 28 Aug. 1669; Matthews, *Cal. Rev.*, pp. 198–9.

[5] *Cal. S.P. Dom., 1661–2*, p. 415.

[6] Worcs. Rec. Office, Quarter-Sessions records, Sept. 1667: depositions of J. Jimcot, W. Perrott, W. Carsdale; *Victoria County Hist., Worcestershire*, ed. J. W. Willis-Bund and W. Page, ii. 75.

[7] SP. 29/275, fos. 214, 216: information of J. Poulter, May 1670.

teachers had become ordinary Congregationalists or Baptists, though probably still millenarians. Anthony Palmer, Cockayne, Taylor, Woodall, Wise, Okey, Squibb, Price, Tunman, Steed, Skinner and Adams were all licensed. Helme was dead, but his widow took out a licence, as did the survivors of Pendarves's congregation at Abingdon. Feake, Rich and Spencer were all mentioned as teachers in 1669, but did not apply for a licence. Danvers and Thomas Palmer were conspicuously absent.[1] Since the 'wild principles' of the Fifth Monarchists did not permit them to accept the king's 'act of soe great grace', it must be assumed that all who took advantage of the Indulgence had adopted a quietist millenarianism compatible with membership of the other sects.[2]

The history of the Fifth Monarchists in the 1670s shows a continuing polarization of the movement, with the majority moving towards quietism and being accepted by other contemporary sectarians, whilst the minority became more deeply involved in violence and plots. Reports of conventicles still reached the government, though less frequently now that persecution was less severe. A meeting of Fifth Monarchists/Seventh Day Baptists was discovered near the Tower, and in 1671 thirty-five members were arrested, including Belcher, Goodgroom, Squibb and John Jones. All refused the oaths. Thirty-one were brought to trial, and twenty-seven of them were sentenced to imprisonment at the king's pleasure. The fate of the four leaders is not recorded, but Secretary Williamson thought Goodgroom was 'mad, no fighter', and with the king planning his Indulgence, they were probably released quite soon. One Squibb, probably the same, was licensed in 1672.[3]

In 1675 a Fifth Monarchist weaver named John Mason, one of the group arrested in 1671, achieved some notoriety by playing a leading part in the machine-breaking riots of the London silk-weavers.[4] But the following year a list of 47 London conventicles included only two described as Fifth Monarchist. Widow Brome held a meeting in Tuttle Street, and the church of Glasse and Vernon, now dead, held meetings in Glovers' Hall, Beech Lane, Cripplegate.[5]

[1] Turner, *Orig. Recs.*, i. 33, 84, 87, 105, 112, 566, 575, 576; ii. 951, 980, 984, 1017, 1051, 1075, 1204.   [2] *Cal. S.P. Dom., 1671–2*, p. 217.

[3] SP. 29/277, f. 4: information, 1 July 1670; SP. 29/291, fos. 176, 179: Sir J. Robinson to Williamson, 2 July 1671; *Cal. S.P. Dom., 1671*, pp. 386, 496; Jeaffreson, *Middx. Recs.*, iv. 29–31.   [4] *Cal. S.P. Dom., 1675–6*, pp. 258–9.

[5] Hist. MSS. Comm., xxii, *Leeds MSS.*, pp. 15–16; W. T. Whitley, *The Baptists of London* (1928), pp. 106–7.

The last sign of Fifth Monarchist activity in the north was an episode involving Richard Whitehurst, an ejected minister licensed as a Congregationalist in 1672. A fierce quarrel developed in 1679 between him and his congregation at Lydgate, Yorks., over his millenarian ideas. Part of the congregation was hostile to millenarianism altogether, wishing to study 'more profitable subjects', so that Whitehurst may have been only a passive millenarian. But since Marsden and Astley were called in to mediate in the dispute, and Anthony Hatfield was Whitehurst's protector, he may well have acquired Fifth Monarchist ideas from them. He was forced to leave the district as a result of the dispute, and died at Darlington in 1697.[1]

In 1676 one Studesbury of Broadley, Worcs., was tried at Worcester and ventured to justify Venner and boast of his own participation in the execution of Charles I. Greatly to the annoyance of the judge, the jury twice chose to irritate the government by finding the accused insane, and he thus escaped sentence.[2]

Fifth Monarchist conventicles survived into the 1680s. Christopher Feake appeared for the last time in 1682 preaching in a cellar on London Bridge. Henry Danvers and Richard Adams led two conventicles in the same year with a total attendance of one thousand.[3]

Not all the saints were prepared to follow the path to quietism. In 1674 William Medley, Venner's son-in-law, emerged after thirteen years' obscurity. He went to London as a Dutch agent, spreading propaganda pamphlets and meeting leaders of the Country Party, trying to influence Parliament to end the Dutch war and break the Anglo-French alliance. The efforts of Medley and other agents did apparently contribute to the Anglo-Dutch treaty of that year, but it is clear that Medley's group saw these activities only as a first small step towards the re-establishment of a republic in England.[4]

Another line of action was that adopted by Richard Halliwell, a former soldier, who in 1670 or '71 broke with his Fifth Monarchist

---

[1] J. Hunter, *The Rise of the Old Dissent* (1842), pp. 295–6; O. Heywood, *Autobiography, Diaries, Anecdote and Event Books*, ed. J. Horsfall Turner (Brighouse and Bingley, 1881–5), ii. 99, 101, 112, 240–3; J. Lister, *Autobiography* (1842), pp. 50–1; Matthews, *Cal. Rev.*, pp. 17, 526. For Astley and Whitehurst see Biog. App.

[2] J. Pollock, *The Popish Plot* (1913), p. 390.

[3] SP. 29/421, f. 324: information, 1682; SP. 29/419, f. 102: information, (11) June 1682.

[4] K. H. D. Haley, *William of Orange and the English Opposition* (Oxford, 1953), pp. 55–6, 164, 172–4, 179, 185, 188, 193–5, 200–1.

group 'on account of their apostacy and subservience to the Monarchy', and called for a return to the spirit of the Musselburgh
Declaration of 1650. Halliwell's response was to join Blood. In 1670
they kidnapped the duke of Ormonde in the centre of London, intending to hang him at Tyburn. The following year, with the Fifth
Monarchist Robert Perrott, they stole the crown and sceptre from
the Tower, and nearly escaped. Yet Blood was able to win the king's
favour, secured the release and pardon of himself and his friends, and
in return for supplying some information became a court favourite.[1]

Several other Fifth Monarchists refused to moderate their principles. In 1669 Jeremiah Marsden was offending more cautious
sectarians by 'preaching up the 5th Anarchy'. 'As for our rulers', he
prayed, 'what shall wee say unto thee O Lord, Our rulers are rulers
of Sodome and of Gomorrah.'[2] Danvers too was irreconcilable. In
1670 the government ordered the arrest of Danvers and Blood, so he
may have been involved in the attempt on Ormonde, but as usual he
proved elusive. In 1675 he was reported to be preaching in Staffordshire, but not until 1676 was he captured and put in the Tower for
treasonable practices. He was freed in April '76 after giving £1,000
security.[3] In 1677 Edmund Chillenden, now a coffee-house keeper,
was in trouble for publishing and spreading seditious pamphlets.[4]

The later 1670s were a period of increasing turbulence and tension
produced by the facts that the heir-apparent, the duke of York, was
a Catholic, that the king wanted toleration for the Catholics, and
that the court favoured a French alliance and admired the absolutist
regime of Louis XIV. To meet the threat of James eventually using
French aid to subvert Protestantism and the constitution, opposition
leaders moved towards the idea of excluding him from the succession.[5] Naturally the remaining Fifth Monarchists took a militant
position. In 1678 Marsden was comparing the times to the reign of
Bloody Mary, and condemning a 'great duke' who was the enemy
of God's people.[6] The previous autumn Blood had reported the

---

[1] Hist. MSS. Comm., vii, *Appendix to the 8th Report*, pp. 154–8; *Cal. S.P. Dom.,
1671*, pp. 237, 247, 385, 409; *ibid., 1671–2*, pp. 45, 65; SP. 29/437, f. 84: . . . to
Jenkins, 22 March 1684. Cf. Abbott, *Blood, passim*.

[2] Bodl. MS. Rawl. D 1347, fos. 25–30: S. Mather to Marsden, 12 Nov. 1669.

[3] *Cal. S.P. Dom., 1670*, p. 239; *ibid., '75–6*, pp. 419, 516; *ibid., '76–7*, p. 90; Hist.
MSS. Comm., xxv, *Le Fleming MSS.*, p. 124.

[4] *Cal. S.P. Dom., 1677–8*, pp. 338, 643; see also Biog. App.

[5] See generally D. Ogg, *England in the Reign of Charles II* (Oxford, 1955), and
J. R. Jones, *The First Whigs* (1961).

[6] SP. 29/404, f. 18: memorandum, about 26 May 1678.

Fifth Monarchists and 'Atheists' (Sir Robert Peyton and republican groups) meeting to condemn Popery and France. They had been stirring up their friends in Bucks., Berks., and Bedfordshire, and were planning an attack on the Tower, perhaps setting up Richard Cromwell as nominal ruler. William Smith, a Fifth Monarchist veteran of Blood's exploits against Ormonde and the crown jewels, was sent to London to reconnoitre for an assassination bid. The plan, which in fact fell through, was to kill Charles and James at Newmarket or in London, and murder William of Orange on his way from Harwich. Danvers and Axtel (son of the regicide) were implicated in the plot.[1]

In 1678 Oates revealed the great Popish Plot, a fantasy of lies with a modicum of truth, according to which the papists were plotting to murder Charles and declare James as king. The exclusionist leaders naturally made great capital out of the ensuing panic, pressing still harder for exclusion and a purge of the Catholics.[2] The king was forced to feign belief in the plot, but declared that the Fifth Monarchists were a greater danger, and that the campaign against popery was the first stage of an attempt to restore the republic.[3] Bedloe, one of the leading informers, attempted to please all parties by describing the plot as a conspiracy between the Jesuits and the Fifth Monarchists.[4]

The king's intention was to launch a counter-attack on the Whig exclusionists as soon as his position was strong enough. Although some of the Whig leaders, such as Essex, Russell and Sidney, were respectable figures, the earl of Shaftesbury's following included many extremists, and here the Whigs were vulnerable. Richard Mayhew, a Fifth Monarchist preacher, dedicated his books to Shaftesbury, who was presumably his patron.[5] L'Estrange claimed that the whole exclusionist cause was dominated by Fifth Monarchists and sectarians, and he published extracts from their sermons and writings of

[1] SP. 29/397, f. 9: notes by Williamson, Sept. 1677; SP. 29/396, f. 294: T. Barnes to . . ., 30 Sept. 1677; *Cal. S.P. Dom., 1678*, pp. 290, 291, 299, 300; J. Macpherson, *Original Papers; containing the Secret History of Great Britain* (Dublin, 1775), i. 86.
[2] Ogg, *op. cit.*; Jones, *op. cit.*; J. Pollock, *The Popish Plot, passim*; K. H. D. Haley, *The first earl of Shaftesbury* (Oxford, 1968), *passim*.
[3] Hist. MSS. Comm., xxxvi, *Ormonde N.S.*, iv. 486, 496.
[4] W. Bedloe, *A Narrative and Impartial Discovery of the Horrid Popish Plot* (1679), sig. A1v., p. 14.
[5] R. Mayhew, *Sichah: Or a Tract of Meditation* (1678), sig. A1; *Cal. S.P. Dom., 1678*, p. 246.

the 1640s and '50s as a reminder that they were republicans and social revolutionaries.[1]

In the spring of 1681 Charles felt sufficiently independent financially to be able to dispense with Parliament and go on to the offensive. In July Shaftesbury was charged with treason and put in the Tower. A jury—nearly all Fifth Monarchy Men, according to Secretary Jenkins—rejected the charge against him, and he was freed in 1682 and went into exile in the Netherlands, where he was welcomed by, among others, Medley and a 'Mr. Venner'. Despite Shaftesbury's release, the Whig cause was collapsing, and it was discredited completely by the alleged Rye House Plot of 1683 to assassinate the king and/or to stir up a general rising to put Princess Anne on the throne. Most of the details of the plot were, as usual, fictitious, but they provided an excuse for renewed persecution of the dissenters and for the execution of the Whig leaders Russell and Sidney. Essex committed suicide.[2]

There was no real evidence to connect the Whig leaders with the extremists, except that Danvers was an associate of Sidney and acted as his election agent in 1679.[3] But there is little doubt that the extremist groups were plotting violence. In 1682 meetings were reported between Danvers, Thimbleton and Fifth Monarchist followers of Blood, Halliwell, Perrott and Cary, and members of Shaftesbury's organization, the Green Ribbon Club. They intended to seize and probably kill Charles, James and as many as possible of the Privy Council, and hoped that Monmouth and Shaftesbury would then take up arms against the regime. Danvers was said to be looking forward to regaining the lands he had lost in 1660. Their plans however were betrayed to the government, and the scheme was dropped.[4]

In February 1683 several long-standing plotters were named in

---

[1] R. L'Estrange, *Citt and Bumpkin, in a Dialogue over a Pot of Ale* (4th edn., 1680), pp. 3, 12; *The Dissenter's Sayings* (1681), *passim*.

[2] Ogg, *op. cit.*, pp. 614–15, 628–30, 647–50, 653; D. J. Milne, 'The Results of the Rye House Plot . . .', *Trans. Roy. Hist. Soc.*, V. i (1951), pp. 91–108. *Cal. S.P. Dom., 1680–1*, p. 500; anon., *Memoires of the Life of Anthony late Earl of Shaftesbury* (1683), p. 7.

[3] M. D. George, 'Elections and Electioneering, 1679–81', *Eng. Hist. Rev.*, xlv (1930), p. 565; *Cal. S.P. Dom., 1684–5*, p. 148.

[4] SP. 29/420, fos. 166–8: J. Harris to Jenkins, 18 Sept. 1682; SP. 29/421, fos. 54–59: information of Harris, 24 Oct.; SP. 29/419, fos. 162–3: information of S. Oates, 8 June 1682; SP. 29/420, fos. 73–4: information of Harris, ?Aug. 1682; SP. 29/421, f. 156: Harris to Jenkins, 13 Nov. 1682; SP. 29/422, fos. 148–9: information of J. Harrison, 12 March 1683.

a new design, including Buffett, Cary, 'a Fifth Mon. man & brisk', and John Patshall who was 'as vile as ever' and expressed his readiness to join in killing the king and all the royal family. All these, as well as Danvers, were thought to be involved in the Rye House Plot 'exposed' on 12 June.[1]

The group of militant Fifth Monarchists survived into the reign of James, except for Marsden who died in prison in March 1684 and whose funeral was attended by five thousand mourners.[2] The last bid for the Fifth Monarchy, as for the 'Good Old Cause' in general, was in the rebellion headed by the duke of Monmouth in June 1685. Danvers had planned a rising at the time of James's coronation, and had assembled in London five hundred men from Essex and Hertfordshire, but had postponed action on hearing of Monmouth's forthcoming attempt. He was made head of the group which was to raise London for the duke, and Thimbleton was also involved. Monmouth approved of Danvers's position, though Perrott warned of his former 'Cowardice and Deceit' and general unreliability. Danvers failed to act at the appointed time, ostensibly because of Monmouth's assuming the title of king, though he himself had apparently urged this earlier. He fled abroad to avoid arrest, and died at Utrecht. Perrott sailed with Monmouth and fought at Sedgemoor, where he was wounded and captured, and he was later executed at Taunton. The government sought the arrest of one Ireton, perhaps Clement Ireton, and captured Colonel Buffett and Thimbleton, who was pilloried in 1686 for spreading libels that the earl of Essex had been murdered by the authorities (as Danvers had also done). One Thomas Venner was among the rebels who were transported, and was possibly the 'Mr. Venner' who was a friend of Medley.[3]

Monmouth's ill-fated rebellion marked the end of Fifth Monarchist hopes and, indeed, all the radical hopes aroused in the 1640s and '50s. The Whigs were free to make terms with William of Orange, unembarrassed by their extremist fellow-travellers.

---

[1] *Cal. S.P. Dom., 1683*, i, p. 66; ii, pp. 4, 15, 53, 77, 216–17; ibid., *'84–5*, pp. 145, 148, 268, 292, 296; SP. 29/423, f. 221: . . . to Jenkins, 18 April 1683.
[2] *Cal. S.P. Dom., 1683*, ii. pp. 374–5, 380; ibid., *'83–4*, pp. 332, 335.
[3] Ford, lord Grey, *The Secret History of the Rye-House-Plot; and of Monmouth's Rebellion* (1754), pp. 105, 113, 102 (misprint for 122), 107 (misprint for 123); L. Echard, *The History of England. From the Restoration of King Charles the Second* (1707–18), iii. 757, 764–5, 770; *Cal. S.P. Dom., 1685*, pp. 5, 157, 233, 246, 276, 429; ibid., *'86–7*, pp. 174, 183, 191; *D.N.B.*, H. Danvers.

The nature of the sources after the Restoration, little more than details of plots and conventicles, makes it difficult to solve the problems surrounding the later years of the Fifth Monarchist movement. These sources throw little light on its character, why it faded away, and what became of its members. The only accounts of the saints' beliefs are by outsiders. The most detailed was by Cosmo III, the Grand Duke of Tuscany, who visited England in 1669. He seems to have been informed that the Fifth Monarchists wished to destroy

> the ministry of priests, as being Catholic; the payment of tithes, as belonging to Judaism; the Norman laws of England; the universities and schools, as seminaries of idle curiosity; the nobility and distinctions of birth, as repugnant to natural reason and to Christianity; and they are madly desirous to overthrow . . . all earthly principalities and to prepare the way for the coming of Christ.[1]

Another account in 1669 said the saints expected the return of Christ, the resurrection of saints and martyrs, the end of all afflictions, government by the saints and the replacement of gospel ordinances by Jewish rites.[2] Of the two accounts, only this last detail shows any difference from Fifth Monarchist beliefs in the 1650s, and it may reflect only the deviations of the Tillam-Pooley group. The lawyers certainly believed that they were still the chief objects of the saints' hatred. In July 1671 a cow broke into the Palace Yard at Westminster and, through a misunderstanding of the ensuing commotion, the cry went up in the law courts that 'ye fifth-monarchy men were up and come to cut ye throats of ye lawyers who were ye great plague of ye land.' Flinging away their swords, wigs and gowns, the lawyers fled. Scroggs, later Lord Chief Justice, was supposed to be suffering from gout, but 'wase perfectly cured, stript himself of his gowne and coife, and with great activity vaulted over ye bar'.[3]

The problem of what became of the saints is obscured by the fact that most were humble people who simply disappeared. Few if any seem to have conformed altogether. Squibb remained a Fifth Monarchist, despite pressing his claim to a revision to a tellership

---

[1] *Travels of Cosmo III, Grand Duke of Tuscany*, ed. L. Magalotti (1821), p. 451.
[2] Bodl. MS. Rawl. D 1347, fos. 4–14: 'A Friendly Consideration of some mistakes about the Fifth monarchy'.
[3] *Correspondence of the Family of Hatton (1661–1704)*, vol. i, ed. E. M. Thompson (Camden Soc., N.S., xxii, 1878), pp. 60–1.

at the Exchequer, and Chamberlen continued to proclaim his apocalyptic beliefs when he was a royal physician.[1] The careers of many of the leading saints have already been described in this chapter, but only rarely can the fortunes of lesser members be traced. William Righton returned to Bermuda, where he continued as a Fifth Monarchist. Robert Heyward escaped during Venner's rising, and later grew rich as a tradesman near Shrewsbury, where he died in 1705 without abandoning his beliefs. William Parsons also escaped into the crowd, and emigrated to New England, where he died in 1702.[2]

G. P. Gooch suggested that many Fifth Monarchists, disillusioned because the millennium had not appeared, joined the Quakers who preached an inward kingdom.[3] But none of the leading Fifth Monarchists became a Quaker, and, except for Morgan Llwyd, all the leading writers attacked the Quakers.[4] The rank and file, of course, may not have heeded the denunciations of their leaders. Frederick Woodall admitted that two of his congregation had joined the Quakers. So did John Pennyman, who formerly attended Feake's services, though there is no evidence that he was a committed Fifth Monarchist, and he proved to be far from orthodox as a Quaker. John ap John, a disciple of Llwyd, and Richard Davies and Thomas Ellis, a deacon, both of Powell's church, all became Quakers.[5] An analysis of 141 signatories of the *Word for God* showed that 36 of them later had some Quaker connections, but many of the signatories had not been Fifth Monarchists, and the identifications are often uncertain.[6]

Attempts to measure the movement to the Quakers are not very successful. The lists of Quakers who suffered under the Stuarts'

---

[1] Hist. MSS. Comm., viii, *Appendix to 9th Rep., part ii*, p. 44; *Cal. S.P. Dom., 1663-4*, pp. 121, 582; ibid., *'66-7*, pp. 182-3, 535; MS. Clar. 72, f. 355-*v*.: G. Downing to Clarendon, 30 May/9 June 1662; Bodl. MS. Tanner 35, fos. 2, 95, 104, 133; MS. Tanner 36, fos. 130, 155.

[2] J. H. Lefroy, *Memorials of the Discovery . . . of the Bermudas* (1877/79), ii. *passim*; R. Gough, *Antiquities . . . of Myddle* (Shrewsbury and London, 1875), pp. 124-5, 185; C. E. Banks, 'Thomas Venner', *New England Hist. & Gen. Register*, xlvii (1893), p. 444.

[3] G. P. Gooch and H. J. Laski, *English Democratic Ideas in the Seventeenth Century* (New York, Evanston and London, 1959), p. 233; cf. G. F. Nuttall, *The Holy Spirit* (1947), pp. 111-12.

[4] See above, p. 183.

[5] F. Woodall, *Natural and Spiritual Light* (1655), p. 1; *D.N.B.*, J. Pennyman; W. G. Norris, *John ap John* (1907), *passim*; R. Davies, *An Account of the Convincement . . . of . . . Richard Davies* (3rd edn., 1771), pp. 38, 81 and *passim*.

[6] A. H. Dodd, 'A Remonstrance from Wales, 1655', *Bull. Celt. Stud.*, xvii (1956-1958), pp. 286-91.

persecution, collected by Joseph Besse, reveal only a handful of Fifth Monarchist names: Humphrey Bache, Anne Curtis, Thomas Lacy. Several more are doubtful: John Light (1673), John Marlow (1686), and Clement Plumstead (1686), but the time lapse here makes identification very uncertain.[1]

The 1669 census returns are of some help in showing how many former Fifth Monarchist locations had acquired Quaker groups, though the returns were far from complete, and since the Fifth Monarchists were strongest in large towns, the Quaker groups in 1669 may well have been alongside, not instead of them. In East Anglia, Quakers were reported at North Walsham, Bury and Wymondham, with none at Norwich, Ipswich, Syleham or Woodbridge. They had groups at Skegby, Notts., Southampton and Manchester, but none at Reading, Abingdon, Hull, Lewes or Exeter. In Wales, they were reported only in Glamorgan and Montgomery.[2] These returns, though incomplete, and the fact that the Quaker strongholds (outside London) were in the north and around the Bristol Channel, neither of which were Fifth Monarchist centres, seem to rule out any massive or general swing to the Quakers.[3]

It has also been suggested, by Whitley and Dr. Payne, that many Fifth Monarchists became Seventh Day Baptists. The churches of Chamberlen and Belcher were Seventh Day, and there was a Seventh Day group at North Walsham in 1669. But only a small proportion of the saints were affected, and Belcher, Chamberlen and Pooley seem to have adopted the Seventh Day Sabbath as an addition to their Fifth Monarchist beliefs, not as a replacement.[4]

The outer layers of Fifth Monarchist supporters, those who had been attracted to the movement only at its climax around 1653, may well have drifted on into the next religious novelty, of which the Quakers were the most obvious. For the more deeply committed, a move to the Quakers meant accepting their 'spiritualizing' notions and also reversing in most cases their own predestinarian beliefs. The evidence of 1669 and '72 suggests that most of the saints

---

[1] J. Besse, *A Collective of the Sufferings of the People called Quakers* (1753), i. 366, 392, 437, 480, 481.

[2] Turner, *Original Records, passim.*

[3] W. A. Cole, 'The Social Origins of the Early Friends', *J. Friends' Hist. Soc.,* xlviii (1957), p. 101; H. Barbour, *The Quakers in Puritan England* (New Haven and London, 1964), p. 257.

[4] W. T. Whitley, 'Seventh Day Baptists in England', *Bapt. Quart.,* xii (1946–8), p. 253; E. A. Payne, 'More about the Sabbatarian Baptists', *ibid.,* xiv (1951–2), pp. 161–6; Turner, *Orig. Recs.,* ii. 900.

followed their leaders into the fold of conventional nonconformity, retaining their millenarian faith but in passive form.

The decline and disappearance of the Fifth Monarchists is partly to be attributed, of course, to persecution. Many leaders were arrested, and strict censorship made propaganda difficult. At the same time, critics were free to attack the saints in print. There was a steady stream of dissuasives, from the erudite arguments of the Cambridge Platonist, Henry More, to jibes that the Lord Omnipotent would never be reduced to using such instruments as the Fifth Monarchists. Others simply poured scorn on the 'dark and dubious prophecies' revered by the saints.[1]

More important, probably, was the saints' belief in providence, for it was the amazing series of providences from 1640–53 that had built up the great wave of millenarian excitement. After 1660 providence was consistently hostile, and though preachers might explain the failure of their prophecies, they were unable to generate new excitement. Tillinghast and Rogers had remarked in the 1650s how unfavourable political developments reduced the numbers and zeal of the faithful.[2] After 1660 the movement was always on the defensive.

Assimilation into the Baptist and Congregationalist movements was all the easier because of the long tradition of joint meetings, and because these sects still retained a large amount of their former millenarianism. The Baptists, Knollys and Praise-God Barbone, published several millenarian works in the 1670s and '80s.[3] The most effective propaganda against the Fifth Monarchists was probably the writings of sectarians such as Tombes, Bagshaw and Grantham, who accepted the millennium and only criticized violence.[4]

The spirit of the Restoration may have been hostile to religious 'enthusiasm', but millenarian beliefs remained widespread. William Sherwin, an ejected Presbyterian minister, published numerous millenarian tracts until his death in 1690, and Thomas Beverley,

---

[1] H. More, *Apocalypsis Apocalypseos; or the Revelation* (1680), p. xxxv.; anon., *Mene Tekel to the Fifth Monarchy* (1665), brs.; E. Lane, *Look unto Jesus* (1663), p. 70.

[2] J. Tillinghast, *Knowledge of the Times* (1654), sig. a5-v.; J. Rogers, *Jegar-Sahadutha* (1657), introd., p. 3.

[3] For example, H. Knollys, *An Exposition of the whole . . . of . . . Revelation* (1689); P. Barbone, *Good Things to Come* (1675).

[4] J. Tombes, *Saints no Smiters* (1664), p. 26 and *passim*; E. Bagshaw, *Saintship no Ground of Soveraignty* (Oxford, 1660), p. 13; Bagshaw, *The Doctrine of the Kingdom . . . of Christ Asserted* (1669), sig. A2; T. Grantham, *Christianismus Primitivus* (1675), p. 5.

rector of Lilley, Herts., kept up the stream until the end of the century. The Baptist minister Benjamin Keach hailed William of Orange as a messianic king. Lodowick Muggleton, who claimed to be one of the last witnesses of Rev. xi. 3, found a following from the interregnum till his death in 1698, and the sect lasted into the twentieth century.[1] Even the Anglican church was affected, and in 1691 Richard Baxter alleged of millenarianism that it was not dissenters but 'Conformists that are its strongest Pillars'. The most distinguished Anglican millenarians were William Lloyd, bishop of St. Asaph, and William Sancroft, archbishop of Canterbury.[2] But the most notorious was John Mason, vicar of Water Stratford, Bucks. Mason, who had been subject to depression and pains in the head for many years, declared in 1691 that the Second Coming was at hand, and that Charles II and James II had given the kingdom to the Beast. In 1694 he had a vision in which Christ appeared and revealed that New Jerusalem was to be at Water Stratford, whilst the rest of the world was to be destroyed. Mason was seriously ill, and died in May 1694, but by then a body of four hundred wildly enthusiastic disciples had gathered in the village. They practised common ownership, and spent their time in frenzied singing and dancing. Mason scorned the rich and the educated, and his followers were all from the lower classes.

Dr. Hill rightly contrasts the different reaction of the government to Venner and to Mason, who was allowed to die in his bed, which he ascribes to the fact that 'the age of reason had arrived'. But Mason was also an Anglican minister, not a 'fanatic', which made it embarrassing to magnify the case. Moreover, he had in 1691 condemned the Fifth Monarchists (though not by name) for discrediting millenarianism by drawing '*strange Consequences from this Doctrine to establish seditious Principles and Practices against the* Powers that be'. As a quietist he was hardly dangerous.[3] Even so, there was some alarm. The archbishop of York asked a local minister, Henry Maurice, for an account of the matter, and Maurice

---

[1] Matthews, *Cal. Rev.*, p. 439; B. Keach, *Antichrist Stormed* (1689), p. 188; *D.N.B.*, W. Sherwin and Muggleton.

[2] R. Baxter, *A Reply to Mr. Tho. Beverley's Answer* (1691), p. 1; J. Evelyn, *Diary*, ed. E.S. de Beer (Oxford, 1955), iv. 636, v. 26, 322.

[3] C. Hill, *Puritanism and Revolution* (1962), pp. 328–36; J. Mason, *The Midnight Cry* (2nd edn., 1691), p. 4; anon., *A Letter from a Gentleman in Buckinghamshire* (1694), p. 6; H. Maurice, *An Impartial Account of . . . Mason* (1695), p. 30; F. Hutchinson, *A Short View of the Pretended Spirit of Prophecy* (1708), pp. 44–6; Brit. Mus. Add. MS. 34272, fos. 142–8*v.*: letters concerning Mason, and hymns, 1694.

compared Mason to John of Leyden, Hacket and Venner. Sir Charles Wyndham, a local landowner, thought the saints 'ought to be whipped and dispersed', and the duke of Bolton called for sterner measures, for 'my opinion is, they are fifth monarchy men'.[1]

Village messiahs and popular prophets continued to appear after the seventeenth century, and usually won a following. The line began with the French prophets and John Lacy around 1708, and continued through Richard Brothers, Joanna Southcott and John Nichols Tom, alias Sir William Courtenay, to James White, who was able to win a following in Chatham and Gillingham in the 1870s and '80s.[2] The failure of a resurrected Fifth Monarchy movement to appear in the century or so after 1685 probably owed more to the preservation of political and social stability than it did to the age of reason.

[1] Maurice, *Impartial Account*, pp. 55–6; Hist. MSS. Comm., xxii, *Bridgewater MSS.*, p. 151.
[2] J. Sutherland, *Background for Queen Anne* (1939), pp. 36–74; R. A. Knox, *Enthusiasm: A Chapter in the History of Religion* (Oxford, 1950), pp. 356–71; W. H. G. Armytage, *Heavens Below: Utopian Experiments in England, 1560–1960* (1961), pp. 39ff; R. Matthews, *English Messiahs* (1936); E. P. Thompson, *The Making of the English Working Class* (1968 edn.), pp. 52–5, 127–30, 199, 420–8, 429–31, 865, 877–83; P. G. Rogers, *Battle in Bossenden Wood: the Strange Story of Sir William Courtenay* (1961); Rogers, *The Sixth Trumpeter* (1963).

CHAPTER TEN

Conclusion

The Fifth Monarchist phenomenon is to be explained in terms of both the European situation following the Reformation and the more immediate circumstances of the English civil war. The unparalleled religious and political division of Western Europe, which the Reformation produced, unleashed a period of prolonged tension and warfare. The early Protestants formed a small and precarious minority. They naturally responded favourably to the idea that the Biblical prophecies, speaking of the profanation of the true church, of great calamities and of the vindication of the saints by the Second Coming and Last Judgement, referred to the contemporary situation. Most early Protestants, regarding themselves as the saints and the Papacy as Antichrist, awaited the imminent end of the world. By the 1530s the doctrine of the triumph of the saints on earth before the Last Judgement was already widespread in Germany. Subsequent political events such as the Armada and the Massacre of St. Bartholomew were fitted into the eschatological scheme laid down in Daniel and Revelation. In England, Elizabeth was seen as God's champion, and the concept of England as a chosen nation enabled the fusion of nationalist and apocalyptic enthusiasm. Though dormant under the early Stuarts, the theory of the elite nation emerged even stronger in the 1640s. Though there was no popular millenarian movement in England until the civil war, this was largely because the government was able to maintain political order and a large measure of religious uniformity. The career of Hacket, and the increasing number of millenarian lower clergy, from Durden to Archer and Goodwin, suggests that such a movement could have flourished in more favourable circumstances.

If the Fifth Monarchists are to be seen in a European context, the problem arises as to why there were no comparable movements produced by, for example, the wars of religion in France and the

Netherlands in the sixteenth century. Something similar in many ways had emerged in Germany in the 1530s when the Anabaptists seized control of Münster and tried to erect the New Jerusalem. The Münster episode served to discredit millenarianism completely, branding it as bloodthirsty and socially subversive. The story still provided potent propaganda in the 1640s against religious radicalism, and it must have been overwhelming in the 1560s. Millenarianism flourished in Münster because of the almost total breakdown of political order. Without such freedom, it could spread only with the connivance of some sections of the landed or official classes. The regiments of men like Cromwell provided an ideal milieu for millenarianism in the 1640s. In France and the Netherlands political authority remained mostly, though with some notable exceptions, in the hands of the nobility and local Estates whose objectives were primarily secular. Compared to Cromwell, William of Orange and Henry of Navarre were *politiques*, suspicious of their own more zealous Calvinist supporters. Millenarianism, still associated with Münster, could hope for no official favour. But by 1640 the story of Münster had to be extracted from the history-books and it could be argued (as by the Fifth Monarchists) that the accounts were prejudiced and inaccurate. Moreover millenarianism had been re-discovered at a higher intellectual level by the academics Mede and Alsted. Made thus respectable, it was able to win some support among the gentry and ministry. Cromwell could see no incompatibility between his millenarian sympathies and his defence of existing social distinctions.

The English civil war broke out over largely secular issues, but the Catholic character of the Court and the nature of the Laudian church made it easy to identify the royalist cause with the papal Antichrist. Parliamentary preachers found a ready response when they preached that Parliament and the army had been chosen by God to throw down Babylon and prepare the way for the Kingdom of Christ. Millenarian ideas were widespread among Parliamentary supporters, though it was in the sects and the army that they found their most intense expression. These circumstances meant that millenarianism was given an activist direction: God's wish was for the saints to throw down Babylon and establish the New Jerusalem, not merely to await some divine intervention.

Millenarian beliefs were most widespread in the 1640s, yet it was only after 1649, when the wave was already receding, that the Fifth Monarchist movement emerged. Partly it was a response to the hopes aroused by the execution of King Charles, making way for King Jesus—a development which itself repelled millenarians who were socially conservative. But most important, it was a response to the fact that both the Rump and the Grandees were apostatizing from God's work. The millenarians who became Fifth Monarchists would have been content to watch the Rump or the army set up Christ's kingdom. They formed a separate movement only when it became apparent that God's cause would go by default unless it was upheld by saints who were private citizens.[1]

The emergence of Fifth Monarchism was not the result of a massive switch to millenarianism by Levellers, disappointed at 'the failure of the left-democratic revolution to consummate itself'.[2] The Fifth Monarchists' wish for the tyrannical rule of the elect over the ungodly was diametrically opposed to the Levellers' egalitarian tendencies. Nevertheless, some of the rank and file of the Leveller supporters may have drifted into Fifth Monarchism because the saints shared many of the objectives of the other contemporary radical movements. They called for legal reforms, lower rents and the abolition of feudal relics. They attacked monopolies, condemned tithes, and sought to relieve the plight of the poor. The existence of a body of shared objectives may have facilitated movement between the fringe members of the radical groups, but there is no evidence that the Fifth Monarchists owed their rise to the defeat of the Levellers, or that their ideas were derived from the Levellers.

The Fifth Monarchists were an elitist movement, seeing the saints as God's aristocracy and therefore justified in ruling over the reprobate. Divine grace ignored existing social distinctions, and the saints believed that it necessitated a social revolution. But within the ranks of the saints, it made them egalitarian. A journeyman, apprentice or labourer might possess the grace of God, and persons of these social degrees were accepted as equal saints, able to hold office in the congregation.

Fifth Monarchism, and the great millenarian wave of the seventeenth century, was the result of the political and religious crisis,

[1] This was recognized by J. F. Wilson, in 'Comment on "Two Roads to the Puritan Millennium"', *Church History*, xxxii (1963), p. 341.
[2] P. Zagorin, *A History of Political Thought in the English Revolution* (1954), p. 105.

not of economic circumstances. But the Fifth Monarchist form of millenarianism, calling for a social revolution and the confiscation of the lands of the ungodly, appealed particularly to certain social and economic groups. It drew its support largely from the towns and the army, where traditional social patterns had broken down. The saints were mostly artisans, journeymen and apprentices. The cloth and leather industries provided over 30% of the membership. Even though these were not the most capitalized industries, many of the saints were probably wage-earners with no prospect of becoming economically independent. Pamphleteers and preachers attacked the rich, the covetous, great merchants and monopolists. Yet the specific economic proposals of the Fifth Monarchists were not anti-capitalist. There were demands for protection against foreign competition, for a trade-war against the Dutch rivals, and for the reform of the law relating to debt, to protect the creditor as much as to relieve the debtor. Though there were attacks on covetousness, there was no condemnation of usury. There were schemes to use beggars and criminals as a pool of cheap labour. Such proposals looked towards the future.

This is partly to be explained by the dichotomy between the authors of the pamphlets, largely the better-educated and socially superior members of the movement, and the mass of the saints, which was revealed also in the conflicting attitudes towards Münster and the use of violence. Yet even Venner's group called for a programme similar to the one above, and it would appear that even small masters could see the advantages of these schemes. When it was argued that these proposals would bring universal wealth, they could be made generally acceptable. Such generalized promises, and the prospect of a social revolution and retribution falling on the privileged orders, the rich, the lawyers and the clergy, were probably what was most attractive to the majority of the saints. Even the Fifth Monarchist form of millenarianism was sufficiently flexible to embrace visions of varying kinds.

The panic produced in 1653 by the Fifth Monarchists' attempt to throw down tithes and the existing laws was in part responsible for the tide of reaction which flowed through the Protectorate to the Restoration. Millenarianism was once more identified with social and political subversion. The only successful challenge to the restored Stuart regime was the Glorious Revolution of 1688, the leaders of which avoided all contact with the survivors of the radicalism of the 1640s and '50s. Henceforth the landed classes moderated their quarrels sufficiently to prevent any dangerous revival of the millenarian ideas which continued to circulate at those levels of society untouched by the 'age of reason'.

Apocalyptic ideas did survive on the continent after Münster. Prophecies of the impending end of the world were circulated widely throughout Germany in the later sixteenth century. In 1556 Jobus Fincelius of Siebenbürgern reported that the prophetic message, 'Inri DMLVI ein Ende Dieses Reichs', had been seen in the sky. In 1587 fishermen off the coasts of Denmark and Norway caught two herrings, each inscribed with the cryptic word, 'Vici'. The fish were sent to King Frederick II of Denmark who was informed, on taking learned advice, that they were to be interpreted as the two witnesses of Rev. xi, and were a sign of the imminent apocalypse. The end of the world in 1588 was indeed widely foretold, by Regiomontanus, Adam Nachenmoser and others. In 1612 a Lutheran minister, Johannes Gerhardt, wrote that all the biblical prophecies referred to the next fifty years, and that Christ would soon appear.[1]

Brightman's belief in the gradual establishment of the reign of Christ, beginning with the first signs of the Reformation, found a number of supporters on the continent, some of them perhaps influenced directly by Brightman during his exile in the Netherlands. Daniel Cramer, a Lutheran pastor and professor at Stettin, claimed in 1618 that the thousand years' reign of the saints had begun with Luther and would gradually increase in glory. Similar views were held by the French Calvinist, Matthieu Cottière, minister of Tours and deputy at the synod of Alais in 1620, and by several Dutch Calvinists, such as Jacobus Koelman (1633–95), who taught that the millennium had begun in 1560, and that the fall of the Pope and the Turks, and the restoration of the Jews, were all imminent. Johannes Cocceius (1603–69), born in Bremen but later professor at Leyden, thought that the literal thousand years of Satan's binding were over, but that a second, future millennium was to be expected. He saw the Thirty Years' War as the purification of the saints, and contrived to explain the Treaty of Westphalia as corroboration of his beliefs.

[1] H. Corrodi, *Kritische Geschichte des Chiliasmus* (Frankfurt and Leipzig, 1781–3), iii. chapter 2, esp. pp. 38, 42–9, 50–7; J. B. Neveaux, *Vie Spirituelle et Vie Sociale* (Paris, 1967), p. 487.

Conclusion

His disciple, Groenewegen, commented that the approach of Coccieus closely resembled that of Brightman.[1]

The idea of a wholly future Kingdom of Christ was not unknown. Alfonso Corrado, a Mantuan who taught in Switzerland, published in 1574 his belief that Christ would return to destroy Antichrist, and would then withdraw to leave the Church to flourish for a thousand years before the Last Judgement. Johannes Piscator (1546–1625), Calvinist professor at Herborn, in Hesse-Nassau, argued in 1613 in favour of a future millennium in which popery would be destroyed and the godly would live on earth for a thousand years.[2] But the decisive shift from a gradualist millennium to belief in the cataclysmic destruction of the existing order as the prelude to the New Jerusalem, came with the Thirty Years' War. The most important theorist of the new creed was Alsted, who adopted it after the war had driven him into exile from Herborn, where he too had been professor. Another important exposition, drawing heavily on Mede, was the *Clavis Apocalyptica* of the Silesian noble, Abraham von Frankenburg, which was translated into Dutch and English.[3]

Belief in the imminent, violent establishment of the millennium was naturally strongest in the areas most affected by the war. It was especially strong in Bohemia, a Protestant state overrun by the Habsburgs early in the war, where a long millenarian tradition had been kept alive by the Bohemian Brethren. Since the war was fought against external states, millenarian thought on the continent assumed a nationalist character. Echoing the traditions of the 'last Emperor', Protestant princes were seen as the heralds of the Kingdom of Christ. The vision of destruction was of foreign, Catholic states, not of internal institutions or social classes as in the case of the Fifth Monarchists, influenced by the character of the English civil war. The Elector Frederick was the obvious and not unwilling focus for prophetic ideas in the early stages of the war, and the legend survived his rapid defeat. Johannes Plaustrarius of Kaiserslautern in

[1] L. E. Froom, *The Prophetic Faith of our Fathers* (Washington, 1946–54), ii. 608–610; R. G. Clouse, 'The Influence of John Henry Alsted on English Millenarian Thought in the Seventeenth Century' (U. of Iowa Ph.D. thesis, 1963), p. 39; J. Van Den Berg, 'Eschatological Expectations concerning the Conversion of the Jews in the Netherlands during the Seventeenth Century', in P. Toon, ed., *Puritans, the Millennium, and the Future of Israel* (1970), pp. 144–7; G. Schrenk, *Gottesreich und Bund im älteren Protestantismus* (Gütersloh, 1923), pp. 219–38.

[2] Clouse, 'Influence of Alsted', pp. 37–8; Froom, *op. cit.*, ii. 318–19, 601.

[3] Clouse, 'Influence of Alsted', pp. 108–205; *Clavis Apocalyptica* (1651), preface, p. 3; D. Hirst, *Hidden Riches* (1964), p. 88; M. L. Bailey, *Milton and Jakob Boehme* (New York, 1914), pp. 84–8.

the Palatinate published in 1620 or '21 his scheme of a new creation, in which the six years from 1618 represented the six days of the Creation, and would lead to the destruction of the Habsburgs by Frederick, preparing the way for Christ.[1] In 1620 Christopher Kotter (d. 1647), of Sprottau in Silesia, was inspired in a vision to tell Frederick his divine mission, which was to destroy the Habsburgs and Rome by 1624. Later events prompted Kotter to include Frederick's descendants in the prophecy, and to postpone the fall of Rome to 1666. His teachings spread widely in the Sudetenland, the borderland of Poland, Silesia and Bohemia, which became a stronghold of millenarian beliefs.[2] A very different version of the legend was published in 1622 by Philip Ziegler, a Rosicrucian who had earlier proclaimed himself king of Jerusalem, and who now fused the Joachite age of the spirit with the thousand years' reign. Frederick was to be ruler over thirteen peoples in the Kingdom of Christ. In 1625 Ziegler travelled to England to persuade King James to intervene in the war, only to find that James had died during his journey.[3]

The Elector of Brandenburg had in 1625 summoned Kotter to Berlin to hear his prophecies, but when hope faded concerning the Elector Frederick, it was natural that millenarian expectations should be transferred not to Brandenburg but to Sweden. Gustavus Adolphus became the great hope of the Protestant cause, and the concept of Sweden's messianic role (which Gustavus apparently encouraged) outlived his death in 1632.[4] Its most famous advocate was Johannes Warner, a peasant from Bockendorf in Saxony, who experienced visions from 1624. Warner took service in the Swedish army, where he delivered God's message that Gustavus had been chosen as the saviour of Germany and herald of the millennium, and he enjoyed the favour of the Swedish generals Banér and Torstensson. As it became clear that his hopes of Sweden were not being fulfilled, Warner's theories assumed a more nationalist character. His prophecies, published in 1639, envisaged Saxony and Sweden jointly destroying Rome, after which Christ's kingdom would

[1] R. Haase, *Das Problem des Chiliasmus und der Dreissigjährige Krieg* (Leipzig, 1933), pp. 54–60; Corrodi, *Geschichte*, iv. 50–9.
[2] Haase, *Problem*, pp. 63–6; anon., *Prophecies of Christopher Kotterus, . . . Nicholas Drabicius* (2nd edn., 1664).
[3] Haase, *Problem*, pp. 102–3; Corrodi, *Geschichte*, iv. 22–3.
[4] Haase, *Problem*, pp. 64, 68–70; M. Roberts, *Gustavus Adolphus* (1953, 1958), i. 522–6, ii. 406.

spread to include the Ottoman Empire, Russia and America. The Holy Roman Empire would be divided between Saxony and Sweden. This tendency was still more pronounced in his *Schwann-Gesang* (1641), in which he criticized Sweden's pretensions and argued that, though Sweden had been called to assist, the Germans were to free themselves. Sweden would be rewarded with territory, but would be excluded from a reconstructed Holy Roman Empire. It was perhaps a measure of Warner's celebrity that when he fell into Habsburg hands in 1641, he was treated with great respect, and was released after a long discussion with the Imperial general, Piccolomini.[1]

The best known of the continental millenarians of the period was undoubtedly Comenius (1592–1670), famous also as an educator and irenicist, who had studied under Piscator and Alsted. A minister of the Bohemian Brethren, driven into exile by the Habsburg conquest, he was naturally attracted to millenarianism. He became a close associate of Kotter, and accepted the messianic predictions concerning Frederick and Gustavus. From 1643 Comenius was closely connected with Nicholas Drabik (1597–1671), another exiled Bohemian. Drabik's visions, which Comenius came wholly to accept, began in 1638 and revealed that the salvation of Germany and restoration of Bohemia would be achieved by Georg I, Prince of Transylvania. Though Georg died in 1648, Drabik switched his predictions to his sons Sigismund (died 1652) and then Georg II, who showed great favour to both Drabik and Comenius. In 1655 Comenius found a new deliverer in Charles X of Sweden, who launched a triumphant invasion of Poland. Comenius hailed Charles as a second Moses, but within a year the Poles had reoccupied their lands and drove Comenius into exile once more from his refuge at Leszno. The desperation of the messianic cause became apparent in 1658 when Drabik made the astonishing revelation that Louis XIV was to be God's chosen instrument in destroying the Habsburgs and the papacy and preparing for Christ's kingdom. This too was accepted by Comenius, who published the prophecies of Kotter and Drabik in his *Lux in Tenebris* (1664). Johannes Redinger, once of Zurich, a follower of Comenius, travelled to France, Vienna and into the Turkish camp to deliver this message. Drabik fell into Imperialist hands in 1671 and was executed, allegedly at the instigation of the Jesuits.[2]

[1] Haase, *Problem*, pp. 70–6; Corrodi, *Geschichte*, iv. 67–77.
[2] Haase, *Problem*, pp. 107–31; Corrodi, *Geschichte*, iv. 119–32; *The Diary and*

Conclusion

Comenius spent the last years of his life in Amsterdam. Although the Netherlands escaped the disasters of war, its religious tolerance made it a millenarian stronghold by the mid-century. One of the most prominent figures was Paul Felgenhauer (1593–1677), another Bohemian exile, whose works were immensely popular throughout North Germany. Felgenhauer was convinced that the Thirty Years' War, and the English Civil War heralded Christ's coming, the conversion of the Jews and the start of the thousand years' reign. In his later years he came to reject war altogether, and taught that love and toleration were the means to, and the guiding principles of the millennium; his career thus served to spiritualize the creed. But some of his earlier doctrines paralleled those of the Fifth Monarchists, in attacking the rich and covetous, and the universities and scholars who 'filled the World full of Bookes, which are endlesse and numberlesse', but served only to make men 'more and more scattered and confused'.[1] Other Dutch millenarians included Jacobus Alting, in the second half of the century. Slightly earlier, and more important, was Petrus Serarius (?1600–69), son of an Amsterdam merchant, who expected the return of Christ and the conversion of the Jews. Serarius, a friend of Felgenhauer, frequently travelled in England, and was probably born in London; he may well have been influenced directly by English millenarians. His *Awakening Warning* (1662) used astrological calculations to interpret Revelation, and concluded that the establishment of the millennium was imminent. He also followed closely the career of the pretended Messiah, Sabbatai Sevi.[2] At least two Fifth Monarchist works were translated into Dutch.[3]

In France, the Protestant theologian Moïse Amyraut, a fierce opponent of millenarianism, conceded in the 1650s that many of his

---

Correspondence of Dr. John Worthington, ed. J. Crossley and R. C. Christie (Chetham Soc., xiii, xxxvi, cxiv, 1847–86), i., 357n.–36on.; cf. also on Comenius, M. Spinka, *Comenius, that Incomparable Moravian* (Chicago, 1943); H. R. Trevor-Roper, *Religion, the Reformation and Social Change* (1967), pp. 237–93.

[1] H. J. Schoeps, *Philosemitismus im Barock* (Tübingen, 1952), pp. 18–45; P. Felgenhauer, *Postilion, or a new Almanack* (1655), pp. 13, 28, 38, 44; *Neue Deutsche Biographie*, v (Berlin, 1960), p. 69.

[2] Van Den Berg, 'Eschatological Expectations', pp. 147, 150, 152–3; W. Goeters, *Die Vorbereitung des Pietismus* (Weimar, 1909), pp. 47–50; Serarius, *An awakening warning to the Wofull World* (Amsterdam, 1662); *The Correspondence of Henry Oldenburg*, ed. A. R. and M. B. Hall (Madison, Milwaukee and London, 1965–6), esp. iii, 447.

[3] Spittlehouse, *Het legher gewroocken* (1653), i.e. *The Army Vindicated*; O. Lloyd, *Het Gezigt van den Panther* (1688).

friends held the doctrine, and that its revival could be dated to fifty or sixty years earlier. Amyraut felt obliged to refute the writings of its foremost French advocate, Pierre de Launay, sieur de la Motte (1573–1661).[1] One D.R., a French Protestant writing at Mount-Royal in 1645, sent his millenarian work to a German princess to be circulated and forwarded to the Queen-Mother of Sweden.[2] In the latter half of the century, French millenarianism seems to have survived only amongst exiles. The most important was Jean de Labadie (1610–87), a former Jesuit, later a Huguenot minister and pastor of the Walloon church at Middelburg from 1669, and also a friend of Serarius. His tract *Le Héraut du Grand Roy Jésus* (1667) predicted the imminent establishment of the millennium, with the return of Christ and the conversion of the Jews. Labadie appears to have followed closely the career of Sabbatai Sevi, as a possible agent of the Jewish conversion. Pierre Jurieu (1637–1713), pastor of the Walloon church at Rotterdam, continued to teach the millenarian faith towards the end of the century, and several of his works were translated into English.[3]

By the second half of the century, international politics had lost so much of its religious, crusading content that millenarian ideas were no longer utilized by governments even as propaganda. Eva Fröhlichinn, wife of a Swedish noble, who taught the Fifth Monarchy in Stockholm and told Charles XI that he was called by God to restore the Jews to Jerusalem, was deported in 1685, and lived thereafter in Amsterdam.[4] Millenarians who attempted to form a movement which might prove subversive were quickly suppressed. Pell wrote from Cologne in 1655, discussing the Fifth Monarchists, and noted that the people there were 'now and then troubled with men of the like principles, but they soon shut them up, that they may not seduce others'. In 1663 one Morin was burnt at Paris 'for professing himself to be Jesus Christ: he had got many disciples, and among the rest two Priests'. His followers were gaoled or banished. Anders Kempe (1622–89), a Swedish army officer who translated and published Felgenhauer's works in Sweden in the 1660s, found his books burnt and himself exiled. In 1674 it was

[1] E. G. Léonard, *A History of Protestantism*, trans. J. M. H. Reid and R. M. Bethell (1967), ii. 389n.; Froom, *Prophetic Faith*, ii, 632–4; M. Amyraut, *Du Règne de Mille Ans* (Saumur, 1654), pp. 3, 5, 37–44; P. de Launay, *Paraphrase et Exposition sur l'Apocalypse* (Geneva, 1651), p. 517 (misprint for 617).
[2] D.R., *The Morning Alarum*, trans. N. Johnson (1651), *passim*.
[3] Van Den Berg, 'Eschatological Expectations', pp. 149–53.
[4] Corrodi, *Geschichte*, iv. 24–5.

noted that an apparently native Fifth Monarchy movement was spreading rapidly at The Hague, but that the magistrates were about to crush it.[1]

The subversiveness and social radicalism of the English Fifth Monarchy movement were moulded by the particular circumstances of England in the 1640s and '50s. In different circumstances, continental millenarianism took a different, nationalist character, revolving around existing rulers, to whom messianic attributes were ascribed. But despite its peculiarities, Fifth Monarchism was clearly only one manifestation of a millenarian climate of opinion which was deeply rooted in much of Europe in this period.

[1] R. Vaughan, *The Protectorate of Oliver Cromwell* (1839), i. 154; *Mercurius Publicus*, 12 (19–26 March 1663), p. 196; Schoeps, *Philosemitismus*, pp. 45–6; Hist. MSS. Comm., xxv, *Le Fleming MSS.*, p. 109; Newsletter, 14 April 1674.

APPENDIX I

Biographical Appendix

❉❉❉

The appendix gives a brief summary of the careers of the leading Fifth Monarchists, and mentions all whose occupations are known. Where possible, a person's occupation, earlier and later religious/political affiliations, and dates of adherence to Fifth Monarchism have been noted. Individuals whose careers have been described at length elsewhere, such as Harrison, Overton, Rogers and Powell, have been dealt with cursorily here. The italicizing of a name signifies that the person is the subject of a separate entry. Certain Fifth Monarchist declarations have been abbreviated as follows:

Comp. Test. *The Complaining Testimony of some . . . of Sions Children* (1656), after the rally at Abingdon for the funeral of Pendarves.

Declaration *A Declaration of several of the Churches of Christ* (1654), London Fifth Mon. declaration.

Essay *An Essay towards Settlement upon a sure foundation* (1659), London Fifth Mon./Baptist tract.

Word for God *A Word for God* (1655), printed in *Thurloe*, iv. 380–4 (Welsh Fifth Mon. manifesto inspired by Powell).

The abbreviations 'Cong.', 'Ind.' and 'Bapt.' denote respectively Congregationalist, Independent and Baptist; 'lic.' denotes licensed.

ADAMS, Ambrose
Millwright, Abingdon church, fined for conventicling, 1664. (Preston, *Church . . . of St. Nicholas, Abingdon* (1935), p. 121n.)

ADAMS, Richard, d. 1716
Ejected from Humberstone, Leics.; schoolteacher. Licensed (Cong.) 1672. Head of 5th Mon. church in London, 300 strong, 1682. Elder of Gen. Bapt. church in Bermondsey 1689, and pastor of Particular Baptist church at Devonshire Square 1701–12. No other 5th Mon. connections known.

> Matthews, *Calamy Revised* (1934), pp. 1–2; *Bapt. Quart.*, i. 84–5; SP. 29/419, f. 102; Whitley, *Baptists of London* (1928), p. 103.

ADMAN, Ursula
Sister of Anna *Trapnel* (Trapnel, *Report and Plea* (1654), p. 42). Arrested for holding (5th Mon.) meeting at her house in Middlesex, 1669 (Jeaffreson, *Middlesex County Records*, iv (1892), pp. 14–15).

ALLEN, William, 1616–fl. 1667
On fringe of 5th Mon. movement. Originally feltmaker. In Parlt. army

from 1642. Agitator, 1647. Adjutant-General by 1651. Broghill in Ireland said he would only obey Ireton and Allen. Millenarian by '49. Opposed fall of Barebones and very critical of Protectorate, but remained in army, in Ireland, till 1656. At Bapt./5th Mon. meeting at Dorchester, 1658, signed *Essay* '59. Arrested 1660 and '61, released and banished. Published verses on death of *Wigan, Glasse* and *Vernon*, '66–7. A Baptist. Dead by 1679.

> *Thurloe* and *Clarke, passim;* biogs. by Wheeler Robinson and Hardacre, *Bapt. Q.*, iii. 237–40; xix. 292–308; *T. Bapt. H.S.*, iii. 254–5; iv. 130–1; Bodl. MS. Rawl. A 13, fos. 24, 26; Worcester Coll., Oxford, MS. 18, f. 8; Bodl. MS. Ashmole 210, f. 134 gives date of birth; Firth and Davies, *Regimental History* (1940), pp. 613–14; R. Bagwell, *Ireland under the Stuarts* (1909), ii. 267, 349; anon., *Bochim* (1667), *Mite from Three Mourners* (1666).
> Not to be confused with General Baptist minister of same name.

ANDREWES, —
Rich brewer, Limehouse, London, 1661 (SP. 29/44, f. 267).

ARCHER, John, fl. 1629–d. about 1642
Not a Fifth Monarchist. Perhaps educ. Cambridge. London lecturer, 1629; suspended by Laud. Presented to All Saints', Hertford, by Feoffees for Impropriations, 1631. Perhaps left '32, was suspended for long absence by '38 (I. M. Calder, 'A Seventeenth Century Attempt to Purify the Anglican Church', *American Hist. Rev.*, liii (1947–8), p. 769; W. Urwick, *Nonconformity in Herts.* (1884), p. 526). Went into exile, pastor of English church at Arnhem, died about 1642 (G. Hornius, *Historia Ecclesiastica* (1665), p. 331; Alsted, *Beloved City* (1643), suffix, p. xxi; Tillinghast, *Generation-Worke*, 3rd part (1654), p. 47). His *Personall Reigne of Christ* (1641 and many later edns.) made him posthumously famous. His first name appeared as Henry on one edn. Confused with Anglican Aucher in *D.N.B.*

ARMIGER, John, fl. 1653–d. 1683
Shoemaker. Of Knollys's cong., Coleman St., 1653 (ed. Underhill, *Records of . . . Hexham* (1854), p. 340). At Abingdon rally 1656 (*Comp. Test.*, sig. A2). Signed Baptist invitation to Charles II, 1656 (Crosby, *Hist. of the Baptists* (1738–40), i. appendix, p. 84). Presented for absence from church, 1664 (Guildhall MS. 9583, box 1, St. Anne and St. Agnes). In Rye House Plot, '83 (*C.S.P. Dom., 1683,* ii. p. 448 and *passim; A List of all the Conspirators* (?1683), brs.).

ASHTON, William
Silk-weaver. Took part in Venner's plots, 1657 and '61; executed '61. (*Thurloe*, vi. 194; Burrage, 'Fifth Mon. Insurrections', *Eng. Hist. Rev.*, xxv (1910), pp. 737–8/44).

ASPINWALL, William, fl. 1630–62
Settled in Massachusetts, 1630; freeman, deacon, trader and recorder of Boston. Expelled as antinomian, 1637–42. Returned to England 1652. Publ. 5th Mon. and anti-7th Day Sabbath tracts 1653–7. Opposed plots, favoured participation in existing government. Whitley calls him a Baptist and infantry captain, but there is no evidence for either. Minister in Ireland, 1659. One W.A., mercer of Halifax, died 1660; but a W.A. of Chester, '62.

D.N.B. (confuses him with Presbyt. namesake); *T. Bapt. H.S.*, vii. 185; *New Engl. Hist. and Gen. Reg.*, ii. 76; iii. 90; v. 301, 448; vii. 232; xxviii. 47–50; lix. 103; F. C. Gray, *Mass. Hist. Soc. Coll.*, 3rd ser., viii. 193–4; *Canterbury Wills, 1657–60*, ed. T. M. Blagg (1936), p. 24; Aspinwall, *Legislative Power* (1656), pp. 36–7. S. D. Seymour, *The Puritans in Ireland 1647–1661* (Oxford, 1969), p. 206.

ASTLEY, John
Yeoman of Middx. Arrested '69 at *Adman's* house (Jeaffreson, *Middx. Recs.*, iv. 14).

ASTLEY, Richard, fl. 1659–d. 1696
Minister, perhaps educ. Cambridge, ejected from Blackwood, Bolton, '62. Succeeded *Canne* as head of Hull 5th Mon./Cong. church, 1669. Lic. Ind., '72. Mediated between *Whitehurst* and his cong., 1679.

> Matthews, *Cal. Rev.*, p. 17; J. Hunter, *Rise of the Old Dissent* (1842), pp. 295–6

ATWOOD, Thomas
Silverspinner. Defected from *Venner* over 1657 plot (Burrage, 'Insurrections', p. 734). Fined 1663 for conventicling at Spittlefields (Jeaffreson, *Middx. Recs.*, iii (1888), p. 330).

BACHE, Humphrey, d. 1662
Goldsmith, formerly excise-collector. Signed *Declaration*, 1654 as of Fenton's church. Became Quaker, imprisoned after Restoration, died shortly after release.

> His own *Few Words in True Love* (1659); H. Barbour, *Quakers* (1964), pp. 160–1, 168n., 201; *Canterbury Wills, 1661–70*, ed. J. H. Morrison (1935), p. 11; W. C. Braithwaite, *The Beginnings of Quakerism* (1955), pp. 517–19.

BANFEATHER, Joseph
Silk-stocking-maker of Nottingham. Associated with *Pooley*, 1667 (SP. 29/190, f. 189).

BARRETT, George, fl. 1653–d. 1700
Mealman. Assistant to Jessey, 1653; signed *Declaration*, '54. Asked to be called as defence witness at *Canne's* trial, 1658. Arbitrator in breach in *Simpson's* church. Head of cong. of 100 5th Mon. men at Horsleydown, '69. Thereafter head of London Particular Bapt. churches, and not known as 5th Mon. man.

> *T. Bapt. H.S.*, iii. 125; vii. 186; Whitley, *Bapt. London*, pp. 108, 115/18; *Narrative . . . of Canne* (1658), p. 11; *Old Leaven Purged* (1658), p. 28; Turner, *Original Records* (1911–14), i. 69, 144; ii. 990.

BASSE, Jonathan, fl. 1651–d. 1681
Esq.; of *Woodall's* cong., Woodbridge. He and Woodall 'Commonly termed a Jonathan and David' (Dr. Williams's Lib., Harmer MS. 76.5: Woodbridge Churchbook, fos. 2, 4). On county committee, Suffolk, 1657 (Firth and Rait, *Acts and Ordinances* (1911), ii. 1081). Cong. met at his house after Restoration (Turner, *Orig. Recs.*, i. 105; Norwich Rec. Office, VIS/7, box. 411, 31 May 1678).

BAWDEN, Major John, fl. 1650–d. 1685
Gent.; M.P., Cornwall, 1653. Supporter of *Trapnel* during her western tour, 1654. On Cornwall county committees, 1650/2, 1659–60. No other 5th Mon. connections. His will describes him as of Truro.

Glass, *Barbone Parliament* (1899), p. 71; Firth and Rait, *Acts and Ord.*, ii. 463, 659, 1322/66; Trapnel, *Legacy of Saints* (1654), p. 50 and her *Report and Plea*, pp. 13, 25; *Merc. Politicus*, 201 (13–20 March 1654), pp. 3429–30; *Cornwall and Devon Wills*, ed. R. M. Glengross (1929), p. 17.

BAYLIE, Thomas, c. 1582–1663

Minister, ejected from Mildenhall, Wilts. M.A. and B.D., Oxon. Presbyt., member of Westminster Assembly. Became Congregationalist; kept conventicle after ejection. Married daughter of Robert Parker, millenarian author. Called 5th Mon. by Calamy and Wood, but not otherwise known as such.

> *D.N.B.*; Matthews, *Cal. Rev.*, p. 40; A. Wood, *Athenae Oxonienses* (1691–2), i. 217.

BEECH, John

Tailor. In *Rathbone* plot, but acquitted, 1666 (Jeaffreson, *Middx. Recs.*, iii. 376; iv. 269–70).

BELCHER, John, fl. 1658–d. 1695

Bricklayer and pastor. Arrested with *Canne*, 1658. Itinerant 5th Mon. preacher in early '60s, thought likely to rebel. Adopted 7th Day Sabbath by 1664. Led the Bell Lane 7th Day church till death. Arrested with the cong. in 1671 as 5th Monarchists, but not known as 5th Mon. thereafter.

> *T. Bapt. H.S.*, iv. 127–8; vii. 187; *Bapt. Q.*, xiv. 161–6; A. Wood, *Life and Times* (1891), i. 302; *Narrative . . . of Canne*, p. 6; Jeaffreson, *Middx. Recs.*, iv. 31; SP. 29/42, f. 69v.;/44, f. 267;/80, f. 192;/291, f. 176.

BLOXSOM, Barnabas

Tailor. His house in Southwark a 5th Mon./Ind. meeting place 1669. Lic. Cong., 1672 (Turner, *Orig. Recs.*, i. 144; ii. 983).

BRAYNE, John, fl. 1642–d. 1654

Not 5th Mon. Millenarian V. of the Soke, Winchester by 1647 and till death. Earlier min. in Essex and Norfolk. Claimed to have had vision in '47 of fall of all kings. His work on Mosaic law admired by 5th Mon. men. Apparently adopted Seeker ideas by '52.

> Matthews, *Walker Revised* (1948), pp. 166, 186, 204, 264; *A Vision, which . . . Brayne . . . had in . . . 1647* (1649); his own *New Earth* (1653); Spittlehouse and More, *Vindication . . . In Answer to . . . Brain* (1652); SP. 18/74, f. 22; *Canterbury Wills, 1653–6*, ed. T. M. Blagg and J. S. Moir (1925), p. 67.

BREVITER, Richard, fl. 1640–d. 1664

V. of N. Walsham, Norfolk. Educ. Cambridge (M.A., '47). Presbyt. min., '47, joined Norwich Ind. church 1650, at N. Walsham by '51. Nominated members for Barebones '53. Wrote in support of 5th Mon., 1654. Rebaptized and resigned living '56. Lived in Norwich after 1660; millenarian, but no later 5th Mon. activities known.

> Matthews, *Cal. Rev.*, p. 71; *Bapt. Q.*, xviii. 311; Tillinghast, *Generation Worke*, 3rd part (1654), prefatory letter from B.; J. Browne, *Congregationalism* (1877), pp. 297–8; his own *Mighty Christ* (1662), sig. A7v. and *passim*.

BRIERLY, (alias Bradley), Robert

?Tallow-chandler. In *Venner's* rising 1661; death sentence, but suspended (Burrage, 'Insurrections', pp. 744–5). Perhaps the R.B., tallow-chandler mentioned in Interregnum assessment of London (SP. 19/A46)

Appendix I

BROWNE, Capt. John, fl. 1647–75
Gent., of Little Ness, Salop. Of *Llwyd's* cong. 5th Mon. M.P., Barebones.
Officer since 1647. A J.B., sequestrator of Shropshire, died 1654 (*Cal. Cttee for Compounding*, i. 686), but not the same as the 5th Monarchist Browne, who signed the *Word for God* in 1655, and joined *Powell* in criticizing *Llwyd* for drawing back from it. Licensed as Cong. teacher, 1672; still of the Wrexham church, 1675.

> W. R. Williams, *Parlt. Hist. of Wales* (1895), p. 4; Glass, *Barbone*, p. 72; T. Richards *Relig. Developments* (1923), pp. 228, 232; Richards, *Puritan Movement* (1920), pp. 82, 93, 96; R. T. Jones, 'Vavasor Powell', p. 140; MS. Rawl. A 47, f. 30; Dodd, 'Remonstrance', p. 296; Turner, *Original Records*, i. 55, ii. 740. Not the J.B. who wrote *A Brief Survey of the Prophetical . . . Events* (1655), who was of Orpington, Kent, and was not a 5th Monarchist.

BROWNE, Robert, 1633/4–1688
Ejected as Min. of White Lady Aston, Worcs. Educ. Oxford. Described as 'fervent . . . Fifth-Monarchy-man' by Calamy, but no other evidence. Not a Baptist, but later headed Baptist churches in London, Worcester and Plymouth.

> Matthews, *Cal. Rev.*, p. 81; E. Calamy, *Continuation* (1727), pp. 894–5.

BRUNT, Simon, fl. 1671–1711
Tailor. Arrested 1671 as 5th Mon./7th Day man (Jeaffreson, *Middx. Recs.*, iv. 30). Gaoled 1685 as supporter of Monmouth (*ibid.*, p. 293). Member and deacon of Bell Lane church till 1711 (*T. Bapt. H.S.*, iv. 128; Dr. Williams's Lib., 'Mill Yard Minutes', p. 193).

BUNCH, Nathaniel
Cobbler's apprentice, examined 1656 (*Thurloe*, iv. 621). Signed *Rogers's Reviving Word*, 1657.

BUTTEVANT, Capt. Thomas, fl. 1646–61
Of Norwich. In Lifeguards, purged 1656. In Knollys's cong., 1646 and still '53. At Abingdon rally '56. Militant leader in E. Anglia and London 1656. Hiding in London 1661.

> T. Edwards, *Gangraena*, (1646) iii. 49; ed. Underhill, *Hexham*, pp. 311, 340. *Comp. Test.*, sig. A2; *Thurloe*, iv. 629; v. 220, 296–7; SP. 29/44, f. 265.

BYFIELD, Nathaniel, 1602–fl. 1672
Educ. Oxford, R. of Silverton, Devon, 1647–54. Led 5th Mon. cong. in Exeter in 1650s. Arrested 1661 for complicity with *Venner* and preparing a rising. Of Ilfracombe 1665; lic. (Bapt.), Bridgwater, 1672.

> Matthews, *Cal. Rev.*, pp. 96, 560; W. J. Harte, 'Exeter 1640–62', *Rep. and Trans. Devon. Assoc.* (1937), p. 55; *Merc. Publicus*, 4 (24–31 Jan. '61), p. 62; *C.S.P. Dom.*, *1672*, p. 378.

CALEY, Jacob, fl. 1643–d. 1680
Gent.; M.P. for Ipswich, 1653. Portman of Ipswich. On Suffolk county committees 1643, '47–52, '57, and on Eastern High Court of Justice. Of *Stoneham's* cong.; joint author with him of 5th Mon. tract, *A Serious Proposal* (1659).

> Glass, *Barbone*, p. 72; Firth and Rait, *Acts and Ord.*, i. 168, 111–12; ii. *passim*; A. Everitt, *Suffolk and the Great Rebellion* (1961), p. 117; *Canterbury Wills, 1676–85*; ed. C. H. Ridge (1948), p. 61.

Appendix I

CANNE, John, c. 1590–c. 1667
Pastor of English separatist cong. at Amsterdam, 1630–47. Held mill. ideas by 1640. Chaplain to Col. Robert Lilburne 1647, and Robert Overton, 1650. Wrote for the Army and Rump and against the Levellers, 1647–50. Wrote 5th Mon. tracts 1653–9. At Abingdon rally '56. Expelled from Hull '56, went to London. Not involved with *Venner* but suspected of plotting '57. Arrested '58 for seditious words. Editor of *Publick Intelligencer* May–Aug. '59. Still active Nov. '61, but back in Amsterdam by '64 and died there. *Not* a Baptist.

> *D.N.B.; Clarke*, i. lvii; iv. 43, 146; *Thurloe*, vi. 349; *T. Bapt. H.S.*, iii. 212–46; *Church Hist.*, xxxiii. 34–49; *C.S.P. Dom.*, *'56–7*, p. 41; *Comp. Test.*, sig. A2; *Narrative . . . of Canne, passim*; SP. 29/44, f. 267; Burrage, *Early English Dissenters* (1912), ii. 305.

CARDELL, John, 1609/10–fl. 1655
Min. of All Hallows, Lombard St., 1643–55. Educ. Oxford. Lost living 1655 for attacking national ministry. Spittlehouse in 1655 called him 'one of the *late* Fifth *Monarchists*'.

> Matthews, *Walker Rev.*, p. 62; Foster, *Alumni Oxon.* (1891–2), i. 236; *Clarke*, iii. 50, 53; anon., *Cause of God* (1659), p. 7; Spittlehouse, *Royall Advocate*, p. 44.

CAREW, John, 1622/3–1660
Gent., son of Sir Richard C. of Antony, Cornwall. Educ. Oxford and Inns of Court. M.P. 1647–53 and Barebones. On county committees '47–53, '59–60. Gaoled by Cromwell 1655–6. Re-baptized '58. At Dorchester meeting '58. Executed as regicide 1660. Never implicated in plots.

> *D.N.B.;* Firth and Rait, *Acts and Ord., passim*; Foster, *Al. Oxon.*, i. p. 237; F. E. Halliday, *Cornish Chronicle* (1963), pp. 153, 157–60, 165; *Clarke*, ii. 242–6; iii. 23–4; *Thurloe*, vi. 164, 790; vii. 140; G. Bate, *Lives, Actions . . .* (1661); *Merc. Politicus*, 402 (4–11 Feb. 1658), p. 294; *C.S.P. Dom.*, *'56–7*, p. 130.

CARY, Capt. Edward, fl. 1663–83
Brewer of Southwark. In Parlt. army. Involved in 1663 plot, captured but escaped. Follower of Blood. Warrant for arrest, '67. Involved in crown-stealing. Described as 5th Mon. man, 1683, when was implicated in Rye-House Plot.

> *C.S.P. Dom.*, *1663–4*, pp. 259, 375, 652–3; *ibid.* *'64–5*, p. 159; *ibid.*, *'66–7*, pp. 537, 546; *ibid.*, *1683*, i, pp. 105, 185.

CARY, Mary, c. 1621–fl. 1653
Became a millenarian 1636, age 15 (Cary, *Resurrection of the Witnesses* (1653), sig. C4v.). Published tracts 1647–53 in praise of Army and Barebones. Praised 5th Mon. congs. at Christ Church and Blackfriars. Known as Mary Rande after '51, perhaps related to Daniel and Walter Rand, who signed *Rogers's Reviving Word*, 1657.

> Own writings, *passim*.

CASTLE, William
Linen-draper of Abingdon, 1664 (Preston, *Abingdon*, p. 121n.).

CHAMBERLEN, Dr. Peter, 1601–83
Royal physician. Educ. Cambridge and Padua. Published millenarian and 5th Mon. tracts, '49–59, mostly on the law, trade, and the poor. Baptist by

1650, head of Lothbury Sq. church 1652–4. Adopted 7th Day Sabbath by '57. Signed *Declaration*. Not involved in plots. Welcomed Charles II; reappointed royal physician. Not afterwards known as 5th Mon.,but remained in Mill Yard and Bell Lane 7th Day churches, and still preached the apocalypse. Engaged in schemes for union of all Christian churches, and in mechanical projects.

> *D.N.B.*; J. H. Aveling, *The Chamberlens* (1882), pp. 30–122; J. Thirtle, 'Chamberlen', *T. Bapt. H.S.*, iii. 176–89; F. A. Micklewright, *Notes and Q.*, (1946), pp. 95–9, 137–40, 161–3, 185–9; Bodl. MS. Rawl. D 828, *passim*; J. Ives, *Saturday No Sabbath* (1659); SP. 29/31, fos. 141–2;/237, f. 117; Bodl. MS. Tanner 35, fos. 2, 5, 104, 133, 135, 155.

CHANDLER, Samuel
Bricklayer; arrested 1669 at meeting at *Adman's* house (Jeaffreson, *Middx. Recs.*, iv. 14).

CHAPMAN, Livewell, fl. 1650–d. 1664/5
Leading publisher of 5th Mon. tracts. Gaoled '54 and '56. Associated with *Venner*, but broke over '57 plot. Fled abroad, 1660, but returned. Continued to publish anti-govt. tracts, gaoled '61–2, '63–4, and died in prison.

> *C.S.P. Dom.*, *'54*, pp. 378, 389; *ibid.*, *'59–60*, pp. 572/5; *ibid.*, *'63–4*, pp. 71, 180 349, 581–2; *Thurloe*, iv. 379; G. Kitchin, *Sir Roger L'Estrange* (1913), pp. 60–1 115–17; B.M., Add. MS. 4459, fos. 111–12*v*.

CHAPPELL, Thomas, fl. 1648–86
Silk-throwster of Stepney. One T.C. in army '48 (SP. 28/124, f. 206*v*). Of *Simpson's* cong., 1657 (SP. 18/106, f. 109;/156, f. 29). Silk-throwster, gaoled with *Courtney*, '61 (SP. 29/47, f. 104). Received letters indirectly from Serarius 1666, and accepted claims of Sabbatai Sevi (SP. 29/162, fos. 157–8; *C.S.P. Dom.*, *'65–6*, p. 568). Gaoled for conventicling '85/6 (Jeaffreson, *Middx. Recs.*, iv. 302).

CHILD, John
Silk-weaver of Bedford; 5th Mon. agent '56/7 (*Thurloe*, vi. 187).

CHILLENDEN, Capt. Edmund, fl. 1637–78
Originally button-seller; friend of John Lilburne, but testified against him in Star Chamber 1637. Arrested for conventicling 1641. Served in army, captured by royalists, 1643. Agitator '47, but helped to suppress Ware mutiny '47; captain by '50/1. Head of Gen. Bapt. church at Aldgate and then St. Paul's, 1653. Expelled from army and church '53 for immorality, but back in church by '55. Active 5th Mon. '53–9, though claimed to oppose violence. Said during '56 election 'Pish, let religion alone'. Held post connected with admiralty 1670–1, but excluded by D. of York. Coffee-house-keeper 1661 and 1677–8, when arrested for publishing illegal newspapers.

> *D.N.B.*; *C.S.P. Dom.*, *1640–1*, p. 418; *ibid.*, *'52–3*, p. 423; *ibid.*, *'55*, p. 224; *ibid.*, *'70*, pp. 47, 328, 376; *ibid.*, *'71*, pp. 15, 220, 529; *ibid.*, *'77–8*, pp. 338, 643; Clarke, i. *passim*; iii. 162; *Thurloe*, iv. 365; v. 287; J. Lilburne, *Legall Fundamentall Liberties* (1649), p. 21; *Fifth Monarchy . . . Asserted* (1659), p. 24; MS. Rawl. A 8, f. 127; *Phanatique Intelligencer* (1660), p. 8; SP. 29/44, f. 265; Firth and Davies, *Reg. Hist.*, pp. 214–15; J. Nickolls, *Orig. Letters* (1743), p. 122; B. Lillywhite, *London Coffee Houses* (1963), pp. 323–4; his own *Nathans Parable* (1653); H. N. Brailsford, *The Levellers* (1961), p. 225.

Appendix I

CLARKE, John, 1609–76

Emigrated to Boston 1637, settled Newport, R.I. Physician and Baptist pastor, and antinomian. In London 1651 on colony's business, but stayed. In '52 called Rump 'Sword-bearers' to the 'King of Kings'. Became minister of Baptist cong. at Worcester House. Signed *Declaration*, '54; at Abingdon rally, '56; arbitrator in feud in *Simpson's* church. Arrested with *Canne* '58. Arrested '61, but prob. not in plot. Back to Newport '61, no further 5th Mon. activities.

> *Dict. Amer. Biog.*, ii. 154–6; *Bapt. Q.*, i. 368–72; *Comp. Test.*, sig. A2; Tillam, *Lasher proved Lyer* (1657), p. 2; *Old Leaven*, p. 28; *Narrative . . . of Canne, passim*; *London's Glory* (1661), p. 16; own *Ill Newes from New England* (1652), sig. A2v.

CLARKE, Samuel

Labourer, arrested 1671 as 5th Mon./7th Day man (Jeaffreson, *Middx. Recs.*, iv. 29). Became asst. minister at Mill Yard (*T. Bapt. H.S.*, iv. 128).

CLEMENTS, John

Of London. Perhaps the J.C., girdler, d. 1667 (*Canterbury Wills '61–70*, ed. Morrison, p. 54) and/or the J.C., former servant, mentioned 1666 (P. E. Jones, *The Fire Court* (1966), p. 278). At Abingdon '56 (*Comp. Test.*, sig. A2), signed *Rogers's Reviving Word*, '57. One of leaders in radicals' breach with *Simpson* (*Old Leaven, passim*). A J.C. in the army '49 (SP. 28/142 ii, f. 31).

COATES, Thomas

Scrivener of Limehouse, 1661 (SP. 29/44, f. 267v.). Signed *Rogers's Reviving Word*, 1657.

COCK, Henry

'Of quality'; member of Chalfont St. Giles, Bucks., 5th Mon. church, 1669 (Turner, *Orig. Recs.*, i. 78). Head of 7th Day cong., Bucks., 1690 (*Bapt. Q.*, xiv. 165).

COCKAYNE, George, 1619/20–91

Son of Esq.; educ. Cambridge (B.A.); army chaplain. In London 5th Mon. movement '52–3, but not during Protectorate. Condemned *Venner* '61, but associated with *Danvers*, *Glasse*, *Vernon*, and was described as 5th Mon. again in '64. Lic. (Cong.) in '72, and not known as 5th Mon. thereafter.

> *D.N.B.*; Matthews, *Cal. Rev.*, p. 124; J. B. Marsh, *Story of Harecourt* (1871), *passim*; W. Erbery, *Bishop of London* (1653), p. 3; *C.S.P. Dom.*, '53–4, p. 307; SP. 29/71, f. 147;/101, f. 201;/103, f. 262;/105, f. 75.

COLE, John

Tailor; executed 1666 after *Rathbone* plot (Jeaffreson, *Middx. Recs.*, iii. 376; iv. 269–70).

COMBES, John, fl. 1648–c. 1675

Cordwainer and miller of Abingdon. Perhaps in army '48. In Abingdon church from '52, at rally '56. Probably pastor after *Pendarves*. Gaoled at Reading 1660. Fined '64 for conventicling. Lic. (Bapt.), 1672.

> Preston, *Abingdon*, pp. 121n., 130; J. Stanley, *Church in the Hop Garden* (1935) pp. 103–4; E. A. Payne, *Baptists of Berkshire* (1951), pp. 31/3/9, 53; *Comp. Test.*, sig. A2; J. Atherton, *Pastor Turn'd Pope* (1654), p. 1; SP. 28/124, f. 316v.

Appendix I

COOKE, Elizabeth
Wife of mealman; arrested as of *Swift's* cong., Hendon, 1669 (Gter. London Rec. Office, MR/RC–1, no. 46).

COURTNEY, Quarter-Master-General Hugh, fl. 1649–66
Gent. of Cornwall. Made M.A., Oxford, '49, for help in suppressing Levellers. On N. Wales and Cornwall committees '49–52, '59–60. M.P., Wales, 1653. Prominent 5th Mon. leader in Protectorate, gaoled for urging armed resistance '55, and '57/'58–9. Re-baptized '58; signed *Essay* '59; supporter of Vane in '59. Gaoled 1660–3. Reported to be stirring up trouble in Essex/Herts., '66. Possibly same as one Coutnay, arrested 1671.

> Williams, *Parlt. Hist. Wales*, p. 3; Firth and Rait, *Acts and Ord.*, ii. *passim*; Clarke, ii. 242–6; iii. 105–6; *Thurloe*, ii. 214; iii. 140/3; M. Harrison, *Narrative of the Proceedings* (1659), p. 3; E. Pagitt, *Heresiography* (1662), p. 525 (misprint for 285); SP. 29/47, f. 104;/67, f. 103;/144, f. 138; *Pub. Intelligencer*, 120 (1–8 Feb. 1658), p. 286; *C.S.P. Dom.*, '56–7, p. 130; *ibid.*, '70–1, p. 52.

Cox, Nicholas
Bag-mender, of Northants.; swore loyalty to King Jesus, in London, 1670 (SP. 29/275, fos. 214–6).

Cox, Capt. Owen, fl. 1646–d. 1665
Naval captain from '46, served in Mediterranean, won engagement in Swedish service against Danes/Dutch, 1659, was made Vice-Admiral of Sweden. Arrested '61 for seditious words, defending *Venner*. Had ship full of arms at Sandwich '61. Bought own ship. Relative of Wm. Lilly. Died in shipwreck.

> *Letters and Papers relating to First Dutch War*, ed. S. R. Gardiner, i (1899), pp. 18–20; J. R. Powell, *Navy in the . . . Civil War* (1962), pp. 209, 215/17–18; *Loyall Scout*, 18 (26 Aug.–2 Sept. '59), p. 152; *C.S.P. Dom.*, '61–2, pp. 127, 188; SP. 29/44, f. 267v.; J. Gadbury, *Nauticum Astrologicum* (1691), pp. 79–80, 118–19.

CROSSBY, Richard
Cutler; arrested 1671 as 5th Mon./7th Day man (Jeaffreson, *Middx. Recs.*, iv. 29–30).

CROWCH, John
Tailor; 5th Mon. agent at Lewes, 1656/7 (*Thurloe*, vi. 187). Perhaps same or father of J.C. of Lewes, at Oxford Univ. '57–60, writing-master '63, lic. (Cong.), 1672, d. 1691 (Matthews, *Cal. Rev.*, pp. 150–1).

DAFFERNE, Thomas
Leveller, friend of Lilburne, '48. Of *Chillenden's* cong., 1653–4. His house a meeting place for *Harrison, Feake, Rogers*, '57. Prob. same as T. Dafford, arrested for conventicling in London '63. A Mr. Dafferne of London, 1638.

> *Thurloe*, vi. 349; Nickolls, *Orig. Letters*, p. 122; J. Lilburne, *Legall Fund. Liberties*, p. 36; J. More, *Lost Ordinance* (1654), p. 1; Jeaffreson, *Middx. Recs.*, iii. 322; T. C. Dale, *Inhabitants of London in 1638* (1931), p. 131.

DANE, (alias Dild), George
Tailor of London; arrested '71 as 5th Mon./7th Day man (Jeaffreson, *Middx. Recs.*, iv. 29–30).

247

DANVERS, Charles

Merchant of London, fl. '64. Brother of *Henry D.* (SP. 29/105, f. 75; *C.S.P. Dom.*, *'64–5*, p. 555).

DANVERS, Col. Henry, c. 1622–87

Gent., had Staffs. estate of £300 p.a. Educ. Oxford. On Staffs. county committees '47–52, '59–60; Gov. of Stafford, '50; M.P. for Leicester '53, and prominent as 5th Mon. thereafter. Negotiated with Commonwealthsmen '56, arrested '57; signed *Essay*, '59. Elder of *Chillenden's* cong. Prob. leader of *Rathbone* plot, '65; captured '65, but freed by the mob. Arrested '76. Head of 5th Mon. cong., '82. Involved in Rye House Plot and Monmouth's Rebellion; fled abroad to Holland, and died there.

> *D.N.B.;* (but confuses him with Robert D.: see p. 211, above); R. Kidson, 'Gentry of Staffs', *Staffs. Rec. Soc.*, iv. 13; Firth and Rait, *Acts and Ord.*, *passim*; *C.S.P. Dom.*, '50, pp. 211, 595; *ibid.*, *'82*, pp. 237, 358, 405, 495; SP. 29/419, f. 102;/437, f. 84; Clarke, iii. 105–6; Thurloe, iv. 365, 629; D. Neal, *Hist. of Puritans* (1837), iii. 415; Crosby, *Hist. Bapt.*, iii. 90/7; J. Lingard, *Hist. of England* (1849), xi. 290–1; S. Pepys, *Diary*, ed. Wheatley (1893), v. 40; Hist. MSS. Comm., xix. *Townshend MSS.*, pp. 43–4; *ibid.*, xxv, *Le Fleming MSS.*, p. 124; Clarendon, *Continuation* (1759), iii. 550–1; L. Eachard, *Hist. of England* (1707–18), iii. 757, 764–5, 770; Ford, lord Grey, *Secret History* (1757), pp. 105, 113, 122–3 (misprinted as 102, 107).

DAY, Cornet Wentworth, fl. 1647–61

Cornet in *Harrison's* regt., '47; left army '49/50. Arrested '55 for reading *Word for God* in public and attacking govt. In *Venner's* plot '57; arrested '58 with *Canne*, till '59. Signed *Essay*. Gaoled '60–1 for treasonable words.

> Clarke, iii. 62, 146; Thurloe, iv. 321/9, 343/8, 359; vii. 5–6, 18; *Narrative . . . of Canne, passim*; Jeaffreson, *Middx. Recs.*, iii. 306–7/9; Burrage, 'Insurrections' p. 738; *C.S.P. Dom.*, '59–60, p. 47; SP. 29/47, f. 104; Firth and Davies, *Reg. Hist.*, pp. 179, 184–5.

DENTON, Richard, fl. 1652–86

Trumpeter, member of a London congregation (?Knollys's); admitted to *Tillam's* church at Hexham, 1652. At *Pendarves's* funeral, 1656. Member of F. Bampfield's Seventh Day Baptist Church from 1676.

> E. B. Underhill, ed., *Records of . . . Hexham* (1854), p. 290; *Comp. Test*, sig. A2; T. *Bapt. H.S.*, iii. 10.

DYER, William

Yeoman of Abingdon; fined '64 (Preston, *Abingdon*, p. 121n.).

ECRING, Thomas

Tailor of Blackfriars, '64; became govt. informer (SP. 29/99, f. 17;/103, f. 262v.;/449, f. 61v.).

EVANS, Thomas

London milliner; executed '66 after Rathbone plot (Jeaffreson, *Middx. Recs.*, iii. 376, iv. 269–70).

FEAKE, Christopher, c. 1612–fl. 1682

Of Surrey. Educ. Cambridge (M.A., '35). Prob. V. of Elsham, Lincs., '38; Min. at Hertford, '46 (John *Archer's* former parish). Called 'tailor's man' by L'Estrange, but owned considerable property. Interest in Daniel and Revelation first aroused by anti-Prayer Book riots in Edinburgh, 1637.

Pub. millenarian views from '49. Min. of Christ Church, Newgate and lecturer at St. Anne's, Blackfriars from '49, and head of gathered church in Swan Alley and Warwick Lane. Most important 5th Mon. leader in London '51–60. Gaoled '54–5 and lost livings. Thought to be plotting '57; at *Canne's* trial, '58; arrested '58. Left London '60, became itinerant 5th Mon. preacher. Settled in Dorking, arrested '64. Promised not to act against govt. Head of 5th Mon. church on London Bridge '82. Dead before '93. *Not* a Baptist (*Cert. Passages*, 28 (21–8 July '54), p. 220).

> *D.N.B.; 'Vis. of Surrey'*, ed. Bannerman (Harleian Soc., 1899), p. 107; Venn and Venn, *Al. Cantab.*, ii. 128; Urwick, *Noncon. in Herts.*, pp. 526–9; Kitchin, *L'Estrange*, p. 125; *Thurloe*, i. 641; v. 755–9; vi. 349; *Clarke*, iii. 53, 61, 146, 163; *C.S.P. Dom.*, *'53–4*, pp. 304–6, 449; *ibid.*, *'56–7*, p. 194; SP. 29/44, f. 265v., 267;/90, fos. 24–8, 55, 57;/421, f. 324; *Narrative . . . of Canne*, p. 14; BM. Add. MS. 37808, fos. 2–3; his own *New Non-Conformist* (1654), *passim*, and *Oppressed Close Prisoner* (1654).

FENTON, Richard
London labourer; arrested '71 as 5th Mon./7th Day man (Jeaffreson, *Middx. Recs.*, iv. 29).

FINCH, James
Husbandman of Hendon; fined '65 as of Swift's cong. (MR/RC–1, no. 46).

FISHER, James, fl. 1622–d. 1667
V. of Sheffield by '46, ejected '60. Involved in 1663 plot. Reported that he 'preaches up the Fifth Monarchy'. Died at *Hatfield's* house.

> Matthews, *Cal. Rev.*, pp. 198–9.

FITTEN, James
Of Chester. Named in '63 plot (E. Price, *Eye-Salve* (1667), p. 2). Arrested as fanatic, '66; received letters from *Chappell* on Sevi (*C.S.P. Dom.*, *'65–6*, pp. 526, 568). London Baptist pastor 1674–d. 1677 (Whitley, *Bapt. London*, p. 108).

FLY, Timothy
London draper; at conventicle at *Adman's* house and fined, '69 (Jeaffreson, *Middx. Recs.*, iv. 14).

FLYNT, Thomas
Gent. of London; excuted '66 after *Rathbone* plot (Jeaffreson, *Middx. Recs.*, iii. 376; iv. 269–70).

Fox, Capt. Consolation
Maltster and yeoman of Abingdon; fined '64/'69 (Preston, *Abingdon*, pp. 121n., 123n.). In the cong. by 1654 (Atherton, *Pastor Turn'd Pope*, p. 3). Agitator of Ingoldsby's regt., 1647 (*Clarke Papers*, i. 437).

Fox, Edmond
London hat-maker; arrested '71 as 5th Mon./7th Day man (Jeaffreson, *Middx. Recs.*, iv. 29–30).

FOXWELL, John
London weaver; arrested over *Venner* plot, '61 (*London's Glory*, p. 16), and for conventicling '62 (Jeaffreson, *Middx. Recs.*, iii. 313). Presented at visitation '66 as scandalous person (Guildhall MS. 9583, box 1, St. Botolph's without Bishopsgate). Possibly the J.F. who signed Gen. Bapt. declaration

Appendix I

of '54 opposing 5th Mon. men (Whitley, *Minutes* (1909–10), i. 5). Possibly the Foxell who signed 5th Mon. letter 1670 (SP. 29/275, f. 216).

FRITTON, —
Miller of Canterbury; head of 5th Mon. church '65 (SP. 29/136, f. 65). Possibly to be identified with Alexander Tritton, head of a Baptist group in Canterbury in 1669 (Turner, *Orig. Recs.*, i. 13–14; I owe this reference to Dr. M. V. Jones).

GADBERRY, William
London bookbinder; arrested '71 as 5th Mon./7th Day man (Jeaffreson, *Middx. Recs.*, iv. 29–30).

GARRETT, William
Yeoman of Middx.; arrested at cong. at *Adman's* house, '69 (*ibid.*, iv. 14).

GEDDING, Zacharias
Smith of Middx.; arrested at cong. at *Adman's* house, '69 (*ibid.*).

GIBBS, Thomas
London joiner; in *Venner's* risings '57 and '61 (Burrage, 'Insurrections', p. 738; *Last Farewell* (1661), pp. 6–7).

GIBSON, William
London joiner; arrested '71 as 5th Mon./7th Day man (Jeaffreson, *Middx. Recs.*, iv. 29).

GLASSE, Thomas, d. 1666
Baptist pastor of Bovey Tracey in '56; at Dorchester meeting '58. In London after 1660 with *Vernon*, *Strange* and described at this time as a leading 5th Mon. Perhaps the T.G. of Cambridge (M.A., '31).

> T. *Bapt. H.S.*, vii. 203; Whitley, *Bapt. Lond.*, p. 113; *Thurloe*, vii. 138–40; SP. 29/71, f. 147;/99, f. 16; *Mite from Three Mourners*; Venn and Venn, *Al. Cantab.*, ii. 222.

GOFF, James
Portsmouth baker; agent '56/7 (*Thurloe*, vi. 187).

GOODGROOM, Richard
In army in Ireland from 1649, removed for opposing Protectorate (own *Copy of a Letter* (1656), *passim*). At *Canne's* trial, '58. Recommissioned as Capt., '59, then chaplain to *Overton*. Signed *Essay*. In gaol '61–7. Arrested '71 as 5th Mon./7th Day man; described as yeoman, preacher but 'no fighter'. Not the same as R.G., schoolmaster at Usk, 1650.

> *Bapt. Q.*, i. 232–3; xiv. 162; *Narrative . . . of Canne*, p. 14; Worcs. Coll. MS. 33, f. 111v.; *C.S.P. Dom.*, '59–60, pp. 45, 240; *ibid.*, '67, p. 498; *ibid.*, '71, p. 496; SP. 29/43, f. 120;/291, f. 179; Jeaffreson, *Middx. Recs.*, iv. 31.

GREEN, —
Gunsmith of Middx., '61 (SP. 29/40, f. 157).

GREGORY, Lidia
Shoemaker's wife, of Hendon; fined as *Swift's* cong., '65 (MR/RC–1, no. 46).

HABERGHAM, Samuel, 1626–65
Son of Min.; educ. Cambridge (M.A., '48). Follower of Bridge. V. of

Appendix I

Syleham, Suffolk by '52, ejected '62. At E. Anglian 5th Mon. rally '56. Pastor of Cong. church at Syleham till death.

> Matthews, *Cal. Rev.*, p. 240; *Thurloe*, iv. 687; Browne, *Congregationalism*, pp. 220–2.

HAGAR, George
Yeoman of Abingdon, fined '64 (Preston, *Abingdon*, p. 121n.).

HALL, John
Grocer of Abingdon, fined '64 (*ibid.*).

HALLIWELL (alias Holloway), Cornet Richard, fl. 1664–82
London tobacco-cutter. In Parlt. army, then in Flanders and Virginia. Presented for nonconformity '64. Follower of Blood in attack on Ormonde, '70. Broke with 5th Mon. men over their 'subservience'. In Rye House Plot, '82.

> Hist. MSS. Comm., vii. *App. to 8th Rep.*, pp. 155–9; SP. 29/421, f. 156; Guildhall MS. 9583, box 1, Trinity Minories.

HARRISON, Major-Gen. Thomas, 1606–60.
Most prominent 5th Mon. man, but not the leader; was swayed by the preachers. Son of grazier of Newcastle, Staffs. Educ. at Inns of Court. M.P. in '46. Had millenarian views by '49. Head of Propagation scheme in Wales '49–53. Prominent in fall of Rump; sat in Barebones. Dismissed from army Dec. '53 for opposing Protectorate. Gaoled '55–6, '57/8, but made no attempts to organize resistance. Executed 1660 as regicide.

> *D.N.B.*; C. H. Firth, *Life of Thomas Harrison* (Worcester, Mass., 1893); C. H. Simpkinson, *Thomas Harrison* (1905).

HASSELLOPP, Hugh, fl. 1652–74
Apothecary; baptized by *Tillam* into Hexham church '52. In Cheshire '64 (*T. Bapt. H.S.*, iv. 128). Arrested '71 as 5th Mon./7th Day man (Jeaffreson, *Middx. Recs.*, iv. 30).

HATFIELD, Capt. Anthony, fl. 1649–72
Esq., of Hatfield, Doncaster. On county committees, Yorks., '49/50. Said to be 5th Mon. and in 1663 plot. Patron of *Whitehurst* and *Fisher*.

> SP. 29/78, f. 12; Matthews, *Cal. Rev.*, pp. 526, 199; Firth and Rait, *Acts and Ord.*, ii. 297, 1067.

HATSELL, Capt. Henry, fl. 1652–d. 1667
?if 5th Mon. Admiralty commissioner at Plymouth by '52 (*First Dutch War*, ed. Gardiner and Atkinson (1899–1930), *passim*). On Devon/Somerset committees, '52–9 (Firth and Rait, *Acts and Ord.*, *passim*). Arrested at Exeter over *Byfield's* plot, '61 (*Merc. Publicus*, 4 (24–31 Jan. '61), p. 62). Soon released; lost Admiralty post '62 (*C.S.P. Dom.*, '60–1, p. 516; *ibid.*, '61–2, p. 483). Died '67 (*Canterbury Wills '61–70*, ed. Morrison, p. 117).

HAYLE, Richard
Collar-maker of Middx.; arrested at cong. at *Adman's* house, '69 (Jeaffreson, *Middx. Recs.*, iv. 14–15).

HEATH, Robert
Labourer of Abingdon, fined '64 (Preston, *Abingdon*, p. 121n.).

Appendix I

HELME, Camshaw, c. 1622–69
Son of poor gent.; educ. Oxford. Served in army (perhaps as chaplain). Min. from '47/8, V. of Winchcombe (Gloucs.) by '50, ejected '60. Attacked scheme to make Cromwell king, '56. Condemned *Venner* '61, but took over *Feake's* cong., and described as 5th Mon. and likely to rebel '61–5. Head of meeting in London '69.

> Matthews, *Cal. Rev.*, p. 256 and *Walker Rev.*, pp. 174, 192; Calamy, *Continuation*, p. 501; Nickolls, *Orig. Letters*, p. 141; SP. 29/42, f. 69;/44, f. 267;/65, f. 16;/93, f. 167v.;/120, f. 57; Helme, *Life in Death* (1660), sig. A2v.

HEYWARD, Robert, fl. 1657–d. 1705
Apprentice to silver-refiner. In *Venner's* risings '57 and '61. Became rich tradesman and landowner near Shrewsbury, but never abandoned beliefs.

> Burrage, 'Insurrections', p. 738; R. Gough, *Antiquities of Myddle* (1875), pp. 124–5, 182–5.

HICKS, Richard
London hat-maker; arrested '71 as 5th Mon./7th Day man (Jeaffreson, *Middx. Recs.*, iv. 29–30).

HIGGENSON, Thomas, fl. 1653–d. 1659
5th Mon. writer on law and against Quakers; probably a minister. *Feake* supplied an epistle to his *Some Legible Characteristics* (1659).

> Own writings.

HODGKIN, Roger
London button-seller; executed after '61 rising (Pagitt, *Heresiog.*, p. 289).

HONYBURNE, William
London smith; arrested '71 as 5th Mon./7th Day man (Jeaffreson, *Middx. Recs.*, iv. 29–30).

HOPKINS, Robert
London shoemaker; in '57 and '61 plots (Burrage, 'Insurrections', p. 738; Pagitt, *Heresiog.*, p. 289). Arrested as 5th Mon./7th Day man '71 (Jeaffreson, *Middx. Recs.*, iv. 29–30). Still 7th Day man in '85 (*T. Bapt. H.S.*, iv. 127–8).

HUTT, Robert
Basketmaker of Abingdon, fined '64 (Preston, *Abingdon*, p. 121n.).

IRETON, Clement, c. 1612/6–fl. 1667
Gent.; brother of John and Henry. On London and Middx. committees '49–54, '59–60. Associated with 5th Mon. leaders '55. Signed *Essay* '59. Described as friend of *Danvers* '61, and gaoled '66–7 for part in *Danvers's* plot. One Ireton sought by govt. over Monmouth's rising '85.

> R. W. Ramsey, *Henry Ireton* (1949), pp. 1, 207; *Thurloe*, v. 397; Firth and Rait, *Acts and Ord.*, ii. *passim*; *Faithfull Narrative* (1655), p. 41; SP. 29/192, f. 133;/217 f. 48v.;/446, f. 139; *C.S.P. Dom.*, '85, p. 157.

JAMES, Col. John, c. 1610–81
Gent. of Worcs. and Hereford. On committees for both, '47–52, '54, '57–60. M.P. for Worcester '53; on Council of State '53. Follower of *Llwyd*, signed *Word for God*, but was prepared to serve on committees under Protectorate. In London 1670.

W. R. Williams, *Parlt. Hist. of Worcester* (1897), pp. 44–6; T. Richards, *Puritan Movement* (1920), pp. 82, 93, 266; Nickolls, *Orig. Letters*, pp. 120–1; Firth and Rait, *Acts and Ord.*, *passim*.

JAMES, John, d. 1661

Head of 5th Mon./7th Day church in London. Ribbon-weaver, barely literate. Attacked by G. Fox, '58, as critic of Quakers. Executed for treason 1661, though not involved in plots. Elizabeth, prob. widow, in Mill Yard cong. '73.

> *D.N.B.*; T. B. Howell, *State Trials*, vi. (1816), pp. 67–104; *Narrative of the Apprehending of . . .* (1662); *True and perfect Speech of . . .* (1662); Pagitt, *Heresiog.*, pp. 295–7; Fox, *John James, I hearing* (1658), *passim*; 'Mill Yard Minutes', list of members.

JONES, James

Abingdon tailor, at rally '56 (*Comp. Test.*, p. 3). Fined 1664 (Preston, *Abingdon*, p. 121n.).

JONES, John, fl. 1654–d. 1666

Bookseller of St. Botolph's, Aldersgate. Prob. one of 2 J.J.s who signed *Declaration* '54. Released from prison with *Spittlehouse* '55. At Abingdon rally '56, and preacher in Swan Alley that year. Broke with *Venner* over '57 plot.

> *Thurloe*, iii. 149; iv. 650; *Comp. Test.*, sig. A2; *C.S.P. Dom.*, '55–6, p. 155; *True Catalogue* (1659), p. 13; Burrage, 'Insurrections', pp. 732–4; *Canterbury Wills '61–70*, ed. Morrison, p. 139.

JONES, John, fl. 1668–87

Yeoman, of the Bell Lane 5th Mon./7th Day church '68–87; arrested '71. Perhaps one of the 2 J.J.s who signed *Declaration* '54.

> *T. Bapt. H.S.*, iv. 127–8; *Bapt. Q.*, xiv. 161–6.

JONES, Rice

Schoolteacher of Llanfair Careinion, N. Wales, 1653. Signed *Word for God*. Named in fake 5th Mon. plot 1660 (Richards, *Relig. Develop.*, p. 237; *C.S.P. Dom.*, '59–60, p. 407).

JOPLIN, John, fl. 1653–68

Gaoler of Durham under Protectorate. Member of Tillam's church at Hexham from 1653. Formerly cornet in army under Hobson. Signed declaration with Hobson welcoming fall of Rump, 1653. Involved in 1663 plot, and though acquitted '64 was kept in prison. Noted as 'furious' 5th Monarchist '66.

> *C.S.P. Dom.*, *1663–4*, pp. 352, 550; *ibid.*, '64–5, p. 40; *ibid.*, '66–7, p. 318; *ibid.*, '67, p. 463; *ibid.*, '67–8, p. 273; *Sev. Proceedings*, 188 (28 April–5 May '53) p. 2960; Underhill, *Hexham*, p. 293.

KIRTON, Daniel, d. 1674

London liquor-shop keeper and distiller. Spread pamphlets at 5th Mon. meetings 1656 (*Thurloe*, v. 272–3; Jeaffreson, *Middx. Recs.*, iii. 253). Died '74 (*Canterbury Wills '71–5*, ed. J. Ainsworth (1942), p. 123).

KNIGHT, —

One of earliest 5th Mon. leaders at Allhallows, '52 (Erbery, *Bishop of London*, p. 3). Probably Isaac Knight, R. of Fulham from 1652 till Restoration, formerly chaplain to Fairfax (Matthews, *Cal. Rev.*, p. 311). Possibly the Mr. Knight, preacher and former porter, arrested Dec. '60/Jan. '61 with *Courtney* and *Allen* (*Merc. Publicus*, 54 (27 Dec. '60–3 Jan. '61), p. 846).

LABORY, John
London yeoman, arrested '71 as 5th Mon./7th Day man (Jeaffreson, *Middx. Recs.*, iv. 29–30). Still 7th Day '85 (*T. Bapt. H.S.*, iv. 127–8).

LAMAS, Susanna
Wife of Hendon labourer. Of *Swift's* cong., fined '65 (MR/RC–1, no. 46).

LANGDEN, Capt. Francis, d. 1658
Gent., of old Cornish family. On county committees '49–52. J.P., M.P. for Cornwall '53. Re-baptized '51. Chief supporter of *Trapnel* on her tour in 1654. At Abingdon rally '56. 5th Mon. agent, Cornwall, '56/7.

> Glass, *Barbone*, p. 79; Firth and Rait, *Acts and Ord.*, ii. 31, 294, 463, 659; *C.S.P. Dom.*, '49–50, p. 229; Trapnel, *Report and Plea; Comp. Test.*, sig. A2; *Thurloe*, vi. 187; *T. Bapt. H.S.*, iv. 135; *Canterbury Wills '57–60*, ed. Blagg, p. 336.

LAUGHTON, John
Smith of Middx. Arrested '69 at cong. at *Adman's* house (Jeaffreson, *Middx. Recs.*, iv. 14).

LLOYD, Owen
Follower of *Llwyd*. Had vision of black panther in Dec. '53 which he sent to *Rogers*. Published as *Panther-Prophecy* (1662) and used against Charles II (*Het Gezigt van den Panther* (1688), *passim*).

LLWYD, Morgan, 1619–59
Minister of Wrexham from 1646. Of yeoman family, Merioneth. In army, partly as chaplain. Worked with Propagation, and close follower of *Harrison*. Mill. writings from 1647–8. Fierce attack on Protectorate '54. His name on *Word for God*, but soon criticized it, and became quietist. Remained millenarian, but broke with *Powell*. Some disillusionment in later writings. Can be called 5th Mon. in '53–5.

> *D.N.B.;* Richards, *Puritan Movement* and *Relig. Develop.*, *passim*; A. N. Palmer, *Older Nonconformity in Wrexham* (1889), *passim*; Nuttall, *Welsh Saints* (1957), esp. chap. 3; *Thurloe*, ii. 129; A. H. Dodd, *Bull. Board Celt. Stud.*, xvii. 281–2; Llwyd, *Gweithiau* (1899/1908), i. 7, 9, 89; ii. 222–3.

LOCKTON, Philip, fl. 1656–86
Abingdon grocer. 5th Mon. agent '56/7 (*Thurloe*, vi. 187). Fined '62/4/9, 1686 (Preston, *Abingdon*, pp. 119n., 121n., 123n., 124n., 138n.).

LOVEGROVE, Richard
Abingdon labourer, fined '64 (*ibid.*, p. 121n.).

LOVEGROVE, Robert
Abingdon yeoman, fined '64 (*ibid.*).

MACEY, Francis
London scrivener, arrested '71 as 5th Mon./7th Day man (Jeaffreson, *Middx. Recs.*, iv. 29–30).

MALBAN, Robert, d. 1673
Silk-throwster of Shoreditch. Assisted George Masterson, minister of Shoreditch, in spying on a Leveller meeting for the government, Jan. 1648.

Appendix I

Arrested '61 over *Venner* plot (*London's Glory*, p. 16), and again for conventicling (Jeaffreson, *Middx. Recs.*, iii. 311). Involved with *Marsden*, Blood and other plotters '65 (SP. 29/114, f. 210;/121, f. 245). In army 1650 (SP. 28/142 iii, f. 52). R.M., gent. of Covent Garden, d. 1673 (*Canterbury Wills '71–5*, ed. Ainsworth, p. 136).

W. Haller and G. Davies, *The Leveller Tracts, 1647–1653* (1964 edn.), p. 97.

MARSDEN, Jeremiah, 1626–84
Of Lancs. Educ. Cambridge, minister from 1650 (Baptist). Chaplain to *Overton* '59–60. Ejected E. Ardsley, Yorks., '62. In 1663 plot, but in favour at court '64–5. Head of London church in '70s. Active plotter: sought in '67, gaoled '75 and '83–4. 5,000 at funeral. Prob. 5th Mon. by '59, still in '69 and probably till death.

Matthews, *Cal. Rev.*, pp. 339–40; Calamy, *Cont.*, pp. 942–5; Crosby, *Hist. Bapt.*, ii. 374–5; J. Walker, *Yorks. Arch. Journ.*, xxi. 348–59; MS. Rawl. D 1347, fos. 3–31; Worcs. Coll. MS. 52, f. 52; *C.S.P. Dom.*, *'66–7*, pp. 533/7; ibid., *'78*, p. 189; ibid., *'83 ii*, pp. 374–5; ibid., *'83–4*, pp. 332/5.

MARSHALL, Abigail
Presented silver bowl to *Chamberlen's* cong. (MS. Rawl. D 828, f. 11). 5th Mon. agent at Lincoln, '56/7 (*Thurloe*, vi. 187).

MARSHALL, Edward
London labourer, arrested '71 as 5th Mon./7th Day man (Jeaffreson, *Middx. Recs.*, iv. 29–30).

MARTEN, Edward
London tailor, arrested '71 as 5th Mon./7th Day man (*ibid.*).

MASON, John
London weaver, arrested '71 as 5th Mon./7th Day man (*ibid.*). Arrested '75 as prominent in the silk-weavers' riots (*C.S.P. Dom.*, *'75–6*, pp. 258–9).

MASON, William
London upholsterer, arrested '71 as 5th Mon./7th Day man (Jeaffreson, *Middx. Recs.*, iv. 29–30). Prob. the W.M. of Bell Lane church 1711 ('Mill Yard Minutes', p. 193).

MAYHEW, Richard, fl. 1653–83
Minister, ejected from Iken, Suffolk. Nominated M.P. for Barebones. Prob. 5th Mon. in '50s, though not known as such. Pastor of 5th Mon. church in London 1678/80. His *Sichah* (1682) was dedicated to Shaftesbury.

Matthews, *Cal. Rev.*, p. 346; SP. 29/404, f. 303; *C.S.P. Dom.*, *'80–1*, p. 613.

MEDLEY, William, fl. 1654–83
Signed *Declaration* '54 as of *Rogers's* cong. In *Venner's* plot '57, signed its manifesto as scribe. Goaled '57–9. Married *Venner's* daughter. Described in Nov. '61 as scribe and accountant of whole 5th Mon. movement. Acted as Dutch agent in London '72–4. In Amsterdam 1682, welcomed Shaftesbury.

Burrage, 'Insurrections', pp. 738, 746; *Thurloe*, vii. 598–9; SP. 29/44, f. 267; Medley, *Standard Set Up* (1657); K. H. D. Haley, *William of Orange and the English Opposition* (1953), *passim*; *Memoires of Shaftesbury* (1683), p. 7.

Appendix I

MILLES, John
London carpenter, executed '66 after *Rathbone* plot (Jeaffreson, *Middx. Recs.*, iii. 376; iv. 269–70).

MORE, John, fl. 1652–d. 1702
Apprentice/journeyman of Wm. Webb (?the Surveyor-General) in 1652 when joined *Chamberlen's* church. Promptly became prominent member. Broke away '54, signed *Declaration* as of Raworth's cong. Published fierce tracts '52–4, *A Vindication* (1652, with *Spittlehouse*) defending Münster, and *A Trumpet Sounded* (1654) attacking Protectorate. In Mill Yard church till death. Only known as 5th Mon. up to 1654.

> Anon., *Disputes between Cranford and Chamberlen* (1652), *sig.* A2–v.; MS. Rawl. D 828, *passim*; T. *Bapt. H.S.*, iii. 180–2; vii. 221.

NASH, James
Labourer of Whitechapel, of *Malban's* cong. Fined '61 (Jeaffreson, *Middx. Recs.*, iii. 313).

NAUDIN, Theodore
French physician of *Chamberlen's* church, '52–4. Involved in plot with French embassy to subvert army and kill Cromwell, '54. Gaoled, and made abject submission (MS. Rawl. D 828, *passim*; Gardiner, *Commonwealth and Prot.*, iii. 125–6, 136; *C.S.P. Dom.*, '54, pp. 289, 372; SP. 18/74, f. 21).

NEAT, Joseph
Small master, trade unknown. At Abingdon rally '56 (*Comp. Test.*, *sig.* A2). Of Mill Yard 7th Day church '73 ('Mill Yard Minutes', p. 3).

NEWBURY, Francis
Abingdon labourer, fined '64 (Preston, *Abingdon*, p. 121n.).

NORRIS, Henry
Schoolmaster of N. Wales, indicted with *Powell* '54 (*Thurloe*, ii. 226).

OASTLER, —
London cheesemonger; house a 5th Mon. meeting-place for *Strange, Vernon*, '64 (SP. 29/103, f. 262;/105, f. 75;/110, f. 216).

OKEY, Thomas
Woolbroker; head of 5th Mon. group, Devizes, '69 (Turner, *Orig. Recs.*, i. 118).

OVERTON, Maj.-Gen. Robert, c. 1609–c. 1668
Educ. Grey's Inn. Governor of Hull '47, with *Canne* later as chaplain. Dissatisfied at fall of Barebones, but retained position till arrested '54 for allowing officers to criticize govt. Gaoled till '59, when restored. Signed *Essay*. Tried to establish 5th Mon. stronghold at Hull '59–60. In prison '60–1, '63–8. One of most prominent 5th Monarchists, but usually far from centre of action, and political behaviour was ineffective.

> D.N.B.; *Thurloe*, iii. 46–7, 75–6, 110–12, 185; ed. Firth, *Scotland and the Protectorate* (Scott. Hist. Soc., xxxi), *passim*; Firth and Davies, *Reg. Hist.*, pp. 546, 559–60.

PACKER, Col. William, fl. 1644–62
Major of Cromwell's regt. A Baptist; in early 5th Mon. group '52, and

supported Barebones. But loyal to his 'dear friend' the Protector; became deputy maj.-gen., and sat in Commons. Broke with Cromwell over offer of crown. Col. in '59; backed Lambert. Gaoled '60/1, transported '62.

> D.N.B.; T. Bapt. H.S., iv. 58–63; vii. 223; Firth and Davies, Reg. Hist., pp. 8–9, 35, 73; Erbery, Bishop of London, p. 7; Faithfull Scout, 122 (22–9 July '53), pp. 908–9; C.S.P. Dom., '61–2, p. 476; Eng. Hist. Rev., lxxxiii (1968), pp. 692–3.

PALMER, Anthony, 1616/18–79

Minister, ed. Oxford (M.A. '41), Min. of Bourton, Gloucs., '46 till ejected '60. Petitioned against making Cromwell king, '56. Called a leading 5th Mon. man only after 1660, when he went to London. Head of mixed Bapt./Cong. church. Called 5th Mon. only up to 1663; lic. (Cong.) in '72, so views probably moderating by then.

> D.N.B.; Matthews, Cal. Rev., p. 380; SP. 29/34, f. 2;/42 f. 69;/44, fos. 10 267;/65, f. 16;/88, f. 127–v.;/105, f. 75.

PALMER, Thomas, c. 1612–fl. 1667

Minister, son of min. of Leicester. Educ. Oxford (B.A., '35). Chaplain to Skippon's regt., and possibly later a major. Min. of St. Lawrence Pountney London '44–6, and of Aston, Derbys., '46–60, when ejected. Millenarian by '44, 5th Mon. by '54. At Canne's trial '58. Pastor of Cong. church at Nottingham by '59, but also itinerant preacher. Arrested Kent, 1662. Big part in 1663 plot. Gaoled 1663. Went to Ireland '66. Published defence of rebellion '67. (Not to be confused with Capt. Laurence Palmer, R. of Gedling, Notts., 1640–82: see R. A. Marchant, Puritans . . . in . . . York (1960), p. 360; cf. Nuttall, Visible Saints (1957), p. 33n.).

> D.N.B.; Matthews, Cal. Rev., p. 380; Walker, Yorks, Arch. Journ., xxxi. 354; A. R. Henderson, Castle Gate Church, Nottingham (1905), pp. 45–56; Narrative . . . of Canne, p. 11; Intelligencer, 14 (30 Nov. 1663), p. 112; C.S.P. Dom., '63–4, pp. 635, 663; SP. 29/85, f. 103;/92, f. 112;/121, f. 247; Palmer, Saints Support (1644) tit. pag., sig. A2; Palmer, Saints Freedom (1667), passim.

PARNHAM, Richard, fl. 1647–81

London silversmith. Quarter-master in Ireton's regt., '47. At Abingdon rally '56. Joint head with Belcher of 5th Mon./7th Day church at Bell Lane in '68, and still in '81; arrested with cong. in '71.

> Worcs. Coll. MS. 67, f. 17; Comp. Test., sig. A2; Jeaffreson, Middx. Recs., iv. 29–30; T. Bapt. H.S., iii. 188; iv. 128.

PATSHALL, John, fl. 1661–83

Brewer's clerk of Southwark (C.S.P. Dom., '83 i, p. 184; ibid., '83 ii, p. 4). Vennerite '61, acquitted as only one witness (Pagitt, Heresiog., p. 290). In 1663 plot, gaoled '65, escaped '66 (C.S.P. Dom., '64–5, p. 293; ibid., '65–6, pp. 400, 404, 416). In plot 1678 (ibid., '78, p. 290) and Rye House plot 1683 (ibid. '83 i, pp. 66, 104, 184; ibid., '83 ii, pp. 4, 77).

PAYNE, Robert

Abingdon wool-draper; fined '62/4, '86. Excommunicated '70 (Preston, Abingdon, pp. 119n., 121n., 124n., 138n.).

PECK Simon

Abingdon maltster. At rally '56 (Comp. Test., sig. A2). Fined '64, excomm., '69 (Preston, Abingdon, pp. 121n., 124n., 126).

Appendix I

PENDARVES, John, 1622–56
Baptist minister, of Cornish gentle family. Educ. Oxford (B.A., '42). Resigned living at Abingdon '49, and led a gathered church. 5th Mon. by '55; died London '56. Great Baptist/5th Mon. rally at his funeral.

> *D.N.B.*; Payne, *Baptists of Berkshire*, pp. 24–7; Preston, *Abingdon*, pp. 116–17; Nuttall, *Journ. Eccles. Hist.*, xi, p. 214; Wood, *Ath. Oxon.*, pp. 129–30; Foster, *Al. Oxon.*, iii. 1140; *Comp. Test., passim*; W. Hughes, *Munster and Abingdon* (1657), pp. 87ff; J. Atherton, *Pastor Turn'd Pope* (1654); *Clarke*, ii. 243.

PERROTT, Capt. Robert, d. 1685
Silk-dyer of Allhallows and preacher in *Danvers's* cong. In prison in Surrey as 5th Mon. man '62. Arrested for conventicling '63, presented at episcopal visitation '64. Became follower of Blood, involved in stealing crown. In plots '78 and '82. Big part in Monmouth's rising, fought at Sedgemoor, captured and executed.

> Jeaffreson, *Middx. Recs.*, iii. 328–9; SP. 29/56, f. 165;/421, f. 156;/437, f. 84; *C.S.P. Dom.*, '71, pp. 225, 247, 385, 460; *ibid.*, '71–2, p. 65; *ibid.*, '78, p. 320; *Surrey Q.S. Recs.*, '61–3, ed. Powell and Jenkinson (Surrey Rec. Soc., xxxvi), p. 279; Guildhall MS. 9583, box 1: Allhallows the Gt; L. Eachard, *Hist. of England* (1707–18), iii. 757, 765, 770; I. Morley, *A Thousand Lives* (1954), pp. 202, 226.

PLOMSTEAD, Clement
London ironmonger (Jeaffreson, *Middx. Recs.*, iii. 341). Signed *Rogers's Reviving Word* '57. One C.P. a Quaker in '86 (J. Besse, *Collection of Sufferings* (1753), i. 480).

POOLEY, Christopher, c. 1620–fl. 1679
Educ. Cambridge (M.A. '47); C. of Thwaite, Suffolk, '43. Apparently in army '47–51. Head of church at Wymondham '53. Rebaptized '56, and one of leading 5th Mon. militants in Norfolk at this time. Head of 7th Day church in Norwich '61. Involved in *Tillam's* millenarian settlement in Germany after Restoration. On recruiting tour in England '66, gaoled '67–8. Reverted to orthodox 7th Day views by 1677. (Not to be confused with a Norfolk Presbyterian minister of the same names.)

> Venn and Venn, *Al. Cantab.*, iii. 379; Nickolls, *Orig. Letters*, pp. 124–5; *T. Bapt. H.S.* vii. 225; *Bapt. Q.*, xvii. 65; xviii. 364; *Sabbath Memorial*, xlix–l, p. 568; *Thurloe*, v. 188, 219–20, 372; E. Stennet, *The Insnared Taken* (1677/9), p. 7; SP. 28/124, f. 180; SP. 28/125, f. 369v.; SP. 29/41, f. 1;/106, fos. 17–18;/181, fos. 193–5;/190, f. 189;/446, f. 139; *C.S.P. Dom.*, '67, pp. 229, 335; *ibid.*, '67–8, p. 154.

PORTER, John
London labourer, arrested '71 as 5th Mon./7th Day man (Jeaffreson, *Middx. Recs.*, iv. 29–30).

PORTMAN, Edmund
Clerk to Treasurer of Navy in '52 (*First Dutch War*, iii, ed. Gardiner (1906) p. 324). One of leaders, with brother, of breakaway group from *Simpson's* church which negotiated with *Venner* 1657 (Burrage, 'Insurrections', p. 731).

PORTMAN, John, fl. 1652–73
Dep. Treasurer to the Fleet and 'principal secretary to the generals at sea'. Millenarian by '53. Dismissed '56 over 5th Mon./Commonwealthsmen

negotiations. One of leaders of breakaway group in *Simpson's* church '56-8. Negotiated with *Venner* '57, but no part in plot. In gaol '57-8, '58-9 for spreading seditious literature. Signed *Essay*. Named in plot '61, gaoled '61, calling for revenge for *Harrison*. Still in prison '67. One Portman Cashier to victuallers of navy '73 (though could be Edmund).

> *C.S.P. Dom.*, '52-3/53-4, *passim; First Dutch War*, ed. Gardiner and Atkinson, *passim; C.S.P.D.*, '56-7, pp. 149, 391; SP. 29/34, f. 120;/218, f. 142; *Thurloe*, vi·163, 185, 775; vii. 599, 619-20, 623; *Old Leaven, passim; Comp. Test.*, sig. A2; Burrage, 'Insurrections', p. 731; G. Wharton, *Second Narrative of Late Parliament* (1658), p. 36; *Publick Intell.*, 121 (8-15 Feb. '58), p. 321 (misprint for 301), and 122, pp. 333-4; *ibid.*, 157 (27 Dec. '58-3 Jan. '59), pp. 134-5; *Traitors Unvailed* (1661), p. 7; Howell, *State Trials*, vi. 117; T. Carte, *Orig. Letters* (1739), ii. 112; *C.S.P. Dom.*, '73, pp. 259, 271.

POSTLETHWAITE, Walter, fl. 1643–d. 1672
Son of minister; educ. Cambridge (B.A., '46). Convert of H. Peter. At Lewes, Sussex, by '46; Rector till ejected '60. Called moderate 5th Mon. man '55. Took oaths '61, stayed at Lewes as head of Indep. cong. There '69. Not known as 5th Mon. after Restoration.

> Matthews, *Cal. Rev.*, p. 396; *Thurloe*, iv. 151; Edwards, *Gangraena*, iii. p. 105.

POWELL, Vavasor, 1617–70
Son of ale-house-keeper; ?educ. Oxford. Chaplain in Parlt. army. Itinerant N. Welsh preacher, based on Radnor. Leading part on Propagation, and a major influence on *Harrison*. In London '53, supported Barebones. Fierce critic of Protectorate, drew up *Word for God* '55, but opposed plots. Signed *Essay*. Almost always in prison after 1660. Proclaimed his loyalty to 5th Mon. ideas, but his beliefs became more quietist.

> *D.N.B.*; R. T. Jones, 'Life, Work and Thought of Vavasor Powell', Oxford D.Phil., 1947; Richards, *Puritan Movement, Relig. Devel., Wales under Penal Code* (1925), all *passim*; (Bagshaw), *Life and Death of ... Powell* (1671); Powell, *Bird in the Cage* (1661), *passim*.

PRICE, Evan
? if 5th Mon. A 'wandering person', said to spread news and propaganda in the 1663 plot: 'the secrets of the plotters are bound up in the breast of Major *Wigan* and Evan Price'. Gaoled at Lancaster, 1664, and was offered £1,000 to reveal details of the plot. Alleged to have rejected this offer and demanded more (*C.S.P. Dom., 1663-4*, pp. 512, 519, 545). But in his *Eye-Salve* (1667) he denied any connection with the plot.

PRICE, Col. Richard, fl. 1639–d. 1674/5
Small squire of Gunley, Montgom.; in army from '45. On county committees '47-54, '57/9. High Sheriff, Montgom., '50. Supporter of *Powell*. M.P. for Wales '53. Delivered *Word for God* to Cromwell in London. Head of N. Wales militia '59. Signed *Essay*. Ind. preacher after Restoration (lic. '72) until death. Not known as 5th Mon. after Restoration.

> Williams, *Parlt. Hist. Wales.*, pp. 3-4, 144; Richards, *Puritan Movement*, pp. 82, 90/2/4/6 and *Wales under Penal Code*, p. 126; Firth and Rait, *Acts and Ord.*, *passim; True Catalogue* (1659), p. 10; J.W.H., 'Pryces of Gunley', *Arch. Cambrensis*, 4th ser., xiii (1882), pp. 129-37; Dodd, 'Remonstrance', p. 290; Dodd, *Studies in Stuart Wales* (1952), pp. 129, 147, 163.

Appendix I

PRINCE, William

Middx. chandler, arrested '69 as of cong. at *Adman's* house (Jeaffreson, *Middx. Recs.*, iv. 14).

PRITCHARD, Giles

London cow-keeper, executed after 1661 rising (Pagitt, *Heresiog.*, p. 289). Left 15 cows (*C.S.P. Dom.*, *'60–1*, p. 487).

PRYOR, William

Wrote 5th Mon. pamphlet '59. Perhaps the W.P., a 'labouring man' and Quaker who died in Newgate '61 (Besse, *Sufferings*, i. 389).

QUELCH, Richard, fl. 1652–d. 1665/7

Oxford watchmaker and 5th Mon. agent '56/7 (*Thurloe*, vi. 187). At Abingdon rally '56 (*Comp. Test.*, sig. A2). For life see C. F. C. Beeson, *Clockmaking in Oxfordshire*, Banbury Hist. Soc., iv (1962), p. 135.

RATHBONE, Col. John, fl. 1646–d. 1666

Gent.; in army by '46. Associated with *Rogers* in seeking end of tithes during Barebones. Involved in plot led by *Danvers* to seize king and fire the city '65, captured and executed.

> Rogers, *Sagrir*, sig. C2; SP. 28/123, f. 612; Jeaffreson, *Middx. Recs.*, iii. 376; Abbott, *Am. Hist. Rev.*, xiv. 700; Clarendon, *Continuation* (1759), iii. 550–1; *London Gazette*, 48 (26–30 April 1666).

RICH, Col. Nathaniel, fl. 1639–d. 1702

Gent.; educ. Inns of Court. Col. by '45. M.P. '49–53 and in Barebones. Removed from army Dec. '54, arrested with other 5th Mon. leaders '55–6, '57. Restored to command '59, supported Rump, opposed Monk. Gaoled '60, '61–5. Married daughter of E. of Ancrum. Refused oaths but promised not to oppose govt. Kept conventicles, but not politically active after '65.

> *D.N.B.*; *Thurloe*, vi. 185, 251; *Clarke*, ii. 242–6; iii. 69, 105–6, 113; iv. 19; SP. 29/31, f. 154;/84, f. 1;/109, f. 115v.; Ludlow, *Memoirs*, ii. 148–9, 163/5, 183–4, 238; Hist. MSS. Comm., 51, *Leyborne-Popham*, pp. 168–9; Firth and Davies, *Reg. Hist.*, pp. 145, 151/4, 162; Firth and Rait, *Acts and Ord.*, *passim*; Turner, *Orig. Recs.*, i. 112.

RICHARD, John

Apprentice or journeyman; arrested Swan Alley '58 with *Canne* (*Narrative . . . of Canne*, p. 6).

RIGHTON, Capt. William, fl. 1654–85

Tailor and trader of Bermuda; also public preacher till removed as subversive in '57. In England in mid-'50s; signed *Declaration*. Tried in Bermuda '61 for seditious words against king. Also amateur lawyer and smuggler. Associated with another 5th Mon. man in Bermuda (J. H. Lefroy, *Memorials of the Bermudas* (1877–9), i. 741; ii. *passim*).

ROBERTS, John

Servant to Abingdon cordwainer, fined '62 (Preston, *Abingdon*, p. 119n.).

ROBERTS, Richard

Cordwainer of Middx.; at cong. at *Adman's* house, arrested '69 (Jeaffreson, *Middx. Recs.*, iv. 14).

ROBERTS, Timothy, fl. 1651–d. 1665
Minister, educ. Oxford (B.A. '55). V. of Barton, Westmorland, '55 till ejected '62. Described as 5th Mon. '63, discussing rising with other 5th Mon. men, in London. Gaoled at Appleby for preaching. Died of plague 1665.

> Matthews, *Cal. Rev.*, p. 412; B. Nightingale, *The Ejected of 1662* (1911), ii. 1224–6; SP. 29/114, f. 20v.

ROGERS, John, 1627–?d. 1670
Son of Essex minister. Educ. Cambridge (B.A. '46). Presbyt. then Ind. minister in Essex then London. Min. in Dublin '50–2; lecturer at St. Thomas Apostle's, London '53–Restoration. Millenarian by '53, broke with Cromwell '54 and joined with 5th Mon. men. Opposed govt., gaoled 1654–7, and '58. An admirer of Vane in late '50s, combined 5th Mon./Commonwealth principles. Supported return of Rump. Army chaplain '59, in Ireland end of '59, then fled to Netherlands. M.D., Utrecht, '62. Reported as itinerant '61. Head of cong. at Bermondsey '63; practised as physician. A J.R. of that parish died 1670, though a govt. newswriter in Nov. '71 thought he was still alive and still a 5th Mon. man.

> *D.N.B.*; E. Rogers, *Life and Opinions of a Fifth Monarchy Man* (1867); SP. 29/42, f. 69;/44, f. 267;/88, f. 127; *C.S.P. Dom.*, '71, pp. 569–70; Rogers, *Christian Concertation* (1659), pp. 59–60 and *passim*.

RUDDUCK, Thomas, fl. 1650–7
Shopkeeper of N. Walsham, Norfolk. In army (apparently illiterate) in '50. Militant 5th Mon. there in '56, newly re-baptized. At Abingdon rally '56; arrested and gaoled at Windsor. 5th Mon. agent in Norfolk, '56/7.

> SP. 28/142, iii. f. 52; *Comp. Test.*, sig. A2; *True Catalogue*, p. 13; *Thurloe*, v. 220, vi. 187.

RUSSELL, William, fl. 1654–85
Tailor of Southwark. Signed *Declaration* '54; signed *Rogers's Reviving Word* '57. In prison '61 for refusing oaths and conventicling. Arrested '71 as 5th Mon./7th Day man. In Newgate 1685 over Monmouth rising. One W.R. in army 1647.

> *Surrey Q.S. Recs.*, '59–61, ed. Powell and Jenkinson (Surrey Rec. Soc., xxxv), p. 168; Jeaffreson, *Middx. Recs.*, iv. 29–30, 293; SP. 28/124, f. 64.

RYE, John, fl. 1655–67
Thought to be author of *Word for God*. At Abingdon rally '56, as of London. Thought to be author of *Venner's* second manifesto, *Door of Hope* (1661). In prison, London and Hull, 1660–7. A J.R. of Friday St., London, 1638.

> *Thurloe*, iv. 379; *Comp. Test.*, sig. A2; Pagitt, *Heresiog.*, p. 224 (misprint for 284); SP. 29/218, f. 142; Worcs. Coll. MS. 33, f. 111v.; Dale, *London, 1638*, p. 99.

SAMAND, Alexander de
Servant in London, c. 1654/5 (MS. Rawl. A 47, fos. 26–7v.).

SAUNDERSON (alias Sanders), William
London yeoman, executed '66 after Rathbone plot (Jeaffreson, *Middx. Recs.*, iii. 376; iv. 269–70).

Appendix I

SEELE, William, fl. 1654–d. 1667
Shipwright of Wapping (*Canterbury Wills* '61–70 ed. Morrison, p. 216). Signed *Declaration* '54 as of Fenton's cong.

SELLWOOD, Richard
Abingdon baker, fined '64 (Preston, *Abingdon*, p. 121n.).

SHIMMEN, George
London waterman, arrested '71 as 5th Mon./7th Day man (Jeaffreson, *Middx. Recs.*, iv. 29–30).

SHIPPEY, Maria
Wife of Hendon husbandman; arrested as of *Swift's* cong., '65 (MR/RC–1, no. 46).

SIFERWEST, Robert
London glazier. At cong. at *Winch's* house, fined '65 (MR/RC–1, no. 35).

SIMPSON, John, fl. 1642–d. 1662
Baptist/5th Mon. minister. A J.S. of St. Botolph's Aldgate, 1638. Said to be frivolous in youth, but a lecturer by '42. Major in Parlt. army. Antinomian in '40s. Min. of St. Botolph's, Bishopsgate '52–5 (removed by govt.), and '59–62; lecturer of St. Botolph's, Aldgate 'by election of the people' throughout '50s, and at Allhallows the Gt., '47–62. A leading 5th Mon. man from '52. Gaoled '54/6, then moderated views and attacked violence. Part of cong. at Allhallows seceded in disgust. Took oaths at Restoration, but preached against the govt. A major figure, but unstable and lost the confidence of many saints.

> Matthews, *Cal. Rev.*, p. 443; Erbery, *Bishop of London*, p. 3; *C.S.P. Dom.*, '53–4, p. 449; *ibid.*, '54, p. 256; *ibid.*, '55, p. 226; *ibid.*, '55–6, p. 109; *ibid.*, '56–7, p. 272; *ibid.*, '57–8, pp. 62, 64–5; SP. 29/43, f. 105;/44, fos. 10–v., 270; *Thurloe*, iv. 321, 545; *Clarke*, ii. xxiv; *Old Leaven*, *passim*; *Failing and Perishing* (1662); *Merc. Politicus*, 288 (13–20 Dec. '55), p. 5836; *Perf. Diurnall*, 216 (23–30 Jan. '54), p. 3092; J. A. Dodd, *Eng. Hist. Rev.*, x, 41–54; Dale, *London, 1638*, p. 213; Nuttall, *Visible Saints*, p. 36 and n.

SKINER, —
London coffee/strong-water-seller; house a 5th Mon. centre 1660 (SP. 29/1, f. 96).

SKINNER, Capt. John, fl. 1646–d. 1694
Minister by '46; R. of Weston and Hope Mansell, Herefordshire, '49 till ejected '60. Then in London, with *Strange*, and in '63–4 described as a leading 5th Mon. man. Fined at Hereford '65 for conventicling. Lic. (Cong.) '72, though in fact a Baptist. Died at Ross.

> Matthews, *Cal. Rev.*, p. 444; *T. Bapt. H.S.*, iii. 117–20; SP. 29/71, f. 147;/88, f. 128;/99, f. 16;/105, f. 75.

SPENCER, Capt. John, fl. 1639–82
Originally groom to Lord Say and Sele. Baptist preacher from '39. Wrote millenarian defence of civil war in '42. In early 5th Mon. group '52, but loyal to Protectorate. Bought royal estate with *Packer* in Herts. Remained in that area; lic. (Bapt.) '72, last known '82. Not the same as J.S., author of *Short Treatise* (1641).

Appendix I

T. Bapt. H.S., iv. 58–63; vii. 230; Whitley, *Bapt. Lond.*, p. 104; Firth and Rait, *Acts and Ord.*, *passim*; Firth and Davies, *Reg. Hist.*, pp. 75–6; Erbery, *Bishop of London*, p. 3; W. J. Hardy, *Hertford County Recs.* (1905), i. 223, 307, 325; Spencer, *Spirituall Warfare* (1642).

SPITTLEHOUSE, John, fl. 1643–d. 1659
In army 1643–51; deputy to Marshal-General (in charge of military security), but apparently dismissed. In *Chamberlen's* cong. Gaoled at fall of Barebones till April '54, and again '54–5. Signed *Declaration*. Involved in *Sturgeon's Short Discovery* 1655. Published 5th Mon. tracts 1650–6. His widow mentioned '59.

D.N.B.; MS. Rawl. D 828, *passim*; *C.S.P. Dom.*, '54, pp. 61–2, 378, 434; *ibid.*, '55–6, p. 155; *ibid.*, '59–60, p. 39; *Thurloe*, iii. 149; *Perfect Procs.*, 287 (22–29 March '55), p. 4557; Worcs. Coll. MS. 18, f. 10.

SQUIBB, Arthur, fl. 1640s–d. 1680
Of Dorset/Wilts. family, son of Teller of Exchequer. Became a sequestrator. Had gathered church at house by '49. J.P.; M.P. for Middlesex in Barebones, prominent as 5th Mon. man. Removed from office Jan. '54. In 5th Mon./Commonwealth negotiations '56/7. In prison for some time to Dec. '59. Sold reversion to tellership to Edmund Squibb 1654; Edmund tried to claim it in vain, in '63. It was said of Squibb in '62 'surely he is *Harrison* alive'. Arrested as 5th Mon./7th Day man, '71. Lic. (Bapt.), Surrey, '72.

Glass, *Barbone*, p. 84; *T. Bapt. H.S.*, vii. 230; G. Aylmer, *The King's Servants* (1961), pp. 90, 387; *Thurloe*, i. 289; H. Walker, *Spiritual Exercises* (1652), p. 44; *Faithfull Narrative* (1655), p. 41; J. Hall, *Confusion Confounded* (1654), p. 6; *Merc. Politicus*, 600 (22–9 Dec. '59), p. 984; *Weekly Intell.*, 149 (3–10 Jan. '54), p. 117; Abbott, *Writings . . . of . . . Cromwell*, iv. 489; SP. 29/291, f. 176; *C.S.P. Dom.*, '61–2, p. 369; Jeaffreson, *Middx. Recs.*, iv. 31; Turner, *Orig. Recs.*, ii. 1017–18; Hist. MSS. Comm., viii, *App. to 9th Rep.*, part ii., p. 44; *Canterbury Wills '76–85*, ed. Ridge, p. 317; *C.S.P. Dom.*, '54, p. 272; *ibid.*, '61–2, p. 369; *ibid.*, '63–4, p. 121; Bodl. MS. Clar. 76, f. 355*v*.

STARRE, Edward
Abingdon maltster, fined '64 (Preston, *Abingdon*, p. 121n.).

STENNET, Edward, fl. 1654–d. 1705
'Medical man'. Early of Abingdon church, later head of 7th Day cong. At Abingdon rally '56. Married Mary Quelch, perhaps rel. to Richard *Quelch*. 7th Day by '58. Head of 7th Day church at Wallingford (lic. '72), still there in '90. 5th Mon. only '55–8 (if at all); still millenarian in '67.

T. Bapt. H.S., vii. 231; *Bapt. Q.*, xiv. 161/5; Whitley, *Bapt. Lond.*, p. 119; Payne, *Bapt. of Berkshire*, pp. 48–9; *Comp. Test.*, sig. A2; own *Royal Law* (1667), p. 8.

STIBBS, John
Abingdon maltster, fined '64 (Preston, *Abingdon*, p. 121n.).

STIBBS, Thomas
Abingdon labourer, fined '64 (*ibid.*).

STOCKDALE, —
Silkthrowster of Aldgate, '63; meeting place for *Belcher's* cong. (SP. 29/80, f. 192).

Appendix I

STONEHAM, Benjamin, c. 1612–76

Educ. Cambridge (M.A. '46); chaplain before war. C. of St. Peter's, Ipswich, '51-Restoration. Nominated M.P.s for Barebones. Leading 5th Mon. in Suffolk '56, agent at Ipswich '56/7. Published *A Serious Proposal* with Feake, '59. Preacher in London after Restoration; gaoled '65. Remained a millenarian, and possibly a 5th Mon. as not licensed '72.

> Matthews, *Cal. Rev.*, p. 465; Nickolls, *Orig. Letters*, p. 94; *Thurloe*, iv. 687, 727; vi. 187; Browne, *Congregationalism*, pp. 366–7; own *Saul and David* (1676), pp. 145–8, and *Voice of a Cry* (1664), *passim*.

STRANGE, Lt. Nathaniel, fl. 1648–d. 1665

In Army; pastor of Bapt. church at Barnstaple in later '50s; at Dorchester meeting '58. Known as 5th Mon. only after 1660, when moved to London. Often described as such '63–5; tried to stir up rising. Said to be a 'scholler and linguist'.

> Nuttall, *J. Eccles. Hist.*, xi. 213–18; *Thurloe*, vii. 140; SP. 28/124, f. 357;/125, f. 262; SP. 29/71, f. 147;/99, fos. 16–17;/114, f. 19;/121, f. 247; *Memorial on the Death of . . . Strange* (1666), brs.

STRICKLAND, Thomas

London yeoman, arrested '71 as 5th Mon./7th Day man (Jeaffreson, *Middx. Recs.*, iv. 29–30).

STURGEON, John, fl. 1653–62

Of Cromwell's Lifeguard. In *Chillenden's* cong., later said to be head of own Baptist cong. Arrested '55 over anti-govt. pamphlet. In Reading '56 stirring up opposition. Joined Sexby working for restoration of king on terms. Found with copies of *Killing No Murder* and gaoled '57–9. Made Messenger of the Exchequer at Restoration, but resigned '62. Perhaps the J.S., grocer of Westminster, arrested at conventicle '63.

> *D.N.B.*; J. More, *Lost Ordinance* (1654), p. 1; Jeaffreson, *Middx. Recs.*, iv. 324; Clarke, iii. 51; *C.S.P. Dom.*, '60–1, p. 144; *ibid.*, '61–2, p. 513.

SUADON, John

London tailor, arrested '71 as 5th Mon./7th Day man (Jeaffreson, *Middx. Recs.*, iv. 29–30).

SWETMAN, John

Silkman of Cheapside (*Thurloe*, iii. 160); signed *Declaration* '54.

SWIFT, Richard, 1616–1701

Son of Norwich attorney; perhaps in army. An R.S. of Aldgate, 1638. V. of Offley, Herts. 1650; C. of Edgware, Middx. '56 till ejected '60. Lived afterwards as weaver in Middx., also kept school and conventicle. Gaoled several times in Newgate. Called 5th Mon. by Calamy, but for how long is not known.

> Matthews, *Cal. Rev.*, p. 472; SP. 28/124, f. 335*v.*; Dale, *London, 1638*, p. 72; Jeaffreson, *Middx. Recs.*, iii. 343.

SWINFEN, Samuel

London tailor; in *Rathbone* plot '65, but acquitted (Jeaffreson, *Middx. Recs.*, iii. 376; iv. 269–70).

TALBOT, John

Receiver-General in Devon by '55, held similar post in '59 (*C.S.P. Dom.*, '55,

Appendix I

pp. 342/5; *ibid.*, '56–7, pp. 99, 106/8, 155; *ibid.*, '59–60, pp. 221–2). 5th Mon., in London, keeping diary of persecution of saints '64 (SP. 29/99, f. 17).

TAYLOR, John
Shipwright of Wapping, associated with *Day* '60 (Jeaffreson, *Middx. Recs.*, iii. 309).

TAYLOR, Thomas, 1625–1700
Son of royalist gent. of Norfolk. Educ. Cambridge (B.A. '46). Influenced by Bridge of Yarmouth. Schoolmaster. Joined Bury Cong. church '53, pastor Jan. '56. At 5th Mon. meetings '56, agent '56/7. Tobacco-merchant and conventicler in London after Restoration. Lic. (Cong.) '72. Minister in Cambridge in '90s. Not known as 5th Mon. after Restoration, but still millenarian.

> Matthews, *Cal. Rev.*, p. 478; *Thurloe*, iv. 687; Browne, *Congregationalism*, pp. 396–404; 'Bury Churchbook' (transcript) and J. Duncan 'Hist. of Cong. Church in Bury' (typescript), both in Bury Rec. Office; his own *True Light* (1693), Epis. to the Reader.

TEMPEST, Christopher
London butcher, arrested '71 as 5th Mon./7th Day man (Jeaffreson, *Middx. Recs.*, iv. 29–30).

TERRALL, Jonathan
Middx. labourer; arrested '69 for attending cong. at *Adman's* house, died in prison (Jeaffreson, *Middx. Recs.*, iv. 14).

TERRALL, Joseph
Middx. labourer, arrested '69 for attending conventicle at *Adman's* house (*ibid.*).

TESDALE, Joshua
Abingdon yeoman, fined '64 (Preston, *Abingdon*, p. 121n.).

TESDALE, Richard
Woollendraper of Abingdon, fined '64, with wife Elizabeth (*ibid.*). Preacher in cong. '54 (Atherton, *Pastor Turn'd Pope*, p. 4).

THIMBLETON, Capt. Walter, fl. 1653–86
?Merchant. Of *Llwyd's* cong. '53. Signed *Word for God*. Officer under *Overton* '59. Plotting with *Courtney* round Epping '66. In Rye House Plot '82. Holding conventicles '86; pilloried '86 for libels about death of E. of Essex; said to be a poor man. A W.T., merchant of London, '77.

> Dodd, 'Remonstrance', p. 291; Overton, *Letter from Overton* (1659), brs; *C.S.P. Dom.*, '82, p. 405; *ibid.*, '85, p. 136; *ibid.*, '86–7, pp. 174, 183, 191; Jeaffreson, *Middx. Recs.*, iv. 302/4–6; *Little London Directory of 1677* (1863), sig. H2.

THOMAS, (Philip)
One Thomas, tailor of Old Exchange, London, '65 (SP. 29/121, f. 64). Perhaps same as P.T., signed *Declaration* '54.

THORNETON, Henry
Tobacco-pipe-maker of Abingdon, fined '62/4 with wife Mary (Preston, *Abingdon*, pp. 119n., 121n.).

Appendix I

TILLAM, Thomas, fl. 1651–d.c. 1676
On fringe of 5th Mon. movement. Apothecary. Probably Catholic in youth.
Connected with Knollys's church. Lecturer at Hexham, founded Bapt.
church there, but driven out in '55. Knew *Chamberlen, Buttevant, Simpson* by
'53. Adopted 7th Day sabbath by '55, led 7th Day cong. at Colchester.
Millenarian author by '51 (his *Two Witnesses*, 1651). In gaol '60. Friend of
Pooley with whom he set up millenarian settlement in Palatinate, which was
still flourishing in 1668.

> Payne, 'Tillam', *Bapt. Q.*, xvii. 61–6; *T. Bapt. H.S.*, vii. 234; R. Howell, *New-
> castle and the Puritan Revolution* (1967), pp. 249–54; T. Weld, *Mr. Tillam's
> Account* (1657); SP. 29/236, f. 28; Underhill, *Hexham*, pp. 291–346; Tillam,
> *Temple* (1660), epis. to the Reader.

TILLINGHAST, John, 1604–55
Son of Sussex minister. Educ. Cambridge (B.A. '25). Minister by '36,
became an Ind. by '50, assistant to Bridge at Yarmouth '51–2. R. of Trunch
(Norfolk) and head of gathered church there '52–5. Published 5th Mon.
tracts '53–5. Went to London '55, remonstrated with Cromwell, and died
there. Other works pub. posthumously till '63; eulogized in poem, '65.

> *D.N.B.*; Venn and Venn, *Al. Cantab.*, iv. 242; Browne, *Congregationalism*,
> pp. 222–3, 295; own *Eight Last Sermons* (1655), sig. A3–4; B.M. Add. MS.
> 15226, fos. 84–v.

TIRRET, John
5th Mon. preacher with *Perrott* '63 (Jeaffreson, *Middx. Recs.*, iii. 328–9).

TOMKINS, Edward
Broom-man of Abingdon, fined '64 (Preston, *Abingdon*, p. 121n.).

TOMKINS, John, 1632–1708
Brush-maker (and bottle-maker, maltster) of Abingdon, in cong. by '54, at
rally '56. Fined '62/4. Alderman under James II.

> *Bapt. Q.*, xvi. 165; Preston, *Abingdon*, p. 121n.; *Comp. Test.*, sig. A2; Atherton,
> *Pastor Turn'd Pope*, p. 1.

TRAPNEL, Anna, fl. 1642–60
Of Hackney, daughter of shipwright of Poplar. Converted by *Simpson* '42.
Had millenarian visions from '47. Visited celebrated convert Sarah Wight,
'47. Member of Simpson's church from '50. Published 5th Mon. visions
attacking Protectorate, 1654–8. Toured west '54, till arrested, but again in
'55. Attacked in print '60. Just possibly the A.T. who was married at
Woodbridge, Suffolk, '61.

> *C.S.P. Dom.*, '53–4, p. 393; *ibid.*, '54, pp. 86, 134, 436/8; Jessey, *Exceeding
> Riches* (1647), sig. a1; *Merc. Politicus*, 312 (29 May–5 June '56), p. 6998;
> *Publick Intell.*, 13 (24–31 Dec. '55), pp. 193–4; *Bibliotheca Fanatica* (1660), p. 4;
> *Suffolk Parish Registers*, ed. W. Philimore (1912), ii. 46; Burrage, *Eng. Hist. Rev.*,
> (1911), pp. 526–35; own *Cry of a Stone* (1654), pp. 3–4.

TRONKES, Thomas
Husbandman of Hendon; fined '65 with wife Anna as of *Swift's* cong.
(MR/RC–1, no. 46).

TUCKER, Henry
London tailor, executed '66 after *Rathbone* plot (Jeaffreson, *Middx. Recs.*,
iii. 376; iv. 269–70).

Appendix I

TURROLD (alias Terrel), Jonathan
Abingdon yeoman, fined '64 (Preston, *Abingdon*, p. 121n.).

TURROLD (alias Terrel), Richard
Abingdon linen-draper, fined '64 (*ibid.*). In cong. by '54, at rally '56
(Atherton, *Pastor Turn'd Pope*, sig. B1v., *Comp. Test.*, sig. A2).

VENNER, John
Ivory-turner of Whitechapel, in Tong Plot '62, gaoled in Tower (SP. 29/66,
f. 72v.). Perhaps the Mr. Venner with *Medley* in Amsterdam in '82 (*Memoires
of Shaftesbury*, p. 7), but cf. a Thomas V. was transported after Monmouth's
Rebellion (*C.S.P. Dom.*, *'85*, p. 429).

VENNER, Thomas, fl. 1638–d. 1661
Master cooper. Emigrated to Massachusetts by '38, freeman of Salem '39.
In Boston '44, back to England '51. Head of church in Swan Alley, Coleman
St., by '56–61. Dismissed '55 as cooper at Tower for plot to blow it up. In
5th Mon./Commonwealth negotiations '56/7. Attempted a rising '57,
gaoled '57–9. Led a rising '61, wounded 19 times, captured and executed.
Meeting house demolished. His widow's house raided by govt. over *Medley's*
activities, 1674.

> *D.N.B.*; Burrage, 'Insurrections', pp. 722–47; C. Banks, 'Venner', *New Eng.
> Hist. Gen. Reg.* xlvii. 437–44; *Thurloe*, iii. 520; vi. 163–4, 184–6/8, 194; vii.
> 622; Howell, *State Trials*, vi. 105–17; J. Macpherson, *Orig. Papers* (1775), i.
> 16; Haley, *William of Orange*, p. 200.

VERNON, Quarter-Master-Gen. John, fl. 1647–d. 1667
Baptist officer. In army by '47. Brother-in-law of *Allen*. Mostly in Ireland
till resigned commission '56. At Dorchester meeting '58. Signed *Essay* '59.
Gaoled '60–1, banished for life, but in fact lived near London as physician.
Preacher in *Glasse's* cong. '63–5, and described as a leading 5th Mon. man.

> *T. Bapt. H.S.*, iii. 254–6; iv. 129–36; vii. 236; Worcs. Coll. MS. 67, f. 23;
> J. Rogers, *Ohel*, p. 302; *Thurloe*, iv. 327–8, 315, 433; v. 122, 278, 670–2; vi.
> 222; vii. 139–40; *C.S.P. Dom.*, *'61–2*, p. 12; SP. 29/71, f. 147;/99, f. 16;/100,
> f. 19;/121, f. 64; *Bochim* (1667); own *Swords Abuse* (1648) and *Compleat Scholler*
> (1666), pp. 6, 8.

WAINFORD, William
Norwich woolcomber. Joined Cong. church '44, at Abingdon rally '56.
Became Baptist by '67.

> *Bapt. Q.*, x. 227; xviii. 367; *Comp. Test.*, sig. A2.

WARE, Richard
London plasterer, arrested '71 as 5th Mon./7th Day man (Jeaffreson,
Middx. Recs., iv. 29–30).

WESTCOTT, William
London yeoman, executed after *Rathbone* plot '66 (*ibid.*, iii. 376; iv. 269–70).

WHITBY, Nicholas
Gent., of Abingdon, fined '64 (Preston, *Abingdon*, p. 121n.).

WHITE, William
Cutler of Abingdon. In cong. by '54, at rally '56. Fined '64, gaoled '65.

> Atherton, *Pastor Turn'd Pope*, p. 3; *Comp. Test.*, sig. A2; Preston, *Abingdon*,
> p. 121n.; SP. 29/137, f. 240.

Appendix I

WHITEHURST, Richard, 1637–1697
Min. in Notts., '58; at Laughton, Yorks, '59 till ejected '60. Kept conventicle, protected by *Hatfield*. Lic. (Cong.), '72. Feud with his cong. over his 5th Mon. ideas '78–9. At Bridlington '95 and died there.

> Matthews, *Cal. Rev.*, p. 526; O. Heywood, *Autobiography* (1881–5), ii. 72, 99, 101, 112/19, 240–3; J. Lister, *Autobiography* (1842), pp. 50–1; J. Hunter, *Rise of Old Dissent* (1842), pp. 295–6.

WICH, Walter
Labourer of Hendon, of *Swift's* cong. Fined '65 with wife Hester (MR/RC–1, no. 46).

WIGAN, Lt.-Col. John, fl. 1642–d. 1665
Curate near Manchester from '42, Presbyt. then Ind. Became major in Cromwell's regt., but resigned Jan. '54 at establishment of Protectorate. Returned to Manchester area, established 5th Mon./Baptist churches there and Cheshire. 5th Mon. agent '56/7, signed *Essay*. Became Lt.-Col. under Overton '59. In 1663 plot, gaoled '63–4. Died in London of plague '65.

> Matthews, *Cal. Rev.*, p. 529; *Thurloe*, vi. 187; Firth and Davies, *Reg. Hist.*, pp. 333, 484–8; Whitley, *Baptists of N.W. England* (1913), chap. 3; SP. 29/85, f. 103; *C.S.P. Dom.*, '63–4, p. 519; T. Curwen, *This is an Answer* (1665), *passim*.

WILKES, Col. Timothy, fl. 1647–61
Originally a tailor in *Feake's* cong; no other 5th Mon. connections known. Major by '47, supported Protectorate and Monk; gaoled '61.

> Firth and Davies, *Reg. Hist.*, pp. 171, 389, 392/6–7; *Clarke*, iv. 300.

WILLIAMS, Capt. John, fl. 1646–d. 1681
Small squire. Fetched *Powell* from Dartford to Wales '46, and became elder in his church. Worked on Propagation; sequestrator, sheriff of Radnor, M.P. for Wales in Barebones, and on Council of State. Active as 5th Mon. in Protectorate. Signed *Word for God*. Said to be planning rising '58. Not known as 5th Mon. after Restoration. Arrested as conventicler '64. Perhaps lic. (Cong.), '72. Congregationalist till death.

> Richards, *Pur. Movement*, pp. 82, 90, 145, 195 and *Wales under Penal Code*, p. 19; A. H. Dodd, *Studies in Stuart Wales* (1952), pp. 134, 155; *Thurloe*, ii. 46, 93, 128–9; vi. 187; Jones, 'Vav. Powell', p. 47; SP. 29/97, f. 153; Turner, *Orig. Recs.*, ii. 1201.

WILLOUGHBY, Christopher
Officer in London militia, Feb. 1660, and described as 5th Mon. man (Hist. MSS. Comm., li, *Leyborne-Popham* MSS., p. 168).

WINCH, Mary
5th Mon. meetings at her house in London '62–5 (SP. 29/67, f. 7; Jeaffreson, *Middx. Recs.*, iii. 343/5).

WINTER, Thomas
Victualler of Cripplegate; 5th Mon. meetings at house '61. Formerly a trooper (B.M. Egerton MS. 2543, f. 24).

WISE, James
Clothworker; gaoled Southampton for preaching '62 (*Merc. Publicus*, 49 (4–11 Dec. '62), p. 797). Head of 5th Mon. cong. there '69; lic. (Bapt.),

Appendix I

'72 at Cowes, I. of Wight, and Salisbury (Turner, *Orig. Recs.*, i. 143; ii. 1051, 1075).

WISE, John
Clockmaker of Abingdon, fined '64 (Preston, *Abingdon*, p. 121n.).

WOODALL, Frederick, 1614–81
Educ. Cambridge (M.A., '41). Minister from '41. Close associate of Bridge. Pastor of gathered church at Woodbridge '52–81, and lecturer there till Restoration. At E. Anglian 5th Mon. rallies '56. Kept school after '60. Gaoled '66 and presented '78 for conventicling. Lic. (Cong.) '72. Not known as 5th Mon. after Restoration.

> Matthews, *Cal. Rev.*, pp. 542–3; Browne, *Congregationalism*, pp. 231, 285, 343, 453, 467; *Thurloe*, iv. 687, 727; Ipswich R.O., Suffolk Q.S. Minute Book, '62–7, f. 130*v*.; Norwich R.O., Visit. Book of Bp. Sparrow, '77/8, 31 May 1678; Dr. Williams's Lib., Woodbridge Churchbook (transcript), fos. 1–4; Turner, *Orig. Recs.*, i. 105.

WOODWARD, Robert
London labourer, arrested '71 as 5th Mon./7th Day man (Jeaffreson, *Middx. Recs.*, iv. 29–30). Signed *Declaration* '54.

WROUGHTON, Edward
London haberdasher, ex-soldier. Involved with *Sturgeon* and *Kirton* in spreading seditious tracts '56 (*Thurloe*, v. 272–3; vi. 315–17; Jeaffreson, *Middx. Recs.*, iii. 253).

YEWEL, —
Schoolmaster of Epsom, Surrey, late '70s/early '80s (E. Calamy, *Account of My Own Life* (1829), i. 76).

Anonymous 5th Monarchists
(all of London) of known occupations:

Four apprentices, 1671 (SP. 29/291, f. 179).
Cap-maker, follower of *Powell*, preached 1653 (MS. Clar. 45, f. 269).
Glazier, preached at Somerset House '53 (MS. Clar. 45, f. 223).
Goldsmith, 1664 (SP. 29/103, f. 262).
Hotpresser, 1664 (SP. 29/110, f. 216).
Oilman, 1664 (SP. 29/110, f. 216).
Ropemaker, 1664 (SP. 29/110, f. 216).
Master silver-refiner, 1661 (Gough, *Antiquities . . . of Myddle*, pp. 124–5).
Woollendraper, 1661 (*London's Glory*, p. 15).

Two cases of mistaken identity

BOATMAN, James, fl. 1641–*d.* 1658
Described by Gardiner and Braithwaite as leading 5th Monarchist in E. Anglia. Educ. Cambridge, but no degree. Presbyt. minister at Hull, but removed 1650 as supporter of Charles II and for not recognizing Rump. Went to Norwich, became Min. of St. Peter Mancroft. Noted as 'a great enemy to Sectaries' and that he 'declared himselfe for Episcopacy something plainely'. Removal as malignant sought by local Maj.-General.

Appendix I

Gardiner, *Comm. and Protect.*, iv. 267; W. C. Braithwaite, *Beginnings of Quakerism* (1955), p. 164; *Thurloe*, iv. 217, 257, 302; v. 289, 297, 311/13; Venn and Venn, *Al. Cantab.*, i. 172; *C.S.P. Dom.*, '50, pp. 385, 452; *Merc. Politicus*, 20 (17–24 Oct. '50), pp. 327, 334–5; J. Collinges, *Responsoria Bipartita* (1654), sig. b3*v.*–4, c1; W. Rye, 'St. Peter Mancroft', *Norfolk Antiq. Misc.*, ii. (1893), pp. 335, 342; Bodl. MS. Tanner 286, f. 150.

SANDERS, John, fl. 1643–55

Described as 5th Mon. by Hill, following Court. Ironmonger of Harborn, near Birmingham. Urged workers to strike against rich ironmongers. Looked forward to a 'Fifth Monarchy', but one involving return of king and bishops and suppression of sects. Had no connection with the 5th Mon. movement.

C. Hill, *Puritanism and Revolution* (1962), p. 327; W. H. B. Court, *The Rise of the Midland Industries* (1938), pp. 62–3; own *Iron Rod for the Naylors* (1655) and *Iron Rod put into the Lord Protectors Hand* (1655).

Locations of Fifth Monarchist Congregations, Ministers and Agents

⊶⊷⊶⊷⊶⊷⊶⊷⊶⊷⊶⊷⊶⊷⊶⊷⊶⊷⊶⊷⊶⊷⊶⊷⊶⊷⊶⊷⊶⊷⊶⊷⊶⊷⊶⊷⊶⊷

Sources are to be found, except when given here, in the Biographical Appendix, in the section on the saint whose name is italicized here. The congregations frequently changed their meeting-places, especially in London after 1660, and the attempt to distinguish them here is only tentative. The words 'Whitley 8', etc., refer to the numeration of the London Baptist churches listed in W. T. Whitley, *The Baptists of London* (1928).

LONDON AREA

Allhallows the Great, Thames St., from 1652. Under *Simpson*, lecturer there, and flourished till his death in '62; also met at London House. Radical wing broke away '56–8 under the *Portman* brothers and established a separate church.

S. also had livings at St. Botolph's Aldgate and St. Botolph's Bishops-gate but although there were individual 5th Monarchists in these congregations, there do not seem to have been separate 5th Monarchist groups there.

Blackfriars, under *Feake,* from '52. *Feake* was lecturer at St Anne's, Black-friars. Church later met in Swan Alley, Coleman St., and in Warwick Lane (Feake, *New Non-conformist* (1654), *passim*). After 1660 taken over by *Helme,* d. 1669. Helme's widow's house lic. (Cong.), 1672 (*C.S.P. Dom.,* '72, pp. 63, 197).

F. also had living at Christ Church, Newgate; not apparent whether separate 5th Mon. group.

St. Thomas Apostle's, under *Rogers,* lecturer there from '53–9. Headed later by one Needham, prob. Congregationalist (*T. Cong. Hist. Soc.,* v. (1912), p. 345).

Lothbury Square. Chamberlen headed church '52–4. Later at Bullstake Alley under *J. James,* d. 1661, then at Mill Yard as 7th Day Baptist (Whitley 13).

Stone Chapel. Led by *Chillenden* at Aldgate in '53, and perhaps by '50 (Z. Grey, *Impartial Exam.* (1739), iii. appendix, pp. 149–52). At Stone Chapel, St. Paul's in '53. Perhaps led by *Sturgeon* in mid-'50s. Largely army membership. Led by *Glasse, Vernon, Strange* in '60s, by *Danvers* and *Perrott* in '70s/'80s (Whitley 15).

5th Mon. group in Raworth's Baptist cong., signed *Declaration* 1654.

5th Mon. group in Fenton's Baptist cong., signed *Declaration* '54.

5th Mon. group in Knollys's Baptist cong. (Whitley 8), signed *Declaration* '54. 5th Mon. group at Artichoke Lane 1670 probably also part of Knollys's cong. which sometimes met there.

5th Mon. group in Highland's Baptist cong., signed *Declaration* '54.

5th Mon. group in Barbone's Baptist cong., signed *Declaration* '54.

5th Mon. group in Jessey's Baptist cong. (Whitley 9a), signed *Declaration* '54.

All Hallows, Lombard St. *Cardell* minister there until 1655.

Soper Lane. Cockayne minister of St. Pancras, '46–60, and kept conventicle later. He was 5th Mon. '52–3, and around '64.

Swan Alley, Coleman St. *Venner's* church there by '55, destroyed '61. Several of *V*'s church earlier with *Rogers.*

Edgware, Middx. *Swift* curate of Edgware 1656–60.

Worcester House. *John Clarke* head of Bapt. (/5th Mon.) church by '57.

Bell Lane. Under *Belcher*, at Limehouse and Duke's Place, Westminster, '61. At Bell Lane from '66, gradually evolved into pure 7th Day Baptist church (Whitley 18).

New St., Cripplegate. Under *Thomas Winter*, 1661.

Trinity Lane, Stepney. Under *Rogers*, 1661 (SP. 29/47, f. 107).

Broken Wharf. Feake there '61 (SP. 29/47, f. 107). *Mayhew* head of 5th Mon. church there 1678 (*C.S.P. Dom.*, '78, p. 246).

Maiden Head Tavern, Piccadilly. Anon. 5th Mon. meeting there '61 (SP. 29/30, f. 101).

Beech Lane, Cripplegate. 5th Mon. in 1661 (B.M., MS. Egerton 2543, f. 24). Also at Elbow Lane, Cannon St. and elsewhere. Under *Vernon, Glasse, Strange* by '63. Still called 5th Mon. in 1676 (Hist. MSS. Comm., xxii, *Bolton MSS.*, p. 16). (Whitley 7).

White Horse Yard, near Somerset House. Anthony Palmer there '64 (SP. 29/105, f. 75). No doubt part of *P.*'s church, later at Pinners' Hall (Whitley 23).

Shoreditch. Malban head of congregation, '61.

St. Giles, Cripplegate. Congregation at house of *Winch* '62–5.

Hendon, Middx. Swift head of church '65, perhaps since Restoration.

Hillingdon, Middx. Cong. at *Adman's* house '69.

Horsley Down, Southwark. Church led by *Barrett* '69.

St. Mary Overy's Dock, Southwark. 5th Mon./Ind. church '69 at *Bloxsom's* house. (Stephen More's church, Whitley 4a.)

Tuttle St., Westminster. Cong. at house of Widow Brome, 1676 (Hist. MSS. Comm., xxii, *Bridgewater MSS.*, p. 15).

Richard Adams had cong. of 300 in 1682 (SP. 29/419, f. 102).

London Bridge. Feake at conventicle 1682. (SP. 29/421, f. 324).

REST OF COUNTRY

BEDFORDSHIRE

Bedford. John Child agent '56/7 (*Thurloe*, vi. 187).

BERKSHIRE

Abingdon. Church led by *Pendarves*, d. 1656. Survivors accepted Bapt. licence '72, so presumably moderated (Preston, *Abingdon*, p. 130).

Appendix II

Reading. Sturgeon active '56, and Baptist church founded that year (Berkshire R.O.: Book of Records of Reading Baptist Church). 5th Mon. men reported there in 1664 (MS. Clarendon 81, f. 199).

BUCKINGHAMSHIRE
Chalfont St. Giles. Henry Cock active in 5th Mon. group '69.

CHESHIRE
Chester. 5th Mon. men reported '69 (SP. 29/264, f. 206). Cf. *Fitten* of Chester, fl. 1663–6.
Great Budworth. 5th Mon./Bapt. meeting '69 (Turner, *Orig. Recs.*, i. 169).
Nantwich. 5th Mon. agent '56/7 (*Thurloe*, vi. 187). These three churches probably all founded by *Wigan.*

CORNWALL
Tregas. Langden agent there '56/7 (*Thurloe*, vi. 187).

DERBYSHIRE
Aston-on-Trent. T. Palmer minister '46–60. (See also Notts.)

DEVON
Dartmouth. One Slid agent, '56/7 (*Thurloe*, vi. 187).
Exeter. Byfield head of 5th Mon. cong. in cathedral in late '50s. *Carew* sponsored Bapt./5th Mon. church in '50s (Brockett, *Nonconformity in Exeter* (1962), p. 15). One Leap 5th Mon. agent in '56/7 (*Thurloe*, vi. 187).
Tiverton. Rumour of impending Bapt./5th Mon. massacre there '59 (*Merc. Politicus*, 580, (21–8 July '59), pp. 617–18). A Baptist church was there, perhaps it had some 5th Mon. members (Nuttall, *J. Eccles. Hist.*, xi. 213–18).

ESSEX
Epping. Attempted 5th Mon. rising there 1657 (Russell, *Life of William Lord Russell* (1819), pp. 13–14).
Courtney and *Thimbleton* active in Essex/Herts. '66, at Ware, Enfield, Epping, Theobalds (SP. 29/144, f. 138). *Danvers* in 1685 drew 500 supporters from Essex/Herts. to London for projected rising (Grey, *Secret History of Rye-House-Plot* (1754), p. 113.

HAMPSHIRE
Newport, Isle of Wight. Mr. Smith, 5th Mon. agent '56/7 (*Thurloe*, vi. 187).
Portsmouth. J. Goff, 5th Mon. agent '56/7 (*Thurloe*, vi. 187).
Southampton. J. Wise head of 5th Mon. cong. '69. He was licensed in '72 at West Cowes and Salisbury (Turner, *Orig. Recs.*, i. 142, ii. 1051, 1075).

HERTFORDSHIRE (see under Essex)

KENT
Canterbury. Fritton head of 5th Mon. group '65.
Sandwich. Capt. Boys and Mr. Taylor agents '56/7 (*Thurloe*, vi. 187). 'Hundreds' of 5th Monarchists in Kent were mentioned by the *Declaration* (1654), sig. D2v.
A millenarian address from some Kent J.P.s was presented to Barebones in 1653 (*Merc. Pol.*, 165 (4–11 Aug. 1653), p. 2636).

Appendix II

LANCASHIRE
Manchester. Under *Wigan*, d. 1665.

LINCOLNSHIRE
Lincoln. Abigaill Marshall agent '56/7. Abigaill Diodaty, also formerly of *Chamberlen's* cong., there in 1654 (MS. Rawl. D 828, f. 17).

NORFOLK
North Walsham. Breviter head of cong. there 1651–64. Centre of 5th Mon. activity 1655–6 with *Pooley* and *Rudduck*. Independent, Quaker and 7th Day Baptist groups there '69 (Turner, *Orig. Recs.*, ii. 100).
Norwich. Pooley head of church there in 1660. *Wainford* a 5th Mon. there '56.
Trunch. Tillinghast Rector 1652–5 and head of Congregationalist church.
Wymondham. Church headed by *Pooley* in 1653.

NORTHAMPTONSHIRE
One *N. Cox* of Northants., 5th Mon. in 1670.

NOTTINGHAMSHIRE
Nottingham. T. Palmer head of church by 1659, and probably since its foundation in '55 (Nuttall, *Visible Saints*, p. 33). *Banfeather* of Nottingham an associate of *Pooley* in 1667.
Skegby. 5th Mon./Bapt. group 1669 at Mrs. Lindley's house (Turner, *Orig. Recs.*, i. 155). Probably established by *T. Palmer*.

OXFORDSHIRE
Oxford. Quelch agent in '56/7. A 'brother' from Oxford at *Venner's* church '57 (B.M. Add. MS. 4459, f. 111*v*.).

SOMERSET
Bristol. George Packer agent '56/7 (*Thurloe*, vi. 187).
Wells. A number of Fifth Monarchists said to be there, 1656 (D. Underdown, 'A Case Concerning Bishops' Lands', *Eng. Hist. Rev.*, lxxvii (1963), p. 31, but his source, T. Collier, *A Looking Glasse for the Quakers* (1657), p. 16, in fact only mentions Ranters and Quakers).

SUFFOLK
Bury. T. Taylor head of church at Shire House 1653-Restoration.
Ipswich. Stoneham head of church 1651-Restoration; church produced 5th Mon. tract 1659.
Syleham. Habergham head of gathered church 1652–62.
Woodbridge. Woodall head of gathered church 1652–81, but only known as 5th Mon. before Restoration.

SURREY
Dorking. Feake taught there '69 at 'Independent' congregation of 100 (Turner, *Orig. Recs.*, i. 47).
39 Surrey 5th Monarchists, including *Perrott*, in prison in Surrey 1662 (SP. 29/91, f. 165).

SUSSEX
Lewes. Postlethwaite head of church 1646–72. 5th Mon. in 1650s, *Crowch* agent in '56/7; but Congregationalist in '60s.

Appendix II

Horsham (?). Report of assembly of 5,000 5th Monarchists there, 1659 (MS. Clar. 61, f. 103).

WARWICKSHIRE
Warwick. Mr. King, agent '56/7 (*Thurloe*, vi. 187). Perhaps Daniel King, Baptist pastor of Coventry and Warwick to '56 (*T. Bapt. H.S.*, vii. 213, *Bapt. Q., xvi.* 59).

WESTMORLAND
Barton. T. Roberts minister 1655–62.

WILTSHIRE
Devizes. T. Okey head of 5th Mon. group of 40 in 1669.
Mildenhall. T. Baylie minister '47–60, and later held conventicles there.

WORCESTERSHIRE
White Lady Aston. R. Browne minister '46–60.

YORKSHIRE
Hull. Canne chaplain there from '50, and head of congregation until expelled 1656. One Lepington agent '56/7 (*Thurloe*, vi. 187). *Astley* took over church in 1669.
Laughten en le Morthen/Hatfield. Whitehurst minister at Laughton '59 and remained after ejection. Licensed at Hatfield in 1672.
Sheffield. Fisher head of church by '46 till death in 1667.

WALES
The 5th Monarchist centres were *Llwyd's* church at Wrexham and *Powell's* at New Radnor. Powell gathered about twenty churches, many of which were probably imbued with 5th Monarchist ideas (Crosby, *History of the English Baptists* (1738–40), i. 377).

The Schism within John Simpson's Congregation, 1656–8

Only rarely does detailed evidence exist of the internal history of a Fifth Monarchist, or indeed any seventeenth century sectarian congregation. The Churchbook of Chamberlen's congregation is unusual in revealing the inevitable frictions within a body, every member of which could claim divine 'leadings': most Churchbooks suppressed or minimized dissensions.[1] But the internal history of another Fifth Monarchist, or rather Fifth Monarchist/Baptist, congregation, that of John Simpson at Allhallows the Great, Thames Street, can be pieced together from a pamphlet account published by one faction in 1658, *The Old Leaven Purged Out*.[2]

Many Fifth Monarchist groups were not first formed as such, but consisted of members of existing Independent or Baptist churches who had been further enlightened. Simpson's congregation was of this type, with Baptists as well as Fifth Monarchists, and reflected also the earlier connection between sectarianism and the New Model Army, containing a number of officers. Up to 1653 the Fifth Monarchists accepted that the army was doing God's work—the *Old Leaven* cited the Declaration of Musselburgh and Cromwell's speech to Barebones as proof.[3] But the establishment of the Protectorate necessitated a choice between obedience to the new regime and the repudiation of it which the Fifth Monarchists demanded. The majority of the congregation, including the officers, accepted the Protectorate. Simpson himself, with a minority of the church, followed the Fifth Monarchists, and Simpson was imprisoned in 1654 and briefly again in January 1656 for his opposition to the government. The *Old Leaven* later printed his letters from prison in 1654 predicting Cromwell's downfall, attacking the defection of 'rotten-hearted Hypocrites' and calling for fidelity to Christ's cause which would triumph 'let Souldiers, and Devils, and carnal Policy do what they can to hinder it'. But the suspicions of the Fifth Monarchist group were aroused when Simpson prayed *for* the government after his release in mid-1654. They were confirmed in February 1656 when Simpson, shortly after his second release, preached 'against the oppinion of the fifth monarchy' and declared there would be no millennium until Christ appeared in person, for

---

[1] Bodl. MS. Rawl. D 828.
[2] Signed by Humphrey Hathorn, Caleb Ingold, John Seely and John Portmans.
[3] *Old Leaven*, p. 2.

which he 'was sufficiently bayted by his own partye, and so they broke up their meetinge in confusion'.[1]

This defection provoked the Fifth Monarchist group to militant action. On 1 June 1656 the group, numbering seventy-two, presented a paper containing their grievances to the congregation at London House (where the church met on Sundays). They alleged that the army and government had apostatized from Christ's cause, and that God had accordingly deserted it. (This was proved in the later, printed version by references to the Hispaniola expedition launched by Cromwell, and to God's 'frustrating the consultations of both his Parliaments'.)[2] They next made specific charges against 'our dear brethren who wear the Sword', who were guilty of treason (in breaking the Act of 1649 against government by a single person), of breaking their own declarations (notably Musselburgh), and of oppression, in gaoling those whose conscience forbade them to pay tithes or taxes. This apostasy had led to the continuance of 'heathen and Antichristian laws' instead of those in the Bible.[3] Worst of all, perhaps, were the individual acts of oppression and cynicism of which the brethren had been guilty. Col. Kelsey (i.e. Thomas Kelsey, one of the Major-Generals), Major Strange, Captain Harrison, and Col. Baxter, one of the new Lords (i.e. Barkstead) had all justified the imprisonment of Fifth Monarchists. Kelsey had said before the congregation that 'if any should rise up against the present Power, under what pretence soever, he would sheath his sword in their bowels, though his own Brethren'. Kelsey had quartered troops in Col. Rich's house in Kent, for refusing to pay taxes, and had distrained Rich's corn. Capt. Harrison had acted as gaoler to Simpson, his own pastor. Major Strange had been custodian of Maj.-Gen. Harrison in prison, and had refused to accept any of Simpson's followers in his troop, rejecting Humphrey Hathorn, one of the Fifth Monarchists, who tried to enlist. The most poignant illustration of the apostasy from the millenarian ideals of the 1640s was the case of 'our brother *Sumner* [who] being asked what he fought for now, he replyed, *For half Crowns*'. The Fifth Monarchists concluded by demanding the punishment of the soldiers.[4]

The paper was read at the London House meeting, but debate was postponed until a further meeting. This in fact did not take place: Simpson and the majority instead wrote to the pastors and members of other London churches, including Cockayne, Knollys and Jessey, for advice on how to deal with the dissidents. The dissidents themselves, however, came to hear of this, and neutralized the move by persuading Cockayne and the others not to intervene until the issue had been debated by the whole church.[5] An inconclusive debate was held later, and a further unprofitable dispute took place at the house of a member in Coleman Street. Convinced that their opponents

[1] *Old Leaven*, 2nd pagination, pp. 1–27, esp. pp. 9, 11, 19; *Thurloe State Papers*, iv. 545; *Cal. S.P. Dom.,1655–6*, p. 109; see above, pp. 101, 103, 110, 113, 117.
[2] *Old Leaven*, pp. 1–4, 21.
[3] *Ibid.*, pp. 4–11.
[4] *Ibid.*, pp. 10, 12–17.
[5] *Ibid.*, pp. 21–3; the full list of invited arbitrators, as printed, is: Cockayn; Jackson; Roberts; Jessey; Hubbard; Isles (?i.e. Ives); Knowles (i.e. Knollys); Highland; Bradshaw; Jackson, Chir.; Woolaston; Barebone; Taylor.

were hardened in their sins, the Fifth Monarchist group resolved to go *en masse* and lay their faults before them. They invited a number of outside Fifth Monarchists and others, including Canne, Danvers and Squibb, to accompany them as witnesses. But on arrival at London House they found that Simpson refused them entry until Canne and the others were turned away. The militants refused to comply, and instead sent their accusations by letter (repeating largely the contents of the earlier paper).[1]

Confronted with this missive, Simpson wrote again to sectarian church leaders in the city, and this time representatives, led by Philip Nye, did go to London House to discuss the problem, in January 1657. Six of the Fifth Monarchist group also attended, and were able to outmanœuvre their opponents. Having received an assurance from Simpson that they were still regarded as part of the church, they pointed out that Nye and the other outsiders had therefore not been invited by the whole congregation, and so had no moral right to intervene. Nye accepted this reasoning, and the outsiders withdrew.[2] Subsequent negotiations proved futile. The Fifth Monarchists refused to agree to the invitation of outsiders until the majority group recognized the guilt of the army brethren—which it naturally declined to do, though the reasons it gave, that some held the army men guilty, some innocent, and others did not know, revealed the divisions within the majority group itself. In the spring of 1657 the Fifth Monarchists drew up a draft of separation from the main church. This was approved by Canne, Danvers and the others to whom they had appealed, and the formal secession took place on 1 September 1657.[3]

The *Old Leaven's* account of the schism is, though one-sided, of considerable value in illustrating the internal life and problems of a gathered church. It is important too in underlining the fluidity of the sectarian church structure of the period: Simpson could appeal to the prominent Independents Nye and Cockayne to intervene in a Baptist and Fifth Monarchist dispute. Nye and Cockayne were not only prepared to do so, but also to listen sympathetically to the arguments of the militants. That Kelsey, Simpson and Portman could be contained in one congregation as late as 1656 is itself surprising: the schism was indeed one step towards a clearer demarcation of the sects.

---

[1] *Old Leaven*, pp. 24–35; those invited were Cann; Clark; Danvers; Bland; Barbone; Waters; Squibb; Luxford; Barret; (Clement) Ireton. Only Barebone appears on both lists.
[2] *Ibid.* pp. 36–8.
[3] *Ibid.*, pp. 39–63.

Bibliography

❋❋

1. MANUSCRIPT SOURCES

OXFORD

Bodleian Library
Ashmole MSS:
       210, f. 134v.: horoscope of Wm. Allen.
       241, f. 200: 'Of the number 666'.
       427, f. 59v.: horoscope of Owen Cox.
Carte MSS:
       81, fos. 16–17v.: circular letter of J. Owen *et al.*, 9 Jan. 1654.
       fos. 214–15: memorandum (by ?Philip Nye), c. 1664.
Clarendon MSS:
       45–83: royalist newsletters and correspondence, 1653–65.
       74, fos. 418–22: P. Chamberlen, 'A Case of Conscience . . . Concerning The Words of the Oath of Supremacy' (1661), apparently copied from printed tract no longer extant.
Rawlinson MSS:
       A 8, f. 127: S. Otes to R. Jeffes, 15 Nov. 1653.
       A 10, f. 11: J. Vernon to J. Standish, 5 April 1654.
       f. 339: T. — to Monk, 31 Jan. 1655.
       A 13, f. 26: W. Allen to T. Hart, 5 April 1654.
       A 26, fos. 239–51: Account by Col. Whichcote of Feake and Rogers at Windsor, 18 May 1655.
       fos. 252–4: account of same by R. Blande and other Fifth Monarchists.
       A 29, fos. 628–9: J. Rogers to T. Brookes, 29 Aug. 1655.
       A 47, fos. 26–7v.: A. de Samand to — (?1655).
       f. 30: J. Browne to J. Wright (no date, early 1654).
       fos. 32–5: J. Rogers to Cromwell (no date, Dec. 1653 or early 1654).
       A 57, f. 312: H. Smith to Cromwell, 1 Feb. 1658.
       A 61, f. 29: information concerning Powell and Williams (no date, ?Spring 1658).
       D 828, records of the Baptist Church at Lothbury Square, London, 1652–4.
       D 859, f. 162: note on death of Pendarves.

Bibliography

D 1347, fos. 1–31: 'A Friendly Consideration of some mistakes about the Fifth monarchy', containing (fos. 25–31) a letter from S. Mather to J. Marsden, 12 Nov. 1669.

Tanner MSS:

35, 36, 36*, 42, 160: letters from Chamberlen to Archbishop Sheldon.

51, f. 74: J. Ireton to Fleetwood, 6 June 1659.

286, f. 150: 2 letters between J. Collinges and J. Boatman, 20/1 Dec. 1653.

Worcester College

MSS: 16–114: army lists and letters, 1647–62.

LONDON

British Museum

Egerton MS.

2543, f. 24: information of 5th Mon. meetings, 1661.

Sloane MS.

63, fos. 36–57*v*.: Mark Leonard, 'Christs Monarchicall, and personall Reigne uppon Earth', no date.

Stowe MS.

185, fos. 168–70: 'Copy of a Notable Letter . . . to one Linwell (*sic*.) Chapman' (faked evidence of 5th Mon. plot, 1660).

Add. MSS:

4459, fos. 111–12*v*.: minutes of Venner's congregation, 1657 (the remainder was published by Burrage in *Eng. Hist. Rev.*, xxv, 1910).

15226, fos. 80–4*v*.: E.N., 'London's Plague-Sore Discovered' (1665), apparently copied from printed tract. Contains verses on Tillinghast, f. 84–*v*.

34272, fos. 142–8*v*.: letters and hymns concerning John Mason, 1694.

37808, fos. 62–3: land transactions of Feake's family, 1651–82.

38856, fos. 79–80: 'A doore of hope opened into the valley of Achan' (no date, ?1663; manifesto of 1663 rising).

39942, fos. 12–16: sermon by Feake, 10 July 1653.

Thomason

Collection

E. 710, (13): 'Mr Feakes Hymne: August ye 11: 1653'.

Public Record Office

P.R.O. 31/3/90–106: Baschet Transcripts of French Embassy correspondence, 1653–60.

SP. 18/ passim: State Papers, Domestic, Interregnum.

SP. 19/A 46: assessment of London inhabitants, Interregnum.

SP. 28/121b, 123–5, 142: regimental lists, 1645–50.

SP. 29/ passim: State Papers, Domestic, Charles II.

Bibliography

Dr. Williams's Library
> Harmer MS. 76.5: 'Copy of the Records of the Congregational Church
> ... at ... Woodbridge, 1651–1851'.
> MS. 533.B.1.: 'Mill Yard Minutes, being the Church Book of the
> Seventh Day General Baptist Congregation, ... 1673–1840'
> (xerox copy, 1953).

Greater London Record Office, Middlesex Branch
> MR/RC–1, nos. 35, 46: convictions of conventiclers, 1665; congrega-
> tions at the houses of Mary Winch and Richard Swift.

Guildhall Library
> MS. 9583, boxes 1, 1a, 2: churchwardens' presentments at Episcopal
> visitations, London and Middlesex, 1664–85.

NATIONAL LIBRARY OF WALES
MS. HM2. 14/7a, b: 'Of ye late K. Charles of Blessed Memory, by Vavasar
> Powell' (undated copy of verses by Powell, probably composed in or
> soon after 1649).

BERKSHIRE RECORD OFFICE, READING
Book of Records of the Reading Baptist Church ... 1656–1770.

NORFOLK RECORD OFFICE, NORWICH
VIS/7, box 411: Visitation Book of Anthony Sparrow, bishop of Norwich,
> 1677–8.
Court Books 23: Court of Mayoralty Court Book, 1654–66.
Church Book of the Old Meeting, Norwich (transcript).
Church Book of Gt. Yarmouth Congregationalist Church, Middlegate St.,
> 1642–64 (xerox).
Church Book of St. Mary's, Norwich, Baptist Church, from 1691.
MS. 4259–61: M. F. Hewett, 'Collection of Material in Preparation for an
> Historical Record of the Baptists of Norfolk and their Churches'.

SUFFOLK: BURY AND WEST SUFFOLK RECORD OFFICE
Acc. 1231: Bury St. Edmunds Church Book, 1646–1801 (transcript).
Acc. 1339: J. Duncan, 'The History of the Congregationalist Church in
> Bury St. Edmunds' (typescript, 1962).

IPSWICH AND EAST SUFFOLK RECORD OFFICE
Suffolk Quarter-Sessions Minute Book, 1662–7.
Suffolk Quarter-Sessions Order Book, 1665–76.

WORCESTER RECORD OFFICE
Quarter-Sessions Records, 1667: depositions relating to incident at Oldbury,
> 1667.

THESES
Clouse, R. G., 'The Influence of John Henry Alsted on English Millenarian
> Thought in the Seventeenth Century', U. of Iowa Ph.D. thesis, 1963
> (microfilm in Dr. Williams's Library).

Bibliography

Farnell, J. E., 'The Politics of the City of London (1649–1657)', Chicago
    Ph.D thesis 1963, Bodleian microfilm Diss. Film. 175.
Jones, R. T., 'The Life, Work, and Thought of Vavasor Powell (1617–
    1670)', Oxford D.Phil thesis 1947, MS. D.Phil. d. 538.
Woolrych, A. H., 'Politics and Political Theory in England, 1658–1660',
    Oxford B.Litt. thesis 1952, MS. B.Litt. d. 138.

2. SELECT PRINTED SOURCES

A. PRIMARY WORKS

The exact dates are given, when known, of Fifth Monarchist works, and of
other works when relevant. Unless otherwise stated, these are the dates
noted by George Thomason on his copies, now in the British Museum. The
locations are given of works not in the Bodleian, British Museum or Cambridge University Library. The place of publication, when known, is London
except when stated otherwise.

A(spinwall?), W., *Certaine Queries touching the Ordination of Ministers* (1647).
Abbott, W. C., *The Writings and Speeches of Oliver Cromwell* (Cambridge,
    Mass., 1937–47).
An Advertisement as touching the Fanaticks Late Conspiracy (28 Jan. 1661).
An Alarum to Corporations (1659).
An Alarum to the City and Souldiery (6 June 1659).
Allen, William, *The Captive Taken from the Strong* (1658).
—— *A Word to the Army, Touching their Sin and Dutie* (1660).
All the Proceedings at the Sessions of the Peace holden at Westminster (1651).
Alsted, J. H., *The Beloved City; or, the Saints Reign on Earth a Thousand Yeares
    asserted*, trans. W. Burton (1643).
Amyraut, Moise, *Du Règne de Mille Ans* (Saumur, 1654).
*Animadversions upon a Letter and Paper, first sent to His Highness by certain Gentle-
    men . . . in Wales* (1656), opposing *A Word for God*.
An Answer to a Paper entituled A True Narrative (1653).
Antipharmacum Saluberrimum; or, A Serious . . . Caveat to all the Saints (1664).
Archer, John, *The Personall Reigne of Christ upon Earth* (1642). 1st edn. 1641,
    and many subsequently. One gives Archer's first name as Henry.
Aspinwall, William, *The Abrogation of the Jewish Sabbath* (1657).
—— *A Brief Description of the Fifth Monarchy, or Kingdome* (1 Aug. 1653).
—— *An Explication and Application of the Seventh Chapter of Daniel, wherein is
    briefly shewed . . . the Beheading of Charles Stuart, who is proved to be the
    Little Horn* (20 March 1654).
—— *The Legislative Power is Christ's Peculiar Prerogative* (20 Aug. 1656).
—— *A Premonition of Sundry Sad Calamities Yet to Come* (30 Nov. 1654). Re-
    issued in 1655 as *Thunder from Heaven*.
—— *The Work of the Age* (14 April 1655).
Atherton, John, *The Pastor Turn'd Pope. Or, a Declaration of the Proceedings of
    John Pendarves* (1654). Listed as anonymous in S.T.C.; in Cambridge
    Univ. Lib.
B., T. (?R. le Wright), *Nuncius Propheticus* (1642).

Bibliography

Bache, Humphrey, *A Few Words in True Love written to the Old Long Sitting Parliament* (1659).

Bagshaw, Edward, *The Doctrine of the Kingdom and Personal Reign of Christ* (1669).

(——) *The Life and Death of Mr. Vavasor Powell* (1671).

—— *Saintship No ground of Soveraignty* (Oxford, 1660).

Baillie, Robert, *Letters and Journals* (Edinburgh, 1775).

Banaster, Thomas, *An Alarum to the World, of the Appearing of Sions King* (1649).

The Banner of Truth Displayed . . . Being the Substance of severall Consultations, . . . kept by a Certain Number of Christians, who are waiting for the visible appearance of Christ's Kingdome (24 Sept. 1656).

Barbone, P. G., *Good Things to Come* (1675). Congregationalist Lib., London.

Barksdale, Clement, *The Disputation at Winchcombe Nov. 9. MDCLIII* (1653).

Barrow, Henry. *The Writings of Henry Barrow, 1587–1590*, ed. L. H. Carlson (1962).

Bate, George, *The Lives, Actions, and Execution of the prime Actors . . . of that horrid Murder of . . . King Charles* (1661).

Baxter, Richard, *Reliquiae Baxterianae*, ed. M. Sylvester (1696).

—— *A Reply to Mr. Tho. Beverley's Answer* (1691).

—— *Which is the True Church* (1679).

Bedloe, William, *A Narrative and Impartial Discovery of the Horrid Popish Plot* (1679).

Bernard, Richard, *A Key of Knowledge For the Opening of . . . Revelation* (1619).

Beware of False Prophets, or, A true Relation of . . . Roaland Bateman (1644).

Bibliotheca Fanatica. Or, The Fanatick Library (1660).

Birkenhead, Sir John, *Bibliotheca Parliamenti* (1653).

—— *Paul's Churchyard. Libri theologici* (1652 and 1659).

B., Ro. (?Robert Blackborne or Cornet Blackwell), *A Letter from a Christian Friend in the Country to another in the City* (no date, signed 24 Nov. 1655).

Bochim. Sighs poured out . . . [for] John Vernon (1667). Verses by J.T., J.M., W.A. (?Wm. Allen) and A.C. (?Abraham Cheare).

Boehme, Jacob, *Mysterium Magnum* (1654).

Booker, John, *The Bloudy Almanack. Being a perfect Abstract of the Prophesies proved . . . by . . . Napier* (1647).

Boon or Booth, A., *Examen Legum Angliae* (1656).

Brayne, John, *The New Earth, or the True Magna Charta of the . . . World to come: Called the Jews Commonweal* (3 Oct. 1653).

Breviter, Richard, *The Mighty Christ the Saints Help* (1662).

Bridge, William, *Babylons Downfall. A Sermon lately preached . . . before the . . . Commons* (1641).

—— *Christs Coming Opened in a Sermon* (1648).

Brightman, Thomas, *Apocalypsis Apocalypseos* (Frankfurt, 1609).

—— *An Exposition of the 11th Chapter of Daniel* (1644).

—— *The Revelation of St. John Illustrated* (4th edn., 1644).

Brightman Redivivus: . . . in IIII Sermons (1647).

Brightmans Predictions and Prophesies (1641).

Brocard, James, *The Revelation of S. Ihon reveled* (1582).

Bibliography

Bunyan, John, *The Whole Works*, ed. G. Offor (1862).

Burrough, Edward, *Good Counsel and Advice, Rejected* (1659).

Burroughes, Jeremiah, *Moses his Choice* (1641).

Burton, Henry, *The Seven Vials* (1628).

—— *The Sounding of the Two Last Trumpets* (1641).

Burton, Thomas, *Diary of Thomas Burton, Esq.*, ed. J. T. Rutt (1828).

Butler, Samuel, *A Proposal Humbly Offered for the Farming of Liberty of Conscience* (1663).

Calamy, Edmund, *An Account of the Ministers . . . Who were Ejected* (2nd edn., 1713).

—— *A Continuation of the Account* (1727).

—— *An Historical Account of My Own Life*, ed. J. T. Rutt (1829).

Calendar of State Papers, Domestic, Elizabeth, Charles I, Interregnum, Charles II, James II.

Calendar of State Papers, Venetian, 1653–61.

Calendar of the Committee for Compounding.

The Camp of Christ, and the Camp of Antichrist (1642).

Campanella, Tommaso, *A Discourse Touching the Spanish Monarchy* (1654).

Canne, John (or ?S. Butler), *The Discoverer* (1649).

Canne, John, *The Discoverer . . . The Second Part* (1649).

—— *Emanuel, or, God With Us . . . at Dunbar* (1650).

—— *The Golden Rule, or Justice Advanced* (16 Feb. 1649).

(——) *The Grand Informer* (Oxford, 1647).

—— *The Improvement of Mercy* (1649).

—— *A Seasonable Word to the Parliament-Men* (20 May 1659).

—— *A Second Voyce from the Temple to the Higher Powers* (15 Aug. 1653).

—— *The Snare is broken* (1649). Against the Covenant.

—— *The Time of Finding* (1658). Regent's Park College, Oxford.

—— *The Time of the End* (1657). Epistles by Feake and Rogers.

—— *Truth with Time: or, certaine Reasons proving, that none of the seven last Plagues, or Vials, are yet poured out* (1656).

—— *A Voice from the Temple to the Higher Powers* (13 June 1653).

Cardell, John, *Gods Soveraign Power over Nations* (1648).

—— *Gods Wisdom Justified* (31 Jan. 1649).

Carte, Thomas, *A Collection of Original Letters and Papers . . . 1641 to 1660* (1739).

Cary *alias* Rande, Mary, *The Little Horns Doom & Downfall: or a Scripture Prophesie of King James, and King Charles* (17 April 1651). Epistles by Peter, Jessey and Feake.

—— *The Resurrection of the Witnesses* (1648; 2nd edn., much enlarged, 14 Nov. 1653).

(——) *Twelve [New] Proposals to the Supreme Governours* (signed 7 July 1653). (The second word is missing and is hypothetical.)

—— *A Word in Season* (1647).

The Cause of God, and of these Nations (1659).

Certain Quaeres Humbly presented in way of Petition, by many Christian People . . . throughout . . . Norfolk and . . . Norwich, to . . . the Lord General and . . . General Councel of War (19 Feb. 1649).

Chamberlen, Peter, *The Declaration and Proclamation of the Army of God* (May 1659).

—— *Legislative Power in Problemes* (3 Dec. 1659).

—— *A Letter to Mr. Braine . . . Concerning Water-Baptisme* (signed 3 Aug. 1650).

—— *Non Inventus* (?1665). Contained in SP. 29/142, fos. 41–3.

—— *Plus Ultra: To the Parliament of England* (10 April 1651).

—— *The Poore Mans Advocate* (25 April 1649).

—— *A Scourge for a Denn of Thieves* (16 June 1659).

—— *The Sober Man's Vindication* (1662).

—— *A Speech Visibly Spoken . . . in Parliament, by a Ghost* (1662).

Chambers, Humphrey, et al., *An Apology for the Ministers of . . . Wilts., in their Actings at the election of Members for . . . Parliament* (12 Aug. 1654).

(Chestlin, W.), *Persecutio Undecima* (1648).

Chillenden, Edmund, *Nathans Parable. Sins Discovery* (3 Dec. 1653).

—— *Preaching without Ordination* (1647).

Clarendon, Edward Hyde, earl of, *Calendar of the Clarendon State Papers*, vols. 2–3, ed. W. D. Macray (Oxford, 1869, 1876), vol. 4, ed. F. J. Routledge (Oxford, 1932), proof copy of vol. 5, ed. Routledge (1963).

—— *The Continuation of the Life of Edward Earl of Clarendon, . . . written by Himself* (Dublin, 1759).

Clarke, John, *Ill Newes from New-England* (1652).

The Clarke Papers, ed. C. H. Firth (Camden Soc., new ser., xlix, liv, lxi, lxii, 1891–1901).

Clarke, Samuel, *A General Martyrologie, . . . Whereunto are added two and twenty Lives of English Modern Divines* (2nd edn., 1660).

Cockayne, George, *Flesh Expiring, and the Spirit Inspiring . . . or God himself . . . inheriting all Nations* (1648).

Collier, Thomas, *A Vindication of the Army-Remonstrance* (1648).

Collinges, John, *Responsoria Bipartita* (1654). Against Boatman.

The Complaining Testimony of some . . . of Sions Children . . . occasioned at their Meeting to seek the Lord at Abingdon (1656). Regent's Park Coll., Oxford.

The Confession of Faith, of those Churches . . . called Anabaptists (1644).

Cornewell, Francis, *The Vindication of the Royall Commission of King Jesus* (1644).

Cornubiensis, Johannes (probably John Carew), *The Grand Catastrophe, or the Change of Government* (18 Jan. 1654).

Cosin, Richard, *Conspiracie, for Pretended Reformation* (1592).

Cotton, John, *An Abstract of Laws and Government Wherein . . . may be seen the . . . perfection of the Government of Christs Kingdome* (1655). Published by Aspinwall.

—— *An Abstract of the Lawes of New England* (1641).

—— *An Exposition upon the Thirteenth Chapter of the Revelation* (1655).

—— *The Powring out of the Seven Vials; preached in sermons at Boston in New England* (1642).

Cowell, John, *Divine Oracles* (1664).

—— *The Snare Broken* (1677).

Cradock, Walker, *The Saints Fulnesse of Joy* (1646).

Crowne, William, *The Catalogue of our English Writers on the Old and New Testament* (1668).

A Cry for a Right Improvement . . . With some Cautions touching the election of the (expected) New Representative (1651).

Curwen, Thomas, *This is An Answer to John Wiggan's Book* (1665).

Danvers, Henry, *Certain Quaeries concerning Liberty of Conscience* (1649).

—— *The Mystery of Magistracy Unvailed* (1663). Congregationalist Library.

—— *Theopolis, or the City of God, New Jerusalem* (1672).

—— *A Treatise of Baptism* (1675, 1st edn. 1673).

Davies, Richard, *An Account of the Convincement . . . of . . . Richard Davies* (1771).

A Declaration from the Harmles and Innocent . . . Quakers (1661), against Venner.

A Declaration of divers Elders and Brethren of Congregationall Societies, in . . . London. Decrying . . . A Cry; and . . . A Model (1651).

A Declaration of Maj. Gen. Harrison Prisoner (2 Aug. 1660).

A Declaration of several of the Churches of Christ . . . concerning the Kingly Interest of Christ (2 Sept. 1654).

A Declaration of the English Army now in Scotland, to the people of Scotland (1 Aug. 1650). The 'Musselburgh Declaration'.

A Declaration of the Faith and Order . . . in the Congregational Churches (1658).

De la March, John, *A Complaint of the False Prophets Mariners* (1641).

De Launay, Pierre, *Paraphrase et Exposition sur l'Apocalypse* (Geneva, 1651).

Dell, William, *The Way of True Peace and Unity* (1649).

Denne, Henry, *The Man of Sin Discovered* (1645).

A Discourse Between Cap. Kiffin, and Dr. Chamberlain, About Imposition of Hands (9 May 1654).

The Disputes Between Mr. Cranford, and Dr. Chamberlen (8 June 1652).

Doe, Charles, *A Collection of Experiences of the Work of Grace* (1700).

Doomes-day: or, the great Day of the Lords Iudgement . . . With the gathering together of the Jews under Josias Catzius . . . for the Conquering of the Holy Land (1647).

A Door of Hope: or, A Call . . . unto the Standard of our Lord, King Jesus (1661). Venner's manifesto.

Douglas, Lady Eleanor, *Bethlehem Signifying the House of Bread* (1652).

—— *The Dragons Blasphemous Charge against Her* (1651).

—— *The Excommunication out of Paradise* (1647).

—— *From the Lady Eleanor, Her Blessing* (1644).

—— *Sions Lamentations* (1649).

—— *Strange and Wonderfull Prophesies* (1649).

—— *A Warning to the Dragon* (1625).

The Downfall of the Fifth Monarchy (20 April 1657).

Durham, James, *A Commentarie Upon the Book of the Revelation* (3rd edn., Amsterdam, 1660).

Edwards, Thomas, *Gangraena* (1646).

Eliot, John, *The Christian Commonwealth: or the Civil Policy of the Rising Kingdom of Jesus Christ* (1659).

Ellis, Humphrey, *Pseudochristus, or a True and faithful Relation . . . of William Frankelin and Mary Gadbury* (1650).

Bibliography

Englands Alarm to War against the Beast (1643).

English Liberty and Property Asserted (March 1657).

Erbery, William, *The Babe of Glory* (1653).

—— *The Bishop of London* (8 Jan. 1653).

—— *A Call to the Churches . . . of Wales* (1653).

—— *The Mad Mans Plea: or, a Sober Defence of Captaine Chillintons Church* (28 Oct. 1653).

—— *An Olive-leaf: or, Some Peaceable Considerations to the Christian Meeting at Christ-Church in London, Munday, Jan. 9. 1653* (1654).

—— *The Testimony of William Erbery* (1658).

An Essay towards Settlement upon a sure foundation (19 Sept. 1659).

Evans, Arise, *The Bloudy Vision of John Farley* (1653).

—— *Mr. Evans and Mr. Penningtons Prophesie* (1655).

Evelyn, John, *Diary*, ed. E. S. de Beer (Oxford, 1955).

—— *The History of the Three late famous Impostors* (1669), i.e. Sabbatai Sevi, Padre Ottomans and Mahomed Bei.

The Failing and Perishing of Good Men (1663). Funeral sermon of Simpson.

The Faithfull Narrative of the late Testimony and Demand made to Oliver Cromwel . . . on the Behalf of the Lords Prisoners (i.e. Feake and Rogers) (21 March 1655).

A Faithfull Searching Home Word, Intended for the view of the remaining Members of the former Old Parliament, shewing the Reasonableness . . . of their first Dissolution (13 Dec. 1659).

False Prophets Discovered. Being a story of . . . Farnham and . . . Bull (1642).

Feak, — (pseud.), *A Word for All: or, the Rumps Funerall Sermon* (1660).

Feak, John (pseud.), *A Funeral Sermon Thundred forth . . . for the Loss of . . . Harison* (23 Oct. 1660).

Feake, Christopher, *A Beam of Light, shining in the midst of much Darkness* (2 May 1659).

—— *The Genealogie of Christianity* (1650).

—— *The New Non-conformist* (24 May 1654).

—— *The Oppressed Close Prisoner in Windsor-Castle, his Defiance to the Father of Lyes* (19 Dec. 1654).

Felgenhauer, Paul, *Postilion, or a new Almanacke* (1655).

The Fifth Monarchy or Kingdom of Christ, in opposition to the Beast's, Asserted (23 Aug. 1659).

Finch, Heneage, earl of Nottingham, *An Exact and most Impartial Accompt of the . . . Trial . . . of Twenty-nine Regicides* (1660).

Firth, C. H. and Rait, R. S., eds., *Acts and Ordinances of the Interregnum, 1642–1660* (1911).

Firth, C. H., ed., *Scotland and the Protectorate, 1654–9* (Scottish Hist. Soc., xxxi, 1899).

Foster, George, *The Pouring Forth of the Seventh and Last Viall* (1650).

—— *The Sounding of the Last Trumpet* (1650).

Fox, George, *John James, I hearing* (1658). Friends' House Library.

—— *Journal*, ed. J. L. Nickalls (Cambridge, 1952).

Foxe, John, *The Acts and Monuments*, ed. J. Pratt (1877).

Gadbury, John, *Nauticum Astrologicum: or, the Astrologicall Seaman* (1691).

Bibliography

Gardiner, S. R. and Atkinson, C. T., ed., *Letters and Papers Relating to the First Dutch War*, 1652–4 (Navy Records Soc., xiii, xvii, xxx, xxxvii, xli, lxvi, 1899–1930).

Gataker, Thomas, *Gods Eye on his Israel* (1645).

The Generall Signes and Fore-runners of Christs comming to Iudgement (no date, c. 1620). In Bodleian, but not in S.T.C.

Goodgroom, Richard, *A Copy of a Letter from an Officer of the Army in Ireland, to . . . the Lord Protector, concerning his changing of the Government* (19 March 1656).

Goodwin, John, Ευγκρητιōς. *Or Dis-satisfaction Satisfied* (1654).

Goodwin, Thomas, *A Glimpse of Sions Glory* (1641).

—— *A Sermon of the Fifth Monarchy* (1654).

—— *The World to Come, or, the Kingdome of Christ asserted* (1655).

Gouge, William *et al.*, *Annotations Upon all the Books of the Old and New Testament* (2nd edn., 1651).

—— *The Progresse of Divine Providence* (1645).

—— *Workes* (1627).

Gough, Richard, *Antiquities & Memoirs of the Parish of Myddle, County of Salop* (1700) (Shrewsbury and London, 1875).

Grantham, Thomas, *Christianismus Primitivus* (1675).

Graunt, John, *Truths Victory against Heresie* (1645).

Grey, Ford, lord, *The Secret History of the Rye-House-Plot: and of Monmouth's Rebellion* (1754).

Griffith, Alexander, *Mercurius Cambro-Britannicus. Or, News from Wales* (1652).

—— *Strena Vavasoriensis . . . or a Hue and Cry after Mr. Vavasour Powell, Metropolitan of the Itinerants* (1654).

A Ground Voice, or some Discoveries offered to the view . . . of the whole Army (16 Nov. 1655).

Hall, Edmund, *Lingua Testium* (1651).

Hall, John, *Confusion Confounded: . . . Wherein is Considered the Reasons of the Resignation of the late Parliament* (18 Jan. 1654).

Hall, Joseph, *The Revelation Unrevealed* (1650).

Hall, Thomas, *Chiliasto-mastix redivivus . . . A confutation of the Millenarian Opinion* (1657).

Harrington, James, *A Parallel of the Spirit of the People, with the Spirit of Mr. Rogers* (18 Oct. 1659).

Harrison, Mark, *A Narrative of the Proceedings of the Fleet* (22 Dec. 1659).

Haughton, Edward, *The Rise, Growth, and Fall of Antichrist* (1652).

Hatton. *Correspondence of the Family of Hatton (1661–1704)*, ed. E. M. Thompson (Camden Soc., n.s., xxii, xxiii, 1878).

Heath, James, *Flagellum: or the Life and Death . . . of Oliver Cromwel* (1663).

Hell Broke Loose (1661).

Helme, Camshaw, *Life in Death, or Support for souls* (1660). Dr. Williams's Lib.

Heywood, Oliver, *Autobiography, Diaries, anecdote and event books* (Brighouse and Bingley, 1881–5).

Heywood, Thomas, *A True Discourse of the two infamous upstart Prophets . . . Farnham . . . and . . . Bull* (1636).

288

Higgenson, Thomas, *Glory sometimes afar off, Now stepping in* (1653).
—— *Sighs for Righteousness* (2 June 1654).
—— *Some Legible Characters of Faith . . . Towards the . . . Kingdom of Christ* (1659). Epistle by Feake, signed 6 June, giving a list of Higgenson's publications. Regent's Park College, Oxford.
—— *A Testimony to the True Jesus* (1656).
Hill, William, *A Brief Narrative of that Stupendious Tragedie Late intended to be Acted* (1662), i.e. Tong's Plot.
Historical Manuscripts Commission. iv, *App. to 5th Report*.
—— vii, *App. to 8th Report*.
—— viii, *App. to 9th Report*.
—— xv, *Abergavenny and Braye MSS.*
—— xix, *Townshend MSS.*
—— xxii, *Leeds and Bridgewater MSS.*
—— xxv, *Le Fleming MSS.*
—— xxxiii, *Lonsdale MSS.*
—— xxxvi, *Ormonde MSS., New Series*.
—— xliii, *Somerset MSS.*
—— xlv, *Buccleuch MSS.*
—— li, *Leyborne-Popham MSS.*
—— lv, *Various Coll., II.*
—— lxiii, *Egmont MSS.*
—— lxxi, *Finch MSS.*
Holinshed, Raphael, *The Laste volume of the Chronicles of England* (1577).
The holy Sisters Conspiracy against their Husbands and the City of London (26 Jan. 1661).
Homes, Nathaniel, *The Resurrection Revealed* (1654, 1st edn. 1653).
—— *A Sermon, Preached Before . . . Thomas Foote, Lord Maior* (1650).
Hornius, Georgius, *Historia Ecclesiastica et Politica* (Leyden and Rotterdam, 1665).
Howell, T. B., *A Complete Collection of State Trials*, vi (1816).
Hughes, George, *Vae-Euge-Tuba. Or, the Wo-Ioy-Trumpet* (1647).
Hughes, William, *Munster and Abingdon, or the Open Rebellion there, and Un-happy Tumult here* (Oxford, 1657).
The Humble Apology of some . . . called Anabaptists (1661). Against Venner.
The Humble Remonstrance . . . of Col. Overtons Regiment (20 June 1649).
The Humble Representation and Address to His Highness of severall Churches and Christians in South-Wales . . . Presented . . . January 31 (1656).
Hutchinson, Lucy, *Memoirs of the Life of Colonel Hutchinson*, ed. C. H. Firth (1906).
Isham, Sir Giles, ed., *The Correspondence of Bishop Brian Duppa and Sir Justinian Isham, 1650–1660* (Northants. Record Soc., xvii, 1955).
Ives, Jeremiah, *Saturday no Sabbath* (1659).
James I., *A Fruitefull Meditation* (1603).
Jeaffreson, J. C., ed., *Middlesex County Records*, vols. iii and iv (1888, 1892).
Jessey, Henry, *The exceeding Riches of Grace Advanced . . . in Mris. Sarah Wight* (1657).
—— *The Lords Loud Call to England* (14 Aug. 1660).

Bibliography

Johnson, Edward, *An Examination of the Essay: or, an Answer to the Fifth Monarchy* (1659).

Jones, Roger, *Mene Tekel; or, the Downfall of Tyranny* (1663).

Josselin, Ralph, *Diary, 1616–1683*, ed. E. Hockliffe (Camden Soc., 3rd ser., xv, 1908).

Journals of the House of Commons, vii (1813).

Joye, George, *The exposicion of Daniel* (Geneva, 1545).

Keach, Benjamin., *Antichrist Stormed* (1689).

Κλεὶς Προφητείας, *or, the Key of Prophecie* (1660).

Knolles, Richard, and Rycaut, Sir Paul, *The Turkish History, . . . with a Continuation to . . . MDCXXXVII* (1687).

Knollys, Hanserd, *An Exposition of the whole Book of the Revelation* (1689).

Lane, Col. Edward, *An Image of our Reforming Times* (14 Aug. 1654). Epistle by Rogers.

The Last Farewel to the Rebellious Sect Called the Fifth Monarchy Men on Wednesday January the Ninth (1661).

L'Estrange, Sir Roger, *Citt and Bumpkin, in a Dialogue* (1680).

—— *A Compendious History of . . . the last Fourteen Years* (1680).

—— *The Dissenter's Sayings* (1681).

A Letter from a Gentleman in Buckinghamshire, . . . giving an Account of Mr. Mason (1694).

Ley, William, 'Υηερασπιστὴς, *or, A Buckler for the Church of England Against . . . Pendarvis* (Oxford, 1656).

Lilburne, John, *The Afflicted Mans Out-Cry* (1653).

—— *The Legall Fundamentall Liberties of the People of England* (1649).

Lilly, William, *A Collection of Ancient and Modern Prophesies* (1645).

—— *A Prophecy of the White King* (1644).

—— *William Lilly's History of his Life and Times, from the Year 1602 to 1681* (1826).

A List of all the Conspirators that have been Seiz'd (1683).

A List of some of the Grand Blasphemers and Blasphemies (1654).

Lister, Joseph, *Autobiography*, ed. T. Wright (1842).

Llanvaedonon, William, *A Brief Exposition upon the Second Psalme* (23 June 1655).

Lloyd, Owen, *Het Gezigt van den Panther* (1688).

—— *The Panther-Prophesy* (1662).

Llwyd, Morgan, 'The Book of the Three Birds', trans. L. J. Parry, *Trans. Nat. Eisteddfod of Wales, Llandudno, 1896* (Liverpool, 1898).

—— *A Discourse of God the Word*, trans. G. Rudd (1739).

—— *Gweithiau Morgan Llwyd*, ed. T. E. Ellis and J. H. Davies (Bangor and London, 1899, 1908).

The Londoners Last Warning (15 Aug. 1659).

Londons Glory, or, the Riot and Ruine of the Fifth Monarchy Men (25 Jan. 1661).

Ludlow, Edmund, *Memoirs*, ed. C. H. Firth (Oxford, 1894).

Lupton, Thomas, *Babylon is fallen* (1597).

Machyn, Henry, *The Diary of Henry Machyn, . . . 1550–1563*, ed. J. G. Nichols (Camden Soc., xlii, 1848).

Magalotti, L., ed., *Travels of Cosmo the Third, Grand Duke of Tuscany, through England* (1821).

Bibliography

Mall, Thomas, *The Axe at the Root* (1668).

Mason, John, *The Midnight-Cry* (2nd edn., 1691).

Maurice, Henry, *An Impartial Account of Mr. John Mason* (1695).

Mayer, John, *Ecclesiastica Interpretatio: or the Exposition upon . . . Revelation* (1627).

Mayhew, Richard, *Sichah: or a Tract of Meditation* (1682).

Mede, Joseph, *The Apostacy of the Later Times* (1641).

—— *The Key of the Revelation*, trans. R. More (1643).

—— *A Paraphrase . . . of the Prophesie of Saint Peter* (1642 and 1649).

—— *Works*, ed. J. Worthington (1672).

Medley, William, *A Standard Set Up: Whereunto the true Seed and Saints of the most High may be gathered together* (16 May 1657).

(Melish, Stephen), *Englands Warning: . . . Visions of Stephen Melish* (1664).

Memoires of the Life of Anthony late Earl of Shaftesbury (1683).

A Memorial on the Death of . . . Nathaniel Strange (1666).

Mene Tekel to the Fifth Monarchy (1665).

Milton, John, *Complete Prose Works*, i, ed. D. M. Wolfe (New Haven and London, 1953).

Mirabilis Annus, or, the year of Prodigies and Wonders (1661).

Mirabilis Annus Secundus: or the Second Part of the Second Years Prodigies (1662).

Mirabilis Annus Secundus; or, the Second Year of Prodigies (1662).

A Mite from Three Mourners: In Memorial of Thomas Glass, . . . and John Wiggan (1666). Verses by J.V., W.A., A.C. (probably John Vernon, William Allen and Abraham Cheare).

A Model of a new Representative (1651).

More, Henry, *Apocalypsis Apocalypseos; or the Revelation . . . unveiled* (1680).

More, John, *A Generall Exhortation to the World: By a late Convert* (1652).

—— *A Lost Ordinance Restored: or . . . Laying on of hands* (24 Jan. 1654).

—— *A Trumpet sounded* (signed 14 Aug. 1654).

N., J., *Proh Tempora! Proh Mores! Or an unfained Caveat to all True Protestants, Not in any case to touch . . . Mr. Christopher Feakes Exhortations* (29 Jan. 1654).

Napier, John, *A Plaine Discovery of the whole Revelation* (Edinburgh, 1593).

Napiers Narration (1642).

A Narrative of the Apprehending . . . and Execution of John James (1662).

A Narrative; wherein is faithfully set forth the sufferings of John Canne, Wentworth Day, John Clarke (1658).

Nickolls, John, ed., *Original Letters and Papers of State* (1743).

Nuttall, G. F., ed., *Early Quaker Letters from the Swarthmore MSS. to 1660* (typescript, 1952).

Observations Upon the Last Actions and Words of . . . Harrison (26 Nov. 1660).

Oldenburg, Henry, *The Correspondence of Henry Oldenburg*, ed. A. R. Hall and M. B. Hall (Madison, Milwaukee and London, 1965–6).

The Old Leaven Purged Out. Or, the Apostacy of this Day (1658). Signed by John Portman *et al.*

Osborne, John, *An Indictment against Tythes* (1659). Epistle by Canne.

Overton, Robert, *The Humble and Healing Advice of Collonel Robert Overton* (1659).

Bibliography

Overton, Robert, *A Letter from Ma. Gen. Overton* (signed 11 Oct. 1659).
—— *More Hearts and Hands Appearing for the Work* (7 June 1653).
Owen, John, Οὐρανῶν Οὐρανια. *The Shaking and Translating of Heaven and Earth* (19 April 1649).
—— *A Sermon preached to the Honourable House of Commons . . . 31 Jan.* (1649).
—— *A Sermon preached to the Parliament, Octob. 13. 1652 . . . Concerning the Kingdome of Christ* (Oxford, 1652).
Pagitt, Ephraim, *Heresiography* (2nd edn., 1645, 6th edn., revised, 1662).
A Paire of Spectacles for the Citie (1648).
Palmer, Anthony, *A Scripture-Rale to the Lords Table* (1654).
Palmer, Herbert, *The Duty and Honour of Church-Members* (1646).
Palmer, Thomas, *A Little View of this Old World* (30 June 1659).
—— *The Saints Freedom from Tyranny Vindicated* (1667), Congregationalist Lib.
—— *The Saints Support in these sad Times, Delivered in a Sermon at Tiverton* (16 Oct. 1644).
Parker, Robert, *An Exposition of the Powring out of the Fourth Vial* (1650).
—— *The Mystery of the Vialls Opened* (1651).
Parker, Thomas, *The Visions and Prophecies of Daniel Expounded* (1646).
Peck, Francis, *Desiderata Curiosa* (1732).
Pendarves, John, *Arrowes against Babylon* (1656).
—— *The Fear of God: What it is* (1657). Preached 10 Aug. 1656.
Pepys, Samuel, *Diary*, ed. H. B. Wheatley (1893).
A Perfect Diurnall: or the Daily Proceedings in the Conventicles of the Phanatiques (19 March 1660).
Perkins, William, *Workes* (1612–13).
Peter, Hugh, *Gods Doings and Mans Duty* (1646).
—— *Good Work for a Good Magistrate* (1651).
Postlethwaite, Walter, *A Voice from Heaven: or, A Testimony against . . . the Court of Tryers* (15 April 1655).
Powell, Vavasor, צוֹפֵר בפח *or the Bird in the Cage, Chirping* (1661).
—— *Common-Prayer-Book no Divine Service* (1660).
—— *God the Father Glorified* (1 Dec. 1649).
(——) *The Sufferers-Catechism* (1664). Ascribed to P. by Anthony a Wood.
Price, Evan, *Eye-salve for England: or, the Grand Trappan Detected* (1667).
A Prophesie that hath Lyen hid, Above these 2000 yeares (1610).
Prophecies of Christopher Kotterus, Christiana Poniatovia, Nicholas Drabicius, trans. R. Codrington (2nd edn., 1664).
The Prophets Malachy and Isaiah Prophesying to the Saints (22 Sept. 1656). Epistles by Feake and Pendarves.
The Protector (So called,) In Part Unvailed (24 Oct. 1655).
Prynne, William, *The Popish Royall Favourite* (1643).
—— *A true and perfect Narrative* (7 May 1659).
Pryor, William, and Turner, Thomas, *The Outcries of the Poor, Oppressed, and Imprisoned . . . presented to the Council of Officers, Nov. 24.* (1659).
R., D., *The Morning Alarum*, trans. N. Johnson (1651). Friends' House.
R., J., (?John Rye), *The sad Suffering Case of Major General Rob. Overton* (3 March 1659).

Bibliography

A Renunciation and Declaration of the Ministers of Congregational Churches (1661). Against Venner.

A Revelation of Mr. Brightmans Revelation (1641).

Reverend Mr. Brightmans Iudgement or Prophecies (1641).

Richardson, Samuel, *Plain Dealing* (23 Jan. 1656). Against *A Word for God.*

Rogers, John, *Analecta Inauguralia* (1664).

—— Διαπολιτεία. *A Christian Concertation* (20 Sept. 1659). On pp. 26, 69 Rogers mentions his authorship of *A Reviving Word* and *The Plain Case.*

—— *Jegar-Sahadutha: An Oyled Pillar: Set up for Posterity* (28 July 1657).

—— *Mene, Tekel, Perez . . . a Letter written to, and lamenting over Oliver Lord Cromwel* (10 June 1654).

—— *Mr. Harrington's Parallel Unparallel'd* (22 Sept. 1659).

—— *Mr. Pryn's Good Old Cause Stated and Stunted 10. years ago* (May 1659).

—— *The Plain Case of the Common-weal . . . Stated* (3 March 1659).

—— *Ohel or Beth-shemesh. A Tabernacle for the Sun* (7 Nov. 1653).

—— *A Reviving Word from the Quick and the Dead* (11 Oct. 1657).

—— *Sagrir. Or Doomes-day drawing nigh, with Thunder and Lightening to lawyers* (7 Nov. 1653).

—— *To His Excellency the Lord Generall Cromwell. A few Proposals, relating to Civil Government* (27 April 1653).

—— *To His Highnesse Lord General Cromwel, Lord Protector, &c. The humble Cautionary Proposals of John Rogers* (Dec. 1653).

(——) *A Vindication of that Prudent and Honourable Knight, Sir Henry Vane* (7 June 1659).

Rogers, Thomas, *The Catholic Doctrine of the Church of England*, ed. J. J. S. Perowne (Parker Soc., lii, 1854).

Salmon, Joseph, *A Rout, A Rout* (1649).

Sanders, John, *An Iron Rod for the Naylors* (1655).

—— *An Iron Rod put into the Lord Protectors Hand, to break all Antichristian Powers in pieces* (1655).

Sedgwick, William, *The Leaves of the Tree of Life* (1648).

—— *Zions Deliverance* (1642).

Serarius, Petrus, *An awakening warning to the Wofull World* (Amsterdam, 1662).

—— *The Last Letters to the London-Merchants* (1665).

Simpson, John, *The Great Joy of Saints* (1654). Basically a rearrangement of the contents of the next. Microfilm copy now in Regent's Park College, Oxford.

—— *The Perfection of Justification maintained* (1648).

Sixe strange Prophesies (1643, 1st edn., 1642).

Some Considerations by way of Proposal . . . for the . . . uniting of all the Faithful in this Day (9 March 1658).

Somers. A Collection of Scarce and Valuable Tracts of the late Lord Somers, ed. Sir W. Scott (2nd edn., 1809–15).

The Speeches and Prayers of Some of the late King's Judges (1660).

Spencer, John, *The Spirituall Warfare: A Sermon Preached . . . 30 of March* (1642).

Spittlehouse, John, *An Answer to one part of the Lord Protector's Speech . . . the 4 of September 1654* (1654).

Bibliography

Spittlehouse, John and Saller, W., *An Appeal to the Consciences of the chief Magistrates* (1657).

—— *The Army Vindicated, in their late Dissolution of the Parliament* (24 April 1653).

—— *Certaine Queries Propounded to . . . those Persons Now in Power* (1 Sept. 1654).

—— *An Explanation of the Commission of Jesus Christ* (22 Sept. 1653).

—— *The first Addresses to . . . the Lord General* (5 July 1653).

—— *A Manifestation of sundry gross absurdities* (1656). Trinity Coll., Cambridge.

(——) *The Picture of a New Courtier* (11 April 1656).

—— *A Return to some Expressions* (1656). Trinity Coll., Cambridge.

—— *Rome Ruin'd by Whitehall* (31 Dec. 1650).

—— *The Royall Advocate: or, An Introduction to the . . . Laws of Jehovah* (1655). National Library of Scotland.

—— and More, John, *A Vindication of the Continued Succession of the Primitive Church* (1652). Xerox copy now at Regent's Park College, Oxford.

—— *A Warning-Piece Discharged: . . . in relation to the election of a New Representative* (19 May 1653).

Sprat, Thomas, *A True Account . . . of the Horrid Conspiracy Against the King* (1685).

Stennet, Edward, *The Insnared Taken in the Work of his own Hands; or an Answer to Mr. John Cowell* (1677/9).

—— *The Royall Law Contended for* (1667). Xerox copy now in Brit. Mus.

Sterry, Peter, *England's Deliverance from the Northern Presbytery* (1652).

Stoneham, Benjamin, *The Parable of the Ten Virgins* (1676).

—— *Saul and David, Compared together* (1676).

—— *A Serious Proposal* (also signed by J. Caley and N. Cook) *To which is added, The Serious Proposal Promoted, by . . . Chr. Feake, and the Congregation with him* (1659).

—— *The Voice of a Cry at Midnight* (1664).

Stoughton, John, *Felicitas Ultimi Saeculi* (1640).

Stow, John, *A Summarie of the Chronicles of England* (1598).

Strange Newes from New-Gate (1647).

Strong, William, *XXX Select Sermons* (1656).

Sturgeon, John, *A Plea for Tolleration* (1661).

The Swedish Discipline (1632).

T., D., *Certain Queries, or Considerations* (1651).

Tany, Thomas, *Hear, O Earth* (1654).

—— *The Nations Right in Magna Charta* (1651).

—— *Thau Ram Tanjah his Speech* (1654).

—— *Thearauiohn High Priest to the Iewes* (1652)

Taylor, Thomas, *Jacob Wrestling with God* (1692, 1st edn. 1663).

—— *The True Light Shining in Darkness* (1693).

Three Hymnes, . . . composed by . . . John Goodwin, . . . Powel, . . . Appletree (1650).

Thurloe, *A Collection of the State Papers of John Thurloe, Esq.*, ed. T. Birch (1742).

Bibliography

Tichborne, Robert, *The Rest of Faith* (1649).

Tillam, Thomas, *Banners of Love Displaied* (16 Jan. 1654).

—— *The Fourth Principle of Christian Religion; or . . . Laying on of Hands asserted* (25 July 1655).

—— *The Lasher proved Lyer* (1657). Xerox copy now in Bodleian.

—— *The Seventh-Day Sabbath Sought out* (1657).

—— *The Temple of Lively Stones* (1660). Epistle by Pooley.

—— *The Two Witnesses* (1651).

Tillinghast, John, *Elijah's Mantle* (30 Jan. 1658).

—— *Generation-Worke* (1653–4).

—— *Knowledge of the Times* (9 Dec. 1654).

—— *Mr. Tillinghasts Eight Last Sermons* (1655). Epistle by Feake.

—— *Six Severall Treatises* (1663).

Tombes, John, *Saints no Smiters* (1664).

To the Honest Souldiers of the Garrison of Hull (25 Sept. 1656). In favour of Canne.

To the Officers and Souldiers of the Army, more specially to those that sit . . . at White-Hall (1657). In favour of Biddle.

Townshend, Henry, *Diary*, ed. J. W. Willis Bund, vol. i (Worcs. Hist. Soc., xxxi, 1920).

Trapnel, Anna, *Anna Trapnel's Report and Plea* (1654).

—— *The Cry of a Stone* (1654).

—— *A Legacy for Saints* (1654).

—— Untitled book of verse in Bodleian (1658). Shelf-mark S. 1.42. Th.

—— *Voice for the King of Saints and Nations* (1658).

The Traytors Unvailed (18 April 1661).

A True Catalogue . . . of . . . where, and by whom Richard Cromwell was Proclaimed Lord Protector (28 Sept. 1659).

A true Copie of a Paper delivered to Lt. G. Fleetwood (26 April 1659).

A true Discovery of a Bloody Plot (17 April 1661).

A True Narrative of the Cause and Manner of the Dissolution of the late Parliament, upon the 12. of Decemb. 1653 (1653).

A True State of the Case of the Commonwealth (8 Feb. 1654).

Truths Conflict with Error . . . In three Publike Disputations. The first between Mr. John Goodwin and M. Vavasour Powell . . . The other two between M. John Goodwin, and M. John Simpson (28 March 1650).

The Tryal of Sir Henry Vane (1662).

Turner, G. L., *Original Records of Early Nonconformity* (1911–14).

Underhill, E. B., ed., *Records of the Churches of Christ gathered at Fenstanton, Warboys, and Hexham, 1644–1720* (1854).

—— *The Records of a Church of Christ meeting in Broadmead, Bristol, 1640–1687* (1847).

Vaughan, Robert, ed., *The Protectorate of Oliver Cromwell* (1839).

Vavasoris Examen, et Purgamen: or, Mr. Vavasor Powells Impartiall Triall: Who . . . is found Not Guilty (30 March 1654).

Vernon, John, *The Compleat Scholler* (1666).

—— *The Swords Abuse Asserted* (1648).

A Vision, which One Mr. Brayne . . . had in September, 1647 (1649).

295

Bibliography

Von Frankenburg, Abraham, *Clavis Apocalyptica: or, A Prophetical Key*, trans. S. Hartlib (1651).

Von Kerssenbroch, Hermann, *Anabaptistici Furoris . . . Narratio*, ed. H. Detmer (Münster, 1899–1900).

Walker, Henry, *Spirituall Experiences, of sundry Beleevers* (1653). Epistle by Powell.

A Warning-Piece to the General Council of the Army (1659).

Weemse, John, *An Explication of the Iudiciall Lawes of Moses* (1632).

Weld, Thomas, *Mr. Tillam's Account Examined* (1657).

(Wharton, George), *A Second Narrative of the Late Parliament* (20 April 1659).

Whitelocke, Bulstrode, *Memorials of the English Affairs* (1682).

Whitgift, John, *Works*, ed. J. Ayre (Parker Soc., xlviii, l, 1851–3).

Whitley, W. T., ed., *Minutes of the General Assembly of the General Baptist Churches* (1909–10).

Wigan, John, *Antichrist's Strongest Hold overturned* (1665). Attacking the Quakers.

Wilkinson, Henry, *Babylons Ruine, Jerusalems Rising* (1643).

Wilkinson, John, *An Exposition of the 13. Chapter of the Revelation* (1619).

Williams, Griffith, *The Great Antichrist Revealed* (1660).

A Witnes to the Saints in England and Wales . . . By some of the Mourners in Zion (15 June 1657).

Wood, Anthony a, *Athenae Oxonienses* (1691–2).

—— *The Life and Times of Anthony Wood*, ed. A. Clark (Oxford Hist. Soc., xix, xxi, 1891–2).

Woodall, Frederick, *Natural and Spiritual Light distinguished* (1655). Yale.

—— and Petto, Samuel, and Martin, John, *The Preacher sent: or, A Vindication of . . . Publick Preaching by some men not Ordained* (1658).

—— and Petto, Samuel, *A Vindication of the Preacher Sent* (1659).

Woodcock, Francis, *Christ's Warning-Piece* (1644).

A Word in Season Unto All (1650).

The Worlds Proceeding Woes and Succeeding Joyes . . . or, the Triple Presage of Henry Alsted (1642).

Worthington, John, *Diary and Correspondence*, ed. J. Crossley and R. C. Christie (Chetham Soc., xiii, xxxvi, cxiv, 1847–86).

The Year of Wonders: or, the glorious Rising of the fifth Monarch (1652).

B. NEWSPAPERS

The dates refer to the years in which the newspaper has been cited as a source, not to the total length of its publication.

Certaine Informations (1643).

Certain Passages (1654).

The Faithfull Scout (1652–5).

The Grand Politique Post (1654).

The London Gazette (1666).

The Loyal Intelligencer (1654).

The Loyall Scout (1659).

Mercurius Fumigosus (1655).

Mercurius Jocosus (1654).

Mercurius Politicus (1651–60).
Mercurius Publicus (1660–3).
The Moderate Intelligencer (1653–4).
The Moderate Publisher (1653).
The Observator (1654).
Occurrences from Foreign Parts (1659).
The Parliamentary Intelligencer (1660).
A Perfect Account (1653–5).
A Perfect Diurnall (1649–54).
Perfect Occurrences (1649).
Perfect Passages (1651).
Perfect Proceedings (1655).
The Phanatique Intelligencer (1660).
The Publick Intelligencer (1655–60).
Severall Proceedings in Parliament (1651–4).
The Weekly Intelligencer (1654).
The Weekly Post (1655–9).

C. SELECT SECONDARY WORKS

Abbott, W. C., *Colonel Thomas Blood, Crown-Stealer, 1618–1680* (New Haven and London, 1911).
—— 'English Conspiracy and Dissent, 1660–1674', *American Hist. Rev.*, xiv, (1908–9).
Armytage, W. H. G., *Heavens Below: Utopian Experiments in England* (1961).
Bagwell, R., *Ireland under the Stuarts* (1909).
Bailey, M. L., *Milton and Jakob Boehme* (New York, 1914).
Banks, C. E., 'Thomas Venner', *New England Hist. & Gen. Reg.*, xlvii (1893).
Baptist Historical Society, Transactions (1908–21), *passim*.
Barbour, H., *The Quakers in Puritan England* (New Haven and London, 1964).
Barclay, R., *The Inner Life of the Religious Societies of the Commonwealth* (1876).
Barker, A. E., *Milton and the Puritan Dilemma* (Toronto, 1942).
Besse, Joseph, *A Collection of the Sufferings of the People called Quakers* (1753).
Brailsford, H. N., *The Levellers and the English Revolution* (1961).
Braithwaite, W. C., *The Beginnings of Quakerism* (2nd edn., Cambridge, 1955).
Brockett, A., *Nonconformity in Exeter, 1650–1875* (Manchester, 1962).
Brown, L. F., *The Political Activities of the Baptists and Fifth Monarchy Men* (1911, reissued New York, 1965).
Browne, J., *History of Congregationalism in Norfolk and Suffolk* (1877).
Burrage, C., *Early English Dissenters* (1912).
—— 'Anna Trapnel's Prophecies', *Eng. Hist. Rev.*, xxvi (1911).
—— 'The Fifth Monarchy Insurrections', *ibid.*, xxv (1910).
Burrell, S. A., 'The Apocalyptic Vision of the Early Covenanters', *Scottish Hist. Rev.*, xliii (1964).
Calder, I. M., 'John Cotton and the New Haven Colony', *New England Quart.*, iii (1930).

Calder, I. M. 'A Seventeenth Century Attempt to Purify the Anglican Church', *American Hist. Rev.*, liii (1947–8).

Cohn, N., *The Pursuit of the Millennium* (1962).

Cole, A., 'The Quakers and the English Revolution' in T. Aston, ed., *Crisis in Europe*, 1560–1660 (1965).

—— 'Social Origins of the Early Friends', *Journ. Friends' Hist. Soc.*, xlviii (1957).

Collinson, P., *The Elizabethan Puritan Movement* (1967).

Cooper, B. G., 'The Academic Re-discovery of Apocalyptic Ideas in the Seventeenth Century', *Bapt. Quart.*, xviii (1959–60).

Corrodi, H., *Kritische Geschichte des Chiliasmus* (Frankfurt and Leipzig, 1781–1783).

Cragg, G. R., *Puritanism in the Period of the Great Persecution* (Cambridge, 1957).

Crosby, T., *The History of the English Baptists* (1738–40).

Davies, Godfrey, *The Restoration of Charles II, 1658–1660* (San Marino, California, 1955).

Debus, A. G., *The English Paracelsians* (1965).

Dexter, H. M., *The Congregationalism of the last three hundred years* (New York, 1880). Contains valuable bibliography.

Dictionary of American Biography.

Dictionary of National Biography.

Dodd, A. H., 'A Remonstrance from Wales, 1655', *Bull. Board of Celtic Studies*, xvii (1956–8).

—— *Studies in Stuart Wales* (Cardiff, 1952).

Dodd, J. A., 'Troubles in a City Parish Under the Protectorate', *Eng. Hist. Rev.*, x (1895).

Dodds, M. H., 'Political Prophecies in the Reign of Henry VIII', *Mod. Lang. Rev.*, xi (1916).

Dunlop, R., *Ireland under the Commonwealth* (Manchester, 1913).

Evans, E. L., 'Morgan Llwyd and Jacob Boehme', *The Jacob Boehme Society Quarterly*, i (1953).

Everitt, A., *Suffolk and the Great Rebellion* (1961).

Farnell, J. E., 'The Navigation Act of 1651, the First Dutch War, and the London Community', *Econ. Hist. Rev.*, xvi (1963–4).

—— 'The Usurpation of Honest London Householders: Barebone's Parliament', *Eng. Hist. Rev.*, lxxxii (1967).

Firth, Sir C. H., 'Cromwell and the Expulsion of the Long Parliament in 1653', *Eng. Hist. Rev.*, viii (1893).

—— *Cromwell's Army* (1902).

—— *The Last Years of the Protectorate, 1656–1658* (1909).

—— *The Life of Thomas Harrison* (Worcester, Mass., 1893).

—— and Davies, G., *The Regimental History of Cromwell's Army* (Oxford, 1940).

Fortescue, G. K., *Catalogue of the Pamphlets . . . collected by George Thomason* (1908).

Foster, Joseph, *Alumni Oxonienses: the Members of the University of Oxford, 1500–1714* (Oxford, 1891–2).

Bibliography

Foster, Sir W., 'Venner's Rebellion', *London Topog. Rec.*, xviii (1942).

Froom, L. E., *The Prophetic Faith of our Fathers: the Historical development of Prophetic interpretation* (Washington, 1946–54).

Gardiner, S. R., *History of the Commonwealth and Protectorate, 1649–1656* (1903).

George, M. D., 'Elections and Electioneering, 1679–81', *Eng. Hist. Rev.*, xlv (1930).

Glass, H. A., *The Barbone Parliament* (1899).

Gooch, G. P., and Laski, H. J., *English Democratic Ideas in the Seventeenth Century* (New York, Evanston and London, 1959).

Greene, C. H., and Gamble, J. L., eds., *Seventh Day Baptists in Europe and America* (Plainfield, N.J., 1910).

Haase, R., *Das Problem des Chiliasmus und der Dreissigjährige Krieg* (Leipzig, 1933).

Haley, K. H. D., *The First earl of Shaftesbury* (Oxford, 1968).

—— *William of Orange and the English Opposition* (Oxford, 1953).

Haller, W., *Foxe's Book of Martyrs and the Elect Nation* (1963).

Hardacre, P. H., 'William Allen, Cromwellian Agitator and "Fanatic" ', *Bapt. Quart.*, xix (1961–2).

Harris, V., *All Coherence Gone* (Chicago, 1949).

Harte, W. J., 'Ecclesiastical and Religious Affairs in Exeter, 1640–62', *Report and Trans. Devon. Assoc.*, lxix (1937).

Haskins, G. L., *Law and Authority in Early Massachusetts* (New York, 1960).

Hill, (J. E.) C., *Puritanism and Revolution* (1962 edn.).

—— *Society and Puritanism* (1966 edn.).

Howell, R., *Newcastle Upon Tyne and the Puritan Revolution* (Oxford, 1967).

Huehns, G., *Antinomianism in English History* (1951).

Hunter, R., and Macalpine, I., *Three Hundred Years of Psychiatry* (1963).

Hutin, S., *Les disciples anglais de Jacob Boehme* (Paris, 1960).

Ives, E. W., ed., *The English Revolution, 1600–1660* (1968).

James, M., 'The Political Importance of the Tithes Controversy in the English Revolution, 1640–60', *History*, n.s., xxvi (1941–2).

—— *Social Problems and Policy during the Puritan Revolution* (1932).

Jewson, C. B., 'Norfolk Baptists up to 1700', *Bapt. Quart.*, xviii (1959–60).

—— 'St. Mary's, Norwich', *ibid.*, x (1940–1).

Jones, J. R., *The First Whigs* (1961).

Kitchin, G., *Sir Roger L'Estrange* (1913).

Knox, R. A., *Enthusiasm: A Chapter in the History of Religion* (Oxford, 1950).

Lamont, W. M., *Godly Rule: Politics and Religion, 1603–60* (1969).

Maclure, M., *The Paul's Cross Sermons, 1534–1642* (Toronto, 1958).

Marsh, J. B., *The Story of Harecourt, Being the History of an Independent Church* (1871).

Matthews, A. G., *Calamy Revised* (Oxford, 1934).

—— 'A Censored Letter', *Trans. Cong. Hist. Soc.*, ix (1924–6).

—— *Walker Revised* (Oxford, 1948).

Matthews, R., *English Messiahs* (1936).

Micklewright, F. H. A., 'Seventh-Day Baptists', *Notes and Queries* (1946).

Milne, D. J., 'The Results of the Rye House Plot . . .', *Trans. Roy. Hist. Soc.*, V. i (1951).

Bibliography

Neal, D., *The History of the Puritans* (1837).

Neue Deutsche Biographie, v (Berlin, 1960).

New England Historical and Genealogical Register, passim.

Nightingale, B., *The Ejected of 1662* (1911).

Norris, W. G., *John ap John, and Early Records of Friends in Wales* (*Friends' Hist. Soc., Supplement 6*, 1907).

Nourse, G. B., 'Law Reform under the Commonwealth and Protectorate', *Law Quart. Rev.*, lxxv (1959).

Nuttall, G. F., 'The Baptist Western Association, 1653–1658', *J. Eccles. Hist.*, xi (1960).

—— , ed., *The Beginnings of Nonconformity, 1660–1665. A Checklist* (1960).

—— *The Holy Spirit in Puritan Faith and Experience* (2nd edn., Oxford, 1947).

—— James Nayler: A Fresh Approach (*Friends' Hist. Soc., Supplement 26*, 1954).

—— *Visible Saints. The Congregational Way, 1640–1660* (Oxford, 1957).

—— *The Welsh Saints 1640–1660. Walter Cradock, Vavasour Powell, Morgan Llwyd* (Cardiff, 1957).

Ogg, D., *England in the Reign of Charles II* (Oxford, 1955).

Palmer, A. N., *A History of the Older Nonconformity of Wrexham* (Wrexham, 1889).

Payne, E. A., *The Baptists of Berkshire* (1951).

—— 'More about the Sabbatarian Baptists', *Bapt. Quart.*, xiv (1951–2).

—— 'Thomas Tillam', *ibid.*, xvii (1957–8).

Pollard, A. W., and Redgrave, G. R., *Short Title Catalogue . . . 1475–1640* (1950).

Pollock, J., *The Popish Plot* (1913).

Prall, S. E., *The Agitation for Law Reform during the Puritan Revolution, 1640–1660* (The Hague, 1966).

Preston, A. E., *The Church and Parish of St. Nicholas, Abingdon* (1929).

Richards, T., *A History of the Puritan Movement in Wales . . . 1639–1653* (1920).

—— *Religious Developments in Wales 1654–62* (1923).

—— *Wales under the Indulgence* (1928).

—— *Wales under the Penal Code (1662–1687)* (1925).

Robinson, H. Wheeler, 'A Baptist Soldier - William Allen', *Bapt. Quart.*, iii (1926–7).

Rogers, E., *Some Account of the Life and Opinions of a Fifth Monarchy Man* (1867).

Rogers, P. G., *Battle in Bossenden Wood. The Strange Story of Sir William Courtenay* (1961).

—— *The Fifth Monarchy Men* (1966).

—— *The Sixth Trumpeter. The Story of Jezreel and his Tower* (1963).

Roth, C., *A History of the Jews in England* (Oxford, 1949).

Schenk, W., *The Concern for Social Justice in the Puritan Revolution* (1948).

Schoeps, H. J., *Philosemitismus im Barock* (Tübingen, 1952).

Shaw, W. A., *A History of the English Church . . . 1640–1660* (1900).

Simpkinson, C. H., *Thomas Harrison, Regicide* (1905).

Solt, L. F., *Saints in Arms* (1959).

Spinka, M., *John Amos Comenius* (Chicago, 1943).

Bibliography

Stanley, J., *The Church in the Hop Garden. A Chatty Account of the Longworth-Coate Baptist Meeting* (1936).

Stark, W., *The Sociology of Religion* (1966–7).

Stearns, R. P., *The Strenuous Puritan. Hugh Peter, 1598–1660* (Urbana, Ill., 1954).

Strype, J., *Annals of the Reformation* (Oxford, 1824).

Taylor, A., *The History of the English General Baptists* (1818).

Thomas, K. V., 'Women and the Civil War Sects' in T. Aston, ed., *Crisis in Europe, 1560–1660* (1965).

Thomson, J. A. F., *The Later Lollards* (Oxford, 1965).

Thrupp, S., ed., *Millennial Dreams in Action* (The Hague, 1962).

Tindall, W. Y., *John Bunyan, Mechanick Preacher* (New York, 1934).

Toon, P., ed., *Puritans, the Millennium and the Future of Israel* (Cambridge and London, 1970).

Torrance, T. F., 'The Eschatology of the Reformation', *Scottish J. of Theology, Occasional Paper no. 2*.

Trevor-Roper, H. R., *Religion, the Reformation and Social Change* (1967).

Troeltsch, E., *The Social Teaching of the Christian Churches*, trans. O. Wyon (1931).

Tuveson, E. L., *Millennium and Utopia* (Berkeley and Los Angeles, 1949).

Urwick, W., *Nonconformity in Herts.* (1884).

Vann, R. T., 'Quakerism and the Social Structure in the Interregnum', *Past and Present*, xliii (1969).

—— *The Social Development of English Quakerism, 1655–1755* (Cambridge, Mass., 1969).

Venn, J., and Venn, J. A., *Alumni Cantabrigienses . . . to 1751* (Cambridge, 1922–27).

Walker, D. P., *The Decline of Hell. Seventeenth-century discussions of eternal treatment* (1964).

Walker, J., 'The Yorkshire Plot, 1663', *Yorks. Arch. J.*, xxxi (1932–4).

Walzer, M., 'Puritanism as a Revolutionary Ideology', *History and Theory*, iii (1963–4).

—— *The Revolution of the Saints* (1966).

White, B. R., 'The Organisation of the Particular Baptists, 1644–1660,' *J. Eccles. Hist.*, xviii (1966).

Whiting, C. E., *Studies in English Puritanism from the Restoration to the Revolution, 1660–88* (1931).

Whitley, W. T., *A Baptist Bibliography*, i (1916).

—— *The Baptists of London, 1612–1928* (1928).

—— *Baptists of North-West England, 1649–1913* (London and Preston, 1913).

—— 'Colonel Thomas Blood', *Bapt. Quart.*, iv (1928–9).

(——) 'The English Career of John Clarke, Rhode Island', *ibid.*, i (1923).

—— *A History of British Baptists* (2nd edn., 1932).

——'Seventh Day Baptists in England', *Bapt. Quart.*, xii (1946–8).

Williams, G. H., *The Radical Reformation* (1962).

Williams, W. R., *The Parliamentary History of the County of Worcester* (Hereford, 1899).

—— *The Parliamentary History of . . . Wales* (Brecknock, 1895).

Bibliography

Wilson, J. F., 'Another Look at John Canne', *Church Hist.*, xxxiii (1964).

—— 'Comment on "Two Roads to the Puritan Millennium" ', *ibid.*, xxxii (1963).

—— 'A Glimpse of Syons Glory', *ibid.*, xxxi (1962).

—— *Pulpit in Parliament: Puritanism during the English Civil Wars, 1640–1648* (Princeton, N.J., 1969).

Wing, D., *Short-Title Catalogue . . . 1641–1700* (New York, 1951).

Woolrych, A. H., 'The Calling of Barebone's Parliament', *Eng. Hist. Rev.*, lxxx (1965).

Worsley, P., *The Trumpet shall Sound* (1957).

Young, R. F., *Comenius in England* (1932).

Zagorin, P., *A History of Political Thought in the English Revolution* (1954).

Index

✠✠✠

Places in England and Wales are indexed under their respective counties, and Biblical characters (except Jesus Christ) under *Bible*. Only the leading reference to each Fifth Monarchist has been included from Appendices I–II.

Index

Barkstead, John, 54, 277
Barnwell, Sarah, 95
Barrett, George, 241, 278n.
Basse, Jonathan, 241
Bateman, Rowland, 42
Bawden, John, 68, 102–3, 124, 241
Baxter, Richard, 28, 39, 123, 226
Baylie, Thomas, 176, 242
Becold: *see under* John of Leyden
Bedfordshire, 219; Bedford 77
Bedloe, William, 21, 219
Beech, John, 242
Belcher, John, 121, 143, 205, 207–8, 216, 224, 242
Bennett, Col., 41
Berkshire, 219; Abingdon, 77–8, 85, 91, 107, 116–17, 128, 173, 216, 224; Eton, 191; Newbury, 35; Reading, 77–8, 119, 215, 224; Wallingford, 44; Windsor, 101–2, 108, 115–16, 191
Bermuda, 223
Bernard, Richard, 34
Berry, James, 110
Beverley, Thomas, 225
Bible: O.T., Aaron, 163; Abraham, 42; Daniel, 103; David, 93; Ham, 43; Isaac, 42; Job, 97; Lot's wife, 126; Moses, 42, 62–3, 138, 162–6, 168–71, 235; Rabshakeh, 162–3; Saul, 140; N.T., Barabbas, 120; John the Baptist, 33, 43; St. Paul, 55, 197; Virgin Mary, 33; *see also* Jesus Christ
Biddle, John 183–4
Bingham, Col., 41
Binns, Otwell, 18
Bishop, Francis, 96
Blake, Richard, 81
Blood, Thomas, 212, 218–20
Bloxsom, Barnabas, 242
Boatman, James, 269
Boehme, Jacob, 37, 112, 185
Bohemia, 213, 233, 235
Bolton, duke of, 227
Booker, John, 188
Books, titles of, 14, 17–18, 20–1, 25, 30, 32, 34, 37, 90–1, 102, 110, 114–15, 119, 170, 185, 206, 214, 233, 235–7; *see also* Fifth Monarchists (v)
Boon, A., 164
Bordeaux, 152
Border, Daniel, 57
Bowling, William, 44
Boyle, Robert, 214

Boys, Capt., 273
Bradshaw, John, 115
Brandenburg, 213, 234
Brayne, John, 44, 50, 150, 159, 164, 166, 242
Breviter, Richard, 64, 111, 176, 198, 242
Bridge, William, 30–1, 37, 39, 79
Brierly, Robert, 242
Brightman, Thomas, 28–9, 34–5, 37, 45, 232–3
Brocard, Jacobus, 26
Brome, widow, 216
Brooke, Lord, 40
Brookes, Thomas, 108
Brothers, Richard, 227
Browne, John, 64, 68, 100, 243; Robert, 176, 243
Bruern, Richard, 190
Brunt, Simon, 243
Brute, Walter, 169
Bucer, Martin, 34, 170
Buckinghamshire, 201, 219; Aylesbury, 201; Chalfont, 77, 215; Water Stratford, 226
Buffett, Francis, 200, 212, 221
Bull, John, 33
Bullinger, Henry, 24
Bunch, Nathaniel, 115, 243
Bunyan, John, 156
Burroughes, Jeremiah, 30, 40
Burton, Henry, 26, 31, 36
Butler, Samuel, 207
Buttevant, Thomas, 92, 112, 114, 116, 207, 243
Byfield, Nathaniel, 200, 243
Bywater, John, 96

Caithness, Cornet, 99
Calamy, Edmund, 39
Caley, Jacob, 68, 243
Calvin, John, 24, 163, 169
Cambridgeshire: Cambridge, 28–30; Ely, 44
Campanella, Tommaso, 21–2
Canne, John, career, 244; in 1649–53, 51, 53, 57–8, 60, 67, 78, 80; later, 114–16, 120–1, 124–6, 197, 207, 278; beliefs, 92, 134, 145, 154, 177–8, 180, 183–5, 187, 192, 213
Cardell, John, 244
Carew, John, career, 244; 41, 68–70, 72, 80, 85, 94; after 1653, 107–9, 111,

Index

Index

Index

Nayler, James, 184
Neat, Joseph, 256
Needham, Marchamont, 162
Nelson, Nicholas, 42
Netherlands: see Dutch
Newark, Henry, viscount, 41
Newbury, Francis, 256
New England, 51, 97, 140, 164, 170
New Haven, 139, 170
newspapers, millenarian, 57, 124
Nicholas, Sir Edward, 203
Norfolk, 64, 76, 87–8, 108, 114; Fifth Mon. petitions from, 52, 55, 138, 147, 165; N. Walsham, 64, 77–8, 92, 111–113, 176, 224; Norwich, 64, 77–8, 92, 111, 224; Trunch, 77; Wymondham, 64, 78, 224
Norris, Henry, 256
Northamptonshire, 215
Northumberland, 190, 202; Hexham, 92
Norway, 232
Nostradamus, 187
Nottinghamshire, 202; Nottingham, 77; Skegby, 77, 98, 210, 215, 224
Nye, Philip, 59, 101, 278

Oastler, —, 256
Oates, Titus, 219
Oecolampadius, Johannes, 25
Okey, John, 106, 114–15, 118; Thomas, 215, 256
Oldenburg, Henry, 214
Ormonde, duke, of 218–19
Osborne family, 28
Oseander, Andreas, 24–5
Ottoman Empire: see Turks
Overton, Richard, 171; Robert, career, 256; 41, 51, 63, 78, 92–3, 99, 106, 123–4, 126, 128–9, 183, 196, 199
Owen, John, 50, 53, 59, 93–4, 101
Oxfordshire, 200; Oxford, 77–8; University, 50, 92, 171, 189

Packer, William, 60, 93, 127, 256–7
Pagitt, Ephraim, 44
Palatinate, 201, 234
Palmer, Anthony, career, 257; 138, 176, 182, 203–4, 206–7, 209, 216; Herbert, 37–8
Palmer, Thomas, career, 257; 77, 80, 98, 133, 173, 176, 203, 207–8, 210, 212, 215–16

Papacy, Rome, 20–2, 28, 30, 34, 43, 67, 151–4, 184, 189, 192–3, 232, 234
Paracelsus, 19, 37, 185, 187
Parker, Robert, 34, 40, 152, 242; Thomas, 40, 193n.
Parliament, Long, 13, 18, 38–9, 40, 193–4; Rump, 50, 53, 55–63, 66, 72, 123; restored, 124–9, 158, 167, 171; Barebones, 14, 64, 66–75, 99–103, 113, 138, 143, 153, 158–9, 162, 276; in the Protectorate, 43, 105–6, 114, 158, 277; of Rd. Cromwell, 123–4; under Charles II, 204, 217, 220
Parnham, Richard, 257
Parsons, William, 223
Patshall, John, 210, 221, 257
Payne, Robert, 257
Peck, Simon, 257
Pell, John, 237
Pembroke, Philip, earl of, 40
Pendarves, John, career, 258; 91, 107, 116, 132–3, 141, 173, 175, 178, 181, 216
Pennoyer, Alderman, 204
Pennyman, John, 223
Pepys, Samuel, 206
Perkins, William, 94, 163, 169
Perrott, Robert, 212, 218, 220–1, 258
Pestell, William, 81, 205, 207
Peter, Hugh, 37, 44, 53, 90, 93, 148, 151, 159, 170, 189
Peterborough, countess of, 205
Peyton, Sir Robert, 219
Piccolomini, Gen., 235
Pickering, Sir Gilbert, 69
Piscator, Johannes, 233, 235
Placentinus, 23
Plaustrarius, Johannes, 33
Plomstead, Clement, 224, 258
Poland, 214, 234–5
Pole, Cardinal, 161
Pooley, Christopher, 64, 112, 201–2, 207, 222, 224, 258
Pope: see Papacy
Popish Plot, 21, 219
Porter, John, 258
Portman, Edmund, 81, 258; John, career, 258–9; 63, 81, 113–15, 116–17, 120–2, 126, 196, 200, 209, 276n., 278
Postlethwaite, Walter, 111, 133, 176, 178, 197, 259

Index

314